babycentre™

Baby

the all-important first year

London • New York • Munich • Melbourne • Delhi

For BabyCentre
Project editor Victoria Farrimond
Contributing editor Marie Kreft
Editor Sasha Miller

For DK
Project editor Claire Cross
Project designers Hannah Moore and Kevin Smith
Senior editor Helen Murray
Senior art editor Isabel de Cordova
Designer Saskia Janssen
Photographer Ruth Jenkinson
Photography art direction Isabel de Cordova
Production editor Maria Elia
Senior production editor Jennifer Murray
Production controller Seyhan Esen
Creative technical support Sonia Charbonnier
Managing editor Penny Warren
Managing art editors Glenda Fisher and Marianne Markham
Category publisher Peggy Vance

First published in Great Britain in 2010 by Dorling Kindersley Limited
80 Strand, London, WC2R 0RL

Penguin Group (UK)

A CIP catalogue of this book is available from the British Library

ISBN 978-1-4053-4126-4

Colour reproduction Colourscan, Singapore
Printed and bound in Singapore by Tien Wah Press

Discover more at
www.dk.com

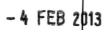

Contents

Your older baby
Six months to one year

Holidays and festivities

Baby healthcare
0–12 months

Newborn health

General health

Special care babies

Returning to work
Your options now

Foreword

Having a baby will probably be the most wonderful, exciting and joyous thing you will ever do. It can also be worrying, at times overwhelming and often downright exhausting. Here, we join you on this unique journey.

When you become a parent, your life changes for ever, and although that's an incredible thing, adapting to those changes can be a real challenge. As a mum myself, I understand that having access to the best information and support makes those changes so much easier to cope with. The moment you become a parent your mind is filled with questions: How is my baby developing? Is this safe? Is that normal? There are also lots of decisions to be made: Should we try to develop a routine? Or not? Should I breastfeed? And how long for? As your baby grows and develops, you'll find that every day you are facing new decisions and dilemmas.

Having a source of information you can really trust will give you the answers to all these questions and more. It will also give you the confidence you need to make choices that are right for you and your baby. And that's exactly what BabyCentre is all about. BabyCentre is the UK's number one website for new and expectant parents. Since we launched in the UK in 2000, our trusted advice and friendly community have supported millions of mums and dads on their journey through parenthood.

This book, with its in-depth information and beautiful photographs, is an exciting new venture for us. We're delighted to be working with Dorling Kindersley to create such a fantastic publication. It brings together BabyCentre's expert content plus the voices of real mums and dads from our online community in a gorgeous book that takes you from those first precious weeks with your newborn to his first birthday. You may want to put your feet up (go on, you deserve it!) and read it cover to cover, or dip into it as your baby develops. Whether this is your first baby, or you are adding to your family, *Baby, the all-important first year* will be your perfect companion.

Sasha Miller

Sasha Miller, Editor
www.babycentre.co.uk

Introduction

Baby, the all-important first year is designed to accompany you all the way through your baby's first year of life, from the moment your baby is born, through those hectic first weeks and all the way to the important first birthday.

How the book works

Through each stage of your baby's first year, you'll find information on feeding, sleeping and development, with tried and tested tips throughout. At BabyCentre, we want to be your most trusted parenting resource – that's why we offer practical advice from expert sources, such as doctors, midwives and fellow parents.

Welcome to parenthood! The first six weeks

The first six weeks with your baby are the most magical, overwhelming and ever-so-slightly terrifying for parents. This section is a survival guide to help you cope. We take you through the first hours and days, outlining all the tests and checks your baby will have, how you'll both feel and how your body recovers. You'll find practical babycare advice, with handy photo sequences showing you how to hold your baby, change his nappy, wash, swaddle and dress him, and soothe him.

Whether you breastfeed or formula feed, we help you get started with information on latching on and positioning, and making up feeds. In these early weeks, your newborn will sleep a lot, but not for long stretches, and not always at night! Our newborn sleep chapter helps you make important decisions about your baby's sleep, from when to start a routine to co-sleeping. You'll also find advice on how to ensure your baby sleeps safely.

Your baby goes through incredible changes as he develops from a "scrunched up" newborn to a smiling, inquisitive six-week-old, and we help you encourage his development. He isn't the only one going through immense changes, so you'll also find a chapter dedicated to you and how to cope with your new life as a parent.

Your growing baby – six weeks to six months

By now, the initial rush of adrenalin that carried you through the first few weeks may have worn off and life may seem like a non-stop cycle of nappy changes, feeds and soothing sessions. However, freedom from the chaos of these days is in sight. Your baby may have started napping about the same time each day, or, if not, it's only a matter of weeks before a pattern emerges. Here we explore the development of a routine, and introduce the concept of sleep training.

Feeding patterns change in the first six months as your baby has growth spurts. We explore feeding ups and downs, and provide advice on problems such as breast refusal, mastitis and keeping up with the demands of your breast- or bottle-fed baby.

You'll be amazed how quickly your baby changes in his first six months. We explain how he achieves exciting milestones, such as rolling over, sitting and imitating sounds. Playing with your baby becomes even more important the older he gets. Here, you'll find great games to help your baby develop new skills. And as your baby starts exploring his world, we advise you on how to babyproof your home.

In this section, you'll also find advice on how to care for your growing baby, with useful tips on bathing, skin care and baby massage.

Your older baby – six months to one year

At six months, you can introduce your baby to the wonderful world of solid foods. Here, you'll find all you need to know about weaning your baby, from the first soupy spoonful to what foods to introduce when, and safe finger foods. There's information on what feeding equipment you'll need, and how to keep it all clean and hygienic.

Sleep is essential for your older baby's growth and development. We outline how much sleep he needs, and explore how to overcome problems that arise now, such as early waking and resisting bedtime.

Your baby's independence grows as he learns to crawl, cruise and eventually walk. He'll communicate more successfully, responding to questions and following simple directions. His personality starts to shine through, but he may also show signs of separation anxiety, as he realises that he's independent of you. We examine these important developmental milestones, and give advice on how to help your baby. We also help you understand his behaviour and set boundaries for when he's older.

Baby healthcare

It can be heartbreaking looking after an unwell baby. Our health section helps you to deal with common concerns, such as colds and fevers, to recognise childhood illnesses and decide when to call a doctor. We also chart childhood immunisations. A special chapter on newborn health deals with early concerns such as umbilical stump problems, colic and jaundice. We've divided health concerns in the first year into infections; allergies and allergic conditions; infectious diseases; gastrointestinal illnesses; and minor concerns. Though we hope you'll never need to deal with them, it's wise to be prepared for accidents and emergencies, so you'll find comprehensive and practical first-aid information too. Our section on special-care babies outlines the needs of premature babies and those with a condition that needs early treatment.

Returning to work

Juggling work and bringing up your baby can be done, but it takes planning. We can help. Our guide to work and childcare helps you choose the right childcare for your baby, gives you tips on being a working parent and helps to make the transition back to work as smooth as possible for both of you.

"Your baby goes through constant **changes** throughout his first **amazing** year of life."

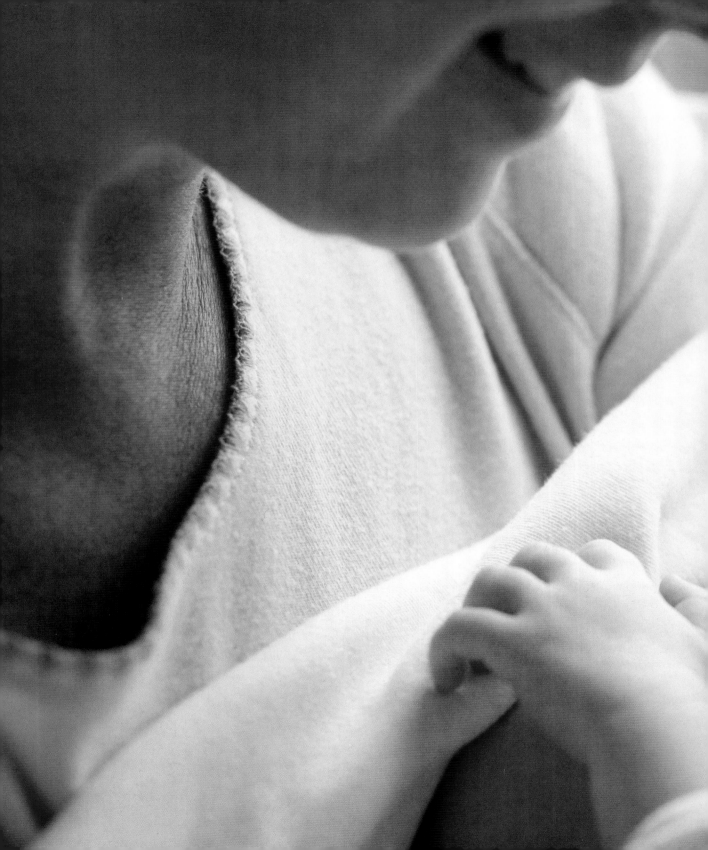

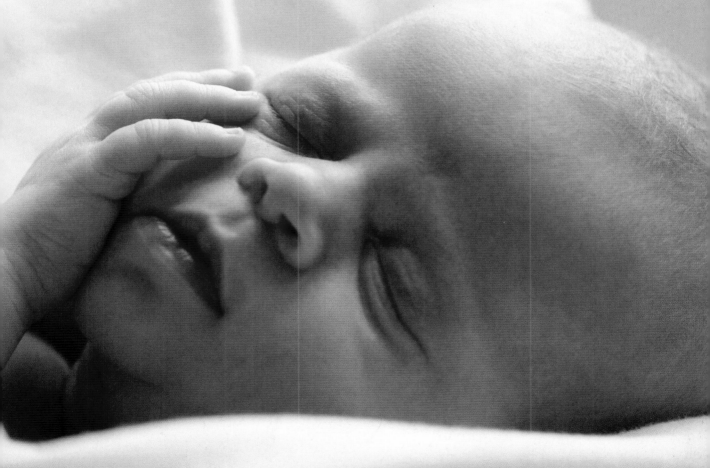

Welcome to parenthood!

0–6 weeks

Your baby's arrival

The first moments

You will never forget the moment when you see your baby and cuddle her for the very first time. You may feel elated or simply exhausted; you might want to laugh or cry. One thing is for certain: as her life begins, your life has changed forever.

Finally face-to-face

How quickly you can cuddle your baby will probably depend on the type of labour you had. If you had a straightforward vaginal birth and your baby is well, you can ask for her to be placed on your tummy straightaway. If you or your baby need medical attention after the birth, for example if you need to have stitches, you may have to wait a little longer.

After the shock of her arrival, your baby will be reassured by contact with your warm skin. If you cuddle her and hold her to your breast, she may start "rooting", which means she's feeling for your nipple with her mouth.

Your baby will probably still have her cord attached and be covered in a layer of grease called vernix caseosa, which protected her in the uterus. The midwife or your partner will clamp the cord after a few minutes, or once it's no longer pulsating. This can be done while you're cuddling your baby – there'll be plenty of time for the midwife to clean her up after you've had a chance to hold her.

Early bonding

When you look into your baby's eyes you may find them wide open and locked onto yours. In the first hour or so of her life, she may be more awake than she will be for many days to come. At this early moment, you may feel a huge rush of love for your baby. Or you may not. Though many mums describe bonding as a feeling of love at first sight, don't panic if that's not how you feel (see p.24). You'll probably find that your love builds over the days and weeks, and in a few months' time, it will be no less intense than if it had begun instantly.

The anticipation is over – holding your baby in your arms is an incredible moment for you, your partner and your baby.

In these early moments, skin-to-skin contact can make a huge difference to developing a close bond. It's also one of the best ways to encourage your baby to breastfeed (see pp.45–6). Not all babies get the hang of breastfeeding immediately. Holding your baby to your bare skin so that she can smell you, and your milk, will encourage her.

Of course, it's not only your life that changes forever with the arrival of your baby. Your partner, too, has been on an incredible journey in the preceding hours and will be adjusting to his new role as a dad. Your partner can play a role in the birth by cutting the cord, but he shouldn't feel any shame if he doesn't do this. However, taking time to cuddle and hold your baby is really valuable. Sharing this very special time gives you all the best possible start to family life.

Parents**Talk...**

"After carrying a baby around for nine months, the moment I finally held him felt like I was welcoming someone I already knew so well."
Aimee, 28, first-time mum

"It was love at first sight with my baby. Before we saw any visitors, we savoured some quiet family bonding time."
Zoe, 35, first-time mum

"I didn't feel an instant connection. I felt shattered after a hard labour, but after resting, the magic began to work. Now I'm totally in love!"
Melissa, 38, mother of two

Welcome to parenthood!
0–6 weeks

Your growing baby
6 weeks to 6 months

Your older baby
6 months to one year

Baby healthcare
0–12 months

After the birth

The first few hours after the birth can feel overwhelming. You are likely to feel an array of emotions and your baby is adjusting to his new world. As well as getting to know each other, this is also an important time for newborn health checks and for you to establish breastfeeding.

Your baby's first checks

Straight after the birth, your baby will be weighed, and his length and head circumference measured. Between four and 48 hours after the birth, your baby will have his newborn tests. A paediatrician, specially trained midwife or, if you had a home birth, your doctor, will do the tests and may ask questions about your family medical history.

What is checked

The examiner will check your baby's heart and lungs. She'll put a finger in his mouth to check that his palate (the roof of his mouth) is complete and will check that his tongue is anchored to the bottom of his mouth correctly. His genitals and anus will also be checked. Your baby's hips will be manipulated to check for instability, or dysplasia, known as "clicky" hips (see p.248). She'll also check his arms, hands, legs and feet, counting his fingers and toes and looking for signs of webbing.

The straightness of his spine will be checked. It's quite common for babies to have a dimple at the spine's base called a sacral dimple. Usually this causes no problems, but occasionally it indicates a problem with the lower part of the spinal cord that could affect nerve function and needs further investigation.

Apgar score

The Apgar score is a simple, visual test to measure your baby's health at birth. The midwife checks his skin colour, heart rate, responses, breathing and muscle tone at one minute after the birth and again after five minutes. An experienced midwife does this in a few seconds, so you may not even notice that it has been done.

A score between seven and 10 means your baby is fine. Between five and seven may mean that your baby needs some oxygen or a quick rub to stimulate breathing. A score of less than five will usually need the attention of a paediatrician.

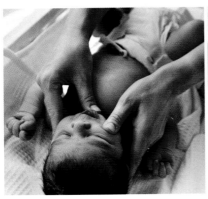

Your baby's mouth will be examined to check that there is no cleft – or split – in the palate and that the tongue is anchored.

Your baby's spine will be examined to ensure that it's straight and that there are no visible abnormalities.

Your baby's heart and lungs will be checked with a stethoscope to ensure that the heartbeat is normal and the lungs are clear.

How your newborn looks

We're so used to seeing chubby, cherub-like newborns in pictures and films, that the reality can be surprising. True newborns have big heads, short necks and legs, and distended torsos.

Your newborn's appearance

Babies born by caesarean section tend to fare better initially in the looks department because they haven't been squeezed down a birth canal. If your naturally delivered baby has a pointy or squashed head, don't worry! This is perfectly normal and his head will become more rounded in a day or two.

Don't be alarmed by the soft spots on your baby's skull. These are called fontanelles and they allow his head to compress during birth. Also, don't worry if his genitals (or breasts) are swollen: this is from the rush of female hormones he got from you before the birth. His

If your baby has a head of hair, its colour may bear no resemblance to yours or your partner's. Newborn hair often isn't an indicator of how a child's hair will turn out: raven-haired newborns can grow up to be blonde, blondes to be brunettes. Of course, some babies are born bald, which is also normal.

Most Caucasian babies are born with dark blue eyes. Their true eye colour – be it brown, green, hazel or blue – may not reveal itself for a few months. African and Asian babies usually have dark grey or brown eyes at birth, which become a true brown or black after six months to a year. Mixed-race children could have any of these colours.

However squashed, pointy-headed or bald your baby looks now, he'll change rapidly. In the meantime, you may already be in love with everything, from his wispy hair down to his tiny toenails.

"He may be **wrinkly**, but to you he's the most **beautiful** baby."

face and eyes may be swollen, too, due to the pressure of squeezing down the birth canal, and he might have pink lips and blue hands and feet.

If your baby was premature, he may have thin, transparent-looking skin. He may be covered with lanugo – a fine, downy hair that insulates babies until they build up body fat. He may also be covered in a greasy white substance called vernix, which protected his delicate skin from the amniotic fluid.

Full-term or late babies may have less vernix. Late babies have little, if any, lanugo and also may have a slightly wrinkly appearance.

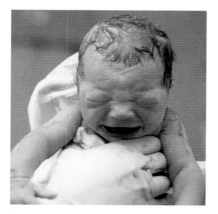

Covered in vernix, blood and amniotic fluid, and looking somewhat squashed, your newborn's appearance can be a shock.

Birthmarks

These may be permanent, or fade over time. The most common ones, sometimes called "stork bites" or "angel kisses", are caused by a collection of tiny blood vessels just below the skin. These red, mottled spots are harmless and often disappear. It's good to get your baby's birthmark checked by a doctor, though, especially if it is large and/or near the eyes, nose, mouth or bottom, in which case it may be wise to have it removed later. But generally birthmarks are harmless.

Other types of birthmark

● Strawberry haemangiomas are raised, crimson-coloured marks that appear a few days or weeks after birth, often on the head or neck. They tend to grow quickly for about six months, but usually disappear by seven years.

● Cavernous haemangioma, a lumpy, bluish or purplish mass, grows quickly in the first six months, then starts to shrink at about 18 months. It's deeper than strawberry haemangioma, but usually disappears by five years of age.

● Congenital moles are brown, or almost black; usually less than 2.5cm (1in) in diameter. They're most common on the back and may be raised or hairy.

● Mongolian spots are bluish or greenish bruise-like marks a few centimetres diameter often on the back or bottom. They can be present at birth, or appear within weeks, but usually disappear by school age.

● Port-wine stains are flat red or purple marks, ranging from a few millimetres to several centimetres in diameter. Light port-wine stains may fade, but most enlarge as your child grows, deepening in colour and becoming raised or bumpy.

Welcome to parenthood! 0–6 weeks

Your growing baby 6 weeks to 6 months

Your older baby 6 months to one year

Baby healthcare 0–12 months

How you might feel

How are you feeling now you've given birth? Don't worry if you haven't felt the joys of motherhood instantly. It's likely that you're a bit shaky at the moment, due to the adrenaline from the birth and the sudden changes to your body (see p.23). You're probably feeling quite emotional – happy and exhilarated one moment and dazed or even depressed the next. All of these emotions are perfectly natural and understandable.

Some new mums find they're on a high, wanting to crack open the champagne and share their joyful news with the rest of the world. Others, though, find it hard to pay attention to their new baby, especially if they had a long and difficult labour or used opiate drugs such as Pethidine, which has a sedative effect and can cause nausea and disorientation.

Taking time to adjust

If you feel bruised and battered, tired or disappointed, don't worry and don't be hard on yourself. It doesn't mean that you won't love your baby, or you won't be a wonderful mum.

However you are feeling, it's important to remember that you're recovering from a huge physical upheaval. You may have had a tear or an episiotomy (an incision made in your perineum to assist the birth), or both, and you may have stitches. All of these things can make you feel uncomfortable and down. If you gave birth by caesarean, you've just undergone major abdominal surgery. Be kind to yourself and your body, and give yourself time to relax and regain your strength. With plenty of rest and support, most women recover quickly.

However you're feeling, it's likely that you'll be unable to take your eyes off the tiny bundle that's your newborn baby.

Single mum

You're likely to feel a range of emotions after the birth, from exhaustion and relief that it's over to elation and pride.

"I've never been so scared as when I went into labour. This was it, I was going to meet my baby and life was never going to be the same again. My mum was there for me throughout my pregnancy, and the labour, too. She held my hand and massaged my back as she had learned in the antenatal classes. My midwife was amazing, too. She encouraged me and told me that she believed in me and that I could do it. She was right, because after eight long hours I gave birth to my daughter, Millie. She weighed 3.35kg (7lb 6oz) and had the biggest set of lungs on her! After the birth I just felt so utterly relieved that the pain had stopped, even though I was completely exhausted. More than anything, though, I was so proud that I'd given birth to such a beautiful baby. "

How your baby might feel

For the last nine months, your baby has had all her needs met inside you – warmth, food and comfort from the cushioning fluid surrounding her, the thump of your heartbeat and the sound of your voice. As her head is born, she's in a half-way place, moments from becoming a separate being, the pressure on her chest stopping her breathing just yet. As her body is born, the pressure is gone, and her lungs, which were previously filled with fluid, fill with air – her very first breath.

She may cry immediately, or cough and splutter, as she clears the fluid from her mouth and throat. Once the cord is cut, her breathing, circulation and digestion work entirely independently of you. Some babies need a little help with breathing, and your midwife or doctor may need to take her aside for a few moments to help clear her airways so that she can breathe.

How your baby adapts

As your baby adjusts to this new world full of light, sound and sensations that are unfamiliar to her, she may calmly take it all in, or she may make her presence felt the only way she knows how, by crying lustily. You can help her adjust by asking for the lights to be dimmed as she is born, by soothing her with the sound of your voice and by

holding her skin-to-skin as soon as you can, so that she can absorb your warmth and hear your heartbeat once more.

Newborns can't regulate their own temperature and can easily become chilled, so covering the rest of her body with a blanket and covering her head will help her keep warm. Your baby will be taking in your scent, and will be fascinated by your face or your partner's face. You may see her instincts kick in as she searches for your nipples and moves towards one. She's also born with several reflexes (see p.64) to help her survive. For example, she'll turn her head towards you if you brush her cheek, and grasp your thumb if you put it in her palm.

Sometimes, the force of the contractions alone, or the use of instruments for an assisted birth, can leave your baby feeling bruised and swollen. She may not be able to open her eyes properly if her face is congested and she may also have a headache if she's sustained grazes or bruising to the head during birth. Handle her gently and help her to feel safe and secure by keeping her warm and comfortable.

Your baby will probably be quite alert for the first hour or so after the birth, but will soon need a long sleep to help her recover from the physical strain of birth and the new experiences she has gone through. If you had any sort of opiate drug, such as Pethidine, in your system towards the end of your labour, either as part of an epidural or as an injection, your baby may be drowsy at first. The effects of opiates may weaken her sucking reflex for several days, so breastfeeding may be trickier to get going. In the meantime, she'll benefit from skin-to-skin cuddles.

As your baby adapts to her strange new world, holding her in a warm embrace will help her to feel secure.

Vitamin K

This vitamin plays an important role in making our blood clot. Babies without enough Vitamin K can develop a very rare, but serious, condition called Vitamin K deficiency bleeding (VKDB). For that reason, newborn babies are now given an extra dose of vitamin K shortly after the birth.

How it's administered

The vitamin K dose can be given by mouth or via a single injection. Both ways are effective if given correctly, but experts agree that an injection is probably best as it gives your baby immediate protection against VKNB. If you opt for an oral dose, the number of doses will vary according to whether you breast- or bottle feed.

Your preference

As with any jab, the injection can be a little painful and leave a bruise. Some parents find it upsetting to see their baby in pain, even momentarily. If you have concerns about an injection, or you're unclear about your options, check with your doctor or midwife.

Fact: In the first hour after birth, your baby's vision is a little blurry.

She can see to a distance of 20 to 30cm (8 to 12in), so hold her close so she can see your face. She may feed within minutes of birth and this could last for an hour or more.

Welcome to parenthood!
0–6 weeks

Your growing baby
6 weeks to 6 months

Your older baby
6 months to one year

Baby healthcare
0–12 months

Your baby's first feed

Once you've delivered the placenta, your hormone levels change dramatically. Levels of progesterone and oestrogen fall and levels of prolactin and oxytocin, released from the pituitary gland, rise. These hormones stimulate your body to produce breastmilk to feed your baby.

Getting started

It's good to offer your baby the breast soon after he's born as babies are often very alert at this time and feed well. Your midwife will be able to help you find a comfy position and will help you get your baby "latched on" (see p.46) so he feeds effectively and doesn't make your nipples sore. Although feeding your baby early and often is ideal, don't worry if at this stage, all your baby wants is to lick a little and enjoy the close, loving cuddle he gets when you hold him.

When you start to breastfeed, it's best to bring your baby to the breast rather than the other way around. You may need a pillow or two on your lap to raise him high enough. To feed well, your baby needs to use his tongue to scoop in a big mouthful of breast to help him latch on. His bottom lip and tongue need to get to your breast first. Bring him to your breast with his head tipped back, so that he leads with his chin, then let his lips touch your nipple. He'll respond by dropping his lower jaw. Move him quickly and smoothly to your breast, aiming his bottom lip as far away from the base of your nipple as you can.

Feeding on demand

It's important to feed your baby as often as he wants to, as feeding works on a supply and demand basis, so your breasts produce milk in response to his sucking. It's not a good idea to wait until he's yelling before you feed him. No one learns well when they're upset and, because of the crying, his tongue will be in the wrong position – it needs to be in a forwards position, and crying makes it go too far back. Relax and soothe and calm your baby before trying to feed him, especially in the early days. As you get to know your baby, you'll soon be able to spot the signs that he's hungry before he starts crying.

Your baby will instinctively "root" for your nipple when he is first placed near to your breast after the birth.

A side-by-side feeding position can be comfortable after a caesarean, avoiding pressure being put on the wound.

The first breastmilk

In the first days, your breasts produce a creamy-looking, high-protein, low-fat "pre-milk" called colostrum. You may have leaked a few drops of this thick, whitish substance in the final weeks of pregnancy (some women notice it in the second trimester). This easily digestible liquid is full of disease-fighting antibodies, immunoglobulins, which strengthen the immune system, and it's the best possible food for your newborn.

About 30 to 40 hours after you deliver the placenta, your hormone levels adjust (see opposite) and transitional milk production begins. For first mums, milk comes in around three to four days after the birth, and your breasts will feel full and tender. With second or subsequent babies, you may notice this happens earlier, at around two to three days. These are averages, though; for some, milk comes in earlier or later. The more you feed your baby in the first 48 to 72 hours, the quicker your milk comes in. This is because your baby's suckling stimulates your body to make prolactin, the hormone that produces milk.

You may have heard stories about breastfeeding being more difficult after a caesarean. Don't let these worry you. Women who've had a caesarean are less likely to start breastfeeding straightaway, but once you've started, your chances of success are the same as for a woman who has given birth vaginally. If you want to breastfeed, get help from the outset from a midwife or a breastfeeding counsellor.

Each time your baby sucks, your body is stimulated to release hormones that trigger the production of more milk.

Parents**Talk...**

"I was in labour for 16 hours with my son. It wasn't the easiest of births and at one point, it looked like I'd need a caesarean section. To say that I was completely exhausted was an understatement. When the midwife placed my baby on my chest and he latched on to feed for the first time though, sleep was the last thing on my mind. I could have stayed like that for hours. It was the perfect time to look down at him and take in everything about him. It's one of my most precious memories."
Shola, 39, second-time mum

"I had a difficult time establishing breastfeeding with my daughter. I had a caesarean and my milk didn't come through until five days later. By that point, my little girl had lost just over 10 per cent of her weight. She was also a little resistant at first, but at four months old she's now a healthy weight. I'm so happy that, despite a tricky beginning, I've been able to give my daughter the best start in life."
May, 24, first-time mum

"The first time I breastfed my baby was just a few minutes after the birth. She was put into my arms and I remember staring at her in awe. Not only had my body made her, but I was now able to feed her as well. It amazed me how instinctively she knew what to do when she fed. She looked so perfect, it was as if we were the only two people in the world."
Fran, 22, first-time mum

Welcome to parenthood! 0–6 weeks

Your growing baby 6 weeks to 6 months

Your older baby 6 months to one year

Baby healthcare 0–12 months

Your recovery time

Make the most of the days after the birth to recover and bond with your baby. If you had a straightforward birth at hospital, you and your baby could go home that day. If not, you may need to stay in for a day or two. After a caesarean, you'll be in hospital for around three days.

Laid-back mum

Not all mums have their babies in hospital.

"I had a fairly straightforward hospital birth with my first child, but decided that I'd really like to give birth in the comfort of my own home with my second, and I'm so pleased that I did. I spent much of early labour in the bath and ended up giving birth on our bathroom floor!

After Ellie was born, we both had a quick dip in the bath and we were then escorted to the bedroom where I tried to feed her while my midwife checked us over and waited for me to deliver the placenta naturally. After 15 minutes, Ellie had latched on and the placenta was out. My midwife then left us to it and went to clean the bathroom for me.

It was so nice to be able to get up and walk around after the birth and I enjoyed being able to go and have a shower. Plus the tea and toast from my own kitchen tasted amazing. My midwife was here for a few hours after the birth writing her notes and checking all was OK.

My homebirth was so relaxed and natural – a very memorable experience for me and my partner."

What to expect

You'll probably feel extremely tired after giving birth. Postnatal wards with other babies and mothers can be noisy, so you might want to bring some earplugs! Whether in hospital or at home, try to sleep when your baby sleeps, as it's harder to bond when you're physically exhausted. Once you feel ready, the midwives will encourage you to walk around, which will speed your recovery.

Asking for help

If you need to stay in hospital for a while, take advantage of the midwives and nurses who are there to help you with babycare basics. If you're not sure about how to hold your baby, ask the staff to show you. Also, if you need help with breastfeeding, don't struggle on alone: one of the midwives can assist you, or your hospital may have a breastfeeding counsellor who can advise you.

Holding your baby skin-to-skin after the birth will help to encourage bonding (see p.24), and the midwives in hospital will show you how to do this. Don't worry if you don't bond with your baby straightaway – everyone is different.

During your time in hospital, you'll learn how to keep your baby clean (see pp.38–9) and how to care for her umbilical cord stump (see p.38).

Before you leave hospital, a paediatrician or specially trained midwife will carry out some routine checks on your baby (see p.16) and her weight will be recorded. In some hospitals, she may also be given a hearing check.

Take advantage of the first few days to rest as much as possible and enjoy some skin-to-skin cuddles with your baby.

Getting the most out of your time in hospital

Being aware of what you can do or request while in hospital can help you to have the best possible experience.

Tips for a hospital stay

- If you're struggling with breastfeeding, ask your midwife to show you how to latch your baby on, and ask if there is a breastfeeding counsellor or infant feeding specialist at the hospital who you can talk to. Don't suffer in silence.
- If you've had a caesarean, it will be fairly painful afterwards. Don't be afraid to ask for pain relief if this isn't already in place. It's best to keep your pain relief topped up, rather than waiting for pain to creep up on you.

- If you need to go to the loo or to have a shower, it's OK to leave your baby, but make sure she is safe in her cot – never leave her alone on the bed, not even for a minute.
- If you really don't want to go onto the postnatal ward after the birth, it may be possible for you to have a side room or private room if there's one free, but you will need to request this as soon as possible (or in advance of your labour) and you will have to pay for it.
- Finally, if you're not sure, just ask! There is a buzzer beside your bed – don't be afraid to use it. However, midwives are busy people so don't expect someone to see you straightaway.

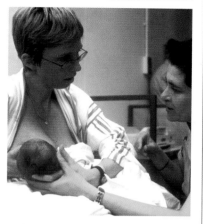

Make good use of your time on the postnatal ward by enlisting the help of midwives while you have them to hand.

Physical changes in you

Now you've given birth, many of the changes that happened to your body during pregnancy are abruptly reversed.

How your body adapts

Your uterus (womb) gets rapidly smaller after the birth and contracts back to its normal size and position. Breastfeeding speeds up this process and, within six weeks, your uterus returns to its pre-pregnancy size.

You may feel "afterpains" as your uterus shrinks, especially if this is your second or subsequent baby. These feel like labour contractions and are common during breastfeeding, as the hormone oxytocin that is released when feeding encourages the uterus to contract.

Your vagina will gradually regain much of its former tone, and your pelvic floor, although inevitably stretched, will return to near its usual position. You can

help this process by practising regular pelvic floor exercises (see pp.78–9) as soon as possible after the birth.

You'll have a discharge called lochia for a while. For about 10 days, this is like a heavy period, then it turns brownish and, finally, yellowish white. You'll need to wear sanitary towels, as tampons aren't advised until at least six weeks after the birth to minimise the risk of infection. Lochia can continue for up to six weeks: the more you rest, the lighter it will be.

Straight after birth, your breasts will be soft because they contain only a little colostrum (see p.21). After three or four days, your milk will arrive, making your breasts feel swollen, tender and hot. This should ease after about the fifth day, by which time both of you will be more used to breastfeeding. Feeding your baby as often as she wants will make you feel more comfortable.

Dad's **Diary**

An introduction to fatherhood

"My wife lost a lot of blood after our baby was born, so she had stay in hospital for a couple of days after the birth. With Jane being told to rest, this meant that I was the one being given the basic lessons in bathing, dressing and nappy changing, so I had the opportunity to get to know my baby son and to be of some practical use.

I felt terrible leaving them both in the hospital as my baby's birth day drew to a close. We'd just experienced the most momentous day in our lives, and there I was, at home alone.

A day or so later, though, Jane had recovered and we were able to go home as a family – it was at this point I finally felt able to realise that I'd become a father. When I look at Daniel now, the whole birth episode seems totally remarkable. Also, watching his mother with him is one of the most wonderful experiences in the world and makes me so happy to be part of our family."

Welcome to parenthood!
0–6 weeks

Your growing baby
6 weeks to 6 months

Your older baby
6 months to one year

Baby healthcare
0–12 months

Getting to know your baby

When experts talk about bonding, they mean the intense attachment you develop towards your baby. It's the feeling that makes you want to shower your baby with love and affection, and the knowledge you would do anything to protect him.

ParentsTalk...

"I thought my heart would melt when I heard that first cry, and was upset when I didn't feel an instant attachment. No one mentions how medication, nerves and exhaustion can leave you feeling empty."
Jane, 22, first-time mum

"The first few weeks were tough – all I seemed to do was feed and change nappies, and I had no idea how I really felt. It wasn't until my son looked into my eyes and smiled for the first time that I knew I loved him completely."
Sunita, 39, first-time mum

"It was love at first sight with both of my children. The moment had arrived when I finally met the little people I'd been carrying around!"
Mel, 27, mother of twins

"When my first son was born, I felt an instant bond. When I didn't feel that for my second son, I felt awful. I needn't have worried, though; my youngest has planted himself firmly in my heart. Now I can't imagine life without him."
Karen, 29, mum of two

Early bonding

For some parents, strong feelings of attachment towards their baby develop within the first few days – or even minutes – of the birth. For others, bonding may take a little longer.

In the past, researchers who studied bonding thought it was crucial for parents to spend a lot of time with their newborn during the first few days to seal the bond with their baby. We now know that bonding can take place over time. After all, parents who are separated from their babies soon after birth for medical reasons, or those who adopt their children when they're several weeks or months old, can also develop wonderfully close, loving relationships with their little ones.

Fathers may be denied the closeness of breastfeeding, but can still develop a loving bond with their baby early on.

Dad's Diary

Dads can do it too

"We dads forget that there isn't a magical intuition that tells women how to care for a baby. They learn by doing it, as do dads; you've just got to get stuck in. I did fumble a bit at first, but I soon got the hang of it.

As my partner was breastfeeding, I took charge of nappy changing while on leave. It's a dirty job, but someone's got to do it! At first, it was an epic ritual, but soon I was a seasoned pro. Burping is another way to get involved, and it gives Jo a break after a feeding session.

I love reading Sam stories. He doesn't understand a thing, but it soothes him and he's getting to know my voice.

And playtime – well, that's a dad's forte. I'm already trying out funny faces on Sam and singing silly songs. I can't wait until I get the first smile out of him."

Eye contact, talking, laughing and engaging with your baby constantly all work towards developing a deep bond (left).
Your physical closeness is a huge comfort to your baby, who will feel reassured by your scent and secure in your presence (above).

Encouraging bonding

Parent–baby bonding is a complicated process and can take time to develop. As bonding is an individual, personal experience, some parents therefore will find it happens instantly, while for others it will happen over time.

Getting to know you

Your baby may be cute and cuddly, but he's also an entirely new person – and one you'll have to get used to. You can't force yourself to bond and there is no magic formula for it. A true parent–child bond often develops through everyday caring. As long as you take care of your baby's basic needs and cuddle him regularly, he won't suffer if you don't feel that strong bond at first.

Breastfeeding can help you bond with your baby. You will both benefit from the close cuddle and skin-to-skin contact needed to feed him, and the satisfaction he gets from being nourished by you. Touching and stroking your baby is also very important, and so is talking to him. When your baby starts to babble in that strange language of his, babble back to him, gazing into his eyes.

Bonding may sound like a lot of work, but the key to this mysterious process is really enjoyment: simply enjoying being with your baby and caring for him. Babies fall in love with the people who enjoy them, and who help them enjoy themselves. Their "first loves" aren't just the people who feed and change them – they're the ones who are there when they want affection and company, who notice when they smile, and smile back.

Over time, as you get to know your baby and learn how to soothe him and enjoy his presence, your feelings will deepen. One day – it may be the first time your baby smiles at you – you'll look at your baby and realise you're completely filled with love for him. And that's bonding!

The mutual gaze

Although your baby probably won't smile until he's around four to six weeks old, in the meantime, he has an innate desire to communicate with you in whatever way he can.

Mirroring you

From early on, your baby can imitate your facial expressions by, for example, moving his tongue or widening his eyes. Babies are programmed to join in this "social dance" by meeting your eyes in a mutual gaze and taking turns to make facial gestures. If he does this, he'll quickly learn that it's an effective way to attract and hold your attention.

Enjoy every moment of your mutual gazes. These facial expressions are the beginning of your baby turning into a social person. When you feel fraught by the hard work of looking after a baby, that beautiful face will always win you over. It's an important part of the parent–child bonding process.

Welcome to parenthood!
0–6 weeks

Your growing baby
6 weeks to 6 months

Your older baby
6 months to one year

Baby healthcare
0–12 months

Going home with your baby

Whether you had a straightforward birth and can go home on the day of the birth, or you had to stay in hospital for a few days after a more complicated birth, or because one of you has a medical problem, going home can be quite an event.

Leaving the hospital

Before you leave hospital, your baby will be signed off by a paediatrician, and you'll be examined by a midwife or doctor to check that your uterus has contracted, that any stitches are healing properly, that your bleeding isn't too heavy and that you've passed urine. As well as the type of birth you had, your length of stay in hospital may depend on factors such as your support network at home and how restful or otherwise you find hospital. Some women love being looked after and feel safe in hospital. You may be able to stay longer if you don't feel ready to go home or you don't have help at home. Other women find it hard to rest in a noisy postnatal ward, or find that their baby won't settle. You may just feel happier at home. You can talk to your midwife about your preferences.

Your baby's first journey

Most hospitals won't sign you off until your baby is sitting safely in a newborn car seat (see p.100). If this is the only car trip your baby is likely to make, you might consider getting a second-hand car seat, perhaps from friends or family. However, only do this if you are certain of the history of the car seat and are happy that it hasn't been in an accident.

Before you leave hospital, you'll be given a list of contact numbers, should you need help or advice at home.

In your own home

Once you're home, your community midwife will usually visit every day or two until your baby is 10 days old. In some areas, though, midwives run postnatal clinics instead of home visits, or they run breastfeeding clinics. Ask your midwife what happens where you live; it helps to have all the information you need in these first daunting weeks.

If your mum visits, enjoy her making a fuss. Don't feel you must entertain lots of visitors, though – your and your baby's needs come first.

If your baby's first journey is by car, you will need to ensure that you have a suitable newborn car seat to transport her.

Dad's **Diary**

Home comforts

"It was really important to me to get our home ready for Sarah and Elliot when they arrived home from the hospital. They both had to stay in hospital overnight and I was sent home. The last thing I wanted was for Sarah to come home to find the pile of dirty dishes we'd left when the contractions started! I gave the kitchen and bathroom a quick clean, and I put fresh linen on the bed – I knew Sarah would appreciate that. My mum helped out by taking some of the washing and ironing off our hands, which I was extremely grateful for.

Elliot's room had been ready for weeks – mostly my handiwork, I'm proud to say. Sarah had carried our baby for nine months – the least I could do was prepare his nursery."

Quiet family time will help you all adjust to the new arrival, and help your baby to settle into her new home environment.

Welcome to parenthood!
0–6 weeks

Your growing baby
6 weeks to 6 months

Your older baby
6 months to one year

Baby healthcare
0–12 months

Essentials for your baby

Stocking up on the babycare essentials before the birth of your baby will ensure the first days at home go as smoothly as possible. Consult the checklist below.

What you'll need

- a supply of nappies. Newborns need eight to 10 nappies a day, so buy enough to keep you going for at least the first few days
- baby wipes or cotton wool, for nappy changing
- a changing mat, or a changing unit
- four to six babygros or all-in-one newborn sleepsuits
- four to six vests or body suits with poppers underneath
- an all-in-one warm suit with poppers beneath the legs is useful if your baby is born in winter
- one or two cardigans to provide an extra layer of warmth
- a summer or winter hat
- a Moses basket or cot
- a fitted mattress
- cotton sheets and cellular blankets, or a bottom sheet and a baby sleeping bag (see p.56)
- a rear-facing newborn car seat
- a pram, or buggy suitable for a newborn
- nursing bras if you're breastfeeding
- bottles, teats and a sterilisation system if you're bottle feeding
- a baby bath (or a washing up bowl will suffice), or a newborn bath support
- a couple of baby towels and some mild baby bath

 ## Systemised mum

From friends to professionals, a support network is crucial.

"One of the first things I did when we got home was to put a list of useful numbers in an accessible place. I included numbers for NHS Direct, our doctor and the midwife; it was reassuring to know that we could quickly access help if needed.

I added a few numbers of friends with children who I thought would help me put things in perspective if I feel overwhelmed. I also included a good friend who will make me laugh when I'm feeling sleep deprived, as well as the number of my most sensitive friend who'll be sympathetic when I need a cry!"

Special care baby

Some newborns need special attention either because they are premature or need extra medical care. Hospital staff understand that seeing your baby attached to tubes in a neonatal unit can feel upsetting and overwhelming. They will talk you through all you need to know.

The neonatal unit

Premature babies need extra monitoring, treatment and care. The neonatal unit gives expert, around-the-clock care for premature or ill newborns. Specially trained staff will look out for signs of any problems and treat your baby promptly.

It may be a terrible shock if your baby has to go to the neonatal unit, but this is the best possible place for your little one to be if he needs special care and attention.

Levels of care

Neonatal units offer different levels of care depending on your baby's needs.
● Intensive care (neonatal intensive care unit or NICU) provides care for the most seriously ill babies.
● High-dependency (HD) care is for babies who are not critically ill, but still need complex care.
● Special care (SC) is for well babies who are catching up on growth and development after a premature birth, or for those who are getting better after more complex treatment.

You may feel helpless and unable to care for your premature baby, but studies show that your touch, voice and physical presence are hugely beneficial to his development.

Your baby's needs

Around six to 10 per cent of newborn babies spend time in a neonatal unit. All babies need to be nourished and kept warm. If your baby is premature, his body isn't fully developed so he'll need extra help. In a neonatal unit, a special cot, or incubator, radiates gentle heat to create a constant temperature. Small babies may stay in an incubator until they're around 34 weeks post-conception age, or weigh 1.4 to 1.8 kilograms (3 to 4 pounds). Your baby may be given a nutritious mix of fluids through a drip, or a tube may carry milk to his stomach. You can provide expressed milk and can breastfeed when your baby is stronger.

How you can help

There are many ways to care for your baby. Protect him by avoiding close contact with outsiders and wash your hands before touching him. Shield him from bright light, hold him close and talk softly. Becoming used to your scent will help when he starts breastfeeding.

Touching premature babies helps them develop and grow. Stroking can interrupt "stop-breathing" (apnoea) attacks, and holding your finger may calm his breathing. If he needs treatment, rouse him by stroking him, wrapping him in a blanket, raising the light level a little and talking or singing softly.

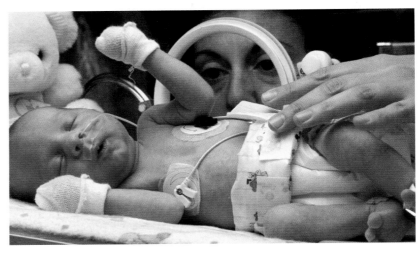

Your baby's care

In the neonatal unit, a skilled team of experts will care for your baby, including specialist neonatal nurses, a consultant paediatrician or neonataologist and other doctors. As your baby's parent, you are also part of this team, so don't be afraid to ask questions or talk about your worries and concerns.

Tests and treatments

During your baby's stay in the neonatal unit, he may undergo various tests and treatments. It can be scary to see your baby attached to all sorts of tubes and machines and you may feel as though you'll never be close to him. However, as he gets stronger, he'll need fewer machines, and soon you'll be able to

hold and care for him. In the meantime, it can be reassuring to be familiar with the procedures that are carried out.

"Vital-signs" machines keep track of your baby's heartbeat, breathing, blood pressure and temperature. Wires from a monitor are attached to your baby's chest with pads. It's normal for the monitor alarms to sound off quite often.

Your baby may have a blood saturation monitor that is strapped to his foot or hand and measures how much oxygen is in his blood.

Some babies need to be on a ventilator. These help babies' lungs to do the work of breathing by pushing air into the lungs through a tube that has been passed into his windpipe.

Oxygen may also be passed to your baby through a see-through head box in his incubator, or he may receive it through a mask or nasal tube. Nasal tubes can gently inflate the lungs and keep them open, a procedure known as continuous positive-airway pressure.

Although you may be unable to hold your baby, enjoying physical contact, however small, is important for you both.

Drips, lines and catheter tubes may be placed in your baby's veins to give him vital fluids, medicine or nutrition. Tubes may also be placed in his arteries to test blood pressure or oxygen levels.

A syringe-like infusion pump makes sure that all medicines are delivered into your baby's bloodstream at the right rate and speed. A feeding (gastric) tube gives your baby milk (once he is OK to receive it) through a tube into his stomach, from his mouth or nose. If your baby has developed jaundice (see p.247), phototherapy lights treat the condition.

Systemised mum

Expressing your breastmilk can give your tiny baby the best possible start

"I knew that breastfeeding Alice was one of the most important things I could do to build up her health and strength and protect her from infection. However, as with most premature babies, getting on to the breast was a gradual and sometimes slow process.

At first, she simply wasn't strong enough to breastfeed. I was told her digestion and sucking ability needed time to develop, and that because of her breathing problems, she would get tired between feeds. However, the staff showed me how to express my milk, which was given to Alice through a feeding tube. I also built up an impressive supply of frozen milk!"

ParentsAsk...

I'm finding it hard to cope with my baby being in hospital. Help!

It's tough when your baby needs special care, especially if you weren't expecting it, but you're not alone. Six to 10 per cent of newborns spend time in a neonatal unit. It's the best place for your baby to be at the moment, and the staff will be very understanding of your anxiety.

Why are there so many machines?

It's upsetting to see your baby wired up to machines via various tubes,

but this means that your baby is being monitored around-the-clock by experts who can deal with problems the moment they occur. As your baby gets stronger, he'll need fewer tubes and machines.

Can I breastfeed my baby?

This depends on how early your baby was born and his overall health and strength. The staff in the unit will be able to advise you. If your baby is too weak to breastfeed, you can express milk for him to take through a tube.

The greener baby

Caring for your baby and the environment at the same time isn't the uphill struggle that some people imagine it must be. In fact, taking on board a greener lifestyle can actually make your life easier – and may even save you money at the same time.

Opting to use washable nappies is an individual lifestlye choice that could have wider implications for your baby's future.

Your choices

As a new parent, you may want to think about the impact of your baby purchases on the environment and whether there are greener options available.

Green purchases
You could choose a crib or Moses basket instead of a full-size cot. Palm and wicker baskets are cheap, made from biodegradable and renewable materials and are easily portable, while recyclable cardboard cribs are becoming popular.

Cloth nappies can be a greener choice depending on how you wash and dry them. Or you can buy eco-friendly disposable nappies, which are more biodegradable than regular ones.

Shopping for newborn clothes can be hard to resist, but for the green-minded there are many options. Organic and fair trade cotton, hemp and bamboo materials are environmentally and ethically sound. There's also a wealth of second-hand clothes shops, auction sites and clothing exchanges, not to mention hand-me-downs from friends and family.

When it comes to toys, there's a wide range of green choices. Toys made from sustainably sourced wood are ideal, as they're hard-wearing, germ-resistant and free from potentially harmful toxins. Like clothing, there's a thriving second-hand market, both on the high street and online. But for the greenest and most fun option, why not make your own? Hand-made toys like rag dolls and finger puppets are simple to make, and a great way to encourage creativity.

4.5 trees are pulped for a baby's supply of disposable nappies.

From birth to toilet training, at two to three years of age, a baby goes through an average of 8,000 nappy changes. That's a lot of nappies if you choose to use disposables, and a lot of washes if you opt for cloth reusuable nappies.

Parents**Talk...**

"We use cloth nappies, and when we do need the odd disposable one we use a biodegradable brand. They break down completely if you have a wormery to put them in."
Lesley, 23, first-time mum

"I use cloth nappies and do a wash once every two days. I then dry the nappies on the washing line rather than use a tumble drier. We also use washable baby wipes, and put them in with the nappies."
Jenny, 34, first-time mum

"I cut up old towels to make my own baby wipes. When you're using cloth nappies, they can all be kept, and washed, together."
Helen, 40, mother of two

A simple, colourful mobile is easy to make and stops you purchasing a manufactured product.

Save energy by drying clothes the good old-fashioned way – on the washing line – and enjoy the freshness this lends to your and your baby's clothes.

Greener practices

As well as the purchases you make, there are a number of ways to employ more environmentally friendly practices when caring for your baby.

What you can do

Cut down on using disposable baby wipes, which end up in landfill, by using alternatives wherever possible. For example, a damp flannel in a plastic bag can be used for quick clean-up jobs when you're out with your baby.

You can also be greener by washing clothes at cooler temperatures. The Energy Saving Trust points out that washing clothes at 30°C (86°F) is an easy energy saver, using around 40 per cent less electricity than higher temperatures. Modern powders and detergents are formulated to work just as effectively at lower temperatures, so unless clothes are heavily soiled, it's fine to select a warm or even a cold wash. This makes

your clothes last longer, too. If you can, wait until you have a full load, or choose a half-load or economy programme.

The greenest clothes dryer is the washing line. If you have the space, hang your washing out to dry. If you have a tumble dryer, cleaning the fluff out of the filter before each load reduces your energy use by up to 30 per cent.

You can even be green in the way you feed your baby. Each bottle of formula affects the environment – from boiling the water, to the tinplate, paper and plastic used to package the powder. Not only that, but cattle farming needs large areas of pasture and significantly contributes to the problem of acid rain. Breastfeeding eliminates all of that. It's also estimated that if all new mums in the UK breastfed their babies, the absence of their periods would result in a saving of 3,000 tonnes of paper-based sanitary products every year!

 Green mum

Eliminating toxic products from your cleaning cupboard is kinder to the environment and better for your baby. Green alternatives work well and can be cheaper.

"I try not to use commercial products on my baby's skin. Soaps, shampoos and lotions often irritate his skin, and in the early months I think that plain warm water or some organic baby soap is sufficient.

I also avoid toxic products that could pollute his environment. My cupboard used to be full of chemical products, which I've since dispensed of in favour of gentler alternatives. Diluted white vinegar is great for cleaning glass, and neat can be used to unblock showerheads and sinks. Lemon juice is an alternative to de-greasers and bleaches, and bicarbonate of soda is great for removing stains on the carpet – or cleaning the toilet seat."

Welcome to parenthood! 0–6 weeks

Your growing baby 6 weeks to 6 months

Your older baby 6 months to one year

Baby healthcare 0–12 months

Babycare basics

When you first come home with your new baby, there seems to be so much to do and remember. Most of this will come naturally, but it's always good to get a few pointers from friends and family, and be reassured that you're a great mum …

Caring for your baby

Over the coming days and weeks, you'll learn how to care for your baby: how to hold him, change his clothes and nappy, keep him clean and respond to his cries.

As a new parent, it's natural to feel overwhelmed, confused and slightly scared. Don't worry – you and your baby will learn together.

First and foremost, your baby needs your love. Caring for your baby's basic needs and showing your love – by talking to your baby and holding and cuddling him – will make him feel secure and loved and help him to thrive.

Babycare basics

Even holding your wriggly, fragile baby will seem difficult at first, but you'll soon get used to it. Remember to support

your baby's developing neck muscles at all times (see opposite). You'll learn how to keep your baby clean in the first few weeks with simple "topping and tailing" (see p.38), and how to look after his umbilical stump.

When you first bath your baby, you may find it a little scary, and newborns can often object quite noisily to bathtime. Following the advice on pages 38–9 will help to ensure that your baby's bathtimes are as stress-free as possible for you both.

Your newborn baby will need frequent nappy changes (see pp.36–7) – before or after each feed, and when his nappy is dirty. You may find at first that it takes you ages to change his nappy, but you'll get quicker with practice!

As you get to know your baby, you'll work out the best ways to respond to his cries (see pp.34–5). If you've met his basic needs, it may be that your baby simply wants some comfort. Some babies like to be swaddled or rocked, others enjoy being carried close to you in a sling.

As your baby grows, you'll find caring for him gets easier – and is second nature before you know it.

Besides his practical care, your baby's most basic need is an abundance of love.

ParentsTalk…

"I'll never forget the first time I bathed my baby. Even in our sink, he looked tiny. I expected him to cry when I first lowered him into the water, but he was as good as gold. He's a real water baby now; he never wants to get out of the bath. I love holding him close when he's clean and wrapped up in a towel. It's a lovely time of day."
Carrie, 29, first-time mum

"I didn't realise it would take so long to get the hang of nappy changing, what with all the unfastening, wiping and lifting. I learnt fast, though, to cover my little boy's willy with a clean cloth or nappy while I wiped him to avoid an unexpected shower!"
Fernanda, 19, first-time mum

"While pregnant, I couldn't stop shopping for my baby. I knew I was having a boy and bought him lots of outfits. Mad, I know, because he seemed to grow out of them overnight! When I first dressed him in a tiny sleepsuit, he looked so sweet. I can't believe I made him!"
Sally, 24, first-time mum

Holding your baby

Your midwife will reassure you that your little wonder won't break if you touch him: just support his head and body and you're away! Babies love feeling secure, so wrap him snugly in soft clothing or a swaddling blanket if he enjoys this (see p.40), and hold him close. Or hold him skin-to-skin to reassure him.

Your baby won't judge you on how well you pick him up, and instinctively you'll do it with care, so have confidence.

Careful cradling

Until about four weeks, your baby won't have head control and will gain neck strength slowly. Support his head when holding him, especially when picking him up and putting him down. Use one hand and arm to cradle his back and bottom (the other hand under his head), and draw him to you in a fluid motion, embracing him gently to your chest. Or hold him with his head on your shoulder,

his bottom in the crook of your arm and your forearm supporting his back. Reverse the steps to put him down, smoothly lowering him onto his back.

When cuddling him to your chest, keep his head slightly higher than his body. When he's tiny, you can do this with an arm supporting the length of his body, or with both arms encircling him. You can also carry him in a sling, as long as his neck and head are supported and his body fits securely into the carrier.

As your baby gains head control, you can pick him up under his armpits and carry him facing inwards. Also, once his head is stronger he can face out: his back to your chest, straddling your hip; or in a "rugby" hold: a hand under his chest and armpits and a hand under his legs. Always mind your back! Never keep your legs straight and bend at the waist to pick up your baby: keep your back straight and bend your legs as if settling into a seat.

Laid-back mum

At first, you may feel awkward and unsure picking up your baby, but before long it will feel totally natural.

"The first few times I picked up Jack I felt clumsy. He was so tiny, and his head looked heavy compared to his body. I was terrified of not supporting his head properly. So most of the time I sat and held him, or lay with him on my chest. It was lovely having him so close, smelling his smell and hearing the snuffling noises that he made.

I feel a bit more confident now, so I can pick him up and carry him around. I prop him on my shoulder, supporting his bottom with one arm and his back with my other. Sometimes he looks around, but often he nods off to sleep. He seems happiest when I hold him and I love it too. I'm getting a sling so that I can carry him all the time!"

Welcome to parenthood!
0–6 weeks

Your growing baby
6 weeks to 6 months

Your older baby
6 months to one year

Baby healthcare
0–12 months

How to pick up and hold your baby

Use one hand to support your baby's head and neck, and the other hand to cradle both his back and bottom.

Once your baby is strong enough, he can face out with his back to your chest and may enjoy being cradled facing downwards.

Always support your baby's head during the early weeks, especially when picking him up and putting him down.

Why your baby cries

All babies cry sometimes – they have to. Even entirely healthy newborns will cry for somewhere between one and three hours each day. This is because babies rely on someone else to provide them with food, warmth and comfort, and crying is their way of communicating these needs.

 Single mum

Caring for a baby on your own can be hard work, so don't hesitate to ask for help from family and friends.

"Jack is a bit colicky in the evenings and he can cry and cry. Sometimes I just want to pass him to someone else, shut myself in a room and scream. Or listen to some really loud music! My mum often comes around in the evenings to help out. She can't stop him crying either, but just having someone else who can walk up and down with him gives me a bit of a break and helps me cope.

Gradually, I'm getting to know other new mums in the area and that's making a big difference. There's a mother-and-baby group that meets round the corner, which my health visitor told me about. The other mums are really nice, and it makes me feel better when I hear that I'm not the only one struggling.

The other thing that has made life easier is just getting to know Jack. I'm more confident and trust my instincts more. At first, I felt like I didn't know what he wanted or needed. Now I know if he's crying for something, or whether he's just fussing."

Deciphering your baby's cries

As a new parent, it can be hard to work out exactly what your baby is telling you when she cries. Is she hungry, cold, thirsty, bored, or in need of a cuddle? In the early days, when you haven't learned to work out what your baby needs, her crying can be upsetting. However, you'll soon start to recognise her different crying patterns and, as you get to know her, will be able to anticipate her needs.

In the meantime, is your baby hungry? This is the most common reason why a newborn cries, and she'll calm down as her tummy fills up with milk. If she's still crying, check that she is comfortable, warm and rested. Maybe her nappy is wet, or her clothes are restricting her movement. It could be that she's fussing from being awake too long, or having had too many visitors. Or perhaps she just needs attention from you – some babies need lots of cuddles and reassurance.

If your baby has been fed and is comfortable but is still crying, you may wonder if she's ill or in pain. First-time parents can find it hard to tell if their baby is crying because she's an unsettled baby by nature (some just are as it takes them a while to adjust to being in the world) or whether there's something wrong. However, you know your baby best, so if you feel there may be a problem, call your doctor, midwife or health visitor. Health professionals will listen to your concerns, and can usually reassure you that there isn't a physical cause for her crying.

As babies develop, they learn other ways to communicate – through eye contact, noises and even smiling, all of which reduce the need for crying.

"As your baby grows, you'll get better at **anticipating** her **needs**."

Responding to your baby's cries straightaway gives her the security of knowing that her needs are always met.

Being carried close to the warmth of your body is incredibly soothing and comforting for your baby.

Soothing your baby

There are many techniques for calming babies. Not all of them will work for you as all babies are different, but as you get to know your baby's personality, you'll find the best ways to soothe her.

Calming techniques

Some newborns like feeling secure and snug, just as they were in the uterus, so you could try swaddling your baby by wrapping her gently in a light blanket (see p.40). She may find it soothing, too, if you hold her close, perhaps in a sling.

Many babies respond well to rhythm – probably because they could hear the regular beat of your heart in the uterus – so regular, repetitive noises can be calming. Try playing soft music, singing a lullaby, or letting her listen to the steady rhythm of the washing machine.

Most babies love movement and enjoy being gently rocked. Try walking around while cradling your baby, or sit

with her in a rocking chair. Special baby swings soothe some babies, while others drop off to sleep almost as soon as they're in a moving car or buggy.

Giving your baby a massage (see p.164) or gently rubbing her back or tummy can be comforting. Babies with colic (see right) are sometimes calmed by having their tummies rubbed.

Some babies have a strong need to suck, and sucking a dummy, finger or thumb brings great comfort. Sucking may steady your baby's heart rate, soothe her digestion and help her settle.

Most importantly of all, don't blame yourself for your baby's distress. Being the parent of a newborn is hard work. If it gets too much, try some of the coping techniques in the box, above. Also, don't be afraid to ask for more support; it's important to get help and support from friends and family when you need it, rather than letting things build up.

Coping strategies

If you sometimes find your baby's crying exhausting and frustrating and wonder about your ability to cope with her, it can help to develop some coping strategies.

Remember that all babies cry, and all mums go through this. Take comfort from the fact that each day, as your baby grows, she will learn new ways to communicate her needs to you. Gradually, as she gets bigger, the crying will reduce.

- Put your baby down safely in her cot, take a few deep breaths and take some time out in another room if you need to. It's OK to put your baby down for a few minutes and give yourself some time to regain your composure.
- Accept any offers of help from others when you need it, rather than struggling on your own.
- Phone a friend or family member for a chat and a moan.

Is my baby colicky?

Around 20 per cent of all babies get colic: uncontrollable crying in an otherwise healthy baby (see p.245). All babies cry a lot, but a baby with colic will cry or fuss for over three hours a day and more than three days in a week. Colic can occur at any time, but is most usual in the evenings.

Signs of discomfort

As well as persistent crying, a baby with colic looks uncomfortable. She may extend or pull up her legs and pass wind. It's upsetting to see your baby in distress, but she won't harm herself. The good news is, colic usually goes away by about three to four months.

Welcome to parenthood!
0–6 weeks

Your growing baby
6 weeks to 6 months

Your older baby
6 months to one year

Baby healthcare
0–12 months

Changing a nappy

Once you've got the hang of it, nappy changing will become second nature, and you'll have plenty of chances to practise, because your little one will need eight to 10 changes a day at first! Expect to change your baby's nappy before or after every feed, and whenever he has done a poo. Leaving him in a soiled or wet nappy for too long can make his skin sore.

Getting started

It's wise to wash your hands and get everything ready before you start. Whether you choose disposable nappies or cloth ones is up to you; both have pros and cons (see right). You'll need a safe changing area, a bucket or bag for disposing of the dirty nappy, baby wipes or cotton wool and warm water, nappy cream and a change of clothes, in case the old nappy has leaked.

Cleaning your baby

Wipe away poo with the old nappy. If you have a boy, cover his penis with a clean cloth or nappy to avoid a sudden shower! Lift the legs and clean the bottom and genitals with a wipe, or wet cloth or cotton wool. If you have a girl, wipe from front to back and away from her vagina to prevent infection. Once your baby is clean, thinly apply barrier cream, if you like, to prevent nappy rash.

If you're using cloth nappies, put the dirty one in the nappy bucket and close the lid tightly! If you're using disposable nappies, re-tape the soiled nappy around its dirty contents, put it in a plastic bag, if necessary, and pop it in the bin.

Fitting a clean nappy

Position the nappy so that just over half of it is under your baby's bottom and the other half is under his legs, making sure

Choosing nappies

This is one of the great parenting debates. The advantages of cloth nappies are that they can be cheaper and may cause less nappy rash, but disposables are more convenient.

Nappies and the environment

Many parents choose reusable nappies because they're worried about the environment, but it's unclear whether reusables are the most ecological choice. Using cloth nappies means much less waste is sent to landfill sites: about eight million nappies are thrown away each day in the UK and it's thought they could take hundreds of years to decompose. However, cloth nappies need to be washed and dried, which uses a lot of energy. They're more environmentally friendly if you have an energy efficient washing machine and you line dry rather than tumble dry.

How to change a disposable nappy

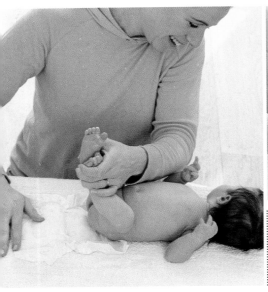

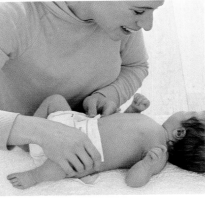

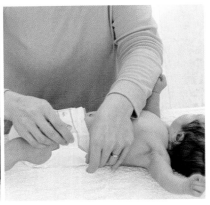

Gently hold your baby's legs by the ankles, lift up his bottom and place the nappy so that just over half of it is under your baby's bottom and the other half is under his legs (left). **Keeping half of the nappy** under the bottom, bring the front half of the nappy up between your baby's legs to just below his navel and hold this in place ready to secure the nappy (top left). **Fasten the nappy securely** with the sticky tabs so that it fits snugly, but is not too tight or restricting (top right).

that the front piece won't irritate his cord stump. For boy babies, tuck the penis down so moisture is less likely to escape through the top of the nappy.

Try not to bunch the nappy between the legs, as this can cause chafing and discomfort. When you fasten the nappy, make sure it's snug, but not so tight that it pinches the skin – there should be space for the skin to breathe. Once the new nappy is secure you're all done! It's time to wash your hands and dress him.

Dealing with nappy rash

Not changing your baby's nappy often enough can lead to nappy rash, which is caused by wetness and bacteria and is sore and uncomfortable. If your baby has nappy rash, you'll see that the skin covered by his nappy, probably the genital area and the folds of the thighs and the buttocks, looks inflamed and red. The affected areas may be dry or moist, and sometimes pimply. The best remedy for nappy rash is to keep your baby clean and dry by changing his nappy often. If it's warm enough, leave his nappy off for a while as the air will speed up the healing process. Use water and cotton wool to clean your baby and apply a barrier cream. If you suspect a rash is allergy-related, use fragrance-free and additive-free detergents and nappies.

A normal nappy rash should clear up after three or four days. If a rash persists, spreads or gets worse, mention it to your doctor or health visitor.

Welcome to parenthood! 0–6 weeks

Your growing baby 6 weeks to 6 months

Your older baby 6 months to one year

Baby healthcare 0–12 months

Cloth nappies

Once, cumbersome terry towelling nappies were the only cloth ones you could buy. But nappies have come a long way, with new designs that are less likely to leak, fastenings and clips instead of pins to hold them in place and lightweight materials that dry easily. They come in cute designs, anything from blue gingham to shocking pink, and can be more cost-effective than disposables, especially if you plan to have more children.

The perfect fit

Shaped washable nappies are cloth nappies designed to fit around your baby, which you use with a waterproof outer wrap. They resemble disposable nappies in their shape and can be fastened with Velcro tabs or poppers.

What's right for you

Send off for trial packs of nappies from different suppliers. This can be a huge help as the last thing you want to do is shell out and then decide you don't like the system you've invested in.

If you're worried about the practicalities of using washable nappies, you could use disposables for some of the time, for example at night, or when you're out with your baby. There are also businesses that offer a nappy-laundering service; they collect dirty nappies and drop off clean ones once a week.

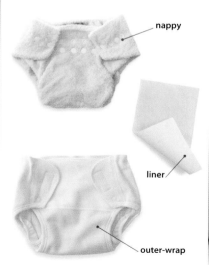

nappy

liner

outer-wrap

Cloth nappies are usually made up of three parts: the nappy, the waterproof outer wrap and the liner.

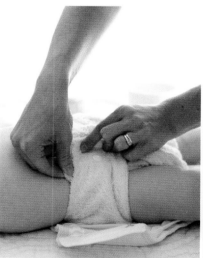

Put a liner (if using) inside the nappy. Lie the nappy on top of the wrap under your baby's bottom. Secure the nappy.

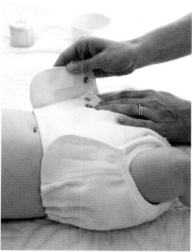

Place the outer wrap over the nappy and secure the poppers or velcro. Or if you're using plastic pants, put them on baby now.

Topping and tailing

At first, you may find it easier to stick to sponge baths – "topping and tailing" – rather than immersing your baby in water. To do this, you'll need a clean, wet, warm sponge or flannel and cotton wool.

What to do

Remove your baby's clothes apart from her vest. With a sponge or flannel, clean around her ears and neck and her hands and feet. Use a new piece of damp cotton wool to clean around each eye and wipe from the inner to the outer corner. Use a separate flannel or damp cotton wool for the nappy area.

When washing a boy, don't retract his foreskin. This won't be possible for a few months or even years and isn't necessary. With girls, wipe from front to back to avoid transferring bacteria from her bottom to her vulva. Pat your baby dry, put on a nappy and dress her.

How to top and tail your baby

Wash your baby's face and hands with a clean, warm, wet flannel or cotton wool. Use a fresh piece of cotton wool for each eye.

Clean your baby's bottom with a moist wipe or a piece of cotton wool. Pat her bottom dry before putting on a clean nappy.

Protecting the cord stump

Your newborn's umbilical cord stump (see p.244) must be kept clean and dry to prevent infection . Always wash your hands before handling it, especially before and after nappy changes.

Keeping the cord stump clean

You can make sure that the cord stump doesn't get any urine or poo on it by folding the front of your baby's nappy down and away from it so that it doesn't become soiled and the area around the stump is exposed to the air. If the stump does get mucky with urine or poo, though, you can simply wash it off using clean water and a mild soap.

In the past, cord stumps were routinely cleaned with antiseptic tissues or powder. Nowadays, though, in most Western countries where there are high standards of cleanliness, this is no longer considered necessary. Studies of the healing process of the stump found that there was no advantage to using antiseptics over simply keeping the cord clean. Using water and gentle soap is sufficient, or even just water alone.

Bathing your baby

You don't need to wait for your baby's umbilical cord stump to fall off, or for the area to heal completely, before you give her a bath. The most important thing when bathing your baby is to keep her warm so she doesn't lose body heat.

Newborns don't need a daily bath. Until your baby is crawling around and getting into a mess, a bath isn't really necessary more than once or twice a week, but do top and tail each day. Some parents bath their babies each day for the pleasure of it, and you may enjoy incorporating it into an evening routine.

Gaining confidence

You may be nervous when you first bath your newborn. Handling a wriggling, wet, soapy baby takes confidence and practice, so stay calm and maintain a

Test the temperature of the water with the front of your wrist, where the skin is more sensitive than on your hands.

How to bath your baby

Wrap your baby in a warm towel and support her along your forearm while you wash her hair over the bath or sink (above). **Lower her into the bath** feet first, supporting her head and neck with one hand.

Wash her gently with your free hand, using a flannel if you wish (above centre).
Lift your baby out of the bath using one hand to support her head and neck and the other to support her bottom (right).

good grip. Never leave her unsupervised, even for a minute. If the doorbell or phone rings and you need to answer it, scoop her up in a towel and take her with you.

Preparation is key

Gather together everything you need before you start running the bath: lay out at least one clean towel, a clean nappy and clothes. Ensure the room is warm, as newborns can lose body heat quickly. Also, don't use strong cleansers, as they may damage your newborn's developing skin. Look for pH-neutral cleansers or mild baby soaps instead, and use them sparingly.

While your baby is so tiny, it makes sense to bath her in the kitchen sink or a small plastic baby bath. Fill it with about 12cm (5in) of water, at a temperature that is warm, but not hot (about 38°C/100°F). Test the water with the more sensitive skin on your inner wrist. Also, never put your baby in the bath while the water is still running in case the temperature changes.

Washing your baby

To wash your baby's hair, wrap her in a towel with her head exposed, hold her under your arm supporting her head and wet her hair with your free hand. Dry her hair, remove the towel and gradually slip her into the bath feet first, supporting her neck and head. Pour cupfuls of bath water over her so she doesn't get cold. Wash her gently with your hand or a flannel, from top to bottom, front and back. Some babies find warm water soothing. Others cry the entire bathtime, or when you lift them in and out.

As you lift your slippery baby out of the bath, use one hand to support her neck and head, and your other hand to support her bottom, with your thumb and forefinger around one thigh.

Wrap her in a soft towel, pat her dry and put a nappy on. Then wrap her in a blanket or a dry towel and cuddle her for 10 minutes to keep her warm. If she has dry skin, you could apply a mild lotion or oil before dressing her in clean clothes. Wrap her again in a dry, warm blanket.

Bathing checklist

Use the list below as a quick reference to ensure that your baby's bathing sessions run smoothly.

Tips for successful bathing

- Don't feel you have to bath your newborn every day – once or twice a week is OK while she's still very tiny.
- A plastic baby bath or even the kitchen sink may be easier at first.
- Gather up everything you need before you start running the bath.
- Use mild and pH-neutral products to protect your baby's delicate skin.
- Newborns lose body heat rapidly, so make sure the room is warm.
- The water should be comfortably warm, but not hot.
- Never, ever let go of your newborn in the water or take your eyes off her.
- Pour cupfuls of water over your baby's head and shoulders regularly so she doesn't get chilly.

Welcome to parenthood!
0–6 weeks

Your growing baby
6 weeks to 6 months

Your older baby
6 months to one year

Baby healthcare
0–12 months

Swaddling your baby

Swaddling is the ancient art of wrapping up your baby snugly to help him feel safe and secure. It can stop him disturbing himself with his own startle reflex – those alarming, but perfectly normal, jerks of the body he makes sometimes (see p.64). Swaddling may also help your baby to settle down when he's over-stimulated.

What to do

Before you swaddle your baby, check that he isn't hungry or wet. Then place a light cotton blanket on a flat surface and fold down the top-right corner by about 15 centimetres (6 inches). Put your baby on his back with his head on the fold, and pull the corner near your baby's left hand across his body, tucking the leading edge under his right arm and

around under his back. Pull the bottom corner up under your baby's chin and bring the right-hand corner over and tuck it under his back on the left side. Some babies prefer to have their hands free; if your baby prefers to keep his hands free, swaddle him under his arms.

Make sure you don't cover your baby's face or head and that the room isn't too warm as he may overheat. Once swaddled, he usually won't need another blanket on top.

Not all babies enjoy being swaddled, although many do. It's important to stop once your baby is around a month old, though, because after this time it may interfere with his development and mobility. When he begins to kick off the covers, he is saying that he no longer appreciates being bundled so snugly!

How to swaddle your baby

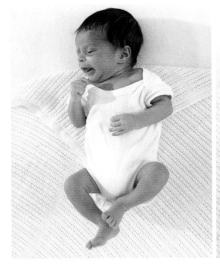

Put a light blanket on a flat surface and then fold over one corner of the blanket. Lie your baby on top of the blanket with his head above the top edge.

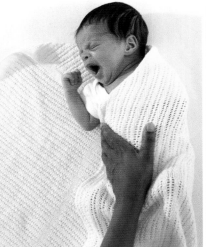

Gently place your baby's arm by his side and then pull over one side of the blanket so that it covers your baby's body and holds his arm securely, but not tightly, by his side.

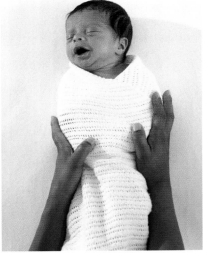

Bring the other side of the blanket over your baby's body, so that both arms are by his sides. Tuck in the bottom of the blanket so that your baby is completely swaddled.

Using slings and carriers

When you were pregnant, the gentle swaying motion as you walked and the bigger movements as you sat down or got up were a normal part of your baby's life. Carrying your baby in a sling can recreate these comforting movements.

Some babies love to be close all the time and so do some mums, but it's not for everyone. You or your baby may get too hot, and some new mums get

can carry him to the shops, or around the home, leaving your hands free to carry shopping, make a meal or hang out washing, while your baby is comforted by your warmth, scent and closeness.

The right sling for you

There are lots of designs of sling, so think about how you want to use one before buying it. Will it be just for walks

Some slings are like roomy hammocks that fit around you. In this type, your baby can lie down and you'll be able to feed him easily without having to extricate him from the sling. Others are like pouches or wraps. Baby carriers hold your baby in an upright position; some adapt from facing you when your baby is tiny to facing out as your baby grows. Most upright carriers can be used for newborns, but not all.

"A sling is **easy** to use and your baby **loves** being snuggled close."

"touched out" and need some space. When your baby's having a clingy day, though, and you've got things to do, a sling can be just what you need. You

or for anytime? Do you want to be able to breastfeed easily? Do you want it to adapt as your baby grows? Is it for your partner to use too?

You may find certain slings easier to get the hang of than others. If you know some other mums with baby slings, ask them for a demonstration. Alternatively, do as much research as you can before you buy one and give it a thorough road-test, either in a shop or at home, before you commit. Practicality and comfort are key when it comes to slings.

Hammock-like slings allow your baby to lie down while you carry him around and enable you to breastfeed your baby while he remains in his sling (left).
Slings that hold your baby in an upright position are popular for newborns and enable

you to carry your baby while keeping your hands free to do other tasks, such as shopping or household chores (centre).
Rucksack baby carriers are great for older babies who have sufficient head control to hold their heads up unsupported (above).

Welcome to parenthood!
0–6 weeks

Your growing baby
6 weeks to 6 months

Your older baby
6 months to one year

Baby healthcare
0–12 months

How to put on a sleepsuit

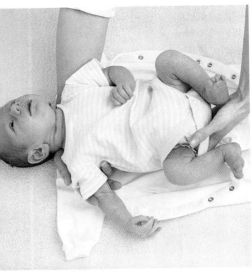
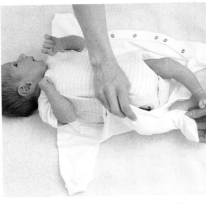

Spread out your baby's sleepsuit, with the poppers open, and lay your baby down on top of it (left).
Gently put your baby's legs into the sleepsuit legs (above centre).

Gather up the fabric on the arms and reach through to hold your baby's hand. Use her grasp reflex to guide her arm along the arm of the sleepsuit. Once both arms and legs are dressed, fasten the poppers (above right).

Dressing your baby

Dressing your baby can feel daunting at first because newborns can seem very fragile, and often cry when they're undressed. You can make the process much simpler for both of you by choosing clothes for your baby that are quick and easy to put on and take off.

Your baby's clothes

The best clothes for newborns are all-in-one, stretchy outfits made of natural fabrics. Choose vests that have poppers under the crotch, and sleepsuits (also called babygros) with poppers down the front, to make nappy changing easy. For most of the year, your baby can wear a sleepsuit with a vest underneath. If your baby is too warm, she could wear a sleepsuit on its own, or if it's really hot, a vest may be all that she needs.

Newborn babies generally need one more layer of clothing than adults. This is because young babies can't regulate their temperature very well. Feel the back of your baby's neck or her chest to assess if she is too hot or cold, and then adjust her clothing accordingly.

If your baby is born in the summer months, buy a sunhat to keep her face out of the sun. It's useful to have some cardigans or jackets so that you can add another layer if your baby is too cold. In the colder winter months, a padded snowsuit and a woolly hat are handy for trips outdoors.

Your baby won't need shoes for a while yet, but socks are handy when your baby isn't wearing an all-in-one outfit. Socks can also double up as scratch mitts if your baby has a tendency to scratch her face.

If your baby has delicate or dry skin or eczema, stick to cotton fabrics and avoid wool and synthetics, which can make your baby itch. If you would like to buy ethically produced clothes or are concerned about pesticides used in clothing, it's possible to buy organic cotton baby clothes, although these can be more expensive.

When your baby is out and about in her pushchair, you might find it handy to have several cellular blankets to hand, which you can then layer on if she gets too cold. Also, always carry a spare set or two of clothing with you, just in case of accidents.

Putting on clothes

As some babies dislike being dressed, try to have everything to hand before you start. Keep the room warm – it's thought that the reason babies often become upset when being undressed and dressed is because they dislike the feel of the cold air on their skin. Put your baby on a changing mat or another soft surface on the floor with a towel over it, in case of little accidents! Make sure your baby is wearing a clean nappy before you start, and massage your baby with a little moisturising lotion or oil if her skin is dry.

First, put on your baby's vest over her nappy. Her neck muscles aren't properly developed yet, so gently support her neck as you carefully place her vest over her head, lifting it over her face and stretching it over her body, then do up the poppers at the crotch. Next, lie your baby carefully on top of her undone sleepsuit, ease her arms and legs in gently, and do up the poppers all the way down the front. If the weather is cold, you could add a cardigan or jacket. Talk or sing to your baby as you get her dressed and tell her what you're doing – don't worry about sounding silly, your baby will love to hear your voice.

You don't need to dress your baby in trousers, shirts, pinafores and tights in the early days – it's best to leave these until she's a bit older. Your newborn will spend a lot of time sleeping, so it's fine to let her wear sleepsuits day and night!

Tips on choosing clothes and dressing newborns

Before succumbing to the tempting array of baby clothes on the high street, wise up to the best buys for your baby, and follow the tips for stress-free dressing and garment care.

● Don't bother with dresses, tights, trousers and shirts for babies under three months – you won't have time to put them on! If a relative or friend buys your baby a fancy outfit, ask them if they could change it to an older size, when your baby will be easier to dress.

● Your baby may have worn a hat in hospital if she was premature or a low birthweight, but unless a midwife or doctor tells you otherwise, she doesn't need one indoors at home.

● If you buy an outfit for a 3 to 6-month-old baby, bear in mind that it might be a different season by the time she wears it.

● Always carry a spare set of clothes with you when you're out and about, or even two spare sets. It's possible to have

one nappy explosion followed by a vomit in a short space of time (sorry!)

● Don't buy more baby clothes than you need before your baby is born as your baby will outgrow them quickly – you can always buy more later. Four to six vests, four to six babygros, plus a couple of cardigans and a hat is all you need.

● Find out about second-hand sales of baby clothes (NCT sales are great), and ask friends and relatives for their cast-offs.

● When you're dressing your baby, have everything you need to hand, including a spare nappy. If she dislikes being dressed, try changing her clothes when she's under a mobile, or play some of her favourite music to distract her.

● Wash new clothes with a gentle washing powder before use to avoid irritating your baby's sensitive skin.

● Don't unwrap everything, and keep your receipts, in case you want to take any spare clothes back.

All-in-one body suits with poppers around the crotch are ideal for babies. Short-sleeved ones are perfect for the warmer months.

Dressing in layers allows you to add or take away clothes as needed. A warm hat keeps your baby insulated outside when it's cold.

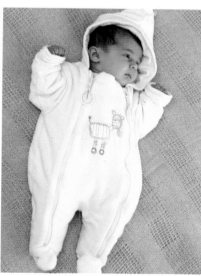

A cosy snowsuit is just the job when you're taking your baby out in the winter. Choose one with easy access to the nappy area.

Welcome to parenthood! 0–6 weeks

Your growing baby 6 weeks to 6 months

Your older baby 6 months to one year

Baby healthcare 0–12 months

Feeding your baby

Breast or bottle

Breast or bottle – that is the question! There is no doubt that "breast is best" for your baby – it is also free, while formula milk and bottles are expensive. However, this is your baby and only you can decide what's best for both of you.

Breastfeeding your baby

There are numerous benefits to breastfeeding. Breastmilk has all the nutrients in the correct quantities that your baby needs to thrive for the first six months; after this, alongside other foods, it's an important part of your baby's diet.

Breastmilk has antibodies that protect against infections such as respiratory illness, gastroenteritis and urinary and ear infections. It may also reduce the risk of childhood diabetes and leukaemia. Breastmilk also has long-chain polyunsaturated fatty acids that are essential for brain development. Breastfeeding is the healthiest choice

for you, too, reducing your risk of pre-menopausal breast and ovarian cancer and of osteoporosis.

Lastly, breastfeeding is very convenient. It's ready at the correct temperature whenever you need it, with nothing to wash, sterilise or prepare.

Feeding on demand

In the past, mums were encouraged to feed their babies every four hours. We now know there is nothing to be gained by this. Sticking to a rigid timetable may mean that your baby simply becomes hungry and therefore distressed, so at first it's better to feed your baby on demand, when he's hungry and fussing for food or "rooting" for your nipple.

Newborn babies need to feed little and often because their stomachs are too small to digest large amounts of milk. As your baby's digestive system matures, he will go for longer between feeds. Try to let your baby set the pace. You may find he has growth spurts where he's hungry and needs extra feeds for a day or two. Trust yourself to respond to his needs – you know him better than anyone else.

For the first few days, your breasts produce colostrum (see p.21), the rich, high-protein pre-milk. You may have

Breastmilk is the ideal first food for your baby, providing a catalogue of benefits for both your baby and you.

Laid-back mum

Breastfeeding allows you to feed your baby as soon as he needs it.

"The first few weeks with my new baby were chaotic: the house was a mess, I looked a mess and, despite the help of my husband, meals were makeshift and sleep was scarce. There's no way, in my zombie-like state, that I would have been able to cope with sterilising bottles, waiting for the kettle to boil and attempting not to spill formula powder everywhere while coping with a crying, hungry baby. Thank goodness for breastfeeding! As soon as my baby was hungry, a quick adjustment of clothing was all that was needed. Also, breastfeeding gives me a few moments of relaxation during the day, when I can sit on the sofa, put my feet up and enjoy some quiet time while my baby feeds."

leaked a little of this before your baby was born. It's the best possible food for your newborn baby. Around three to four days after the birth, your breastmilk will come in and your breasts may feel uncomfortably full and tender. Feeding your baby on demand will also help to reduce any discomfort and avoid your breasts becoming engorged (see p.48).

Welcome to parenthood!
0–6 weeks

Your growing baby
6 weeks to 6 months

Your older baby
6 months to one year

Baby healthcare
0–12 months

How to breastfeed

Breastfeeding your baby can take anything from seven to 40 minutes, so make sure you find a comfortable place to sit before you start. Atmosphere is very important, especially in the early days when you're still trying to get the hang of feeding. If you're easily distracted and disrupted by noise, find somewhere quiet. If you are easily bored, you may want to feed in front of the television, but only if breastfeeding is going well for you and your baby (as otherwise the television may distract you from the task at hand). Try different spots until you find what works for you.

Getting comfortable

Hold your baby in a position that won't leave your arms and back sore. Add support around you with cushions and perhaps a pillow under your baby. Many women find cradling their baby works well, although it really depends on what is most comfortable for you both. Make sure you and your baby are both in a relaxed position before you start feeding.

Latching on

Pay attention to how your breasts feel when your baby latches on. If it hurts when she latches on, break the suction by inserting your little finger between your baby's gums and your nipple, and try again. To latch on well, her mouth should be as wide open as possible as she comes onto the breast. Her tongue, bottom lip and chin should touch your breast first, and you should aim her bottom lip as far as you can from the base of your nipple. This will help her to get a good mouthful of breast tissue (the nipple and the areola, the dark part of the breast) when she starts to feed.

Once your baby has latched on properly, she will be able to feed more easily. On the other hand, if you carry on breastfeeding her while it's hurting because she hasn't latched on well, you are likely to end up with sore nipples.

If your baby starts to feed almost immediately, this is a good sign that she has latched on well. Her feeding pattern should change from a few short, quick sucks to slow deep sucks. During the feed, she will probably pause a few times and then start sucking again without you having to prod her or coax her into feeding again. If she takes a few sucks and then "goes to sleep", she is probably not latched on properly.

When you look down at your baby while feeding, her head should be tipped back and her chin be touching your breast. Her nose should be free so that she can breathe easily without you needing to push your breast away from her nose. If you can see any areola, there should be more visible above your baby's top lip than below her bottom lip.

How to latch your baby on

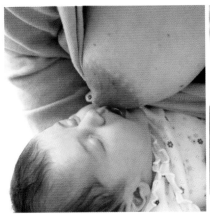

Bring your baby to the breast with her head tipped backwards, so that she leads with her chin. Then let her lips come forwards to touch your nipple.

Your baby will respond by dropping her lower jaw. Move her quickly and smoothly to your breast, aiming her lip as far as possible from the base of the nipple.

To remove your baby from the breast, gently insert your little finger into the corner of her mouth to break the seal. Never try to remove her without first breaking the seal.

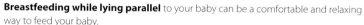

Breastfeeding while lying parallel to your baby can be a comfortable and relaxing way to feed your baby.

A "rugby hold", with your baby underarm, can be comfortable after a caesarean.

Finishing a feed

Once your baby has started to feed, she should relax and stay relaxed until the feed has finished. If she is wriggling, she is probably not latched on well. (Sometimes babies need to stop after a few minutes, when your milk is flowing at its fastest, to bring up wind.) She should let go of the breast on her own when she's finished, or fall away naturally if you raise your breast. Never pull your nipple away as this will be painful. If you need to remove her from the breast, gently insert your little finger into the corner of her mouth to break the seal.

Have a look at your nipple at the end of the feed. If it's compressed at all, it means that it probably wasn't far back enough in your baby's mouth.

Asking for help

Some women adjust to breastfeeding very easily, encountering no major hurdles, but many find it hard and not at all "natural". If you're feeling discouraged, contact a breastfeeding counsellor or infant-feeding specialist. These experts can watch you feed your baby and make recommendations. You could also talk to your doctor, midwife or health visitor about any health concerns that may impede successful breastfeeding of your baby.

Breastfeeding takes practice so give yourself time. Take it a week, a day or even just a feed at a time. If you've had a bad day, tell yourself that tomorrow will be better. Keep in mind that problems are likely to be temporary. By the time of your six-week check, you'll probably be breastfeeding without a second thought. If not, don't hesitate to ask for support.

Parents Talk...

"I found out about baby cafés from my health visitor. Talking to the breastfeeding counsellors there and being told well done when I felt like giving up was all the encouragement I needed to keep going. The cafés are a great way to meet mums, too."
Monica, 25, first-time mum

"Be aware of organisations such as The Breastfeeding Network, the NCT and La Leche League, and don't be shy about asking for help."
Terri, 39, mother of two

At first, feeding is a 24-hour job, so ask your partner to do the rest. Feed the baby, feed yourself and sleep!"
Sonja, 40, first-time mum

"Don't keep formula milk 'just in case' – it's more tempting to use it when you know it's there."
Geraldine, 30, mum of two

"I found lanolin ointment fantastic for cracked nipples. It helped them to heal and meant that I could carry on feeding at the same time."
Suzy, 35, first-time mum

"My breastmilk supply is low in the evenings, but expressing helps. I use an electric pump and clear my breasts after the first feed in the morning and before I go to bed. After a week's expressing, I produced surplus milk and now I freeze some every day."
Yvonne, 29, first-time mum

Welcome to parenthood!
0–6 weeks

Your growing baby
6 weeks to 6 months

Your older baby
6 months to one year

Baby healthcare
0–12 months

Breastfeeding concerns

One of the main concerns for new mums is whether their milk supply is adequate. This may be exacerbated by worries about discomfort and sore nipples. Many experts, though, say that it's rare for a mother not to have enough milk.

Your milk supply

You may think your milk supply is low if you stop feeling a strong letdown reflex (the tingly feeling in your breasts caused by the release of oxytocin) or lose the feeling of fullness, or if milk stops leaking. However, these are signs that your body has adjusted to your baby's requirements.

Breasts produce milk to match a baby's demands. The best way to be reassured that your baby is getting enough milk is his weight gain. Newborns typically lose five to 10 per cent of their birth weight in the first days, but should then start to gain weight. Also, if he has enough milk, he'll have about eight wet nappies a day. He'll be healthy, alert and have yellowy-mustard stools that lighten in colour about the fifth day after birth.

If you feel you're not producing enough milk, it may be that your baby isn't latching on properly (see p.46). If he's sucking on the tip of the nipple, it will probably hurt. Sore nipples are common in new breastfeeding mums, but they aren't a normal part of feeding. If the pain is intense or lasts longer than a few days, you should seek advice.

Specific concerns

Engorged, or swollen, breasts can occur when your milk comes in: more blood flows to your breasts, surrounding tissue swells and you may get a temperature. Feeding on demand helps. A supportive bra, even at night, also helps, as can taking paracetamol. If your breasts are overfull, expressing excess milk can help. While your baby feeds, it may be helpful to gently massage the breast he is on to encourage milk to flow and help relieve the discomfort. It's important to carry on breastfeeding to reduce the risk of developing mastitis, a painful inflammation of the breast (see p.112).

Drinking plenty of fluids helps to replenish fluids lost during breastfeeding.

Expressing breastmilk

If you're going to be away from your baby, you can express and store your milk. Expressing also relieves engorged breasts and increases your supply. When expressing, relax and think of your baby to stimulate your letdown reflex.

Expressing by hand

This takes practice and can be time-consuming, but some mums find this easier than using breast pumps.

Wash your hands and put your thumbs 4 to 5 centimetres (1½ to 2 inches) from the nipple, your fingers below. Squeeze fingers and thumbs together in a circular motion around the areola. If your finger and thumb are too close to the nipple, it will hurt and be ineffective. Use a sterile, wide-rimmed container to collect milk.

Using a breast pump

Some women find pumps faster and more efficient. An electric pump has a suction cup attached to the pump over your breast; you turn on the machine and milk is extracted into a container.

Manual pumps also use a suction cup, but you extract milk by using a squeeze mechanism. Good pumps mimic the sucking action of a baby, stimulating your letdown reflex, and aren't painful.

Storing your milk

Store breastmilk at 4°C or lower in feeding bottles with secure tops, or use plastic bags designed to store milk, or disposable bottle liners and store in the fridge or freezer. Use refrigerated milk within three to five days. Frozen milk lasts a week in the ice box of a fridge, and three to six months in a freezer set no higher than minus 18°C (0°F) (then up to 12 hours refrigerated after thawing). The freezing process destroys some antibodies, but frozen breastmilk is still healthier than formula.

Using a manual or electric breast pump is an efficient and comfortable way to express breastmilk to use as a back-up supply.

Expressing manually can take time, but some mothers find that with practice this is their preferred method of expressing.

Welcome to parenthood! 0–6 weeks

Your growing baby 6 weeks to 6 months

Your older baby 6 months to one year

Baby healthcare 0–12 months

ParentsTalk...

"Breastmilk is the best food for your baby at first. It's nutritionally balanced and builds up the immune system. It's also great for your health. It helps prevent breast and ovarian cancer, and you'll get your figure back more quickly, as it helps the womb contract and burns calories."
Tracey, 27, first-time mum

"There's no faffing about at two in the morning making up a bottle if you're breastfeeding – you can deal with your baby's hunger immediately, or express some milk before you go to bed, ready for your husband to step up and deal with the night feed."
Ruth, 29, first-time mum

"I tried to breastfeed, but had bad mastitis and sore nipples, so after a couple of weeks I switched to formula. I've heard that if you persevere it gets better, but having a new baby was enough to deal with."
Caroline, 31, first-time mum

"I prefer bottle-feeding as my partner can be involved. He enjoys giving our baby her bottle, and it's a chance for father–daughter bonding. He can also do night feeds, which is wonderful."
Susan, 34, mother of three

"My baby has formula and she does sleep for long stretches, but the downside is that she gets constipation regularly, which makes her uncomfortable and irritable."
Hazel, 38, first-time mum

Bottle-feeding your baby

Although experts agree that "breast is best", the decision of whether to breastfeed or bottle-feed is entirely yours. If you opt for bottle-feeding, you can be confident that your baby is receiving high-quality food that is designed to meet her nutritional needs.

Combining breast and bottle

It's perfectly possible to combine breastfeeding with bottles of formula milk. You will need to cut down on breastfeeds gradually, though, to stop your breasts from becoming engorged and leaky. Give yourself time to adjust and try dropping just one feed per week.

Some breastfed babies are reluctant to take a bottle at first and can be confused by the different sucking actions that are required, so perseverance is needed. It can help to warm the teat first and to get someone else to offer the bottle, because your baby may not take a bottle when she can smell your breastmilk.

Choosing formula

You'll need to decide which formula is right for your baby and you, which means considering your baby's health, age and dietary needs, as well as the cost of the formula and preparation time involved in making up bottles.

Most infant formula milks are based on cow's milk, which is modified to resemble breastmilk as closely as possible. Manufacturers modify cow's milk for babies by adjusting carbohydrate, protein and fat levels and adding vitamins and minerals.

The quality of traditional infant formula has improved greatly in the last decade. However, researchers have yet to reproduce the unique qualities that make breastmilk the ideal first food.

Soya-based formula is made from soya beans which, like cow's milk, are modified for use in formula with vitamins, minerals and nutrients. However, the UK Department of Health and the British Dietetic Association do not recommend soya formula for babies under six months. Babies who have a cow's milk intolerance or allergy should be referred to a dietitian. Your baby will probably need a formula that is hypoallergenic, meaning she won't react to it. This will be in the form of an amino acid-based or highly hydrolysed formula milk, which you can get on prescription.

Making up formula

Follow the instructions carefully. Use cooled, boiled water that has been left to cool no longer than half an hour. Fill the bottle to the marked level. Measure the milk powder with the scoop provided. Add this to the bottle. Put the teat and cover on and shake well. Don't add extra scoops as this could make your baby ill. Make up each feed fresh when you need it.

Fill the bottle with the correct amount of water. Add the powder according to the instructions, levelling off the scoops.

Once you've added the specified amount of scoops of formula, shake the bottle well so that the formula is properly mixed.

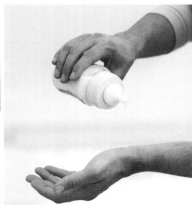

Test the temperature of the milk on your wrist to make sure it's not too hot for your baby; it should feel tepid on your skin.

Storing feeds

It's important to be aware that powdered infant formula milk isn't sterile and there is a small risk of contamination from micro-organisms if made-up formula is stored. For that reason, the UK Department of Health and the Food Standards Agency advise that feeds are made up fresh each time. If you need to prepare a feed for later, they suggest that freshly boiled water is kept in a sealed flask and fresh formula milk is made up when required. Avoid making up enough feed for a day in advance, or warming up bottles of formula milk that have been made in advance.

When bottle-feeding, tip the bottle upwards so that milk covers the teat and your baby doesn't swallow air.

Bottle-feeding and winding are ideal opportunities for dads to take a nurturing role in their baby's care, strengthening their bond.

Bottle-feeding when out and about

- You can buy ready-to-feed formula that comes sealed in little cartons. Although these can be expensive, they're handy for decanting into a sterilised feeding bottle when you're out and about.
- If your baby doesn't like milk at room temperature, you could carry an insulated bottle carrier for holding just-boiled warm water. Water needs to be 70°C (158°F) or hotter to destroy potentially harmful bacteria.
- Don't carry around made-up bottles of formula as this encourages bacteria.
- You can buy small screw-on sterilisable containers, which hold the required amount of formula powder.
- Before feeding your baby, test the temperature of the milk on your wrist.

Welcome to parenthood!
0–6 weeks

Your growing baby
6 weeks to 6 months

Your older baby
6 months to one year

Baby healthcare
0–12 months

Cleaning and sterilising

In the first year of life, babies are at their most vulnerable to viral, bacterial and parasitic infections as their immune systems are immature. These infections can lead to anything from a mild attack of thrush to the more serious condition of gastroenteritis, which causes vomiting and diarrhoea and can result in dehydration. It's important therefore to clean and sterilise all feeding equipment before making up feeds and dummies.

Cleaning your equipment

Before sterilising, your baby's bottles and teats need to be cleaned thoroughly with a bottle brush in warm, soapy water so that any trace of milk is removed. Carefully rinse off the detergent and run water through each teat to ensure that the hole is not clogged with milk curds.

Sterilising

There are different ways to sterilise feeding equipment. A popular method is electric steam sterilising, which is based on hospital methods and takes around eight to 12 minutes, plus cooling time. You can buy steamers for microwaves, too, which take around five to eight minutes to work, plus the required cooling time.

Another form of sterilising is boiling the feeding equipment for at least 10 minutes in a pan used exclusively for that purpose. Be warned that the teats will get sticky and unusable more quickly with this method than with other methods.

You can also buy bottles that can be sterilised in the microwave on their own in just 90 seconds. Lastly, there is cold-water sterilising, using a non-toxic solution, which comes in handy tablet form.

A steam sterilising unit is a popular and efficient way to sterilise equipment.

Avoid leaving sterilised empty bottles out on work surfaces for long as they will quickly lose their sterility. Most sterilisers have built-in storage facilities, which solves this problem.

Sleep and your baby

Your newborn's sleep

Your newborn will sleep a lot during his first few weeks. However, because he sleeps in short bursts – and almost never for more than a few hours at a time even during the night – you might not get much shut-eye for a while. Don't worry, this will get easier …

 Laid-back mum

When it comes to sleep and routines, following your own instincts is often the least stressful path.

"We made the decision when Maya was born to trust our instincts, to listen to what Maya was telling us, and if something wasn't working to try something else – especially when it came to sleep.

On our first night at home, I fed Maya and put her down in her Moses basket and she began to cry. I picked her up and put her next to me in my bed. Waking the next morning with my tiny, new treasure nuzzling to my breast was, I think, the most moving moment of my life.

We continued as we began and Maya has spent every night since in our bed. During the day, she often sleeps in her sling, snuggled up to my body, which we both enjoy.

We're always careful and take all the recommended precautions to make sleeping with our baby safe. We have a big bed and a firm mattress. She sleeps on top of the duvet with her own blankets so that she doesn't overheat. We don't smoke, and we've stopped drinking while we're co-sleeping, too."

What your baby needs

Newborns sleep a lot – about 17 to 18 hours a day for the first few weeks. However, they almost never sleep for more than three to four hours at a time, day or night, so you won't be getting much uninterrupted sleep, either.

While some babies sleep through the night at just eight weeks, most don't reach that milestone until five or six months, or later. If your aim is to get your baby to sleep through, you can get him there sooner by teaching good sleeping habits from early on (see p.54).

A newborn's sleep pattern
For the first six to eight weeks, your baby won't be able to stay up for much more than two hours at a time. If you wait much longer than that to put him

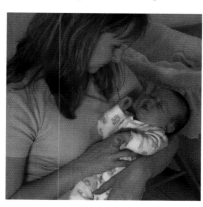

down, he'll be overtired and won't be able to fall asleep very easily. Watch your baby for signs that he's sleepy. Is he rubbing his eyes, pulling on his ear, or developing faint dark circles under his eyes? If you notice these, or any other signs of sleepiness, try putting him down in his cot or Moses basket. You'll soon develop a sixth sense about your baby's daily rhythms and patterns, and you'll know instinctively when he's ready for a nap.

The beginnings of a routine
The long-term key to helping your baby to settle is to establish a consistent bedtime and daytime nap routine (see p.54) and try to put your baby down to sleep at night while he's still awake. However, during the early weeks, you may feel more comfortable following your baby's pattern.

It's important to know that there is no "right" way to encourage your baby to settle and sleep through the night. As he grows and develops, you need to settle on an approach to sleep that works for you all as a family.

In the early weeks, your newborn won't distinguish between night and day, but will have a 24-hour sleep-feed-sleep cycle.

Welcome to parenthood!
0–6 weeks

Your growing baby
6 weeks to 6 months

Your older baby
6 months to one year

Baby healthcare
0–12 months

Establishing good sleeping habits

Your baby can start to develop good sleeping habits from when she's about six weeks old. First, you need to set the stage with a regular bedtime and a consistent bedtime routine. A bedtime that happens at the same time every night will set your baby's internal clock so that she starts to be naturally sleepy at a predictable time.

Overcoming pitfalls

Getting your baby to settle and sleep well, even after six weeks, can seem an uphill struggle, but there are ways to help achieve this over time.

● Once you find a routine, stick to it! Each time your baby wakes at night, repeat whatever you do to help her fall asleep each evening.

● Give your plan time to work – at least one or two weeks – and don't confuse your baby by chopping and changing tactics. Ensure that you and your partner follow the same routine.

● Try not to let you baby doze off late in the afternoon, as she may find it harder to sleep at bedtime.

● If your baby is used to falling asleep after a feed, discourage this by gently waking her before you put her in her cot so that she learns to settle herself. Remember to wind her after a feed.

● Start to teach your baby to tell night from day by keeping daytime naps shorter and letting her sleep in a bright room. Make night-time feeds quiet and comforting, then day feeds can be more sociable and chatty.

● Know that no one approach works for every baby and you may have to try several different plans before your baby becomes a model sleeper.

Early routines

Your baby's bedtime routine should happen in the place you want her to sleep and include three or four soothing activities (see p.121) that let your baby know it's time for "night-night". When the routine is finished, put your baby down in her cot, drowsy but awake. Some babies will surprise you and drift off to sleep without much protest. Other babies, especially those who are used to being fed or rocked to sleep, will require more practice in learning to soothe and settle themselves.

If your baby usually falls asleep in your arms while you're feeding her, you'll need to start gently waking her up before putting her down in her cot to settle. Although waking your soundly sleeping baby may seem mad (especially when you're exhausted and have a million things to do before

80%
of a premature baby's sleep is REM sleep.

The stage of sleep in which we dream is called rapid eye movement (REM). Young babies have considerably more of this REM sleep than adults do. And premature babies spend the majority of their sleeping time dreaming!

turning in yourself), it's well worth doing this to help your baby learn to settle herself.

The idea behind a bedtime routine is that your baby will be more relaxed if she knows what's coming next. The more relaxed she is, the more likely she will be to go to bed without a fuss and fall asleep easily. What you include in your routine is up to you, but focus on calming activities. Popular routines

"A **fixed routine** and a newborn don't go **hand in hand**."

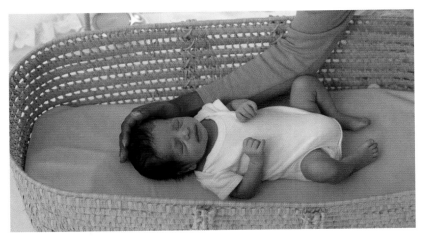

Putting your baby down in her sleeping place at around the same time every evening will help her start to recognise that this is bedtime.

During the day, your baby can sleep through all manner of household noises and activities.

Welcome to parenthood! 0–6 weeks

Your growing baby 6 weeks to 6 months

Your older baby 6 months to one year

Baby healthcare 0–12 months

Systemised mum

For some, just the glimpse of a routine can be a help.

"I'm amazed at what hard work it is looking after a newborn. It's lovely, but exhausting. My midwife said it's too soon to get Megan into a routine, but I find the chaos of my days hard to cope with. So I've established some pattern so that at least I'll know what happens next. It goes something like: sleep, nappy change, feed, nappy change and so on. I don't bath her daily, but we do have a little 'bedtime' routine of washing her face and hands. I say bedtime, but really there's little difference between night and day. We do the same thing at night as we do in the day, only with the lights low. When she wakes for a feed at night, I don't do anything to excite her. I'm hoping I can bore her into sleeping through!"

include bathing, putting on pyjamas, reading your baby a story, giving a "bedtime" feed and having a cuddle.

Making bedtime a pleasurable event, with time, attention and cuddles in strong supply, means that your baby will love the whole process. If she gets upset as she sees you leave after putting her down, tell her you'll be back to check on her in a few minutes. She'll probably be fast asleep by the time you return.

Night waking

Does your baby seem nocturnal? You're not alone! Lots of babies, especially newborns, are night-time creatures, sleeping all day and staying awake much of the night.

When your baby is a few weeks old, you can start to reset her body clock by getting her up in the morning at a normal waking time, rather than letting her sleep in for longer. This may be a hard thing to do at first – and of course you'll miss out on some quiet time – but it will be worth the effort in the long-term. During the day, play with your baby as much as you can so that she's ready for sleep in the evening. During her daytime naps, keep the curtains open and be your usual noisy self. Don't turn the ringer off the phone or avoid turning on the dishwasher. This will also help ensure that she doesn't become the world's lightest sleeper. At night, keep her room dark, with the minimum amount of lighting for feeds and nappy changes. Be quiet and soothing. Move and talk in slow motion – essentially, be as boring as possible. Gradually, your baby will learn that daytime is for fun and night-time for sleeping. This may take days or even weeks, but if you stick to it, you'll have a daytime baby.

Safer sleeping

To ensure that your baby sleeps safely, put her on her back, with her feet at the foot of the crib, cot or pram ("feet to foot"). This practice is recommended to help decrease the risk of cot death – or sudden infant death syndrome (SIDS).

Cot death isn't a single illness or disease. Rather, it's a diagnosis that is given when an apparently healthy baby dies without any prior warning signs. Cot death is most common during the second month of a baby's life, with the risk reducing as the baby grows older. You can find out more about SIDS – and ways to reduce the risks of this happening – on pages 60–1.

Sleeping basics

Where should your baby sleep? What does he need in his cot? Should he sleep in your room, or in your bed? Sleep probably never seemed so mysterious, or so precious, until your baby came along …

What your baby needs

The list below tells you what your baby needs to ensure he sleeps comfortably and safely.

- A cot, or a Moses basket, crib or carrycot for the first few months.
- A new cot mattress. It's not advisable to use a second-hand mattress, unless you know its history and you're sure that it's clean and isn't damp. Even if it's the mattress of your older child, it may be dusty or damp by now and so you may need to invest in a new one.
- Cotton sheets (you could cut and hem sheets from an adult bed if you don't want to buy cot sheets).
- Cotton cellular blankets (or acrylic cellular blankets if your baby's bedroom is cold).
- An optional item is a baby sleeping bag (one without a hood that is the right size around the neck, so your baby won't slip down inside it).
- Another optional item is a baby monitor, which enables you to hear your baby crying from another room.
- Duvets and pillows are not recommended until your baby is at least a year old.

A Moses basket is a convenient and popular choice of bedding in the early weeks and months, being easily transportable and snug for your baby.

Getting equipped

Your baby will probably have a cot until he's two or three years old. You can use a cot from the day he is born, although many parents choose a Moses basket, crib or carrycot for the first few months.

Buying a cot

Cots can be an expensive purchase so you might like to buy one second-hand. The Foundation for the Study of Infant Deaths states that it doesn't matter what kind of cot mattress you use, as long as it's firm, not soft, doesn't sag at all or show any signs of wear and tear. Unless you know the history of a second-hand mattress, buy a new one.

Cots come in many shapes and sizes, including corner-shaped cots that sit neatly in the corner of your baby's room, and oval-shaped cots that can be converted into a junior bed later on. You can also buy bedside cots with a side that drops down (see opposite), which are useful for night-time feeds as they sit right next to your bed.

Your baby's bedding

Although you can buy baby sleeping bags for newborns, most parents start off with cotton sheets and cotton cellular blankets. These keep your baby at the right temperature and are easy to layer: you can simply add or take away a blanket if your baby is too hot or cold.

Duvets and pillows are not recommended for babies under a year because they can restrict their movement and make them too hot.

Welcome to parenthood!
0–6 weeks

Your growing baby
6 weeks to 6 months

Your older baby
6 months to one year

Baby healthcare
0–12 months

A bedside cot is an ideal arrangement during the first six months as it keeps your baby reassuringly close while allowing you to sleep without fear of disturbing him.

Keeping your baby close

The Foundation for the Study of Infant Deaths (FSID), which funds much of the research into cot death, recommends that your baby sleeps next to you, rather than with you, for the first six months of his life. That way he can sleep under his own bedding, but within sight and sound of you and your partner. Sleeping near to your baby also allows you to respond quickly if he starts to cough or cry in the night, and is less disturbing for you when you need to feed your baby during the night.

Easy access
Although it's not crucial, you'll have an easier time touching or soothing your

baby if you can adjust his mattress to the same height as yours. If your baby is a wriggler, this approach can be preferable to having your baby in bed with you, as he's still at arm's length, but not kicking you all night long.

To do this, you can use a bed-side cot. This type of cot can be adapted to fit snugly against your own bed with one side removed. That way, you are near to your baby, but in separate beds. Alternatively, you can use a regular cot, but just keep it close to your bed. Most cots have drop sides – a railing that can be adapted and lowered to make it easier to get your baby in and out when he wakes during the night.

Dad's **Diary**

Essential rest
"I booked as much time off as I possibly could after the birth. As well as my paternity leave, I took another week of holiday time. During this period, my partner and I found that we needed to snatch as much rest as we could in the day when our baby was asleep so that we could cope with the broken nights.

At first, Lauren slept a lot in the day and was awake for much of the night, so we shared the night shift duty: I'd let Amy sleep for a couple of hours while I took care of Lauren, and then we'd swap. At the weekends, we took it in turns to have a lie in.

To help Amy grab more rest, I took charge of the feeding whenever I could. Snuggling up with Lauren while I fed her expressed milk was a wonderful way to build a father–baby bond."

Co-sleeping

If you and your partner both work during the day, co-sleeping with your baby can give you extra time to spend with her. The nurturing and closeness can help create a stronger relationship between you and your child. However, co-sleeping isn't for everyone …

Some couples find that a "family" bed is the perfect arrangement, allowing them to tend to their baby with the minimum disruption.

Sharing your bed

Co-sleeping has pros and cons; while some swear by the closeness it brings to the family, others find it's not for them.

The benefits
Some studies show that babies who co-sleep tend to breastfeed more, yet disrupt their mother's sleep less, than babies who sleep alone. It's thought that mothers who sleep with their baby tend to breastfeed them for longer periods of time, perhaps because they find it easier to feed in the night while lying in bed.

Babies who sleep with their parents tend to stay awake for shorter periods of time in the night than solitary sleepers, and may cry significantly less. Also, sleeping close allows you to respond quickly if your baby coughs or cries in the night.

Furthermore, some studies suggest that, on average, babies who co-sleep wake less often, and go back to sleep more easily, than babies who sleep alone in another room. However, some babies simply are better able to soothe themselves to sleep, so it's misleading to think that co-sleeping will influence when your baby starts sleeping through.

The disadvantages
The downside can be that sharing your bed with a wriggling, kicking baby takes some getting used to, and you may not sleep as well. Also, if your baby gets used to falling asleep next to you, she may have trouble sleeping when you leave her with a relative or babysitter. Later on, making the transition from family bed to her own bed can be a long and drawn-out process.

Sleep sharing can affect your love-life, too. Spontaneous lovemaking with your baby in the bed isn't an option. At times, one or both of you may resent having to make this kind of compromise.

Parents**Ask**…

Is co-sleeping safe?
Some research suggests that co-sleeping can be safe, and that our bodies are designed for close proximity or contact with our babies throughout the day and night for at least the first six months of life.

However, the Department of Health recommends that you should never share your bed with your baby if either you or your partner smokes, as this increases the risk of cot death, or Sudden Infant Death Syndrome (SIDS), see pages 60–1. Neither should you share your bed with your baby if either of you has taken drugs or has been drinking alcohol, or if you are very tired, as you may roll onto your baby in your sleep.

The Foundation for the Study of Infant Death (FSID), which funds much of the research into cot death, actually recommends that your baby sleeps next to you, rather than with you, for the first six months of life. That way she can sleep under her own bedding, but within sight and sound of you.

To make this easier, you can use a bed-side bed. This is a cot that can be adapted to fit snugly against your own bed with one side removed so that you are near your baby, but in separate beds. Or you could simply place your baby's cot right next to your bed. As with most parenting decisions, it's up to you.

Taking precautions

If you decide to co-sleep, there are precautions you should take to make this as safe as possible.

Beds and bedding

First, ideally you'll need a big bed. King-size is best, or consider a cot that attaches to the bedside (see p.57). Never co-sleep on a sofa together as your baby can get wedged between the cushions, or between you and the back of the couch. Waterbeds are too soft and may have crevices around the frame in which a baby could get trapped.

Make sure your mattress is firm. This is because your baby could suffocate or overheat on a soft mattress. Ensure too that she isn't surrounded by pillows and loose bedding. If your bed has a frame, a headboard or is against a wall, check that your baby can't fall into the gap.

Your baby must not overheat. Dress her lightly. Put her on top of the duvet, and use as few blankets as possible, ensuring they're lightweight to reduce the risk of smothering or overheating. Never put her on top of a pillow as she could roll off or be smothered. Check her head often to ensure it isn't covered by a blanket.

While your baby may be safe between you, she could easily fall out if one of you gets up. Some parents put pillows either side of their baby when they leave them unattended, but this isn't ideal as your baby could roll into them. So while you're out of the room, put your baby in a Moses basket or cot.

When to avoid co-sleeping

There are some people who should avoid co-sleeping. If you have a sleep disorder, such as sleep apnoea, where you sleep very deeply, you're at risk of not waking up if you roll onto your baby. Alcohol and drugs can have a similar effect. You should also not sleep in the same bed as your baby if you smoke. Nobody knows exactly why, but the risk of cot death is higher.

You can share a bed with both a baby and a toddler as long as they don't sleep next to each other. Toddlers are not aware of the need to watch out for babies, so your older child may accidentally roll over onto the infant.

Co-sleeping checklist

Following the guidelines checklist below will help your baby to sleep safely with you and your partner if you decide to co-sleep.

Safe co-sleeping

● Never share your bed with your baby if either you or your partner smokes, even if you don't smoke inside the house.
● Don't share your bed with your baby if either of you has taken drugs or has been drinking alcohol, or if you are very tired.
● Don't give your baby a pillow. Ensure that her head is not covered by the blanket or sheets.
● Ensure that your baby sleeps on a firm mattress and use bedding that fits tightly to the mattress.
● Don't co-sleep on a sofa.
● Ensure there are no gaps where your baby could get trapped.
● If your toddler also shares your bed, don't let her sleep next to the baby as she could roll onto her.
● Put your baby to sleep on her back.

Sleeping with your baby can be perfect for breastfeeding mums, allowing them to feed their baby effortlessly during the night.

Welcome to parenthood!
0–6 weeks

Your growing baby
6 weeks to 6 months

Your older baby
6 months to one year

Baby healthcare
0–12 months

Safe sleeping

No one really knows what causes cot death and, sadly, there is no way to be sure that it won't happen. Fortunately, it's quite rare, and there are some measures you can take to reduce the risk for your baby.

Sudden infant death syndrome (SIDS)

Cot death, or sudden infant death syndrome (SIDS), is a diagnosis given if a healthy baby dies with no warning. About 340 cot deaths occur each year in the UK. In 1991, the Foundation for the Study of Infant Deaths (FSID) raised awareness of cot death, cutting deaths by 75 per cent.

Looking at the data
No one knows why some babies die without any warning. Research is

Placing your baby with his feet at the foot of the cot reduces the risk of him working his way down under the bedclothes.

continuing and doctors believe that there may be a combination of factors involved in cases of SIDS. One theory is that certain babies have a problem with the part of the brain that controls breathing and waking, which means

> "Doctors believe a **combination** of factors is **involved** in cot death."

that they don't respond normally when, for example, the bedclothes come loose and cover their nose or mouth.

Cot death occurs most often, though not always, during sleep. This may be at night in a cot, but it could be during a daytime nap, in a pram or even in a parent's arms. It's more common in winter, though it's not understood why.

Cot death is uncommon in babies less than a month old. It's most common during the second month, and almost 90 per cent of cot deaths occur in babies who are under six months old. The risk reduces over time – very few cot deaths occur after the age of one. Cot death can affect any family, although it is rare for it to occur twice in the same family, and

it's rare in Asian families, for unknown reasons. The rate of cot death is highest for babies of mothers aged under 20 at the time of the birth. Other unalterable factors that increase the risk of cot death include being a boy; being premature (born before 37 weeks gestation); and having a low birthweight (under 2.5 kilograms/5 pounds 6 ounces).

Parents**Ask...**

Can sleep monitors help?
A breathing monitor is an electronic device that sounds an alarm if your baby stops breathing. It may have a sensor attached to the baby, an ultrasound ray or pressure pads in the cot. Some parents find them reassuring, but there's no evidence they prevent cot death.

Premature babies may be discharged from hospital with monitors, and parents who've lost a previous baby from cot death can hire them from a local CONI (Care of the Next Infant) representative.

If your baby has had a life-threatening breathing incident or has cot death risk factors, a monitor may be recommended.

Reducing the risks

There's no guaranteed way to prevent cot death, but there are many things you can do to decrease your baby's risk. The Department of Health recommends the following steps to help mimimise the risk of cot death.

● Put your baby down to sleep on his back in a cot in a room with you. Positioning your baby on his back is thought to reduce the risk of your baby getting "stuck" under bed covers and suffocating. Contrary to previously held beliefs, healthy babies placed on their back to sleep will not choke.

At around five or six months, babies start to roll over, but at this age the risk of cot death reduces and it's safe to let your baby find his own comfortable sleeping position. Initially, though, you should always put your baby down on his back to sleep.

● Ensure that your living environment is a smoke-free zone. Don't allow anyone to smoke around your baby. Cot death is more common in babies of mothers who smoked or who were exposed to smoke during their pregnancy, and in babies who are exposed to smoke themselves after the birth. The risk to your baby is increased if anyone in the house smokes, even if they smoke in another room, with a window open or with a fan or ioniser in the room. Ask visitors to smoke outside, and always keep the air around your baby smoke-free.

● Keep your baby's environment at a constant recommended temperature, and don't allow your baby to become too hot. Keep the room that your baby sleeps in at a comfortable temperature (ideally 18°C/64°F). Furthermore, babies shouldn't sleep next to a radiator, heater or a fire, or be placed in direct sunlight. Also, never put a hot water bottle or an electric blanket in your baby's cot. Use lightweight blankets and don't use duvets before your baby is one year old.

● Place your baby "feet to foot" in his cot, Moses basket or pushchair. Placing your baby with his feet at the foot of his cot or other sleeping place ensures that he can't wriggle down under his bedding and suffocate. Keep his head uncovered. If you use a baby sleeping bag, make sure it's well-fitting so that he can't slide down inside.

● Don't let your baby sleep on soft surfaces. Never sleep on a sofa or armchair with your baby. After a cuddle or a feed, put him back in his cot. Also, waterbeds, beanbags, baby nests, fleeces and other soft surfaces aren't suitable for a baby to sleep on. Furthermore, the outside of the mattress should be waterproof and covered with a single sheet.

● Breast is best. Breastfeed your baby. There is new evidence that breastfeeding reduces the risk of cot death in babies. Breastmilk gives babies all the nutrients they need for their first six months of life and helps protect them from infection.

● Keep up to date with your baby's health checks. Take your baby for regular check-ups. Keep up to date with his immunisations, which reduce the risk of cot death, and seek medical advice if he's unwell.

Tip: Some studies suggest that using a dummy may be safer for babies.

Using a dummy when you settle your baby to sleep, even for a nap, may reduce the risk of cot death. One theory is that the dummy handle may help air to get to the baby's airways.

Daytime sleeping

Recent research suggests the safety advice on your baby's night-time sleep should apply to daytime naps, too. In particular, you should put your baby to sleep on his back and ensure he can't cover his head with bedclothes. For the first six months, it's wise to keep him in the same room as you while he naps.

Keeping your baby close

Many mothers put very young babies down in a Moses basket or pram and take them with them as they move around. Babies can sleep through a lot: the noise of washing machines, vacuum cleaners and dogs barking. Most will get used to whatever is normal in their house, including noisy games with older children.

Putting babies down on their own is a fairly recent practice in developed countries and is more unusual in developing countries. There's evidence that, when they wake, babies benefit from the stimulation of being moved around to where the action is occurring.

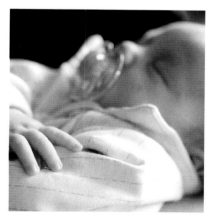

Helping your baby to settle with the aid of a dummy is now thought to promote safe sleep and help reduce the risk of cot death.

Welcome to parenthood!
0–6 weeks

Your growing baby
6 weeks to 6 months

Your older baby
6 months to one year

Baby healthcare
0–12 months

Your baby's development

KEY MILESTONES

* Develops head control
* Eyes focus on objects
* First proper smile

	1 week	2 weeks	3 weeks	4 weeks	5 weeks	6 weeks
	MAKES EYE CONTACT AND RESPONDS TO FACIAL EXPRESSIONS		MAY LIFT HEAD BRIEFLY WHILE ON TUMMY	CAN FOCUS WITH BOTH EYES	FOLLOWS OBJECT WITH EYES	MAY HOLD HEAD UNSUPPORTED FOR SHORT PERIODS
					MAY MAKE FIRST SMILE	
				STARTS TO COO AND GURGLE		

How your baby develops

It doesn't take long for your baby to lose her "newborn" qualities and turn into a tiny human being. Her hearing and eyesight are sharpening up and she's learning all about the world. There are plenty of things you can do to help her to develop.

Helping your baby to thrive

You don't have to be a child-development expert to give your baby a great start in life. Love, attention and basic care are the only things your baby really needs and wants.

Your loving care

All children need love. Your support and care give your baby a secure base from which to explore the world. This isn't just touchy-feely advice. Love, attention and affection in the first years of life have a direct and measurable impact on physical, mental and emotional growth.

So how do you show love to your baby? Smile, cuddle, touch, listen to and play with her. Answering her cries promptly won't spoil her. Experts say that responding to a baby when she's upset (as well as when she's happy) builds trust and a strong bond. One study suggests that if you respond quickly to cries in the early months, she'll cry less as she gets older.

Talk talk talk

The best way to stimulate your baby's brain is to talk to her constantly. She'll respond more easily if she knows the words are directed at her, so look directly at her while you're speaking. Simply describe what you're doing and how it relates to her: "Mummy is putting warm water in the bath so she can get you nice and clean."

Don't worry about using baby talk either. "Motherese", as it's known, is used worldwide (see p.153). Studies have shown that young babies actually prefer to listen to the higher pitch and slower speech patterns that parents use when talking to them.

Parents**Talk...**

"My friend often boasts about how well her son is doing in comparison to my daughter, even though he's four weeks younger. I don't let it get to me – I know that he'll walk and talk when the time is right."
Sarah, 19, first-time mum

"I started to worry about all the things my baby wasn't doing yet. So much so in fact that I went to see my health visitor and she reassured me that development is different for each

baby and that they all catch up in the end. She was right, of course."
Kate, 24, first-time mum

"My friend and I gave birth two weeks apart. Her daughter advanced faster physically, while my daughter moved ahead mentally. It's hard if your baby is behind, but it's also hard to hide your pride when she's ahead. Understanding this, and that all babies get there in the end, helps."
Mahira, 33, mum of two

Your baby will flourish with your love and attention; the knowledge that you are always there is the basis of her secure world.

Learning from day one

Your baby learns from the day he is born, and there are lots of ways you can encourage him. Look out for those brief periods of time when your newborn is quiet but alert as this is his prime time

From the very beginning, your baby has the capacity to interact. His grasp reflex is his first basic form of communication.

for learning. Play and talk to your baby as much as you can. If you try to interact with him and he doesn't seem receptive, he may have become sleepy or moved into a state of active alertness, when he's too distracted by his surroundings to pay attention to you.

Interacting and stimulating

Very early on, babies intuitively recognise faces and gestures, and sometimes even imitate them. You can give your newborn a chance to imitate your facial expressions by putting your face close to his and sticking out your tongue or raising your eyebrows a few times. It's good to repeat these gestures and then give your baby time to mimic them. It may take him a few minutes, or he may not do anything, but he'll definitely be watching you.

Babies are drawn to patterns and lines. Bedroom mobiles with high-contrast patterns, and picture books with strong line drawings will captivate him.

Be alert to the way your baby reacts to stimulation and interaction. While it's great to help your baby learn all about his world, some babies can tolerate only brief periods of interaction, or stimulation of just one sense at a time. If your baby becomes over-stimulated, he will communicate this to you by yawning, averting his gaze, arching his back, turning his face or fussing or crying. He'll also indicate what he enjoys and, believe it or not, you'll understand his signs in no time.

Babies find their own reflections fascinating. You can amuse your baby by propping up a baby mirror by his cot for him to focus on. Although he won't

Your baby's reflexes

Your baby is born with reflexes that are designed to protect him during his first few weeks of life. Some of these reflexes disappear within the first few days or weeks and will then be replaced by voluntary movements.

● **Startle reflex** When your baby is startled, he'll throw his arms out and arch his back, and may also curl up and clench his fists. This is a primitive reflex that lasts until he's around four to six months old.

● **Grasping reflex** If you stroke your baby's palm with your finger, he'll grip your finger firmly. This is thought to originate from prehistoric times, when babies had to cling to their mothers. It usually lasts until he's about three months old.

● **Rooting reflex** This is one of the first reflexes you'll notice from your baby. If you gently touch the side of your baby's mouth with your nipple, a bottle teat or your finger, he'll turn towards it and open his mouth. He's looking for food.

● **Sucking reflex** Your baby was born with the natural instinct to suck anything that is placed in his mouth. This ensures that he can feed.

● **Crawling reflex** When you place your baby on his tummy, he'll bring his knees under his body into a crawling position. After a few months, he'll lie flat and hold his head up.

● **Walking reflex** If you hold your baby upright, his legs will make a stepping motion as though he's trying to walk. This reflex lasts for around two months.

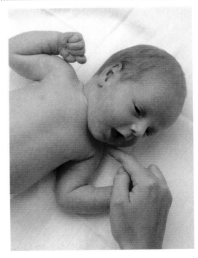

Brushing your newborn's cheek triggers his rooting reflex, the reflex that gives him the innate ability to seek out food.

recognise himself just yet, he'll no doubt find the movement and reflections in the mirror fascinating.

A play gym with lots of compelling things to watch, swipe at and listen to allows your baby to practise his arm, hand and finger coordination skills. It also makes lying down less boring! In the first few months, he won't move his arms purposefully to reach particular objects – this sort of movement will come when he's a few months old.

Motor skills

A motor skill involves the movement of muscles. Gross motor skills are larger movements involving the arm, leg or feet muscles, or the entire body, such as crawling, running or jumping. Fine motor skills are smaller actions, such as picking up between the thumb and finger or wriggling toes, or moving the lips and tongue to taste and feel objects.

You can encourage your baby to develop his fine and gross motor skills by watching to see how he uses his fingers, his arms and his legs, and then providing other opportunities for him to use his body in similar ways, perhaps with different toys or from a different position. A good activity will stretch your baby's abilities a tiny bit.

Your baby's senses

As he grows, your baby will use his eyes and ears to take in massive amounts of information about the world around him.

24%
of babies smile within the first three weeks.

According to parents, around a fifth of babies reach this significant milestone earlier than expected. However, 40 per cent smiled for the first time when they were six weeks or older.

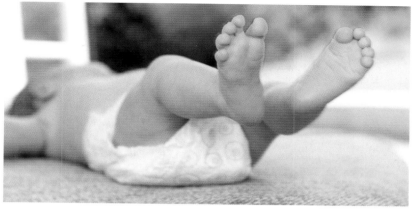

Giving your baby plenty of "floor time" helps his muscles to develop, increasing the strength in his legs and preparing him for that all-important skill of crawling.

In turn, this will stimulate his brain development and lead to physical accomplishments such as sitting, rolling over, crawling and walking.

Your baby's hearing will be fully mature by the end of his first month, but understanding and appreciating what he hears will take a little longer. From the beginning, he'll pay close attention to voices, especially high-pitched ones, and will respond to familiar sounds, such as your or your partner's voice, or a frequently read story. He may startle at loud or unexpected noises.

Your baby's sight develops gradually. At birth, his vision is fuzzy, though he can make out light, movement and shapes. He can see only about 20 to 30 centimetres (8 to 12 inches) – just far enough to make out the face of the person holding him, which suits him because your face is the most interesting thing to him and he'll love to see you gazing at him. At this early stage, he'll like high-contrast items, such as black and white chessboard patterns.

Your baby's eyesight will continue to sharpen as he grows. When he's about six or eight months old, he'll be able to see the world just as well as you do.

Your baby's early development

Your baby is constantly developing. Even in his first few weeks, he will be reaching milestones.

● At birth, your baby's neck muscles are fairly weak, so he'll rely on you to support his head and neck for at least the first month or so. As you cradle him in your arms, enjoy the chance to gaze into his eyes. This will help you bond and make your baby feel loved.

● At birth, your baby doesn't know how to use his eyes together, so they may wander randomly. By the time he is one or two months old, he'll have learned to focus both eyes and will be able to track a moving object.

● From the moment he's born, your baby will notice different voices; he'll pick out high-pitched ones and will respond to familiar sounds. Loud or sudden noises can startle him.

● Your newborn may look "scrunched up" at first, with his arms and legs not fully extended. This is normal, and his limbs will gradually uncurl as he gets used to being outside your tummy.

Welcome to parenthood! 0–6 weeks

Your growing baby 6 weeks to 6 months

Your older baby 6 months to one year

Baby healthcare 0–12 months

To your tiny baby, touch is a hugely important part of his world, forming the foundation of his early communication with you and your partner.

Laid-back mum

Babies love close contact and to be touched and stroked

"Our favourite thing is for me to lie in bed with her resting on my tummy while I gently stroke her back. She likes it best if we're skin-to-skin, so I put a soft blanket over her to make sure she doesn't get cold. Sometimes when I change her nappy, I stroke her tummy and her arms and legs; she really seems to relax, and she stares at me in an intense way while I'm doing this. I can't wait until she's a little bit older so that I can take her to baby massage classes. I think she's going to love it!"

Your social baby

A newborn baby doesn't have much of a personality yet, or at least one that you might recognise. He expresses himself in the only way he knows how: crying. He spends his time moving in and out of the different states of sleepiness and quiet and active alertness.

When will your baby know where you end and he begins? At birth, he thinks he's a part of you and doesn't have a sense of himself as an individual. Babies don't even realise that the tiny hands and feet they see before them are their own. In fact, babies under six months completely identify with their primary caregivers. They don't think about themselves, only what they need: food, love and attention. In the first months, your baby can't think about tackling the process of forming his own identity. He's too busy gaining control over his basic movements and reflexes.

However, even newborn babies are innately social creatures. They love to be touched, held, cooed to and smiled at – touch is a very important means of communicating for your baby. Some newborn babies need a great deal of cuddling and reassurance, and new babies often need close physical contact for comfort. Don't think that you'll "spoil" your baby if you hold him too much or pay him too much attention; during the first few months of his life that's impossible. If your baby needs a lot of holding, a sling might be a solution to keep you both happy (see p.41), allowing you to keep him close while leaving your hands free for other tasks.

Dad's Diary

Shared emotions

"I remember watching a football match on television – an early group game in the World Cup Finals, North Korea vs Portugal – with my six-week-old daughter sitting happily on my knee. Involuntarily, when the underdogs North Korea scored, I leapt up with my daughter, and suddenly saw that she had a big smile on her face. I grinned back and her smile then turned into a giggle. In that moment, the endless duties of the last six weeks were paid back and a few tears welled up! Maybe it's because we're shallow and easily pleased, but the emotion of making your child laugh is one of the most incredible you will experience.

I found that my daughter's first smile was such a significant milestone (see p.68). Once she had started smiling and responding with giggles, I found lots of other ways to make her laugh – simple things such as nodding my head, rustling a paper bag, putting on a jumper, genuflecting, sucking my thumb or blowing raspberries on her tummy. When all else failed, playing peekaboo was the one form of physical slapstick that was guaranteed to work every time."

Play and learn

Even at this early stage, play is crucial for your baby's social, emotional, physical and cognitive growth. It's his way of learning about his body and the world, and he'll use all five senses to do this, especially during the first year. What does this feel like when I touch it? What will this sound like when I squeeze it? What happens if I push this or pull that, crawl over there, or pull myself up on this?

A tactile world

Your baby wants to experience everything up close, and he does this in particular by using his sense of touch. You can encourage his curiosity and tactile talents by touching him with differently textured objects. One at a time, brush each item ever so gently across his skin, describing the sensation as you go: "Can you feel the silky scarf? It's very slippery. Can you feel the toy lamb? It's fuzzy, isn't it?"

Visual games

You could also explore your baby's developing visual skills with a simple game of finger puppets. Lie your baby on his back or put him in a reclining bouncy seat. Put a finger puppet (you

Saying something simple like, "Hello, I'm Clover the cow" will do. As each puppet speaks, bend your finger forwards so the puppet bows to your baby. Wait a moment, as if your baby were answering, then continue conducting a one-sided conversation between him and each puppet. Finally, arrange the puppets to form a parade, bobbing up and down, in and out of your baby's sight.

Your baby's favourite toy

While colourful toys and objects have their place in your newborn's development, don't forget that you're the best toy he has. You can do so much for your baby's developing brain and senses simply by interacting with him and holding him close to you.

Try playing copycat games. It's fun to gaze into your baby's eyes, slowly poke out your tongue and see whether he responds. Of course, he may not just yet, but he'll definitely be observing you! And he loves looking at your face while you're close to him.

Talk to your baby often, telling him what you're doing. Don't be afraid if you slip into that strange, high-pitched way of speaking known as "Motherese" (see p.153). Your baby will also appreciate

"Your newborn is dealing with an **onrush** of **stimulation**."

can buy these in many toy shops, or make your own from felt or even cardboard) on the index finger of each hand. Bring your fingers slowly into your baby's line of sight and wait until he focuses on the faces. Then, speaking slowly, introduce each puppet to him.

you singing to him, or even reading him a story. It's never too early to introduce your baby to first books and he'll gradually start to recognise the same familiar story. H may not be reacting much yet, but everything is being absorbed in his rapidly developing brain.

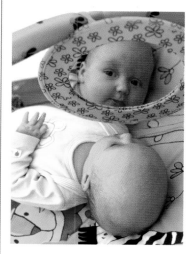

Your baby won't yet recognise his reflection in a mirror, but he's likely to be fascinated by the moving image.

Welcome to parenthood!
0–6 weeks

Your growing baby
6 weeks to 6 months

Your older baby
6 months to one year

Baby healthcare
0–12 months

Your baby's first smile

There's lots of evidence to show that babies are born with an innate desire to communicate and that they interact with us long before their first proper smile. From very early on, they can imitate the facial gestures of their parents by, for example, moving their tongue and widening their eyes.

Not just wind

A baby's first proper social smile occurs around four to six weeks, but may be seen earlier and dismissed as wind. Psychologists say that, as newborns, boys make less eye contact and smile less than girls, which means we have to be extra sure to interact with boys.

Your baby sends signals all the time and, without being aware of it, you respond by echoing back sounds and expressions. In a Canadian study of dads, all said that an important stage in their relationship with their baby was when they were first smiled at. The smile is the start of being a social person: enjoy that first smile. When you feel fraught, the power of those first smiles will always win you over.

That first magical smile can make all those broken nights and endless nappy changes seem utterly worthwhile.

As your baby approaches two months, she'll seem far removed from the helpless newborn you held in your arms not so long ago.

Reaching milestones

By six weeks, your baby may already have reached certain milestones, or be on her way to reaching them.

Physical changes

Your baby's neck muscles are getting stronger and she can hold up her head briefly. She may also hold it up for a few moments while lying on her stomach, and may even turn it to the side.

At birth, your baby had no idea her arms and legs were attached to her. That's all changing now as she explores her body. First, she'll discover her hands and feet. Encourage her by holding her arms above her head and asking "How big is the baby?" or by reciting 'This Little Piggy" and counting her toes.

Babies love to suck. You may have discovered that a dummy works wonders in calming your baby. When her dummy isn't around, she may start to find her thumb or fingers to suck.

First noises

At one month, your baby may gurgle, coo, grunt, and hum to express her feelings. Be sure to coo and gurgle straight back, and talk to her face to face. A few babies may also start to make early squeals and laugh.

Getting to know you

Even though your baby has been able to recognise you since she was a few days old, by the end of this month she may be able to show it. Many babies now begin to exhibit an obvious recognition of their parents: they react differently to them than they do to strangers. Your baby may quieten down and make eye contact with you; some babies at this age smile when they see their parents. She'll hold your gaze for longer periods now.

Sensory milestones

Once your baby stays awake more in the day, you'll have time to stimulate her sensory development. Nursery rhymes, music, the sound of wind chimes or a ticking clock may all amuse your baby. Inevitably, you'll see her react more pleasurably to one selection over another as she develops preferences.

Once she has learned to focus with both eyes, your baby can track a moving object, something she may have been able to do for brief periods since birth. A rattle passed in front of her will often transfix her. Or you can play "eyes-to-eyes" by moving close to her face and slowly nodding your head from side to side: often her eyes will lock onto yours.

Development chart

Age	Physical/motor	Sensory	Social and emotional
1 week	Your baby is looking less "scrunched up" now as she gets used to the outside world. You'll notice her limbs move in a jerky, uncoordinated way.	Your baby's eyesight is quite fuzzy still. She can focus about 20 to 30 cm (8 to 12 in) away.	Your baby doesn't have much of a personality now, or at least what you might recognise as one. She expresses herself through crying.
2 weeks	Reflexes such as sucking, grasping, rooting (when she searches for your nipple), and blinking, continue to be all-important this week.	Your baby has already developed a sense of taste and will show a preference for your breastmilk over formula.	Your baby probably loves to be held, caressed, kissed, stroked, massaged and carried. She may even make an "ah" sound when she hears your voice or sees your face, and she'll be eager to find you in a crowd.
3 weeks	By the end of this week, your baby may be able to lift her head briefly when lying on her tummy. She may also be able to turn her head from side to side.	Your baby loves the sound of voices, but too much noise may cause her to tune out sounds altogether or start wailing.	Your baby loves and needs to suck, so don't discourage her from doing this. By now, your baby may even be able to find her thumb or fingers to soothe herself.
4 weeks	Your baby's head is steadier now. Short periods of time on her tummy will help her strengthen her neck muscles.	Your baby can focus with both eyes and can hold your gaze steadily. She likes bold lines and shapes and high-contrast patterns.	Your baby is beginning to "talk" – that is, coo, gurgle, grunt and hum to express what she is feeling. Try to coo and gurgle back to your baby and speak to her face to face as much as possible. Keep talking even when you walk away; she'll enjoy hearing your voice from across the room.
5 weeks	Your baby may discover her hands and feet, and is just beginning to realise they're part of her body.	Your baby can focus both eyes on an object and follow its movement.	That smile lighting up your baby's face – and your own – may be the real thing. You can tell it's a social smile if she uses her entire face to tell you she's pleased.
6 weeks	Your baby's neck muscles are getting stronger. She may be able to hold her head up for short periods and when she's in a car seat or front carrier.	Your baby is more sensitive to her surroundings. If you ring a bell, she'll respond by starting, crying or even quietening down. She now notices objects more.	Your baby is experimenting with different facial expressions – pursing her lips, raising her eyebrows, widening or squinting her eyes and furrowing her brow. By now, your baby easily recognises both you and your partner and she openly prefers her mum and dad to strangers. She may smile when she sees you as well as coo and kick with pleasure.

Welcome to parenthood!
0–6 weeks

Your growing baby
6 weeks to 6 months

Your older baby
6 months to one year

Baby healthcare
0–12 months

You and
your family

Becoming parents

Nine months of pregnancy is a long time, but it doesn't always prepare you for the reality of having a tiny, wriggling, crying human being who's entirely reliant on you for love and care. Relax! You just need confidence in your ability to be a great parent.

Getting to know your baby

All babies love close-up time with their parents, learning to recognise facial features, voices and familiar smells. So don't be tempted to do all the housework while your baby's stranded in a pram; you can afford to ignore that pile of laundry and have some cuddle time instead. You'll never get these early days back (and there will always be laundry), so make the most of them. This intimate time will help your baby gain trust and security, and you'll gain confidence in your parenting abilities.

Building a relationship

Making frequent eye contact with your baby is reassuring, educational and fun for you both. While he will thrive on the attention, you'll discover what he responds positively to, or if there are certain things – a noisy vacuum cleaner, perhaps – that he finds unnerving. Just when you think none of your efforts are sinking in, he'll dazzle you with his first smile, followed later by adorable noises, laughs and gestures.

You'll build the bond between you by chattering to your baby as much as possible. It doesn't need to be sensible conversation; if you're at a loss, just talk about what you're doing. A running monologue helps him to recognise your voice, and later to develop connections between words and objects or ideas.

Praising your baby

Offer your baby lots of encouragement. This will give him the confidence to explore and develop, and he'll soon show this by looking to you for positive reinforcement. When he wants to reach for a toy but misses, let him try again and chat to him about the object he's aiming for. Ask what he'd like, as a step towards helping him make independent decisions and learn good manners.

An emerging personality

As your baby starts to display his personality, respond to him, reinforcing his interests and achievements, without pressuring him about dislikes or fears. Within reason, let him find his own way, even if he gravitates towards toy trucks instead of that cuddly bear from Granny.

Laid-back mum

In the early weeks, you'll be following your baby's lead in how you care for her.

"I decided early on that the best way to adapt to parenthood and develop a strong relationship with my baby was to take things in my stride and let her set the pace. I didn't think we would gain anything by sticking to a rigid timetable, and wanted to concentrate on helping my baby to feel relaxed and to avoid her becoming hungry and distressed. Anna went through growth spurts where she was hungry and needed extra feeds for a day or two, then would settle down again. I soon learnt to trust myself to respond to her needs, knowing that I knew her better than anyone else."

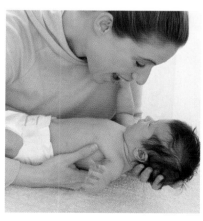

Giving your baby a running commentary of what you're doing, however mundane, will both stimulate and reassure him.

Welcome to parenthood! 0–6 weeks

Your growing baby 6 weeks to 6 months

Your older baby 6 months to one year

Baby healthcare 0–12 months

Your new life together

Remember when your body was your own, you set your own schedule and life with your partner was like one big, carefree, Saturday-night date? Even if, like most couples, you and your partner actually had a weekly showdown over who last emptied the bin or battled nightly for a fair share of the duvet, those bygone days now seem utterly, blissfully serene. Welcome to parenthood – oh, and by the way, could you just grab a cloth to wipe up this bit of sick?

Actually, for the first year at least, you won't have much time or energy at all to gaze back wistfully at the past. However, try not to become completely removed from the life you used to have: it's all too easy to slip into those stereotypical roles of an exhausted, downtrodden, overburdened mummy and a side-lined daddy deprived of appreciation and attention.

Of course, every couple is different. Some women – even those women who previously embraced their independence – just want to nestle in with their baby and dote on her every demand and need. Fathers, too, can assume a newfound sensitivity and compassion for their partner's and baby's needs. The chances are, though, that you and your partner will encounter at least some of the challenges and potential pitfalls that await most new parents. Taking time to develop a few simple coping strategies can make all the difference when everything is transforming around you.

Patience, awareness and understanding

You may feel that the state of your home and baby could bring new meaning to the word "disarray". Likewise, your partner's perfectly innocent question about where he can find that other sock might be just enough to put you over the edge. You're probably both shattered, but that's when it's most important to reach deep into those reserves of patience and understanding to communicate with each other. It might be that one or both of you are being unreasonable – who wouldn't be when you're at the whims of an unpredictable, unrelenting, tiny new boss? But you have to resist the urge to see only your point of view. It's

Try to relax and enjoy spending time with your baby, even if chores go undone.

Single mum

There's no doubt being a single mum is hard, but it can be done.

"I miss not having anyone to share decision making. For example, last night I wondered if Martha needed an extra blanket. It wasn't a big problem, but it would have been nice to have had someone to decide with me.

Friends and family are supportive, but it's hard for them to understand what it's like as they haven't been in my position. The biggest source of help I've had has been from other mums I met at a local group my health visitor told me about. They've all got babies about Martha's age, so there's not a question that one of them won't know the answer to. We get together twice a week. I really look forward to it and they've become good friends."

Introducing siblings

It can be hard for your toddler or older child to welcome a new baby into her home. She won't really understand why

she feels the way she does. Desperate to win back your attention, she may react by misbehaving or regressing into babyhood. Or even try to "punish" her new sibling with a few not-too-subtle prods.

Keep her involved

It may help if you involve her in looking after the baby – holding her towels while you bath her, perhaps, or helping to wash her legs. Ask for her opinion on caring for the baby ("Do you think she would like to wear her red hat or the white hat?") and point out how much her new sibling seems to like her. Most importantly, be sympathetic to her feelings and make time every day just for the two of you.

Make time to help older siblings build a relationship with their new sister or brother.

Coping tips

Despite the rewards, life with a newborn can be hard work. There are ways to ease the load.

- Try to break up your day with a short walk. Whatever the weather, it's good to get some fresh air.
- Don't give yourself extra jobs; let the housework slip for a few weeks.
- Get in touch with other new mums from your antenatal classes or at parent-and-baby groups.
- If friends or family offer to help, say yes! Just a spot of ironing or shopping can make a difference.
- Know that your baby will settle into a routine soon, and these seemingly endless weeks of tiredness will pass.
- While your baby naps, make time for yourself – have a sleep, read a book, wash your hair, phone a friend!

When your baby naps, take the opportunity to catch up on lost sleep rather than busy yourself with tasks.

---

easy to lose sight of how your partner is feeling, and vice versa. This is a new adventure for both of you, and while you might, for example, desperately miss the structure and routine of the workplace, he might be unaware of your conflicting feelings about your new role.

Furthermore, for fathers who have to return to work fairly soon, their partner and new baby can start to seem like an exclusive new unit. After all, the parent who has to leave the house all day doesn't have the chance to experience the intense bonding that comes with all those cuddles and even with the tedious, but necessary, tasks.

What better way to reduce those feelings of alienation than to involve your partner as much as possible in the daily joys and struggles of caring for a new baby? Try to settle on a division of labour that satisfies and fulfils you both (including both of you taking on some of

the less enjoyable parts of babycare). Try to make an effort to be considerate if one of you has had more than their share of bottom-wiping or rush-hour traffic stress for one day. If you both try to be empathetic about the things that are getting on each other's nerves, you'll realise the immediate reasons may be different, but the root causes are probably similar.

Consideration and mutual respect

Not many things manage to soothe the tension of a hard day (or night) better than a meaningful and encouraging kind word. Don't for a moment underestimate the power of even occasional reminders that your partner is doing a fantastic job. Sometimes it can be difficult for each of you to measure your input yourself, which is why you each need to convey what an integral role the other is playing

in raising a healthy, contented little person. Raising your baby really is the toughest, but most rewarding, thing you'll ever do, so try to remind each other how much you admire the effort you're both putting in.

Welcome to parenthood!
0–6 weeks

Your growing baby
6 weeks to 6 months

Your older baby
6 months to one year

Baby healthcare
0–12 months

Your changing body

Your body has just performed an amazing feat of nature – no wonder it's undergoing weird and not always wonderful changes. You will, in the not-too-distant future, feel as though your body is yours again. In the meantime, it's good to know what to expect.

Grazing on healthy snacks during the day will give your body the energy it needs to cope with the demands of motherhood.

How your body adapts

You've just accomplished a strenuous, nutritionally draining feat, so it's important to give your body time to recover. For the first six weeks or so, don't worry about trying to lose weight. Instead, eat a varied, nutritious diet to recover from the birth and keep up with the demands of breastfeeding and being a new parent. Also, although you can start working on your pelvic floor and lower tummy muscles when you feel ready (see pp.78–9), it's not a good idea to do strenuous exercise straightaway.

After birth, your body undergoes changes to revert to its pre-pregnancy state. Giving your body time will help to ensure you recover fully.

Changes to your uterus

Have you been getting crampy stomach contractions since giving birth? Although painful, these are nothing to worry about. They're called "afterpains" and occur as your uterus shrinks back to its pre-pregnancy size.

At the time of your baby's birth, your uterus was about 25 times bigger than normal. Within minutes of your baby's birth, it begins to shrink. Its crisscrossed fibres tighten in the same way they did to push out your baby, and it is this action that causes the afterpains. Afterpains often feel stronger when you're breastfeeding your baby. This is because breastfeeding after the birth

ParentsAsk...

Can I get rid of stretch marks?

Stretch marks, or striae, are caused when skin stretches rapidly over your enlarging body in pregnancy. They can also occur in adolescence or periods of rapid weight gain. They're most common on the abdomen, buttocks, thighs and breasts.

Stretch marks won't disappear, but do become less noticeable over time as the reddish-brown pigmentation fades.

Massaging oils, creams or lotions into your skin may help it feel more supple. Creams or oils derived from vitamin E may help, or even laser treatment, but talk to your doctor first.

The appearance of stretch marks may be exaggerated by the under-use of muscles. Starting an exercise programme in a few weeks' time and eating a sensible diet will help you feel better about the affected areas of your body.

Other skin changes, such as darker pigmentation on your face, known as chloasma, and the dark line in pregnancy that runs down your belly (linea nigra) may never go completely, but like stretch marks will fade over time. The best thing you can do to minimise their appearance is to stay out of the sun, or if you can't avoid the sun, cover up and use sunscreen.

Breastfeeding your baby
triggers uterine contractions after
the birth, helping your body to
return to its pre-pregnancy state.

causes your body to release the
hormone oxytocin, which in turn
triggers uterine contractions.

Adapting to breastfeeding

After the birth, changes carry on
occurring to your breasts. In pregnancy,
hormones transformed your breasts,
causing the development of a network
of ducts and milk-producing tissue.
Once oestrogen and progesterone levels
drop off after the delivery, hormones
called prolactin and oxytocin – in
combination with your baby's suckling
– stimulate milk production (see p.20).

Losing weight

Many new mums worry about losing
their baby weight. At first, weight drops
off rapidly and your total weight loss
shortly after birth is breathtaking.
Subtracting the weight of your baby, plus
the placenta and some blood and amniotic
fluid, leaves most women instantly about
5 kilograms (11 pounds) lighter.

As well as losing the weight of the
baby, placenta and amniotic fluid, you'll
also lose a lot of excess water at first, so

if you feel as though you're peeing all
the time, don't worry, this is completely
normal! During pregnancy, your body's
cells were hard at work retaining water,
and now all that extra fluid can be
released out in the form of sweat and
urine. New mums perspire a lot and
often produce an astounding 3.4 litres
(or 6 pints), of urine a day – twice the
usual amount!

Don't expect your body to snap back
to its pre-pregnancy shape within a
matter of weeks. It took nine months to
get to where it is, so you should allow
the same length of time to get back your
shape after the birth. On a positive note,
if you breastfeed, you should find that
you start to lose weight again easily,
naturally and gradually.

Fact: Your body is efficient
at producing milk, so
you shouldn't need more calories.
There's no right answer about how many
calories a day you need. It's best to be guided
by your appetite and to eat when hungry.

Recovering after
a caesarean

A caesarean is major surgery, so it's
important to go easy on yourself as
it can take up to six months for your
body to recover completely. Accept
offers of help from kind friends and
family members whenever you can!
Here are some ways you can help the
healing process along and get back to
normal faster.

● Trapped wind is a common
problem after a caesarean. Tightening
your abdominal muscles on an
outward breath may help, as does
peppermint water.

● The sooner you get out of bed
and walk around, the better for your
circulation and recovery. You'll be
encouraged to start gentle postnatal
exercises the day after your operation
– a physiotherapist will show you
what to do. These will help speed your
physical recovery; you shouldn't start
any more strenuous exercise until six
to eight weeks after the birth.

● Your first bowel movement may be
painful, so eat lots of high-fibre foods
and drink plenty of water to make it
easier. Holding a pillow over your
wound when you pass wind, laugh or
open your bowels will make you feel
more comfortable.

● Avoid lifting anything heavy as this
could strain your stitches.

● Your scar will start to itch in the
first week. It's a sign that it is healing,
but resist scratching. The stitches need
to either fall out on their own once
your skin is ready, or be removed by
your doctor at your check-up.

● Wait for five or six weeks before
driving, as twisting may hurt, and
having to do an emergency stop
would be very painful.

Welcome to parenthood!
0–6 weeks

Your growing baby
6 weeks to 6 months

Your older baby
6 months to one year

Baby healthcare
0–12 months

Your healing body

With all the strange things that happen to your body during the first few days after your baby's birth, you may start to think that pregnancy wasn't so bad after all! Give yourself time, though – just as your life is changing dramatically now with a new baby in tow, your body is also making huge physical and hormonal adjustments.

How your body recovers

Although giving birth is an amazing and miraculous process, it's also painful. If you gave birth to your baby vaginally, you'll probably feel at least some discomfort in the perineum (the area between the vagina and anus) for a while. If you had an episiotomy or a tear, you will also have to contend with the

pain of the wound and the discomfort of the stitches during the early days. The perineum is an extremely sensitive site for a cut or stitches, and women report a wide range of pain, from mild to excruciating. Most women find that it takes seven to 10 days for the wound to heal, though some pain may persist for up to a month.

It will hurt to cough or laugh if you've had a caesarean birth, but less if you support your wound (with your hands or by holding a pillow over your stomach) as you do so. Wearing bigger knickers that come over, rather than cut into, your scar will feel more comfortable.

Whether you had a natural vaginal birth or a caesarean birth, you'll need to use sanitary pads after the birth because the lochia, or bleeding from the uterus (see p.23), occurs whichever way you gave birth.

Urinary problems

Urinary stress incontinence (involuntary leaks of urine when you laugh, sneeze, cough or exercise) is still one of the least talked about side-effects of pregnancy and giving birth. If you had trouble

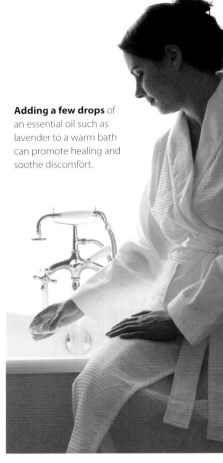

Adding a few drops of an essential oil such as lavender to a warm bath can promote healing and soothe discomfort.

and urethra weakened during the labour and birth. Now, however, it's thought that urinary incontinence after the birth may be the result of changes to a woman's body during pregnancy, rather

> ## "For **most** women, stretch marks **fade gradually** over time."

controlling your urine while you were pregnant, you're likely to have the same problem after you've had your baby. Rest assured though that this is a relatively common problem after giving birth and usually only temporary.

It used to be thought that stress incontinence happened when the pelvic floor muscles that support the bladder

than the result of damage to the pelvic floor during childbirth.

In some women, the problem resolves within a few weeks of giving birth, while in others it can persist for several months. If you're still having urine leaks when you have your postnatal check at six to eight weeks after the birth, do talk to your doctor.

Green mum

Many mums find natural remedies help the healing process after the birth.

"I used arnica tablets, which a friend told me could help to reduce bruising and soothe the discomfort from stitches. Other recommended healing remedies are creams containing calendula and comfrey. Also, I was a little anaemic following the birth, so I took an iron tonic to help restore my iron levels and to ease tiredness – I did check that my doctor was OK with these remedies. Above all, I ate a healthy, nutritious diet, tried to get plenty of rest and got lots of fresh air and a bit of exercise once I felt up to it. Your body changes after you've had a baby, so you have to be prepared to give it time to heal."

Also, it's entirely normal not to need to poo for a couple of days after giving birth. This delay is due to several factors, including high progesterone levels that may already have caused constipation in pregnancy; your digestive system slowing down during labour; and drugs given for pain relief during labour, such as pethidine, making the action of your bowel slower than usual.

Changing moods

Are you elated one minute and snappy or tearful the next? Postnatal hormonal swings affect the central nervous system, so it's normal and extremely common for women to feel weepy and overwhelmed during the first couple of weeks after the birth, which is known as the baby blues (see p.82). However, if feelings of doubt, despair and malaise don't go away after two weeks, you should talk to your health visitor or doctor. You could be suffering from postnatal depression (see pp.83–5) and may need treatment.

Getting back into shape

It's very normal to feel as though pregnancy has ravaged your body and that you'll never get your old shape back. Your tummy may be flabby and wrinkly at first, and your waistline will still be non-existent. This will, of course, change in time. For the moment though, it's important that you concentrate on eating well and getting enough rest to be able to nurture both yourself and feed your growing baby.

Try not to worry about stretch marks at the moment. For most women, these are simply a fact of pregnancy and will fade gradually over time (see p.74). Although there is really nothing you can do to make stretch marks disappear completely, if you're worried about them, you can try to minimise their appearance by rubbing oil or cream rich in vitamin E over your abdomen to keep the skin supple. In addition, drink plenty of water and eat a diet rich in vitamins E and C, and in the minerals zinc and silica, which help to keep skin healthy.

A good recovery

Help your body on the road to recovery with a few sensible precautions and lifestyle measures.

● Gentle exercise is good for physical and mental health. Take your baby out for walks once you feel ready and start exercising the lower tummy muscles when you're ready (see pp.78–9).
● Get plenty of rest. Your body will heal more quickly if you're well rested, so try to sleep when your baby sleeps.
● Eat healthily. Your body may need up to a year to restock all the nutrients your baby used to grow and develop.
● Exercise your pelvic floor muscles (see p.78). The weight of your uterus and baby may have strained your pelvic floor leading to stress incontinence. Regular pelvic floor exercises should sort this out within a few weeks.
● Keep stitches clean to avoid infection. Change maternity pads often, washing your hands before and after.

ParentsAsk...

I feel very anxious about making my first bowel movement. Should I be worried?

Going to the loo for the first time after giving birth is a source of anxiety for many new mums, especially when your midwife keeps asking "Have you been yet?" In fact, it's usual not to have a bowel movement for the first two days after the birth.

One reason why we tend to get anxious about having our first poo is lack of information. Other aspects of your body after the birth, such as bleeding, baby blues, engorged breasts and breastfeeding, are all discussed at antenatal classes, but no one talks about going to the loo.

You may be worried that it will hurt and that, if you strain too hard, you may cause

injury. Many women worry that their stitches will actually burst. Rest assured that although the first bowel movement may be daunting, it won't cause any physical damage. It may be easier said than done, but try not to worry about going to the toilet.

Is there anything I can do to help my bowel open after the birth?

Eat high-fibre foods and drink plenty of fluids, and then your body should tell you when it's ready. When the urge to go finally happens, don't ignore it. Fold a clean sanitary pad in half and place it on your stitches, holding it in place from the front. This helps support your pelvic floor muscles and gives you the confidence that your stitches won't burst (they won't!).

If you haven't had a bowel movement after three days, you may be temporarily constipated, so talk to your midwife or doctor. He or she may suggest taking a laxative, which can be useful and are safe for short-term relief.

Apricots and other fresh fruits encourage and soften bowel movements.

Welcome to parenthood!
0–6 weeks

Your growing baby
6 weeks to 6 months

Your older baby
6 months to one year

Baby healthcare
0–12 months

Postnatal exercise

Many mums are understandably too exhausted to even contemplate exercise in the first few weeks after giving birth, while others can't wait to get back to the gym. Take it at your own pace, but be kind to your body. Here's how …

Diastasis rectus abdominis

This occurs when the abdominal muscles are over-stretched during pregnancy. Leaving it untreated can increase your chance of developing back pain and make it harder to regain your figure.

Self examination

You'll usually be assessed for this condition just after you've had your baby. If you're unsure whether you were, do the following check yourself. Lie flat on your back with your knees bent. Place the fingers of your right hand (or left hand if you're left-handed), palm down and pointing towards your pubic bone, just above your belly button. Breathe in and as you breathe out, gently lift your head and shoulders off the floor as though you were doing a sit-up. It doesn't matter if you can't get your head or shoulders up, simply trying will make your tummy muscles work. You should be able to feel your tummy muscles coming together as you try to sit up. You may need to try a few times before you feel anything. If you can't feel anything after three attempts, don't carry on. Ask your midwife to check instead.

When is it safe to start?

Getting back into regular clothes is exciting, yet challenging, for most new mums, and don't expect to be able to get into your favourite pair of jeans for several weeks. Keep in mind that it took 40 weeks to gain your pregnancy weight, so it will take time to lose it, too.

As for exercise guidelines, start out slowly, since you need to conserve your energy to recover from the labour and the birth. Many doctors and midwives advise waiting until after your postnatal check-up (see p.104), usually around six weeks after delivery to start a proper exercise routine, but most new mums can begin walking and doing pelvic floor and lower tummy muscle exercises almost straightaway.

Pelvic floor exercises

Exercises to tone your pelvic floor are important. Although they may feel like the last thing you want to do, starting them early will help your perineum and vagina to heal more quickly. They won't rip any stitches, either. In fact, doing the exercises improves the circulation to the area and reduces swelling and bruising.

Parents**Ask...**

Am I overdoing it?

Many new mums are eager to work off pregnancy weight straightaway, but too much activity in the first few weeks can cause your vaginal discharge, or lochia, to turn pink or red and heavier: a signal to slow down. If you had a caesarean birth, allow time for your incision to heal and you should do only gentle exercise before six weeks. Talk to your doctor if you experience vaginal bleeding or lochia restarts.

How quickly can I lose weight?

A sensible goal is to lose no more than half a kilo or pound a week. This is safe and helps to ensure that the weight stays off. The best way to regain your figure is to do some form of aerobic exercise, such as swimming or brisk walking, and eat sensibly. Focus on fast movements with your arms and legs that make your heart beat faster. If you weren't active in pregnancy, start with a 15-minute programme and gradually increase to 30 minutes. If you tapered off your exercise as pregnancy progressed, begin at the level you stopped exercising when you were pregnant and increase the intensity or time as you feel ready. If you develop aches or pains, talk to your doctor.

Begin gentle tummy exercises once you feel ready If you had a vaginal birth. If you had a caesarean, wait at least six weeks. Lie flat on your back and, as you exhale, lift your chest and head up, arms stretched out in front. Touch your knees, then relax.

Sit upright with your legs stretched in front of you. Extend from your lower back and stretch one arm forwards, touching your toes if possible. Repeat with the other arm. Try not to arch your back and avoid putting your back under any undue pressure.

It's best to start exercising your pelvic floor muscles while lying on your back or side. In the past, women were advised to do this while urinating, but this is no longer recommended. Some women find it easier to do the exercises in the bath as they feel more relaxed. The feeling of doing them is one of "squeeze and lift", closing and drawing up the front and back passages. (Imagine that you are trying to stop yourself from passing wind and trying to stop your flow of urine mid-stream at the same time.)

Some women feel more happening at the front and some feel more happening around their bottom. Don't worry too much, as long as you can feel a squeeze, tightening or a lift somewhere between your front and back passages!

Over the next few weeks, try to hold a pelvic floor contraction for longer while breathing normally. Start by tightening for a couple of seconds, then four or five seconds, and eventually for 10 seconds.

For the first few days or weeks, you may find that you can't feel the pelvic floor muscles working and think that

nothing is happening; don't worry, this is normal. Keep trying, as the feeling in the pelvic floor will return after a few days and it will work even if you can't feel it.

Taking it gently

In the first six weeks, try some gentle exercise such as brisk walking to increase your circulation. Do only as much as you can manage, even if it's just 10 to 15 minutes, and increase your time as you get stronger. Avoid weighing yourself each day, as this can cause frustration if weight falls off slowly.

Aerobics or running aren't advised for the first three months to allow your muscles and joints to recover fully from the pregnancy and birth. If you're a competitive athlete, you may be able to begin earlier, but talk to your doctor first. Also, don't swim before six weeks as there's a risk of infection from the water.

Begin exercise steadily, listen to your body and increase the amount that you do gradually. If you experience pain, stop exercising until you have seen your doctor or a physiotherapist.

 Active mum

It's fine to exercise while you're breastfeeding. Avoid exercises that make your breasts sore or tender, though, and try to exercise after feeding your baby so your breasts won't feel full.

"I wait for an hour after strenuous exericse before giving my baby his next feed as I've heard that babies can feed less vigorously or shun the breast after a mum exercises. I always wear a sports bra, especially now my breasts are bigger, and often need to wear breast pads! At first, I had to resist overdoing things. Apparently, trying to speed up weight loss while breastfeeding can cause your milk to contain chemicals called ketones that are potentially unhealthy for a baby. I make sure that I eat healthily, as I did when I was pregnant, to provide enough breast milk for my baby and meet my own nutritional needs."

Welcome to parenthood!
0–6 weeks

Your growing baby
6 weeks to 6 months

Your older baby
6 months to one year

Baby healthcare
0–12 months

Getting out each day for a brisk walk with the buggy is the perfect, no-hassle way to introduce exercise into your daily routine.

Active mum

You may be able to find a great postnatal class that takes into account the upheaval your body has been through during the labour and birth.

"For the first few weeks, I did some brisk walking with my baby in the buggy, which really toned my muscles and got my heart beating faster.

After about six weeks, I was able to start doing some simple stretches, sit-ups and toning exercises at home. I did take care when I exercised. I started each session with a gentle warm-up: five minutes of walking on the spot or walking up and down the stairs a few times, as well as rolling my shoulders back and forth several times and twisting gently from side to side, hands on my hips.

Now I've joined a really good postnatal exercise class, which works on blitzing the "problem" areas after pregnancy – the tummy, bottom and thighs. The classes are a good way to meet other new mums, and my class has a crèche too."

Postnatal exercise classes

There are plenty of postnatal exercise classes available and, as well as helping you get back into shape safely, they're also a good way to meet other new mums. You don't have to go to a gym and use a crèche, either: pram-pushing exercise classes that take place outdoors in parks around the country have become popular recently.

In fact, one study showed that attending a buggy-based exercise class helped to alleviate the symptoms of postnatal depression. Your midwife or health visitor may be able to put you in touch with an instructor.

Building exercise into the day
You don't need to join a postnatal exercise class to get fit, though – there are plenty of ways to build exercise into your day. Just getting out each day and taking a brisk walk with your baby in her pram or buggy, as well as being excellent exercise for you, can help to lift your mood, help a fractious baby to settle or sleep and give you more energy – and it's completely free!

When you're feeling stronger, you can use an exercise video at home while your baby is nearby. Make sure she's safely sleeping or secure in a baby seat,

high chair or playpen so there is no danger of tripping over her. Chances are she'll enjoy watching you dance!

You can work out with your baby, too. Try abdominal head and shoulder raises with your baby lying on your thighs, or press-ups with your baby lying on a rug between your hands.

Taking it easy
Bear in mind that the joint-relaxing pregnancy hormone, relaxin, stays in your body for around three to five months after the birth, so take care not to overdo it and hurt your joints.

Baby yoga classes

You may be aware of the benefits that yoga can bring to your body and mind, but did you know that you can also practise it with your baby? Baby yoga is a great way for you and your baby to get to relax and have fun together while you get back in shape, too.

What is involved?

Baby yoga involves gentle stretching and relaxing sequences, which are usually coordinated with music and fun songs and rhymes. Importantly, baby yoga encourages communication and bonding between you and your baby through eye contact, touch, movement, talking to and holding your baby. It also gives you confidence in handling her.

The benefits for your baby

Baby yoga has plenty of physical benefits for your baby. As it provides as much physical activity in a short session as your baby might receive in a whole day, many mums find that it helps their babies to sleep more deeply and promotes a more regular sleeping pattern. It can help relieve any tensions your baby may have in her intestines, releasing trapped wind and alleviating the symptoms of colic.

Baby yoga positions also provide your baby with the opportunity for "tummy time", which enables her to lift her head and strengthen her neck muscles, shoulders and arms. It can help her to breathe more deeply, too, which may help her immune system.

Benefits for you

Relaxation is a key feature of yoga, and baby yoga can be as relaxing for you as it is for your baby. It's performed in a calm and soothing environment, so can give you some much-needed time to unwind and re-energise, which will also help to reduce any stress and anxiety you've been experiencing.

Classes often involve yoga exercises for new mothers, too, and can help to tone the pelvic, abdominal and back muscles through postures that involve your baby. Like adult yoga, it can help you to regain strength and maintain posture, and reduce tension in areas such as the neck, shoulders and back. If there are classes in your area, it's also a great way to get out and meet other new mums.

Above all, baby yoga is fun. The yoga movements are like play for your baby, and are designed to be enjoyed by both of you. Once you've mastered the techniques, you and your baby can have fun at home whenever it suits you.

Wait until at least an hour after you've fed your baby before doing baby yoga. If your baby has a health problem, seek medical advice before trying baby yoga, and observe any cautions given to you by your yoga teacher. If your baby seems unhappy or unsettled during yoga, leave your session until another time.

Incorporate stretches into your baby yoga routine. With your baby lying facing you, extend your right leg and bend your left leg, putting your foot flat on the floor. Put your left arm behind you, clasp your left knee with your right arm and rotate your body.

Straighten both legs and put your baby on your lap facing you, her head supported on a cushion. Sit tall and raise your arms, then exhale and extend forwards, keeping your chest open. Your baby may mirror your pose, raising her arms and stretching out her legs.

To complete the series of stretches sit up straight with your legs crossed, your left leg resting over your right knee. Hold your baby on your lap and enjoy the feeling of extension in your posture as you support your baby. Repeat with your right leg over the left.

Welcome to parenthood! 0–6 weeks

Your growing baby 6 weeks to 6 months

Your older baby 6 months to one year

Baby healthcare 0–12 months

How you're feeling

Having a baby brings much joy, but it can also affect you in ways you would never have expected. Quite aside from all the hormonal changes in your body, your life has changed forever. With such a mixture of happiness and anxiety, it's natural to feel up and down.

Systemised mum

It's normal to feel sad a few days after the birth – you've gone through a life-changing event, you're exhausted and your hormones are in a state of flux.

"I think I expected to feel instant love for my baby and was taken aback when this wasn't the case. About four days after the birth, I felt incredibly weepy. I'd known that hormonal changes could have this affect, but initally felt unprepared. However, I knew that there was a lot I could do to help myself feel better. I made sure I rested as much as possible, sleeping in the day when my baby slept and going to bed early. My partner was really helpful, too, taking turns with the baby so that I could rest.

I took care of myself, eating healthily so that I had enough energy. Also, as soon as I felt ready, I did some gentle exercise, and made sure that I took my baby out for a walk each day, which helped mentally as well as physically.

I was lucky, too, as my partner was so supportive. He always made time to listen to how I was feeling, and it was helpful for both of us to talk about the adjustments we were making together as parents."

Baby blues

Soon after birth, many women encounter a spell of weepiness and moodiness, commonly called the "baby blues".

The baby blues often start three or four days after delivery, when pregnancy hormones dissipate and milk production kicks in. They're also linked to a sense of physical and emotional anticlimax after the birth. Returning home from the hospital can also increase your sense of uncertainty about life as a mum.

Many new mums experience mood swings and weepiness caused by a combination of hormonal upheaval and tiredness.

How you might feel

The baby blues are thought to affect 60 to 80 per cent of women. You may feel exhausted, unable to sleep, trapped or anxious. Your appetite can change (you may eat more or less), or you may feel irritable, nervous and worried about being a mum. These feelings are normal in the first couple of weeks, usually lasting for a few days.

Baby blues can be confused with postnatal depression because they share common symptoms. Although emotional upheaval is natural after a birth, if the blues last for two to three weeks after the birth, then you may have postnatal depression (see opposite) and should seek professional help.

A supportive partner

If you're the partner of a mum with the baby blues, the best thing you can do is support her, listen to her and encourage her to cry if she needs to. Tell her what a wonderful mum you think she will be. Help her set limits on activities and rest as much as possible, and keep visitors to a minimum. Above all, let her know you're there for her, no matter what.

The baby blues will go away on their own. No treatment is needed other than reassurance, support, rest and time.

Signs and symptoms of postnatal depression

The checklist below provides a guide to the signs and symptoms of postnatal depression (PND). If you have one or more of these signs, you should seek help.

- feeling miserable for prolonged periods of time
- feeling that life isn't worth living and you've nothing to look forward to
- guilt
- irritability
- tearfulness
- feeling constantly exhausted, yet finding it hard to sleep, or experiencing disturbed sleep and early morning wakefulness
- being unable to enjoy yourself
- anxiety

- loss of sense of humour
- inability to concentrate or cope
- anxiety about your baby; constantly seeking reassurance from health professionals that he is alright
- worried about your own state of health, perhaps worried that you have a serious illness
- feeling that your baby is a stranger and not really yours

You may also have:

- loss of sex drive
- low energy levels
- problems with memory
- difficulty making decisions
- no appetite, or be comfort eating

A supportive, loving and aware partner can be an important factor in dealing with and recovering from PND.

Welcome to parenthood!
0–6 weeks

Your growing baby
6 weeks to 6 months

Your older baby
6 months to one year

Baby healthcare
0–12 months

Postnatal depression

Postnatal depression (PND) is not the same as the baby blues. The baby blues start a few days after the birth (see opposite). Mothers feel weepy and miserable, worried about their baby or themselves, tense, tired and on edge. However, baby blues disappear within a day or two.

PND is far more serious and is thought to affect a significant minority of women with new babies. When other women have got over their weepy patch and are once again full of the joys of motherhood, a mum who has PND becomes increasingly anxious and miserable. You may have begun to feel depressed during your pregnancy or it could have started in the weeks or months after giving birth. The most common time for postnatal depression to develop is when your baby is between four and six weeks old.

Recognising the symptoms

Being aware of the symptoms of PND can help you or your partner to seek help promptly and receive treatment. Symptoms of PND include feeling miserable most of time; feeling guilty and ready to blame yourself for general problems; being irritable, tearful, constantly exhausted (yet unable to sleep) and being unable to enjoy yourself. You may feel as though you've lost your sense of humour, and be constantly anxious about your baby or even feel as though he's not really yours. We all have feelings like these every now and again – becoming a mother is a physical and emotional rollercoaster and tiredness and hormonal changes take their toll. However, if you experience a lot of these symptoms and they're there constantly, talk to your health visitor or doctor.

Risk factors

It's not known why some women become depressed and others don't. One possibility is that our individual brain biochemistry makes some of us more prone to depression than others. There do seem to be some situations, however, that increase the risk of postnatal depression.

You may be more at risk of PND if you have previously suffered from depression, or if you were depressed while you were pregnant. Sometimes, a bad birth experience or having an ill or premature baby can trigger PND. The condition may also be triggered if your mother died when you were a young child, or if you don't have a supportive partner or family or friends living close by. For some, financial or housing difficulties, or other troubles such as redundancy or bereavement, are the cause.

"Being **diagnosed** with PND can be a huge **relief** and help you to believe that you'll feel better again."

Preventing PND

There are several measures you can take to help reduce your risk of developing PND.

- Be aware of the symptoms of PND (see p.83) and be reassured that if you have the condition, you can be treated successfully.
- Do important tasks only (housework can wait!) and make time just for you.
- Sleep if you can, or rest and doze if you can't. Don't panic if you can't sleep, just relaxing in bed will help.
- Eat a healthy diet with plenty of carbohydrates to keep your energy up.
- If you feel down, talk to someone. This could be a friend, family member or health professional.
- Surround yourself with a good support network of friends and family.
- If you feel depressed tell your doctor. Being diagnosed is a big step towards recovery.

Treating PND

Your doctor may offer you antidepressants. These drugs work by balancing the chemicals within your brain. Antidepressants can lift your mood and help you to sleep well and feel less irritable.

If you are given antidepressant drugs, you must take these at the prescribed times. It will be at least a couple of weeks before you start to notice a difference, so don't give up and throw the drugs away because you think they're not doing you any good. They are working, but it takes time for them to build up in your system. You will need to take the drugs for about six months altogether. If you stop before that time, your depression will probably quickly return. If you're breastfeeding and considering taking antidepressants, talk to your doctor to get a clear understanding of the risks involved.

It's worth considering counselling. While offloading onto your partner or best friend may help, they may find it hard to understand what you're going through. Sometimes, talking about how awful you feel to a professional who understands depression can help more. Your doctor may be able to refer you to a counsellor, or your health visitor may have counselling skills.

Helping yourself

There are a few things you can try to help yourself feel better.

Eating a healthy diet is vital. Even if you have no appetite, eat small, regular meals. Breakfast is especially important. Eating carbohydrates, such as bread, cereals, pasta, rice and bananas, will give you energy for the day, and eat plenty of fresh fruit and vegetables. If the occasional bar of chocolate cheers you up, have one.

Rest is important. Sleep if you can, or relax and doze if you can't. If someone can take the baby for a while, go to bed: have a warm drink, put some calming music on, snuggle down and relax.

Talking to your doctor or other health professional is an important first step in successfully treating PND.

Dad's **Diary**

Noticing a change

"My wife's postnatal depression came as quite a shock to us. For the first few months, Helen had adjusted really well to being a mum. She got into a routine quite early on, and was enjoying looking after Lily. However, when Lily was about four months old, things started to change. I'd come home from work and she would still be in her dressing gown. She worried constantly about the baby – even excessively so, and she would break down and cry over the slightest thing. She felt terribly guilty about feeling so low and couldn't understand why she felt that way, but also felt utterly helpless to control the way she was feeling.

It took some time for her to accept she needed professional help to get better. Once she did accept this, we went together to see her doctor. Once treatment had started, it was a huge relief to know we were on the road to recovery. I took some time off work, too, so that we could spend more time together and I could help out with the housework and looking after Lily."

Enlisting the help of willing grandparents can allow you to get some much needed rest and, in turn, feel more able to cope (left).

Getting out with your partner can elevate your mood and help you both to nurture and focus on your own relationship (above).

Welcome to parenthood!
0–6 weeks

Your growing baby
6 weeks to 6 months

Your older baby
6 months to one year

Baby healthcare
0–12 months

Be kind to yourself. You need time and space to recover. Put off major decisions and don't burden yourself with chores.

How partners can help

Speak to your partner's doctor, who can advise you on how to support her. Make sure that she takes prescribed medication, and/or goes to counselling appointments. If she's reluctant to take drugs, get her to talk to her doctor about alternatives and go with her to the doctor if that helps. Help with household tasks and with the baby, but don't take over the baby. Stay with her if she's frightened of being alone and remind her that she will get better.

10%
of new mums are affected by PND.

Although PND usually starts within the first four to six weeks after the birth, it can occur months later, so it's important to be aware of the signs and symptoms.

Puerperal psychosis

This rare, but serious, mental illness typically starts within a week of giving birth. It can come on suddenly, in just a few hours, but can be treated successfully with medication, supported by counselling and other therapies. It's much less common than PND, affecting only one or two mothers per 1,000. It's more likely to develop if you, or someone in your family, has a history of psychotic illness.

Signs and symptoms

Each case of puerperal psychosis differs, but common symptoms include very heightened and changeable emotions, feeling disconnected from reality and hallucinating, for example hearing voices or seeing things that aren't there. Often other people notice that something is wrong before the mother does because it can cause odd and unpredictable behaviour. It's

important to seek help as soon as possible, not only because there's a risk of self-harm the longer the condition is untreated, but also to prevent damage to the mother's relationship with her baby and her partner.

Diagnosis and treatment

Assessment and treatment of the condition often involves going to hospital, in a mother-and-baby unit if available. Treatment is almost always with medication under specialist supervision, with drugs that allow the mother to continue breastfeeding if she wishes to.

If you've suffered from mental illness in the past and are worried about the possibility of developing puerperal psychosis, talk to a midwife or doctor about your concerns. If you think that you, or someone you know, may be suffering from this condition, seek medical help immediately.

Your partner's role

It's sometimes hard for a new dad to know how to get involved with caring for his new baby. However, there are plenty of ways for your partner to help out, allowing him to bond with his newborn baby and giving you some much-needed rest.

Laid-back mum

It's great when a partner is keen to get hands-on with the baby. Not only can it make you feel all warm and fuzzy to see them together, but it takes some of the pressure away from you.

"I think, at first, my partner struggled to feel involved because George was so reliant on me for feeding and nurture. So I resisted the urge to do everything for George and stood back from time to time to let Paul take over. I don't think there's some innate intuition that tells women how to care for their newborns – I think mothers learn simply by practising, and so do dads. Apart from feeding, Paul was able to help out with everything else, such as changing dirty nappies, bathing, dressing, winding and comforting. Finding a balance worked really well as I managed to get some much-needed rest and he really started to bond with George.

Over time, we both developed our own unique relationship with George. I think dads interact differently with their children. Paul's more physical play was the perfect counterpoint to my gentler care – but he enjoys the softer side to parenting, too."

How dads can help

It's easy to feel left out in the first few weeks, especially if your partner is breastfeeding. You may feel as though your partner and baby bond constantly and you have little part to play.

A supportive partner

There are plenty of ways for dads to get involved and help. Most importantly, you can be supportive and thoughtful towards your partner. Ensure that she has time to rest and take responsibility for chores that normally fall to her.

Breastfeeding can be hard work at first. The current recommendation from health professionals is that women should try to breastfeed for at least six months. Studies show that the more supportive their partners, the longer women breastfeed and the more confident they feel about their ability to do so.

You could talk to your partner about giving your baby expressed breastmilk from a bottle. However, don't put pressure on her, as some women find expressing (manually or with a pump) uncomfortable and even painful. If you do both decide that expressing is a good idea, you'll need to wait a few weeks before introducing a bottle so that your baby has a chance to get comfortable with breastfeeding first.

Time together

In the meantime, spend plenty of time with your baby doing activities that involve skin-to-skin contact. Changing nappies, cuddling and winding her, putting her to sleep, bathing her, and even just reading in a chair while your baby naps on your chest, are all great for bonding. Take your baby for walks in the buggy, put her in a sling to go shopping, or do whatever you can think of to be together.

The more you and your baby are together, the more confident you will feel about your own abilities as a parent.

Fathers can play a significant role in the everyday care of young babies.

Taking parternity leave provides an invaluable opportunity for fathers to bond with their baby in the early days and weeks.

Paternity leave and benefits

When your partner has the baby, you will probably be able to take up to two weeks' paternity leave from work in the period immediately after the birth. This not only means you can support her in the tiring first weeks, but also gives you valuable time to get to grips with the basics of baby care.

Your rights

To qualify for paternity leave you will need to be an employee with a contract of employment, and to have worked for your employer for at least 26 weeks by the end of the 15th week before the week the baby is due.

You can take either one or two weeks' leave. If you take two weeks' leave, the weeks must be consecutive – you can't take odd days.

You must inform your employer of your plans for paternity leave, in writing, at least 15 weeks before the week when your baby is due. You can ask for your leave to start immediately after the birth or in the following eight weeks. If your baby is born early, you can still take your leave within eight weeks of the expected week of birth.

You can change your mind about the start date as long as you give your employer at least 28 days' notice, if practical. Check your contract, too, as some employers offer their own paternity benefits, which may suit you better than the statutory arrangements.

Dads of twins, triplets or more are only allowed one period of paternity leave, regardless of how many babies are born as the result of one pregnancy.

Dad's **Diary**

Strengthening the ties

"My baby, Ruth, and partner had lots of close, nurturing time together while she was breastfeeding, so I thought it was important to build my own relationship with Ruth. I had heard that skin-to-skin contact was wonderful for creating an attachment between parents and babies, so I made time to cuddle her, as well as bath her, settle her or just let her sleep on my chest while I relaxed.

Often, I would bring Ruth to my partner for her feed and I also gave her an occasional bottle of expressed milk once she'd established breastfeeding. This gave us quality bonding time together, and my sleep-starved partner was extremely grateful!

I read about some research which suggested that a high intimacy level in the first few months produces a closer attachment and encourages a more rewarding parenting experience in the future. So I figured that each nappy I changed, every cuddle I gave and every game I played, would strengthen our bond for the months and years to come."

Close nurturing cuddles strengthen the attachment between father and baby and form the foundation of a strong, loving bond for the years ahead.

When dad returns to work

Being a new mum is hard: you've been through the emotional and exhausting experience of giving birth; your hormones are rapidly adjusting; you may be recovering from surgery or stitches; bothered by afterpains, and trying to establish breastfeeding while

32% is an estimate of dads' share of parenting.

There are no official statistics, but it's thought that there are around 155,000 stay-at-home dads in the UK. Research shows that parenting has become more of a joint responsibility.

suffering from a lack of sleep. Thank goodness your partner has paternity leave – it's great having someone else to share the dirty nappies and the sleepless nights. And then he goes back to work!

Coping on your own

It's a shock for both of you at first, but you will cope. Don't make too many jobs for yourself: it doesn't matter if the laundry isn't folded or the dishwasher isn't emptied. Your baby would prefer you spent time cuddling him than having perfectly ironed bibs.

Many women find that the long stretch of the day can be more manageable if it's broken up. If you

plan to go for a short walk every day, whatever the weather, this can help to stop you feeling like the four walls are closing in on you. Also, the exercise will make you feel good and your baby will appreciate the change of scenery.

Meeting other mums

Loneliness can be a real problem for many new mothers. A touch of adult company and friendship can be a lifeline. Some women stay in touch with other new mothers they met through antenatal classes, and this can be a valuable way of socialising, sharing experiences and providing the babies with some company, too.

If you don't know any other new parents in your area, going to a parent-and-baby group for the first time can be daunting, but very worthwhile. It will be great to share your experiences of parenthood with people going through exactly the same things as you. Ask your health visitor about local groups and make the effort to go along.

"Me" time

Set aside time for yourself, too. Advice often given to mums is to "sleep when the baby sleeps". If you can't relax enough to fall asleep while your baby has a daytime nap, you can try to award yourself a break. Instead of using any spare time to catch up on chores, refresh yourself each day by doing something just for yourself. Whether you put your feet up and read a book, or call a friend, it's good to remind yourself that you're still a person with your own life.

Mother-and-baby groups can be a lifeline for new mums, giving structure to the day and providing company and support.

Take a break when your partner gets home while he and your baby enjoy some quality time.

Adjusting to the new order

When your partner is at home, make the most of his natural desire to spend lots of time with his new baby and let him take over your parenting duties a little during this time. It's important that fathers have quality bonding time with their baby, which also means that you will get some time to yourself.

Coping on your own will get easier as you get to know your baby and discover his likes and dislikes, and how he needs to be cared for. Gradually, you and your partner will settle into your own routines with your baby. Although life changes forever the moment you become a parent, the stresses of the first weeks do not last all through babyhood.

Dad's **Diary**

A hard adjustment

"Going back to work after a week's paternity leave was tough. I was more tired than I'd ever been in my life. I had averaged three or four hours' sleep a night since Amy was born. My first day started well. I was glad of the change for the first two hours, and happy to tell my colleagues about my early days as a dad. But after lunch I hit a wall. I didn't fall asleep at my computer, I just stared at it with a fixed gaze. My baby-addled brain had forgotten what I actually did at work.

I realised how much I missed Amy. She spent so much time asleep in the early weeks, so when I got home it was tempting to stomp around to wake her. I spent ages watching her sleep, arms above her head, legs curled up.

The realisation of how much I miss Amy makes the time I spend with her all the more special. I take over nappy changing and bathing, and when we go out, I often carry her in her sling. When I'm at work, I remind myself that I'm providing for a family, which feels good."

Parents**Talk...**

"When my partner's leave ended, I felt panicked – I was used to turning to him constantly for reassurance. In the event, leaving me to my own devices soon helped me realise that I could trust my instincts."
Alison, 32, first-time mum

"When my partner went back to work, I felt really lonely. I loved being with our baby, but missed adult conversation, so I joined baby groups and organised lunches with friends. It gave me the balance I needed."
Sheila, 23, first-time mum

"I was surprised to find myself feeling jealous when my husband went back to work – I missed the focus that my job had given me. I decided to set up a baby-and-book group for local mums. It gives me something to look forward to and organise each week."
Pat, 34, mother of two

"I was worried that my partner would miss out on quality time with our son. So each night he does bath and bedtime. It gives them time together, and it's a break for me!"
Emily, 26, first-time mum

If possible, getting out on your own occasionally with friends provides a refreshing and re-energising break.

Welcome to parenthood! 0–6 weeks

Your growing baby 6 weeks to 6 months

Your older baby 6 months to one year

Baby healthcare 0–12 months

You and your partner

With all the change and upheaval that a new baby brings, together with the exhaustion and sheer unrelenting nature of babycare, it's not surprising that many couples find their relationship takes a back seat. It's important to recognise this and make time for each other.

ParentsTalk...

"Go away together for a weekend to get to know each other as lovers again. Leave your baby with a family member for a night or two."
Rosie, 26, mother of two

"Spending time alone together only helps if the mum is genuinely OK about leaving her baby. If not, she'll be stressed and resentful."
John, 36, father of three

"I don't feel sexually confident about my post-baby body two-and-a-half years on! It helps when my partner tells me I look good."
Anna, 31, first-time mum

"Set aside a night a week when the baby is in bed to have a takeaway, a movie and a bottle of wine."
Hannah, 23, first-time mum

"We were often too tired at night to even contemplate sex. One thing that worked for us for a while was to make the most of our son's midday naps – on a Sunday we would go to bed too!"
Lucy, 40, first-time mum

Nurturing your relationship

It's natural to feel overwhelmed, frustrated – even angry or blue – about your new roles and the changing dynamic of your relationship. In addition, sleeplessness and surging hormones add to the anxiety of wanting to get parenthood right. However, presumably, you and your partner didn't start your life together staring vacantly past each other or issuing only an occasional grunt of recognition, so try not to let those lines of communication become victim to your tiredness or aggravation.

Strengthening your bond

Making the leap from a couple to a family of three (or more) requires trust in and respect for each other. The way

you feel about yourself, inwardly and outwardly, has changed and that also affects your relationship with your partner. Remind yourselves of the basic commonalities you've always shared, and trust each other to put the best interests of your family first. You got together for a reason, so try not to lose sight of that.

The power of communication

If you're feeling frustrated and irritated because your baby won't stop crying, no matter how many clever ditties you've sung, don't keep it to yourself. Your feelings are likely to surface in some form, so it's better to explain it to your partner. Pay attention to each other, and try to find the time to talk through things that are bothering you – and also share your triumphs.

Hold on to the thought that eventually you will possess the ability to speak full sentences with no reference to bodily functions or household chores. It won't be easy, but consider it a fun little challenge on your road to recovering from persistent baby-brain.

Talking, laughing and paying attention to each other helps you both to keep hold of the essence of your relationship.

A loving embrace and plenty of affection can help you to maintain feelings of closeness and rebuild intimacy gradually.

Welcome to parenthood!
0–6 weeks

Your growing baby
6 weeks to 6 months

Your older baby
6 months to one year

Baby healthcare
0–12 months

Getting out together

After a few weeks, if you and your partner feel ready to go out alone, your baby may be settled enough for you to leave him with a trusted adult.

Make sure you leave instructions for your baby's care and how to contact you if necessary. Try going out for a short period the first time, and make sure it's easy for you to get back if the babysitter can't cope or you just feel you have to check on things.

Finding a babysitter

If you don't have parents or suitable friends nearby, you need to find someone with the maturity to look after a young baby. Guidelines are that no one under 16 should be left to care for an infant or young child. Age isn't the only consideration. If you don't know a potential babysitter well, ask for references, and then contact those people. Also, your babysitter should ideally have first-aid skills, or be prepared to take a first-aid course.

Resuming intimacy

Many new parents wonder when it's OK to resume sex. There's no right answer, just whenever you both feel the time is right. Some have sex in the first month, many more between one and three months, and a sizeable minority wait till the six-month mark, or even a year.

How you feel

New mums can feel reluctant to have sex for many reasons. The most obvious is soreness from a tear or episiotomy (see p.18) and stitches. Even without a tear, the perineal area can feel bruised and sensitive for a while. It makes sense to let the wound heal and stitches dissolve before you have intercourse.

Tiredness is another factor. Looking after a baby 24 hours a day is physically and emotionally exhausting. For some women, the perception of their body might hold them back. Your body may feel so changed from the pregnancy and birth that you need time for it to recover before you feel like yourself again. Many new mums report a low libido: they just don't feel sexy.

The first priority for couples is to carve out some together-time and build intimacy slowly. Sex doesn't have to mean full penetration. Words and cuddles can do much to convey affection and emotion, and you'll both benefit from the closeness.

Your adopted baby

After months, possibly years, of waiting, the anticipation is over and you'll soon be bringing home your adopted baby. So, how do you prepare for his arrival? And what can you do to help start the bonding process with your new baby?

ParentsAsk...

Can I breastfeed my baby?

Yes, but only half of all adopting mothers who try to breastfeed make any milk, and few produce enough. A baby's suckling triggers milk production, but without the pregnancy hormones that prepare you for breastfeeding, it's harder to start milk flow.

Inducing lactation takes a month or so of pumping with a hospital-grade pump. Timing this with a baby's arrival can be tricky, as you may have little notice. So breastmilk may not be the sole source of nutrition, but it can help with bonding.

Your baby's arrival

If you're adopting, you haven't got the predictability of a nine-month pregnancy to prepare yourself physically and emotionally. Once adoptive parents have been approved, it can take an agency in the UK anything from a year to just a few weeks to match them with a child. Even in private adoptions, where the approximate arrival date may be known in advance, it's normal for prospective parents to feel wary as well as excited. Be reassured that birth parents experience the same self-doubts.

Plan ahead

Even if you're not sure of your baby's arrival date, you can start to look at baby equipment. Make a note of cot or buggy brand names, styles and store phone numbers so that you can place an order as soon as you get confirmation from the adoption agency or lawyer. Although it's tempting when you've waited so long, don't buy lots of clothes: you'll only end up with a drawer full of outgrown outfits.

Do your research

If you're expecting a newborn, read up on childbirth so you know what your baby has gone through. Adoptive parents are often so excited by a baby's arrival, they can overstimulate him instead of letting him rest. Read up on the subject of adoption, too, and talk to other adoptive parents to find out how they coped. The agency can put you in touch with local support groups, or visit the Adoption UK website (see pp.312–13).

Building up confidence

Soon you'll have responsibility for a tiny baby; it's not surprising you feel anxious. Learning a few babycare skills will boost

Previous carers or agencies can give insights into your adopted baby's character.

your confidence. Ask your doctor about postnatal or early days classes, so you know the basics of feeding, bathing, changing and carrying a baby. Or visit a friend with a baby to pick up a few tips.

Go easy on yourself

Don't expect to feel like a mother from day one. Even birth mothers don't adapt to the role overnight. Like any relationship, the mother–baby bond takes time. The important thing is that, to your baby, you're very much his real mum (or dad), who loves him, shelters him and cares for all his needs. Bear in mind, too, that babies have different personalities and some don't like being touched as much; it's nothing to do with you or the fact that your child's adopted.

Meeting your adopted baby can be an overwhelming and wonderful experience as you adapt to your new role as parents.

Bonding with your baby

You know so much about your new baby, but you may worry that you won't be able to bond. Research shows that adoptive parents are as successful at forming attachments as biological ones. In fact, studies show that adopted children see their parents as more nurturing than non-adopted ones do. Just remember that bonding is a journey.

Tune in together

Spend as much time as you can with your baby. As parents, you should be his primary carers at first to give him a chance to focus on you. Limit visitors at first, too. Making lots of eye contact as you hold or feed him will increase feelings of care, pride, wonder and love. Talk or sing to him to develop his language skills and hasten the magical day when he utters his first "mama" or "dada". If he likes being touched, try some baby massage (see pp.164–67).

Comforting your baby

All healthy new babies communicate by crying. You could soothe him by breastfeeding (see opposite), which will enhance the bond between you. If your baby had a carer before, ask them about his habits, likes and dislikes, to help him settle. Remember, too, that colic (see p.245) can cause crying. His cries are no reflection on you or your care.

See the bigger picture

Some adopted babies are developmentally delayed as they lacked stimulation or nutrition in the early days, so don't worry if your baby doesn't seem to reach milestones as quickly as other babies. If he had a hard start in life, he needs the security of a loving family to nurture him throughout childhood and beyond. You can help by surrounding him with familiar objects, such as toys, from his previous environment.

Trusting your "motherly" feelings

It's hard to trust your instincts when you're battling doubts on all fronts. You may worry that your baby's birth mother will change her mind during the waiting period, or that, because you've missed out on pregnancy or your child's first days or months, it will be harder for you to love him. You may feel unsure of yourself as a mother, or wonder if your baby will grow up to be like you or like his biological parents. What's fairly certain is that these doubts will ebb away as your baby comes to feel more and more like your own, and you realise that to him, you are the only parents he has.

Working it out

In the meantime, the fact that you're worried about being a good mother shows that you're concerned about your baby, and that's a great start. Instead of fretting about whether you fulfil a parental standard that experts themselves don't agree on, focus your energy on getting to know your baby.

For example, when your baby is crying, ask yourself, "Is he hungry? Uncomfortable? Needing a cuddle? Overtired?" Only by working through the possibilities and finding a way to comfort him will you learn to understand his needs and trust your motherly feelings next time round.

An abundance of love

By doing the very best you can for your baby (which after all is what most new parents do), you'll soon grow naturally into your role as a mother. The most important thing is to give your baby all the love and affection that he needs.

Welcome to parenthood!
0–6 weeks

Your growing baby
6 weeks to 6 months

Your older baby
6 months to one year

Baby healthcare
0–12 months

Caring for twins

Get ready: here comes a lifetime of strangers cracking well-meant jokes about "double trouble" and "two for the price of one"! Caring for twins is a challenging prospect for any parent, but with planning and support there is no reason why you won't succeed.

Breastfeeding twins can seem challenging, but it's entirely possible with rest and support.

How you'll cope

Caring for one baby is daunting enough, caring for two can be a jolt. With some extra planning and help from family and friends, though, you can and will cope.

Enlisting help

You'll need other people's support! For the first few months, take advantage of offers of help, however small. Also, dads of twins tend to be more involved in their babies' care and upbringing, and most of them find it's a rewarding experience. Even if you're breastfeeding, there's plenty your partner can do to help with the babies and look after you.

Breastfeeding twins

There is no reason why you can't breastfeed two babies. The law of supply and demand applies to all mothers, including those of twins or more. If you breastfeed each time your babies are hungry, you can trust your body to supply enough milk for both of your babies. A low milk supply can almost always be corrected by feeding more often or improving the way your babies latch on (see p.46). Don't feel guilty, though, if you find it easier to supplement your babies' feeds with formula milk (see p.50).

Coping strategies

Being realistic about what you can and can't do with twins and getting help whenever you can will help you to manage your extra workload.

The first few months are the hardest. Take heart that things will become easier with time and you have so much fun and joy ahead of you.

- Establish a routine and stick to it.
- Aim to feed both babies at the same time so you can get more sleep at night.
- Don't feel guilty if you need to supplement breastfeeding with some formula milk. Although you will be able to produce enough milk for your twins if you keep up with their demand, you may find this exhausting.

- Be prepared for stares and stupid comments – you're probably going to hear "buy one get one free"'!
- Always accept offers of help from family and friends – even if it's just bringing you dinner one evening or making you a cup of tea while you sit down.
- Get in touch with support organisations such as TAMBA (Twins and Multiple Birth Association) (see pp.312–13) or a local twins club to share experiences.
- Sleep when your babies sleep. If they nap at the same time, try to rest, too.
- Save housework until later. It can be easier to accept that there are simply not enough hours in the day to keep everything clean (and your babies won't mind if their towels aren't folded).
- Check out Child Tax Credit and Working Tax Credit to see if you're entitled to money towards childcare.
- Try to get out of the house every day.

Up to about three months, your twins will be happy and safe sharing a cot for sleeping, or for some quiet time while you take a break.

Sleeping together

Research has shown that it's safe for similarly sized twins under three months to sleep in one cot. There may even be positive advantages, as the same study showed that putting newborn twins in the same cot helps them adjust to their environment by regulating their body temperatures and their sleep cycles. Put them on their backs with their feet at the ends of the cot: one at each end if they're head-to-head, or the same end if they're side by side.

Take time off

You don't have to be on the job at all times. Sleep when your babies sleep, if you can. Call in support when you're frazzled. Let your partner take over while you take off, even if it's only for 15 minutes. Get out of hearing range of your babies by going for a walk. Once a feeding routine is established, express milk and enjoy a night out with your partner. You were a couple before with your own relationship. Soon you'll continue where you left off.

Dad's **Diary**

An equal partner

"I always wanted to be a hands-on dad, but when we discovered we were having twins, I knew I had no choice in the matter! Twins are at least double the work.

Setting a routine early on was important to us. As I work during the day, I look after the babies for an hour once I get home. It gives Joanna a break, and I'm happy to see them. We bathe them together, one baby each, and we both put them to bed. We alternate babies so that we can spend an equal amount of time with them.

Joanna expresses milk throughout the week and freezes it so that I can share the feeding at weekends. This gives her the chance to catch up on some sleep while I'm at home. We did worry that the twins may have "nipple confusion" adapting to both the bottle teat and the nipple, but it hasn't been a problem. I totally support her decision to breastfeed. It wasn't easy to start with and it was tempting to start formula, but I do my best to help her and boost her confidence when she needs it. She's a great mum and I'm so proud of her."

Bonding with twins

After months of anticipation, you may be surprised if there isn't an instant bond with one or both of your twins. Don't panic: this is a common reaction and it can take slightly longer to bond with two babies than it does with one.

Getting to know each twin

Parents of identical twins say they quickly find 100 ways of distinguishing their babies, but it may help to use distinctive clothing, blankets or even a splash of nail varnish. The sooner you can establish them as individuals, the easier it will be to build those unique bonds. Use their names frequently and find time for plenty of cuddles and close eye contact. This is where you'll need the first in a long line of helpers, so that you can spend time getting to know each baby individually.

Equal love

Other factors might contribute to lacking the closeness you wish for initially. For example, if one of your babies is in a special-care baby unit, you may feel guilty or torn, depending on which baby you are with at the time. Getting involved with the care of both babies – including touching, feeding, changing or holding your baby in special care – will help you feel more in control and capable. It's good for twins to spend time together, so take the well baby into the special-care unit if possible, at least some of the time. If you begin to feel you are favouring one baby over the other, try to make a conscious effort to show that you love them equally. Shower each baby with smiles and try singing a special song that they can later recognise as their own.

Welcome to parenthood!
0–6 weeks

Your growing baby
6 weeks to 6 months

Your older baby
6 months to one year

Baby healthcare
0–12 months

The outside world

Your time at home

Settling in at home with your new baby not only means getting used to nights of disrupted sleep and strange routines, but also dealing with a stream of visitors keen to meet the newest member of your family! Make the most of their kind offers to help you.

Visiting times

Now that you and your baby are home, people will want to come round to see you both. It's not a problem to have close friends and family hold your newborn, as long as they wash their hands first and avoid coughing or sneezing near him. Try not to let too many people handle him for too long. Newborns are more susceptible than adults to bugs going around because their immune systems aren't mature yet. Once he's more than a month or two old, you won't need to be so vigilant about protecting him from germs.

Putting off visitors

If you're tired and really can't face socialising yet, don't be afraid to space out your visitors, or ask people to wait a few more days. Your loved ones will understand. They won't expect you to be the perfect hostess when they do arrive, so don't worry if your hair isn't washed or you're out of tea bags.

Asking for help

The best kind of visitor is one who helps out. Don't be afraid to accept offers of ironing, washing-up or shopping! Also, don't be afraid to ask for help. People may want to help, but may not know how to unless you ask. Even your mum may have forgotten what it's like to have a baby and might need some direction. Some mums and mothers-in-law are reluctant to launch in for fear of being seen as interfering.

Take advantage of the fact that friends and family are coming to meet your baby as well as to see you. Leave them to cuddle him and use the time to take a bath or have a quick sleep.

Laid-back mum

Even if you're normally quite sociable, having a house full of visitors now may be too much.

"I'm usually quite relaxed about friends and family dropping by, but a couple of days after Leila was born it was chaos. My milk had just come in and I think I was feeling a bit tired and emotional anyway. The house seemed full of people and I simply couldn't cope. I found myself sitting in the kitchen crying while what seemed like a party was going on in the living room, with Leila being passed around from person to person. In the end, my partner Mal came and found me and realised he needed to do something. I don't know what he said to them, but they all left, and it was lovely to be on our own at last with Leila."

Family and visitors will be more than happy to lend a helping hand if you point them in the right direction.

Welcome to parenthood! 0–6 weeks

Your growing baby 6 weeks to 6 months

Your older baby 6 months to one year

Baby healthcare 0–12 months

Family time

The first few days at home with your new baby can be a little bit overwhelming for you, your partner and your baby. There's a lot for all of you to get used to. You and your partner have become parents, with the round-the-clock challenges and huge sense of responsibility that it entails. If you're breastfeeding, you and your baby will be learning together. You and your partner will probably be feeling sleep deprived as your baby will be waking regularly for feeds, day and night. Meanwhile, your baby is getting used to the shock of life outside of the uterus. So you've got plenty to be getting on with without entertaining a house full of visitors too, and may simply want some time alone.

Quiet time

If you're finding it hard to say no to visitors, just think about what a difference some time alone will make to you and your baby. Being able to sleep when your baby does will leave you feeling less tired and more able to cope with the challenges and demands of caring for your newborn. This may mean that you don't get out of your pyjamas for several days, but there's absolutely no harm in that. In some cultures, for example China, new mums traditionally stay in bed with their newborns for a whole month after giving birth.

A gentle start

As well as benefiting you, quiet family time is also important for your baby as it will help her to adapt to her new world

"It was a **relief** to finally have **time alone** as a family."

Enjoying exclusive family time helps you to nurture and cherish your new family unit.

Dad's **Diary**

Being the gatekeeper

"We found ourselves to be very popular during the first few days after we brought our baby home – there's no greater attraction than a newborn baby. Of course, we were happy that our friends and family were excited to meet her, but at the same time it was exhausting to have so many people coming and going.

I felt extremely protective of my new family. I had no choice but to put people off if my partner was tired, or if the baby was niggly – or, for that matter, if I felt totally frazzled!

It could be awkward, but most people understood that we needed time alone as a family, especially when we were just getting to know our baby ourselves.

I decided to introduce our own version of hospital visiting hours. Whenever anyone phoned to invite themselves over, I'd tell them we were only available between, say, 2pm and 4pm. It helped to know that we had the rest of the day to ourselves. I even recorded an answer-phone message that included all of our latest baby action. That way, we could call people back when we felt up to it."

and get to know you both. As you care for your baby and get to know her better each day, you'll feel the bond between you grow. You'll begin to understand better her needs and become more confident at interpreting her cries. You'll also learn how she best likes to be soothed. Most babies love to be cuddled and gently stroked or to hear the sound of your voices. Skin-to-skin contact between you and your baby, or your partner and your baby, is a great aid to bonding, but for this you need some privacy. Most of us wouldn't feel comfortable stripping to the waist in front of a room full of visitors!

Midwife visits

If you gave birth in hospital, the midwife who discharges you will hand over your care to a community midwife. A midwife will usually care for you and your baby for 10 to 14 days after the birth. She'll visit you the day after you've come home and will visit or phone you a number of other times, depending on how you feel. Some areas have postnatal clinics that you can visit instead, if you prefer.

What she'll check

At the visits, your midwife will give you advice on keeping and staying healthy, including eating a balanced diet and taking gentle exercise. If you're feeling tearful, anxious or sad, discuss your mood with your midwife. These feelings are normal and usually disappear within a week or two (see p.82). It's important to get out and about when you feel ready, and your midwife should have details of local mother-and-baby groups.

Your midwife will check that your body is returning to normal. She'll feel your tummy to check that your uterus is contracting, and will check your perineum if you tore or had stitches. She will help you with breastfeeding and make sure that your baby is latching on properly. She'll examine your baby to make sure she's healthy and will check her weight regularly.

The heel-prick test

Your midwife will also take a small amount of blood from your baby's heel before she's a week old. This is to screen for an enzyme deficiency, a thyroid disorder, sickle cell disorders and cystic fibrosis. Your baby may cry a little when the blood is taken, but she'll soon recover.

A helpful contact

If you have any concerns or problems, don't hesitate to mention them to your midwife. If she's not due to visit, she'll leave a contact number. Your midwife can care for you and your baby for up to 28 days if you need it. After this time, she'll hand over your and your baby's care to the health visitor.

Feeding in peace

Breastfeeding can be difficult with an audience, particularly in the early days. It can take a while to get breastfeeding right, during which time you may need to try out different positions, different ways of holding your baby and different types of support. The key is to get your baby to latch on well (see p.46), but that often takes practise for both of you. You'll probably find that it won't be long before you feel confident breastfeeding your baby in public if you want to, but while you and your baby are still learning, a peaceful, calm environment will give you the best chance for success.

Your health visitor

Your health visitor

When your baby is around 10 days old, your midwife will discharge you and a health visitor takes over as your key contact. You may have met her already; in some areas, health visitors help out at antenatal classes. If not, your first meeting will be when she comes to see you at home when your baby is between 10 and 15 days old.

Checking your baby

During this visit, your health visitor will examine your baby and test her reflexes and motor skills as well as her responses to light and sound. She'll measure her length and weight and will record these in your baby's red book (her Personal Child Heath Record), which will be the main record of your baby's health, growth and development until the age of five.

Expert advice

If you have any questions about your baby, now's the time to ask. Your health visitor is a qualified nurse or midwife who has been given extra training and can advise on anything from breastfeeding to immunisations.

Focus on you

Your health visitor will also ask how you're feeling. If you're struggling to shake off the baby blues, she is a good person to talk to. She is trained to spot the signs of postnatal depression (see pp.83–5) and can get you support.

Although your health visitor's main function is to offer advice on health issues, she's also a good source of local knowledge. She can tell you about mother-and-baby groups, and drop-in or specialist classes such as mother-and-baby yoga or baby massage.

Welcome to parenthood! 0–6 weeks

Your growing baby 6 weeks to 6 months

Your older baby 6 months to one year

Baby healthcare 0–12 months

Out and about

The first few times you venture out with your baby can be daunting – have you got everything you need? Is he warm enough? Keep a checklist at first and don't worry – you will soon perfect the art of leaving the house with a small person in tow!

Your baby's travel equipment

Slings, carriers, car seats, buggies – there are so many different accessories available to help you transport your baby that it's hard to know what you'll need. Your choice depends on your lifestyle and on how many children you have. There is no right solution except to go with what works for you.

When choosing a buggy, consider your lifestyle and opt for one that suits your individual needs.

Carrying your baby

Slings and carriers (see p.41) keep your baby close and leave your hands free for other activities. Many parents find that shopping or doing chores is easier when their baby is carried in a sling, although in a few months you may find your baby too heavy for a sling. If you have another child, a sling or carrier puts off the cost of buying a double pushchair. Small babies often like the feeling of being carried and may happily go to sleep.

Car safety

By law, your baby must travel in a car seat. Even if you don't own a car, you'll need a seat if you take lifts. Never use a car seat if you don't know its history, in case it has been in an accident. It is safer to buy new. Choose the right seat for your baby's age and weight and make sure that it's properly installed. If it doesn't fit your car perfectly, or it's difficult to fasten, don't buy it.

Your baby's buggy

Whether or not you start off with a sling, you'll eventually need a pushchair or buggy. This is one of the biggest and most confusing baby purchases you'll make. You need to consider comfort and portability. Traditional prams and three-in-one pushchairs and travel systems are sturdy and comfortable, but hard to carry. Lightweight strollers or pushchairs offer the ultimate in portability, but give a less comfortable ride and usually aren't suitable for newborns, who need to lie-flat in a comfortable padded seat.

 Systemised mum

Choosing the right travel system or buggy can be surprisingly time consuming.

"I spent months researching buggies: reading reviews and stopping unsuspecting mums (and dads!) on the street to ask them about prams! I didn't realise how expensive they can be. When I set my budget, I took into account the extras, such as rain covers, parasols and foot muffs. I didn't want to spend a fortune, but I did want a good quality buggy. I visited a few stores to look at the different models in my price range and even ordered brochures from manufacturers. I eventually chose a travel system with a car seat that will last until my baby is a toddler."

Leaving the house

The first rule of leaving the house with your new baby is to keep your expectations low. Of course, you used to hop on your bike, switch trains with ease, nip to the shop and suddenly remember 15 other errands you could do. You will not do this again for a long, long time, and you shouldn't try, because it will lead to anxiety, frustration or worse. The last thing you want when you're taking your first foray into the big world with your baby is to end up in tears because you're too far from home, for too long, without the right stuff.

But don't be discouraged from going out altogether. Staying cooped up at home isn't good for either of you. Just be realistic about your trip. Aim to grab some groceries, or even just stroll through the local park. Once you have your destination in mind, rely on those old planning skills (you do still have them, even if your brain feels fuzzy) and try to be deliberate about getting ready.

Being prepared
Check the weather report and be flexible. If you wanted to casually stroll to the post office where you know lots of old ladies will ooh and aah over your baby, but gale-force winds are expected, go in the car. Or postpone your outing. There will always be old ladies to tell you how beautiful he is.

Make a list: not just in your head, a mental checklist won't suffice. Perhaps keep a sheet of paper or chalkboard near the front door with a checklist of what to take out. It sounds annoyingly organised, but you'll be glad of it when you haven't left without wipes or a sun shade.

Keep a supply of basics in a bag, in the car or the pram. It will never hurt to have an extra nappy, wipes, hat, jumper, blanket or food (for you if you're breastfeeding or a carton of formula for bottle-fed babies).

It's wise to call ahead. Make sure shops or other destinations are open before you trek all the way over with your baby when you're already tired. If you're going to a restaurant, don't just make a reservation, check that they're equipped for and happy to have babies. It might seem offensive to you now, but recall your pre-baby days when you may

ParentsTalk...

"Three-wheelers can be heavy and, unless you walk a lot in the country, most people don't use them for long. If you use public transport, a lighter model is best. Check that whatever you choose fits in the car boot."
Zan 41, mother of two

"With a newborn and an 11-month-old I went through a lot of prams! Side-by-side models couldn't go through doors or up aisles, so I ended up with a tandem."
Sarah 28, first-time mum

"I switched from a 2-in-1 pram to a buggy when my son was five months, as he was so nosey and liked to see what was going on!"
Claire 33, first-time mum

have been annoyed or uncomfortable with a baby at the next table. It's better to go somewhere that welcomes you than to feel the icy disdain of a snappy waiter, or the couple who've just left their own children with a babysitter.

Welcome to parenthood!
0–6 weeks

Your growing baby
6 weeks to 6 months

Your older baby
6 months to one year

Baby healthcare
0–12 months

Ensure you have all the feeding paraphenalia you need for trips, such as a sterilised bottle, powder, bibs – and a snack for you too.

A spare blanket, change of clothes and a favourite toy are all fairly essential when out and about with your baby.

A well-stocked nappy bag with two or three nappies, barrier cream and wipes should be a constant travelling companion.

Your first outings

Everything your baby needs is in a tidy bag and you feel reasonably confident that your shirt isn't hiding any baby sick. Well done. You're both dressed up, but where should you go?

Your destination

Be realistic about the kind of place you might want to visit and what's best for your baby. Will you be carrying her, or will she go in a pram? Can you get to your favourite spot in the park with a buggy, and will the weather be too warm, too wet or too windy? Will people be smoking nearby? A shopping centre is fine for a short browse, but they tend to be noisy, crowded and have bright or flashing lights. If you're anxious about leaving the house, it might be nice just to go out for a piece of cake and a cuddle. Whatever you do, go where you can quickly access a quiet, comfortable spot if you need to feed your baby.

Being realistic

At least for the first outing with your baby, you'll be glad of an extra pair of hands, so go with your partner, family member or a friend to help you figure out the car seat or hold your baby when you're rummaging for a nappy.

You may feel like you want to do much more and get your baby used to your regular life, but bear in mind your baby's ability to cope with lots of new sounds, sights and smells, not to mention strangers who may want a peek. Plenty of old ladies and children won't ask or think twice about stroking your baby's cheek or head; while you don't want to seem rude or startle your baby, be prepared to deal with unanticipated affection from people who might have just finished wiping their nose or stroking a dog. It probably won't do your baby any harm, but then again, would you want that person pinching your cheek?

Meeting other mums

Many new mothers find the most relaxing excursion is a local playgroup, often held in village or church halls, libraries or community centres. Of course, a week-old baby won't have any interest in wooden blocks, but you'll be thrilled to be away from household chores and able to speak to other mothers about your labour and birth – or even about something other than pregnancy, birth or babies!

Playgroups help to reassure you that you're not alone, and provide a safe and nurturing environment for your baby. Many groups have volunteers who help out, answer questions or offer you tea and biscuits. Most areas also have local groups, formed by mothers, where you can get together regularly for a chat and some playtime for older babies. Look for notices at your local health centre, shop, post office, community centre, library, church or even online. If in doubt, ask your health visitor.

Keep it brief: a quick stroll around the park or a meander to the local shops are perfect first outings with your baby, as you adjust to leaving the house with a baby in tow.

Active mum

Being disciplined and getting out of the house each day can be a boost for you and your baby.

"Before I had a baby, I'd always seen myself as a capable person. I could change a car battery and navigate my way across London. But after my son Ollie was born, my can-do attitude disappeared. I couldn't imagine how I'd care for a baby and what I would do with him all day long. I dreaded seeing the door close as my husband hurried to catch the train to work, leaving me alone for 10 hours with my lovely but oh-so-dependent baby. I loved Ollie and we had our blissful moments, but I was frightened by the responsibility.

To make the long stretch of time seem more manageable, I take a short walk with Ollie at least once a day. Sometimes I spend more time getting ready than I do walking, but the change of scenery and fresh air feel like they're doing us both good. We get back to the house refreshed and ready to tackle the rest of the day."

Travelling any distance with your baby requires advance preparation to ensure that your baby travels safely and you have to hand all she might need for the duration of the journey.

Travelling with your baby

If you have a long journey to make, your baby will add a whole new dimension to the trip. You'll need to take a lot more luggage than usual and plan well in advance. On the plus side, young babies are usually good travellers and not as fragile as parents may fear, and a newborn is less likely to be disrupted by travel than an older baby. Also, if you're breastfeeding, you won't need to bring along food for him. So enjoy this period: once he's mobile, travel becomes a far greater challenge.

Advance planning

Being well organised is essential! If you're travelling by car, make sure your baby's car seat is properly installed. Use removable window shades to keep the sun off your child. It's a good idea to bring some things to amuse your baby, too, such as baby-proof mirrors, rattles, musical toys, soft animals, pop-up toys, plastic keys or teething rings.

Bring nappy rash cream, nappy bags, enough nappies for the trip and infant paracetamol for relieving pain and fever. If you aren't breastfeeding, remember to bring bottles, formula and, to make up the feed, cooled boiled water.

Thinking ahead

If you're staying overnight at a hotel or other destination, you'll need to plan ahead to check what facilities are provided. You can usually expect hotels to have a highchair and a travel cot that you can book in advance, but you may need to pay a fee for them. If they don't provide them, this can be a pretty good indicator that they're not geared up for babies and you're probably better off staying somewhere else.

Smaller hotels with fewer facilities may welcome you if you provide your own chair and cot: give them a call to find out. Also check out the washing facilities. If there's a laundry, you won't need to take as many clothes.

Travel essentials

Travelling with a newborn requires a whole new level of organisation. Consult the checklist below to ensure you have all you need.

- nappies – one for each hour you'll be in transit, plus extras in case of emergencies or delays, and for your stay
- baby blanket(s) for comfort, shade and warmth
- resealable plastic bags for dirty nappies, clothes and bibs
- barrier cream for nappy rash
- baby wipes and tissues
- baby bath and lotion
- extra dummies
- clothes – one to two outfits per day
- bibs
- travel wash gel or powder
- "no-water" hand-washing gel
- window shades for the car
- infant paracetamol
- sun hat and sun protection cream, or warm hat
- formula milk (if used), bottles and sterilising system
- breast pump and bottles
- nightlight for night-time feeds and changes (optional)
- baby sling
- travel cot
- baby car seat
- toys for amusing your baby
- baby bag with waterproof lining, strap and plastic changing mat

Welcome to parenthood!
0–6 weeks

Your growing baby
6 weeks to 6 months

Your older baby
6 months to one year

Baby healthcare
0–12 months

Postnatal check-ups

At your postnatal check-up – usually six to eight weeks after you've had your baby – your doctor will give you a thorough examination and make sure you're recovering well. Your baby will also have a check-up around the same time. If you have any concerns, talk to your doctor.

Your postnatal check

Your six-week postnatal check is a routine examination carried out by your doctor to make sure that you're recovering well physically after the birth and that you're coping with your new life as a mum.

It can take months to recover from pregnancy and birth, and six weeks is a good time to review your wellbeing. If you have any problems at this stage, your doctor will be able to arrange appropriate treatment and support for you.

Systemised mum

Your postnatal check is a good time to discuss contraception.

"My doctor advised me which forms of contraception might suit me best now, given my previous medical history and current circumstances. She took into account factors such as when we might want to try for another baby. She warned me that exclusive breastfeeding isn't a guaranteed form of contraception and explained that as ovulation takes place two weeks before a period, you will become fertile again before you realise you are."

Your physical health

Your doctor will ask questions and perform some examinations to assess your physical health.

- She'll feel your tummy to make sure your uterus has contracted to its normal size and position.
- She'll check your blood pressure – particularly if it was previously high.
- She will ask whether your postnatal bleeding has stopped or slowed down.
- She'll ask if your perineum is healing well, and if there are any problems, such as pain or abnormal bleeding, and she may perform a vaginal examination.
- She will check that any caesarean scar is healing well.
- She will ask if your bowel and bladder are functioning normally and remind you to do your pelvic floor exercises (see pp.78–9).
- She'll ask whether you're breastfeeding and, if so, whether you have any problems such as soreness or engorgement. She'll also encourage you to continue breastfeeding and point you in the direction of help and support if you're having problems.
- She will remind you to book a cervical smear test if it's been more than three years since your last one.
- If you smoke, she'll explain the risks

to your baby and advise you to give up.
- Your doctor will also ask if you have had sex since you gave birth and ask if you experienced any pain or discomfort. She can advise you on which forms of contraception might suit you best now, given your previous medical history and current circumstances.

Your baby will have his own six-week-check (see opposite), however, your doctor will want to know if you have any worries about him, how he's growing, and how content and healthy he is.

Your emotional health

It's important for your doctor to review your psychological and emotional health after you've had a baby. She'll ask you how the birth went and if there are any issues concerning it that you'd like to discuss. She'll ask how you're coping emotionally and will try to assess your mood. She may use a questionnaire to assess whether you're suffering from postnatal depression (see pp.83–5).

She'll ask how well you're supported at home and if you're sleeping. If there are problems, she'll offer advice on how you can get support. If you have concerns, such as sore stitches, breast tenderness or you feel very unhappy, don't suffer in silence: talk to your doctor.

Your baby's six-week check

Your baby has his own health check when he's between six and eight weeks old. This may be done at the same time as your postnatal check, but it's usually carried out at a separate appointment. It includes a physical examination of your baby and a review of his development.

Your doctor will ask you to undress your baby down to his nappy so that she can examine him. She'll weigh and measure him and plot the results on a centile chart in your baby's Personal Child Health Record to see how his size compares with the averages for a baby his age. She'll also measure the circumference of your baby's head.

Your doctor will check the following:
- The fontanelles, or the soft spots on your baby's head, to see how they're developing. The posterior fontanelle usually closes by six weeks of age, as the bones of the head grow.
- The hips, to check that the joints are stable and the legs are the same length.

- The eyes, to see if your baby can follow movement. She'll also shine an ophthalmoscope into the eyes to check for cataracts.
- Your baby's heart, to make sure it has a normal rhythm.
- The testes/genitalia. If you have a boy, she'll check that both testes have dropped into the scrotum.
- The spine and joints, to ensure that these have formed and function normally.
- Your baby's head control, which is known as "tone".
- The abdomen, looking for any irregularities such as hernias.

Your doctor will ask how your baby is feeding, how often he wees, what his poo is like and what his vision and hearing are like. If your baby won't give your doctor a smile, she'll ask you whether he smiles in response to you. Finally, she'll ask how you're coping and if you have any questions or concerns you'd like to discuss.

What are centile charts?

Centile charts are height and weight charts, or graphs, on which your baby's developments is plotted. They let your doctor or health visitor know how your baby's growth compares with that of other babies of his age. The centile lines on the chart show the expected range of weight and length. Each depicts the percentage of children expected to be below that line, so 75 per cent of children will be below the 75th centile, and 50 per cent below the 50th.

What is recorded

Your baby's weight, length and head circumference will be recorded on charts in his Personal Child Health Record book at every check-up. Not all babies grow at the same rate, so try not to worry if he's below or above average. Your doctor will let you know if there's a problem.

Welcome to parenthood!
0–6 weeks

Your growing baby
6 weeks to 6 months

Your older baby
6 months to one year

Baby healthcare
0–12 months

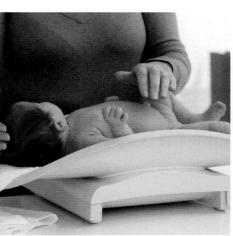

Your baby will be weighed and his weight recorded and plotted on a graph in his Personal Child Health Record book. Any adverse trends in your baby's growth over time will be apparent on the graph.

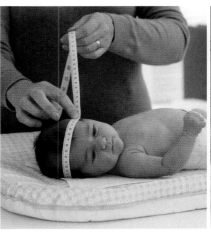

Your baby's head circumference will be measured and the doctor will also examine the fontanelles, the soft spots, on your baby's head to check that these are developing as expected.

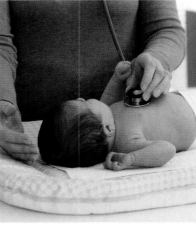

Your baby's heart rate and breathing will be checked to ensure that there are no abnormalities in the heart rhythm that weren't picked up after the birth, or during a pregnancy scan.

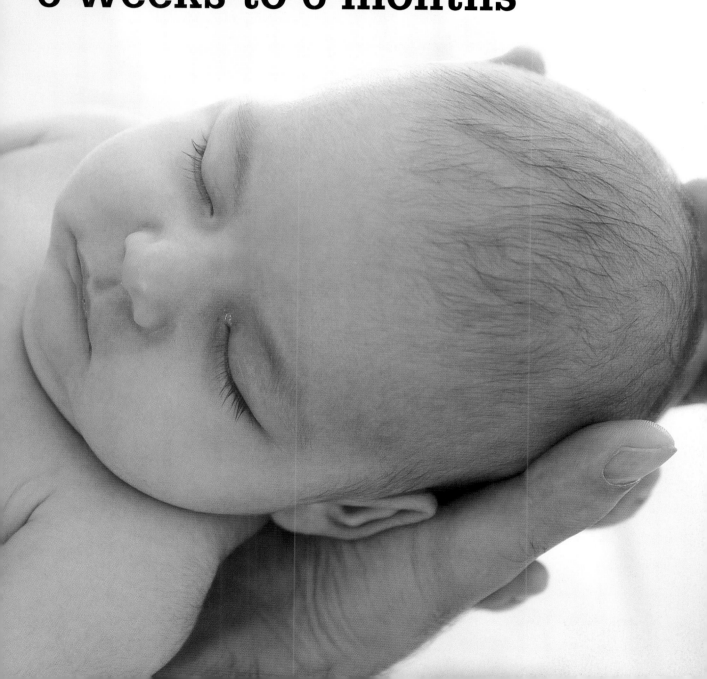

Your growing baby
6 weeks to 6 months

Feeding
your baby

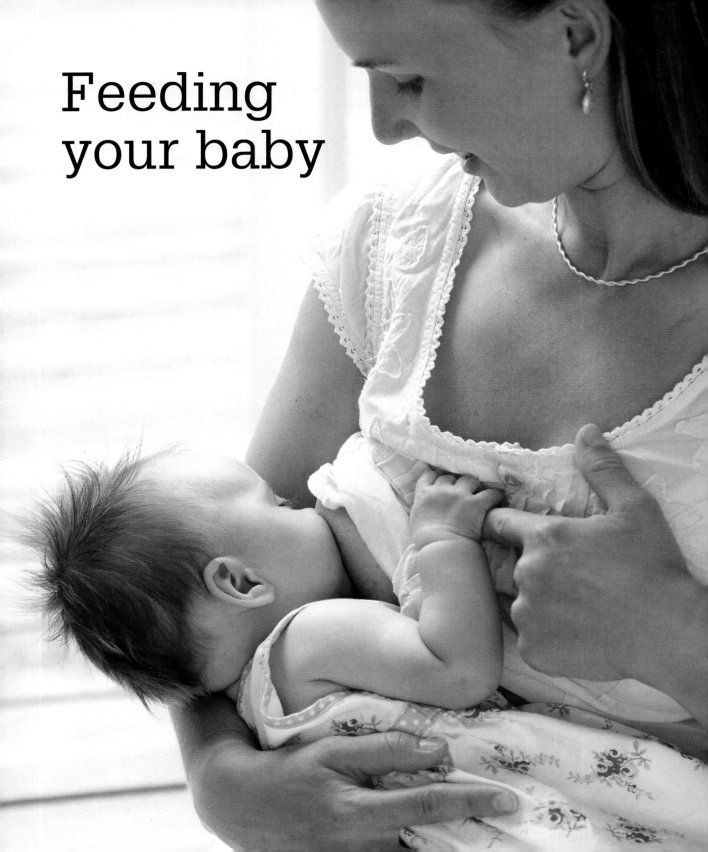

Your growing baby's needs

Until your baby is six months old, breastmilk offers all the food, nutrients and goodness she needs. At six weeks, you'll still be guided by her appetite – routines aren't really possible while she's growing so fast. In the coming months, though, a feeding pattern is likely to emerge.

Developing a routine

At six weeks, it's still too soon to get your baby into a feeding routine. As well as feeding her on demand, your baby needs to determine the length of her feeds herself and regulate her appetite. It's vital that she is able to finish on one breast before starting the next, so that she gets the fattier, more nourishing hindmilk as well as the thirst-quenching foremilk. Sometimes, though, she may prefer a short, rather than a long, feed – opting for a snack rather than a meal.

If your baby is bottle-fed, talk to your health visitor about how much milk she needs. Most importantly, though, be guided by your baby's appetite.

The beginnings of a routine

Over the next few weeks, a feeding pattern may emerge, but don't be disheartened if this takes longer than expected: your baby doesn't eat the same amount every day! Also, at six weeks, her tummy is still tiny and can accommodate only a small amount of food at a time. It may take a bit longer to establish a routine with a breastfed baby, as breastmilk is more easily digested and absorbed, so frequent feeds are needed.

Changing needs

When growth spurts occur at around six weeks, three months and six months, your baby will get hungrier, so it's important to offer her the breast when she needs it so that the quantity of milk you produce changes to meet her needs.

Babies tend to go longer between feeds once they're more proficient at emptying the breast and are more interested in their surroundings. Once solids are introduced, a regular intake of breastmilk is still an important food source, but your baby may choose to cut down naturally after six months of age. She might even be happy with two to three breastfeeds a day. Let your baby set the pace and trust your body to respond to her needs.

ParentsAsk...

My 12-week-old baby is always hungry. Should she have solids?
The Department of Health recommends that babies shouldn't have solid foods before four months (17 weeks) at the earliest, and ideally should be breastfed exclusively for their first six months. Prior to four months, your baby's kidneys are too immature to cope with solid foods, and also it's hard for her gastric juices to digest protein properly. Furthermore, her neuro-muscular co-ordination won't be well developed by this time, which means that she can't maintain the correct upright posture for swallowing.

Your baby may be hungrier now because she's having a growth spurt or she may simply need milk more often. Alternatively, she may be "comfort" sucking – you'll soon distinguish hunger cries from ones indicating a need to be comforted.

Sucking her fists is a clear signal from your baby that she's feeling hungry.

Welcome to parenthood!
0–6 weeks

Your growing baby
6 weeks to 6 months

Your older baby
6 months to one year

Baby healthcare
0–12 months

Combining breast and bottle

It's perfectly possible to combine breastfeeding with bottles of formula or expressed breastmilk. Many mums choose to do this when they return to work so that a carer can feed their baby.

If you would like your baby to have breastmilk when you're apart, you can give your childcare provider bottles of expressed milk (see p.49). Or you may decide on a combination of breastmilk and formula milk – combining breastfeeding with formula feeds means that your baby still gains some of the benefits of breastmilk.

However, if you've breastfed exclusively, it's important not to feel pressurised into introducing bottles before you're ready. Also, before weaning your baby onto formula, bear in mind that breastfeeding becomes easier as your baby gets older, and that making up bottles of formula adds to your workload.

Weaning onto the bottle

If you decide to cut down the number of breastfeeds you give your baby, you'll need to do it gradually to prevent your breasts from becoming engorged and leaky. It takes roughly three to seven days for your breasts to adjust to missing one feed, so try dropping one feed per week.

When it comes to giving a previously breastfed baby a bottle, you may have to persevere. Some breastfed babies are reluctant to take a bottle and confused by the different sucking action. It can help to warm the teat and get someone else to offer the bottle because your baby may not take it when he can smell your milk. Holding him in a different position, such as propped up against your front facing away from you, may also help.

A changing milk supply

Some parents think that giving their breastfed baby a bottle of formula at night helps them to sleep better, but there's no evidence to support this. It's worth bearing in mind that when you substitute a bottle-feed for a breastfeed, the milk supply you would normally have available at that time of day goes down. It's then more difficult to build your supply up if, for example, you want to start doing bedtime breastfeeds again.

Feeding in public

Many first-time mums worry about breastfeeding in public. At first, you'll probably expose a large portion of your breast as you learn how to get your baby to latch on. Once your baby has better head control and can latch on more easily, feeding will become easier and you won't have to show as much skin.

Discreet feeding

You can minimise exposure by wearing a loose top that you can lift easily. You'll find that you soon develop your own discreet technique and will more than likely be comfortable breastfeeding in almost any situation.

Feeding your baby in the night may be tiring, but many women enjoy the quiet closeness they feel to their baby during these pre-dawn feeds.

Welcome to parenthood!
0–6 weeks

Your growing baby
6 weeks to 6 months

Your older baby
6 months to one year

Baby healthcare
0–12 months

Laidback mum

Some mums cherish the quiet closeness they experience with their baby during night feeds.

"Ewan only wakes up for one night feed now, usually at around two in the morning. My friends think I'm mad, but I love our 'dream feeds'. I enjoy the quiet cuddle time that doesn't happen often during the daylight hours. I have a comfy armchair in Ewan's nursery, which I settle into to breastfeed him. I leave the lights off so that he doesn't really wake up. It's so quiet, I can really hear him nuzzling and swallowing – all those noises that let me know he's feeding well and enjoying it.

I'm in no particular hurry to cut out his night-time feed. It is tiring, but I try to catch some sleep during the day when Ewan has one of his naps. My baby knows when he feels hungry, and as long as he needs to be fed at night I'm happy to do it."

Night feeds

Waking up in the night may still be one of the less pleasant qualities of new parenthood. On the other hand, you might relish those predawn snuggles. If so, make the most of this quiet time, but don't get too used to it – you wouldn't want to establish a habit your night-time feeder couldn't break.

Cutting back

When your baby was a newborn, he needed frequent nourishment, so for the first few weeks, night-time feeds were an important part of his weight gain. In the coming weeks and months, you'll be able to cut down on night feeds as he steadily gains weight and sleeps for longer. By six weeks, most babies begin sleeping for more than four hours. When he wakes, offer breastmilk or a little formula, but don't force it; he'll take as much as he needs (and overfeeding with formula can lead to weight problems).

Sleeping on the job

Many sleep experts advise against using feeding as a regular method to get your baby to fall asleep, warning that this could set a pattern that will be hard to undo long after your baby stops actually needing a snack before bedtime. Older babies may become dependent on the breast or bottle to be able to get to – or back to – sleep. Try to be consistent about putting your baby down in his cot or Moses basket while he's tired, but still awake (see p.124).

In reality, like most well-meaning advice, this may be easier said than done. The important thing is to do what works best for you and your baby. It isn't easy to get up in the early hours and feed your baby without falling asleep yourself, much less managing to keep him awake, too. If he does nod off, don't get anxious or startle him awake; a subtle nudge of your nipple or the teat should get him feeding again. Don't forget to put him over your shoulder after a feed to wind him – a baby lying on his back and needing to burp will be unhappy, unsettled and loud!

A quiet time

The same rules that applied to night-time feeds in the early weeks still apply now: you don't want your baby to fall asleep during feeds, but his night-time feeds should be a cozy, rather than a lively, affair. Quietly pick him up and settle down to a feeding position that's comfortable for you both. Hum or whisper a little, but try not to engage him too much. Keep the lighting dim and ensure that both of you are warm and relaxed.

Feeding ups and downs

As many new mums discover, breastfeeding doesn't always go smoothly. If problems do crop up with bottle- or breastfeeding, try not to panic or become dismayed – it's very common to experience the odd hitch, and help is always available.

Gastro-oesophageal reflux

Reflux is when the stomach contents come back up into the mouth or food pipe. In babies, it usually occurs because the diaphragm is too weak to act as a valve between the chest and abdomen.

Your baby may regurgitate milk or have hiccups. This is normal, as long as she's well. If she has reflux over five times a day, cries excessively after feeds, regularly vomits or has a persistent cough, see your doctor. About half of all babies do get some reflux, and most grow out of it.

Overcoming problems

Although breastfeeding your baby is one of the most natural things, it isn't always easy. It's common to encounter some sort of problem, but on a reassuring note, most of them can be overcome.

Dealing with mastitis

About one in 10 breastfeeding mums get mastitis at some point, and some bottle-feeding mothers do, too. Mastitis is an inflammation of the breast, which can become infected. You may have flu-like symptoms, with areas of redness, hardness, swelling, soreness or heat in your breast. It's often caused by "milk stasis", when milk "backs up" because your baby isn't emptying your breasts well. This can indicate a problem with the way your baby latches on.

If you get mastitis, don't stop feeding, as it's vital to drain the breast well. Expressing after a feed can help empty the breast. If it's just too painful to feed, you could express milk and give this to your baby in a bottle or cup. You may feel awful but mastitis won't affect your baby, even when she feeds from the affected breast. Contact your doctor,

Once you overcome feeding hiccups, breastfeeding is a hassle-free way to meet your baby's needs any time or place.

who may prescribe antibiotics and/or refer you to a breastfeeding specialist. If you feel ill, rest as much as you can.

Breast refusal

Babies can go on a "breastfeeding strike", refusing the breast. If your baby does this and she is not in the process of being weaned, it's a sign that something is wrong. It may be that she isn't latching on properly, which may be due to mouth pain, an earache, a cold or a stuffy nose, or she may be distracted.

Breast refusal is upsetting, but can be overcome with support and patience. Keep other elements of your baby's routine as normal as possible. Give her extra attention and physical contact, and call your doctor if you're worried.

Extra demands

It's common to worry about your milk supply when your baby has a growth spurt. Keep your supply up by letting her feed as often and for as long as she wants, and by offering both breasts at each feed. Gauge her hunger by watching her for cues. When she's hungry, she'll "root" (turn her head and open her mouth) towards your breast, bring her hands to her mouth and/or make sucking motions.

Successful breastfeeding

Once you've both mastered the art of breastfeeding, you'll feel a great sense of achievement at being able to provide nourishing food for your baby and bond with her at the same time. It's also more convenient than bottle-feeding: nature gives you food on demand according to your baby's needs, and you don't need to worry about preparing formula milk and sterilising bottles.

Contented feeding

If your baby feeds on demand and starts to feed almost immediately when you put her to the breast, these are signs that she's latched on well. Her feeding pattern will change from a few short, quick sucks to slow, deep sucks. During the feed, she may pause a few times, change her rhythm and start sucking again without you having to prod her or coax her into feeding again. If she is latching on properly, it will not hurt your breasts or nipples and you'll be able to see her swallow. She will let go of the breast on her own when she's finished, or will fall away if you raise your breast.

The signs of success

As you become adept at breastfeeding, you'll become familiar with the signs that your baby is satisfied and is getting enough food. Your breasts will feel empty and softer after feeds. Your baby will have a healthy colour and firmness to her skin, and will produce at least six to eight wet nappies in a 24-hour period. Her urine will be pale and odourless and her stools a yellowy-mustard colour, or dark and frequent. If your baby is showing these signs, then it's very unlikely that she is being underfed.

Ensuring that you and your baby are comfortable and relaxed before a feed will help feeding sessions go without a hitch.

Caring for your breasts

As well as perfecting your breastfeeding technique, looking after your breasts is an important part of successful feeding.

- Don't use soap, alcohol, lotions or perfumes on your nipples. Washing or bathing with clear water will keep your breasts and nipples clean.
- Ease pain or discomfort with warm (or cold) flannels on the breasts, warm baths and gentle massage.
- Using a breast pump incorrectly can damage your nipples, so be careful when you pump (see p.49).
- If you have cracked nipples, use a purified lanolin cream formulated for breastfeeding women to encourage moist wound healing. This forms a semi-permeable layer on the skin, allowing it to breathe. Petroleum jelly is a widely used alternative.

- If you feel your baby hasn't emptied the breast, express milk by hand or with a pump after a feed.
- Wear a properly fitting, supportive nursing bra. Get measured and fitted professionally, either in a store or through a specialist agency, such as the National Childbirth Trust agents, whose staff are specially trained.
- Wearing a "sleep" bra can help your breasts feel more comfortable and supported at night.
- Continue to feed your baby, even if it hurts. Feed as often as you can and avoid long stretches between feeds.
- Above all, if you're having problems get expert help as soon as possible. It's important to sort out your baby's latching on technique so that she is feeding properly without damaging your nipples. Contact a breastfeeding counsellor or infant feeding specialist, or your midwife or health visitor.

A properly fitted feeding bra is essential to give your breasts sufficient support.

Welcome to parenthood!
0–6 weeks

Your growing baby
6 weeks to 6 months

Your older baby
6 months to one year

Baby healthcare
0–12 months

As your baby grows

Your baby is growing rapidly and gaining weight all the time. Don't be surprised if his desire for milk fluctuates as he goes through growth spurts – just keep feeding on demand and your milk supply will adapt to meet his needs.

Feeding at six weeks

Many babies go through a growth spurt at six weeks and need more milk than before. It can come as a surprise if your previously settled baby suddenly wants to feed more, and you may worry that he isn't getting enough nourishment from milk alone. The more often you feed him the sooner you'll boost your supply. Be reassured that breastmilk is the most nourishing, comforting and health-giving food and drink for him. Make sure he empties the breast so he gets the fattier hindmilk towards the end of a feed.

If you're formula feeding, your baby may be ready for a second stage casein-based formula (as opposed to a first stage whey-based milk), or he may need feeding more often. Talk to your health visitor before changing over.

The right teat

Bottle teats come in various "flow" sizes. Generally, newborns start with a slow flow until they get used to feeding, then switch to a medium flow. You can use fast-flow teats if you're confident that your baby can suck at the pace required and isn't overwhelmed by the speed of the milk. If he is choking, spluttering and leaking milk from his mouth, the flow is probably too fast for him.

When he isn't hungry

Occasionally babies "comfort suck" and appear to demand milk when they would perhaps settle for being cuddled and responded to in other ways. As you become more experienced, you'll distinguish a hunger cry from one that indicates a need to be comforted.

Your alert baby

It's normal for your baby's feeding pattern to change at times. As he grows more aware of his surroundings and starts to wriggle and grab for things, his new skills can distract him from his feed. This doesn't mean he's lost interest. You may just have to find a quieter or darker place to nurse until he is less sensitive to environmental changes. Concentrate on him, reassure him quietly, and offer the breast several times before assuming a feed is over.

As your baby becomes more adept at sucking, you may need to change his bottle teat size to one with a faster flow.

Lactose intolerance

Lactose intolerance is an inability to digest the lactose, or sugar, in milk. It's not the same as a milk allergy, which is when a baby's immune system reacts to proteins in milk, causing eczema, a rash or other symptoms. It's rare for babies in the UK to be lactose intolerant; it's more common in parts of the world where adults don't typically drink or cook with cow's milk, such as Asia, Africa and South America.

A short-term condition

Sometimes, babies develop lactose intolerance for a short period after a tummy bug. If your baby is formula-fed, your doctor may recommend a lactose-free formula for a short time. It's rare for this to happen in breastfed babies; if it does, you can keep on feeding as it's a short-term condition.

Feeding at three months

Your baby can now go for longer stretches without a feed, but feeding is still among his list of favourite things (with parents and sleep rounding out the "big three best things" in his life). Mealtimes give him a nice full tummy and time to gaze adoringly at whoever is feeding him – what could be better?

Ups and downs

Often, just when you've got it all figured out, your baby has a day where feeding is less fun and more work, or when it's the only thing he wants to do. That's because babies, like all of us, have days when they're more (or less) interested in their food. It may be the case that your baby isn't feeling well, but it's just as likely that he's too interested in trying out his latest smile!

Keeping up with demand

Three months is another period when your baby is likely to be going through a growth spurt. These spurts can creep up without warning and play havoc with your baby's feeding routine, making him voraciously hungry, even for a couple of days. You can't fight it, so if you're breastfeeding, settle in for some quality time while he gets his fill.

You may not realise how hard you've worked to keep up with your baby's hungry tummy, so try to find some time to put your feet up and rest. All that breastfeeding is demanding on your body, so make sure you're eating enough too. Remind yourself that your body is equipped to produce as much milk as your baby needs, as long as you're looking after yourself.

The right amount

Bottle-fed babies are no less demanding, and bottle-feeding requires you to be prepared to have the equipment to make up a bottle of formula whenever your baby needs it. It's easier to keep track of how much milk your bottle-fed baby receives, but parents of both bottle- and breastfed babies can judge whether their baby is sufficiently nourished by monitoring their weight gain, nappies and behaviour. If you suspect that your baby is getting too little or too much to eat, talk to your doctor or health visitor.

Note: At first, babies may have a bowel movement after every milk feed. As your baby grows, this will settle down and he will work out his own routine, often passing stools at a similar time each day.

As your baby's tummy grows, you may find that he sleeps for longer periods during the daytime.

Systemised mum

For some mothers, establishing a routine is a top priority.

"I was keen to have a routine, and by six weeks a pattern started to emerge as I noticed that Ben gradually went for longer between feeds. I found it helpful to think of the routine as: feed, play, sleep, feed, play, sleep, and so on. It took a while to establish, though, and there are the odd days when I have to be flexible, such as on days out or during a growth spurt, but on the whole, it works really well. It means that I don't mistake tiredness for hunger, or vice versa. Ben is a really happy baby and I've found that I'm a much happier mum, too."

Welcome to parenthood! 0–6 weeks

Your growing baby 6 weeks to 6 months

Your older baby 6 months to one year

Baby healthcare 0–12 months

Feeding from 4–6 months

You want to give your baby the best of everything, and it may seem that now is the time to introduce her to the world of solid foods. However, if possible, hold off on her first taste of solid foods: even if she's expressing an interest in what's on your plate, experts say the weaning process ideally shouldn't begin until your baby is six months old (see p.171) (advice that may run counter to what your parents did). That's because babies get all they need from breast- or formula milk, and their digestive systems often aren't mature enough to handle other foods.

In some cases, your doctor or health visitor may not discourage introducing solids before six months. For example, for babies who are strictly breastfed, this period of rapid growth may also be a time when more calories are needed. If your baby seems unusually hungry, cranky or uncomfortable, has abnormal stools (runny or greenish), is waking more frequently, or has lost weight, discuss weaning with your doctor or health visitor. Counter to this, there is concern, though, that babies who are weaned early risk becoming overweight.

A time of change
By four months, your baby will be able to go for longer between feeds and have extended periods of sleep, sometimes up to eight hours. You can gradually drop a

It's perfectly OK to continue with breastfeeding as much as you and your baby want to, even if she also enjoys the bottle. Your milk supply will keep up with your baby's demand, and your baby will decide herself how interested she is in staying at the breast.

Getting ready for weaning
As you get closer to weaning her onto solid foods, get your baby used to the tricks of eating. Put her in a portable chair, or if she's strong enough, pop her in the highchair (you may need to help her sit with pillows or towels for cushioning, and make sure she's strapped in) and let her play with a baby spoon, cup or plastic dish. Later, it may help to have these distractions to play with while you're trying to tempt her with dinner.

Working mum

If you're returning to work, you may not want to stop breastfeeding your baby. Expressing and freezing your breastmilk can be the perfect solution for you both.

"I began expressing a month before returning to work. I'm glad I did as it took a while to build up enough milk to satisfy my baby for a full day. It also took time for her to get used to a bottle, and for my breasts to adjust to the spaces between feeds. On a slightly unglamorous note, I would recommend that you take plenty of breast pads and a spare shirt to work.

Expressing so much milk can be tiring and it takes a lot of organising. Like any routine, though, once it's in place and after a couple of weeks, it gets so much easier. I love the fact that going down this route means that at the end of a hard day we can still share the closeness of breastfeeding; it's such a special time for us both."

"As your baby nears **six months**, she's becoming **developmentally ready** to start solid foods."

night feed, and give her a feed before you go to bed to last until the morning.

Around this time, some breastfeeding mothers introduce a bottle, either of expressed milk or formula. You might want to consider this if you're going back to work soon. Many babies happily try a bottle, but it's best to introduce one when she's hungry, but not desperate, for a feed. First, let someone other than you be the bottle-bearer, which will be less confusing for your baby.

Freezing expressed milk means that you can build up a supply if you're returning to work or want time off from breastfeeding.

Until your baby can sit up unsupported, a portable baby chair is ideal for first feeds as it keeps her upright enough to facilitate swallowing.

Beginning to wean

You may be thinking of starting your baby on solid foods soon (see p.171). The Department of Health recommends around six months as the right age to gradually introduce your baby to solids.

Additional nutrients

After six months, breastmilk alone doesn't provide your baby with enough nutrients, in particular iron, so other foods are needed. Also, by six months, your baby should be able to hold her head up and sit up if she's supported. She may even have a tooth or two.

Furthermore, waiting until six months to introduce solid foods into your baby's diet may help to reduce the risk of your baby reacting to a food or developing an allergy.

If you feel your baby needs to start solids before six months, discuss this with your health visitor first. This is particularly important if your baby was born prematurely, as her digestive system may be less able to deal with

solids before six months. The official advice is that solid foods should not be introduced before the end of your baby's fourth month (17 weeks). If you do decide to wean your baby onto solids before six months, there are a number of foods that need to be avoided, such as those containing gluten, eggs, milk, nuts, honey, fish and shellfish.

Weaning triggers

The usual triggers for starting weaning are that your baby still seems hungry after a good milk feed, that she wakes during the night having previously slept through and that her weight gain is slowing down. She should also be interested in the solid food that you are eating and may try to pick it up and put it in her mouth, or reach for food from your plate. Even though solid foods will gradually replace some of your baby's milk feeds, breast milk or formula will remain an important source of nutrition until she is one year old.

Signs that your baby is ready for solids

There are several signs which indicate that your baby is developmentally ready to start on solid foods.

● She can hold her head up. It's important that your baby is able to hold her head in a steady, upright position so that she can take food easily from a spoon.

● She sits well when supported. You may have to support her initially – a highchair can be used later when she's able to sit up by herself.

● She makes chewing motions. Your baby should be able to move food to the back of her mouth and swallow.

● She has gained a healthy amount of weight. Most babies are ready to eat semi-solids when they've doubled their birth weight, which usually takes place some time before or around their sixth month.

● Your baby is showing an interest in what you're eating: she begins eyeing your meals and reaches out to try to grab your food.

An interest in food and the utensils used for feeding are signs that your baby is ready and willing to start on solids.

Welcome to parenthood!
0–6 weeks

Your growing baby
6 weeks to 6 months

Your older baby
6 months to one year

Baby healthcare
0–12 months

Sleep and your baby

Your baby's sleep

Young babies need lots and lots of sleep – it's just a shame they don't take it at the same time as adults! By the time your baby is six to eight weeks old, though, you can start to develop a more regular bedtime routine to help him recognise when it's time for bed.

What your baby needs

How much sleep does your baby need? As a new parent, that's probably one of your biggest questions.

From one to three months
Very young babies need a lot more sleep than adults. On average, babies under three months sleep approximately twice as much as their parents, but half of this sleep will be in the daytime.

Every child is different, but as a guide, a one-month-old baby sleeps for around eight and a half hours at night and has three naps a day, totalling about seven hours. Your baby is unlikely to take all of his sleep in one long stretch, though, because he still needs to wake up for frequent feeds, but by six weeks

night. The length of these cycles varies enormously from one baby to another, but on average he will sleep for about two hours at a time in the day, and for a four to six hour stretch at night.

Three to six months
At three months, your baby is likely to sleep for 10 hours at night and five in the day (split between three naps). By six months, most babies sleep for around 11 hours at night and have just two naps a day, lasting about three and a quarter hours in total. By then, he'll be physically able to sleep through the night, but whether he does depends on if he's developed sleep habits that encourage him to sleep through (see p.120).

Keeping your baby's cot close by in the early weeks and months makes it easy to tend to him quickly in the night.

"**Little by little**, your baby will sleep for **longer** periods."

he is becoming more familiar with the long, quiet nights. During the day, don't worry about tiptoeing quietly around the house, as your baby is comforted by all those familiar household sounds.

Up to three months, babies sleep in sleep–wake cycles throughout the day and sleep for longer spells during the

Body rhythms
Like you, your baby's sleep–wake cycle relates to his daily rhythm of feeding, body temperature and hormone release. All of these things influence what is referred to as our "circadian rhythm", which is the natural biological cycle our bodies pass through every 24 hours. We

fall asleep as our level of adrenal hormones and temperature drop, then we come to wakefulness as our hormone levels and body temperature gradually increase.

It's actually quite difficult to fall asleep when your body temperature and hormone levels are high, and equally difficult to wake up if they are low. This is why shift workers have to train themselves to manage their unusual hours. Some individuals are better at this than others, which explains why some parents find it harder than others to cope with the broken nights.

Welcome to parenthood!
0–6 weeks

Your growing baby
6 weeks to 6 months

Your older baby
6 months to one year

Baby healthcare
0–12 months

Laidback mum

As your baby gets older, she will be more active during the day and sleepier at night-time.

"I'm not worried that Masie hasn't slept through yet. She's only four months old, so it's no wonder that she needs me to comfort her when she wakes up. I knew when I was pregnant that she was a little night owl: she was always most active at bedtime! We have a bedtime routine, but I don't have a rigid sleep regime in the night. We're co-sleeping, so when she wakes, it doesn't take long to settle her. She usually needs a feed, or a cuddle. She'll sleep through when she's ready."

A good night's sleep

A decent night of sleep… not too much to ask for is it? Unfortunately, when you're a new parent, this can sometimes seem like an impossible wish.

Coping with sleep deprivation on top of caring for a baby is hard, but this is only a brief spell in parenthood. By the time your baby is six to eight weeks old, you can start to instil good sleep habits in her by encouraging her to settle herself, but starting a sleep-training programme isn't advised until she's about six months (see pp.126–9).

Getting ready to sleep

You may want to start establishing a bedtime routine (see opposite) so your baby knows that it's time for a long sleep, not just a nap. She'll come to feel comforted by the predictability of events, and soothed and happy when she's put down in her cot. It's also important to encourage your baby to settle herself eventually (see p.124). Breastfeeding or rocking your baby to sleep may be a wonderful feeling, but it won't help your long-term goal of helping her to feel happy and secure falling to sleep on her own.

It's essential that you look after yourself, too. Rest whenever you can, eat healthily and don't punish yourself for feeling irritable or tearful sometimes when you're overtired.

Bedtime routines developed now will serve you both well for the years ahead.

Sleeping through

As your baby grows, she'll naturally sleep for longer stretches; here are some tips to help her sleep through.

● Give her a security object, such as a blanket or stuffed animal. Keep it near you for a while so it becomes reassuringly "mum-scented".

● Help her to associate sleep with a proper sleeping place. If she is falling asleep while feeding or being carried, put her in her Moses basket or cot.

● Separate day from night with bedtime routines (see opposite) that indicate it's time for a long sleep.

● When you feed her at night, keep a quiet, sleepy atmosphere. In the day, do the opposite: coo, sing and talk to your baby during feeds.

● Encourage an older baby to fall asleep on her own. By putting her down after a cuddle when she's feeling loved, she'll learn to associate settling herself with such feelings.

An evening bath is a popular way to start a bedtime routine and, for your baby, this will come to signal an end to the day's activities.

Changing your baby, even if just into another sleepsuit, will help her start to distinguish between night and day.

Some quiet wind-down time, with a lullaby, story or quiet conversation will soothe your baby and prepare her for sleep.

Establishing a bedtime routine

When your baby is six to eight weeks old, this is a good time to follow a set bedtime pattern at the same time each night; knowing what's coming next helps her feel more relaxed. The more relaxed she is, the more likely she will be to go to bed easily and fall asleep quickly.

She will quickly come to appreciate the consistency and predictability of a routine. A bedtime routine is good for parents, too – it's a special time set aside for you to spend with your baby.

Crafting your own routine

What you include in your routine is up to you. Typically they include a bath, putting on a sleepsuit, reading a story, having a cuddle or playing a quiet game. Choose whatever helps to calm your baby. A bath, especially, is a soothing experience, and getting your baby warm, clean and dry is a great way to ease her into bedtime. It's also a

wonderful way for your partner to spend some special time with the baby, especially if he can't help with feeds because you're breastfeeding.

While you can certainly start your routine in the bathroom or the living room, aim for it to end up in your baby's bedroom. It's important that your baby's room is a pleasant place to be, not just somewhere she's left at bedtime. Making bedtime a pleasurable event, with time, attention and cuddles in strong supply, means that your baby will come to love the whole process. If she gets upset as she sees you leave after you tuck her in, tell her you'll be back to check on her in a few minutes. She'll probably be fast asleep by the time you return.

Stick to your usual routine as much as you can, even when you're not at home. A familiar routine will make it easier for your baby to settle down in unfamiliar surroundings.

Parents**Talk...**

"My two-month-old baby is more relaxed if she knows what's coming next and is more likely to fall asleep quickly. When her routine is disrupted, she takes a long time to settle and wakes more at night."
Joanna, 34, first-time mum

"I do the same things every night to relax my baby. As well as a story, I play some gentle music, which seems to settle him well."
Christine, 38, mother of four

"We have a bedtime routine for our baby, but don't start it until just before we go to bed, so she sleeps more or less the same hours as us!"
Sarah, 25, first-time mum

"In the run up to bedtime I keep the house quiet and dark: if my baby thinks he's missing out on the fun he won't want to go to bed!"
Natalie, 39, mother of two

Welcome to parenthood!
0–6 weeks

Your growing baby
6 weeks to 6 months

Your older baby
6 months to one year

Baby healthcare
0–12 months

Night waking

It can be extremely disheartening when your good little sleeper starts waking up again frequently in the night, however, this is a fairly common scenario. As your baby grows, although he's capable of sleeping for longer stretches at a time, his sleep patterns are more likely to be

Assessing the situation

If your baby suddenly starts waking in the night, step back and evaluate the situation. First, has there been a change in your baby's environment? Has the weather changed so that he is too cold during the night? Have the neighbours

"A **bout of illness**, such as a bad cold, can **disrupt** your baby's usual **routine** for several weeks."

affected by factors other than hunger, such as illness, holidays or changes in his routine. There are also some physiological and developmental reasons, such as teething, which help explain why babies around six months and beyond, who were great sleepers, start waking again during the night.

started leaving on an outdoor light that is shining into his bedroom? If so, try to remedy the situation. Dress your baby more warmly or put up blackout blinds.

Second, have sudden night-time wakings followed a period of illness or a recent holiday, both of which can be disruptive? Or does your baby's waking coincide with a major developmental change? For example, if your baby has learned a new motor skill, such as learning to sit up unaided, he may want to try this out every chance he gets – even when he wakes in the middle of the night. Furthermore, some older babies enjoy pulling themselves up in their cot to standing, but then can't get back down without help.

Think, too, about whether your baby's daytime routine could be affecting how he sleeps in the night. Is he active enough during the daytime and getting enough fresh air? Also, is he feeding enough during the day to stop him waking up hungry at night?

Take stock if your baby starts waking again during the night and try to identify if there is a new factor disrupting his sleep.

Keep routines going

The best way to deal with a new phase of night-time wakings is to stick to your tried and tested routines. Also, when your baby wakes, try to soothe him first without feeding him to see if he settles back down. Remain consistent for however long it takes to break the cycle of night-time wakings, even if it's several weeks. This will help your baby return to sleeping through once any temporary issues are resolved.

Try not to feel disheartened if night-time wakings are taking a while to cease; or if there's a lapse just when you thought your baby had got the hang of it! It's hard to deal with at the time, but don't be discouraged – these phases will pass and you'll soon forget about them.

Daytime naps are an important part of your baby's sleep routine. In the early weeks, you may want to keep him close by when he sleeps during the day.

Welcome to parenthood!
0–6 weeks

Your growing baby
6 weeks to 6 months

Your older baby
6 months to one year

Baby healthcare
0–12 months

Systemised mum

A daytime sleep routine can help you structure your day.

"I know that some mums find it restricting to work their day around their baby's sleep times, but I love the fact that I can plan my day around my baby's naps. Poppy has three naps a day: a short one in the morning, a long one after lunch and sometimes a catnap in her buggy in the afternoon.

I use her morning nap as a time to have a shower and get dressed. I'm really lucky in that Poppy always has her main nap, which usually lasts one or two hours, after lunch. I use this time to get jobs done in the house, sort washing, prepare meals and make phone calls. When I can, I slot in a bit of 'me time' as well and sit down with a cup of tea and a magazine.

Having a routine doesn't mean that I'm stuck at home all day. After Poppy's nap I take her out in her buggy. I firmly believe that babies who get fresh air in the afternoon sleep well at night, too."

Daytime sleeping

Each baby has a unique sleeping pattern. Some sleep more in the day, whereas others sleep for longer at night. Almost all babies, however, do nap in the day. Most young babies take three naps each day, although some take two longer ones. However, if your baby doesn't seem at all interested in a daytime nap, try to build in some quiet time during the day without any play or stimulation.

As with night-time, developing a daytime routine at two to three months helps your baby to know what to expect, and enables you to structure your day. It also helps you to work out what time of the day he's usually tired, hungry or wanting to play. You don't need to watch the clock, but having certain activites occur at roughly the same time each day helps to keep you and your baby on track.

Where your baby naps
Ideally, your baby should nap in the same room as you in the day. Just as before bedtime, have some quiet time together before naps. You can pull the curtains, read a book or sing a lullaby, or you could leave the curtains open to distinguish daytime naps from night-time sleep.

Timing it right
A mistake many parents make in the day is to wait too long before putting their baby down for a nap. Usually, there is a window of opportunity when your baby will fall asleep easily. If you miss this, he may be too tired and find it harder to fall asleep. Learn to read the signals: he may rub his eyes; get fussy or stare into space.

The gaps between his naps will grow. You may want to avoid late afternoon naps if he's to have an early bedtime.

Settling down
By three months, your baby may begin to soothe himself to sleep in the day as well as at bedtime, whether by sucking his thumb, cuddling a blanket or soft toy, or just drifting off. Instead of rocking or feeding him to sleep, give him the chance to go to settle himself.

If your baby is too young to settle herself to sleep, then don't hesitate to give her a soothing cuddle to comfort her.

Potential pitfalls

Trying to settle your baby to bed can be daunting for new parents. At times it can feel as though you never know whether your baby is going to scream her head off or whimper softly just to get the last word in. By the time she is two or three months old, she may be waking up more frequently than she needs to, or developing sleep associations that may lead to problems for you later on. Be aware of the pitfalls when helping your baby learn to be a good sleeper.

The art of self-soothing

It's not a good idea to breastfeed your baby to sleep every night, as she may continue needing that cue to fall asleep.

developmental ability to self-soothe? In this case, wait a few days, weeks or months before trying again. Maybe she's too tired and overwrought to settle. An overtired baby can make for a difficult bedtime, so put her down an hour earlier than usual. Give her the chance to soothe herself, too; rushing to comfort her at the first peep deprives her of the chance to work it out herself.

Being consistent

Try to have a regular bedtime and a consistent routine (see p.121). This will set your baby's internal clock so that she's naturally sleepy at a predictable time. Stick to the routine even when

Laidback mum

Every baby is different, especially when it comes to sleep. Take her lead and tune into her needs.

"My first baby would sleep anywhere, anytime. We simply took him with us when we went out and moved him into his cot once home. It suited our relaxed attitude to parenting, really. So, I was surprised when my second cried all evening and was generally grumpy. I fed and entertained her more, but she just got crosser and crosser. It took me ages to realise that she was overtired. She needed a regular bedtime and wouldn't sleep anywhere except her cot. Once I stopped thinking about what I wanted (the flexibility to go out) and thought about what she needed – a regular routine and some peace and quiet – she happily went to bed at 6.30pm on the dot and was sleeping through by six months."

"Being able to **settle herself** is an important **skill** for your baby."

Instead, make breastfeeding an earlier part of her bedtime routine, so that she doesn't learn to directly associate it with sleep. After your baby has finished feeding, read her a story, sing her a song or change her nappy one last time. If you separate feeding from the act of falling asleep, even by a few minutes, your baby won't need to feed to drift off.

Learning the art of soothing herself to sleep is a useful tool for your baby. It can help her to rest for longer periods and to get back to sleep when she wakes at night. What's more, it's an important life skill that will serve your baby well in many situations, such as when you're at work or when you momentarily walk out of the room.

If your baby seems unable to soothe herself, think about why she won't settle. Is she too young without the

you're away from home. Avoid, too, overcomplicated ways of getting your baby to sleep. If you drive her around the block before putting her to bed, she will come to expect this and you may find yourself having to do this when she wakes at three in the morning!

Although there is plenty of advice, there's no single "right" way to encourage your baby to settle. You need to choose an approach that will work for you and your family (see p.126).

Fact: As your baby grows, so does her ability to sleep for longer stretches of time.

At around three months, your baby will, on average, be sleeping for twice as long during the night as she does in the day.

Coping with sleep deprivation

Bleary-eyed new parents don't need anyone to tell them that they need more sleep, but how exactly do you cope with feeling sleep deprived?

Rest together

Try to rest during the day whenever possible. Naps, even short ones, are a good way to recharge your batteries, so try to get your head down while your baby is sleeping. If you're back at work, see if you can take a kip in the car or a park during your lunch hour.

At night, take it in turns with your partner to attend to your baby. Of course, this isn't always possible when you're breastfeeding, but can work if you express milk in advance. At the weekends, one of you could lie in for an hour while the other looks after the baby.

Healthy living

Take good care of yourself. Many parents find that what they eat affects how they feel at the end of a sleep-deprived day. Try to avoid heavy meals and junk food, which can give you an energy slump. Eating plenty of fruit and vegetables with bread or pasta is ideal.

Coffee is great for a quick morning pick-me-up, but drinking it during the afternoon and/or evening may affect your sleep patterns, leaving you feeling more tired. If you're breastfeeding, you may be cutting down on caffeine anyway.

It may be the last thing you feel like, but a little bit of exercise each day helps you sleep better at night. Aim to get out at least once a day, even for a short walk.

Winding down

You might have developed the perfect bedtime routine for your baby, but to improve the quality of your sleep, it's important to wind down yourself in the evening before you go to bed. Try a warm bath, a good book and a mug of hot chocolate or herbal tea.

Make time to wind down yourself at the end of the day with a cup of soothing herbal tea before bedtime.

An early start

Many parents complain that their baby wakes up too early. How you address this depends on whether your baby wakes before getting enough sleep, or if she gets enough sleep, but wakes too early for your liking.

Why your baby wakes early

To work out why your baby is waking early, look at her behaviour during the day. Is she sleepy? Does she nap an hour or two after waking? Perhaps she needs slightly shorter daytime naps.

Infants need at least 10 hours' sleep a night. If she's raring to go at 6am, she's probably going to bed at 7:30pm. She can sleep only so much, so a later bedtime might help. Sometimes, though, an earlier bedtime is the answer. If she goes to bed late, she may be sleep-deprived and have trouble sleeping soundly at night.

If she wakes up before a full night's sleep, has she been disturbed, perhaps by sunlight streaming through a window, or a neighbour going to work?

Recharging your batteries while your baby sleeps can make life seem that bit more manageable.

Welcome to parenthood!
0–6 weeks

Your growing baby
6 weeks to 6 months

Your older baby
6 months to one year

Baby healthcare
0–12 months

Approaches to sleep

Do you stay close and comfort your baby or let him "cry it out"? Experts are divided on the best way to teach your baby to sleep through the night, so don't feel pressured and take your time to find a method that both you and your baby are happy with.

Some families relish the closeness and convenience of sharing their bed with their baby in the early months.

What's best for you both?

There is no "right" way to encourage your baby to settle himself and sleep through the night. The most important thing is to choose an approach that will work for you as a family. You may be quite relaxed about night waking, for example and happy to bring your baby into bed with you for a cuddle. Some parents, though, find a more regimented approach works for them. Their aim is to get their baby to sleep through until morning, and so naps and feeds throughout the day and night are planned with that goal in mind.

How sleep training can help

Sleep training (see p.128) – helping your baby to sleep through the night – can make some babies feel secure and happy. Babies can suffer from a sleep deficit, too, if they're waking two or three times a night, so helping them to sleep makes them less tired and irritable in the day.

Moreover, a baby who sleeps through the night also has a parent who sleeps through, and a parent who is rested in the day can only be good for her baby.

All families have different tolerance levels. If you're happy with the way things are, count your blessings. Many, though, try sleep training because they're exhausted by their baby's sleep habits and nothing they've tried works.

When to start sleep training

At around six months, experts say, most babies are ready for sleep training. Of course, some may be ready earlier, others later, and some will sleep seven hours or longer when very young, while others won't do so until they're much older.

Avoid sleep training if your baby has a medical condition that affects his sleep. Be flexible, too, about how you apply your programme and observe how your baby reacts. If he's very resistant or you see a change for the worse in his mood,

When your baby turns over in the night

The Foundation for the Study of Infant Deaths (FSID) states that it's safer for young babies to sleep on their backs (see pp.60–1), and since their campaign started to encourage this, there have been fewer cot deaths each year.

As your baby grows

After a few months, your baby may no longer comply as he becomes more independently mobile; it's part of his normal development to learn to roll. Babies often learn to roll onto their stomachs first, but will usually quickly learn to roll back again. You should still put your baby down to sleep on his back, but as he grows and develops, it's likely that he'll get himself into different positions while asleep: on his side or on his tummy. By all means turn him over, but you can't be there every minute, and the advice is that once he can roll onto his tummy and back again, it's safe to leave him to find his own position.

His sleeping position is just one factor in preventing cot death. It's important, too, to ensure that he doesn't overheat and to lie him at the foot end of his cot.

As your baby grows and learns to distinguish between night and day, he will eventually manage to sleep through the night, leaving you all feeling more rested.

stop and wait a few weeks before trying again. If you're unsure if your baby is ready for training, ask your health visitor.

Your baby's needs

No matter which approach you take, your baby's wellbeing should come first. That includes following the advice of your baby's doctor, if necessary, and using common sense to determine what your baby needs. Follow your instincts; if your schedule says it's time for your baby to sleep, but he's fussier than usual and needs comforting, then he should be comforted. No schedule should supersede the needs of your baby.

Systemised mum

Some parents start a bedtime routine at about six weeks.

"Our bedtime routine is my favourite part of the day. Ours goes a bit like this: we have a bath together at about 6.30pm, then I give Amber a massage and change her into her pyjamas. We have some cuddles and a short story. I think babies are never too young for a story. I did feel a bit silly when she was six weeks old, but she really takes notice of it now! She then has her last breastfeed of the day and I put her to bed at around 7.15pm.

I try to put her down when she's sleepy, but not asleep. I have a little musical toy attached to her cot. I play this so that she associates it with sleep, and it seems to work.

Having a bedtime routine really works for us. Amber settles brilliantly, and she hardly ever wakes up at night."

Twins and sleep

While having twins often means double the fun, getting both your crying babies to sleep – and staying asleep – can seem like double the trouble sometimes.

Sleeping together

To help your babies develop a sleep pattern, and to give you some time off, put them both to bed at the same time. Babies are comforted by close physical contact, so it's fine to let your twins sleep in the same cot. When one cries to be fed, wake the other one and feed both at the same time so that you get more rest.

As with single babies, develop a bedtime routine for your twins and encourage them to learn to fall asleep on their own, rather than putting them down after they've fallen asleep.

Settling down

If one baby is a screamer and the other is calmer, settle your quiet one first. Try not to worry about one baby waking up the other. Most twins aren't bothered by their sibling's crying, even when they're in the same cot.

Your twins will sleep through the night when they're ready, which often depends on their weight, not their age, so if they were premature, you may have to wait a bit longer. Identical twins often sleep through at the same time. Fraternal twins may be more independent, especially if they're very different in size or temperament.

After nine months together in the uterus (womb), sharing a cot is often the perfect sleeping arrangement for many twins.

Welcome to parenthood!
0–6 weeks

Your growing baby
6 weeks to 6 months

Your older baby
6 months to one year

Baby healthcare
0–12 months

Some reassuring words and a gentle touch may be sufficient to settle your baby at bedtime.

Sleep training

This is the process of helping your baby to learn to get to sleep and stay asleep through the night. Some babies seem to develop a regular sleep routine quickly and easily. Many others, though, have trouble settling down to sleep – or getting back to sleep when they've been wakened – and they need help and guidance along the way.

How you go about this is up to you, but it's probably wise to establish a consistent bedtime and daytime nap routine and to put your baby down at night while she is still awake. You may also wish to replace sleep associations that depend on your presence, such as rocking or breastfeeding, with things that will be there when your baby wakes up, such as a toy that smells of you, or a favourite blanket.

Choosing a method

What's the best way to respond to your baby once you've tucked her in? Your overall goal is to help your baby learn to get to sleep alone, but experts are divided on the best approach to take. Some say you should train your baby to go to sleep on her own and to comfort herself when she wakes up. Others say that when she does wake up, which is inevitable, you should use your voice to comfort her, but increase the time you take to respond to her each time she wakes, which eventually will help her learn to settle herself to sleep.

A soothing touch

Another method to help your baby learn to settle down involves comforting her from a distance. Don't let her "cry it out", but don't jump at her first whimper either. Wait a few minutes to see if she's really upset and awake, then go in and reassure and comfort her without taking her out of her cot. Instead, pat and soothe her with your hand and talk to her. At first, go to her every few minutes if she's crying, but eventually call to her from just outside of the room.

When your baby passes six months, you could do a simple checking routine. If your baby is crying, return to her room. Pat her gently and tell her that everything is OK, but that it is time for her to go to sleep. As long as you're sure that she is fed, dry and healthy, don't pick her up or cuddle her; be gentle but firm. Leave the room, wait about five minutes, then check again. Do this repeatedly until she falls asleep, extending the time between each visit, but don't let her get too distressed.

Staying close

Of course, some parents don't feel comfortable with a more distant approach and would rather soothe their baby to sleep with close contact. You could try rocking her, and lying down together until you see that her face is motionless and she's in a deep sleep. Establish and stick with a bedtime routine, and try cuddling up, pretending to sleep, and firmly letting your child know that it's bedtime.

A flexible approach

There is much debate on the best way to sleep train a baby. As even the experts don't agree on any one method, it's up to you to find and settle on an approach that works well for you all as a family. What they do agree on, however, is that the way to ease your baby to sleep changes over time, so while a newborn responds to being cuddled and soothed, a toddler needs a more consistent routine.

Encouraging your baby to adopt good sleep habits takes time and patience, so don't expect too much at once. It's important, too, not to try new sleep-training techniques while there are other disruptions in your baby's life, such as when she is teething or unwell, or if you've moved house, as all your hard work may end up being in vain until she settles down.

Welcome to parenthood!
0–6 weeks

Your growing baby
6 weeks to 6 months

Your older baby
6 months to one year

Baby healthcare
0–12 months

Dad's **Diary**

Finally sleeping through

"After more than four weeks of a consistent bedtime routine, Lauren finally slept right through this week. She's been steadily sleeping for longer at night-time, and now she seems to sleep through from around 10.30 (when she wakes and has a sleepy feed in the darkness of her nursery) through to 6.30, when I get up for work. I really hope it's not just a phase!

Lauren's bedtime routine starts when I get home. I play with her for about half an hour, which usually tires her out, then Janey feeds her. We don't want Lauren to associate feeding with falling asleep, so we feed her early on in the routine. Then I give her a bath, put her pyjamas on and read a story or two. When she's feeling sleepy, but is still awake, we put her in her cot and leave her to fall asleep.

The first night we did the routine, we stood outside the room for 15 minutes, listening to her gurgling and chattering. It's really hard not to rush to her side as soon as she starts whimpering. However, if she cries for more than a couple of minutes, one of us goes in and reassures her, but we try to do this without lifting out of her cot.

Over time, she's really learned to settle herself to sleep, so if she wakes during the night she doesn't automatically cry out for us to come and comfort her."

For fathers out at work, getting involved with baby's bedtime once they're home can become a precious part of their day.

Your baby's environment

Your room or his own room? Moses basket or cot? Whether you're keeping your baby with you still or thinking about moving him to his own room, his environment should be comfortable, safe and right in temperature – a soothing and pleasant place to go for "night-nights"!

Single mum

Many second-hand baby goods are in excellent condition.
"I've bought quite a few second-hand things for my baby. I bought my cot from a friend of mine whose toddler has long since outgrown it. It seems a waste of money to buy a new cot when he'll grow out of it in a relatively short space of time, and this one is as good as new. I'll buy a new mattress, though, which will be safer for my baby. My friend's mattress was showing its age, and she wanted to throw it away anyway. I can't wait to set up the cot in my bedroom."

Where your baby sleeps

Most babies outgrow a Moses basket by the time they're three months old. Once your baby can move around, a Moses basket is just too small for him to sleep in comfortably or safely, and once he can sit up, cradles, baskets and even some co-sleeping cots become dangerous as they're so shallow: it's easy for a sitting baby to fall out of one and be injured.

Choosing a cot
Your baby's cot needs to be sturdy, without cracked or broken slats, and it should have no jagged points or edges. Cots come in many shapes and sizes, including corner-shaped cots that sit in the corner of a room, and oval-shaped cots that can be converted into a junior bed, chair or even a sofa, later on.

Your baby may look a bit lost in a big cot at first, but resist the urge to put in pillows, duvets and bumpers, as these increase the risk of SIDS (see pp.60–1).

Most cots have drop sides: a railing that can be lowered to make it easier to get your baby in and out. They also have an adjustable mattress height, which can be lowered as your baby grows. To help your baby get used to his new sleeping arrangements, play with him in his cot during the day, or put him in the cot while you tidy his room.

A safe environment

Whether you're moving your baby into a cot and/or planning a move into his own bedroom, there are several safety issues to consider first.
● All cots sold in the UK should conform to British Standard/BSEN716. This specifies that cots should be deep enough to be safe for your baby, that cot bars are less than 45–65mm (2–2½in) apart to prevent your baby's head from slipping between them (a drink can wouldn't fit between the bars) and that there are no steps,

corner-post extensions or decorative cut-outs in the headboard or foot board that could trap your baby's limbs. If your cot is second-hand or borrowed, make sure it complies with these criteria.
● If a very old second-hand cot has been painted, strip the paint so that your baby doesn't breathe in lead dust or fumes or swallow any lead from the old paint. Re-paint with lead-free paint.
● Check that the cot mattress fits snugly within the cot and isn't at all damp. Your

baby needs a firm, dry, flat surface to sleep on. Don't use pillows, cushions or a duvet in the cot.
● Position your baby's cot out of direct sunshine, and away from windows, radiators and lamps to prevent overheating. Once he's mobile, position the cot away from any furniture that he could climb onto.
● Ensure shelves are totally secure, and avoid curtains and blinds with cords, which carry a risk of strangulation.

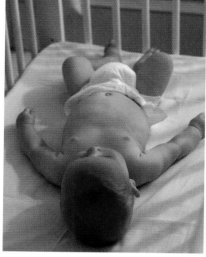

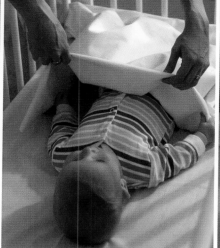

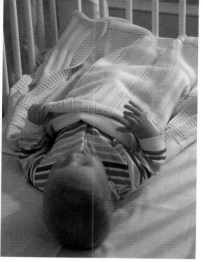

In hot summer months, keep an eye on how comfortable your baby seems at night and take off blankets and clothes if necessary. Sometimes, a nappy may be all he needs.

Blankets and sheets can be added and taken away easily depending on the weather, ensuring that your baby is neither too hot nor too cold during the night.

During the colder months, a lightweight cotton blanket can be added to your baby's bedding. Until your baby is one year old, avoid using duvets.

Adapting to the seasons

As the seasons change, it's important to make sure your baby is not cold or too warm. He'll sleep most comfortably in a room heated to 16–20°C (60–68°F).

Keeping your baby cooler

In the warmer months, make sure your baby doesn't overheat at night by removing unnecessary bedding. The Department of Health recommends that a baby wearing a nappy, vest and sleepsuit only needs a sheet as bedding if the temperature in his room is 24°C (75°F). If your baby is still too hot, he could sleep in his vest or just his nappy.

You should remove any padding from around his cot to allow the air to circulate, and open windows in several rooms to encourage a breeze to pass through. Fans are useful for cooling a room down, but do not direct them at your baby. Turn the fan on before your baby's bedtime to allow the room time to cool down. You could also try hanging wet towels over chairs or windows to cool the air, as the evaporating water

causes a cooling effect. Keep curtains drawn during the day to prevent the sun from heating up the room.

If you use a waterproof sheet in your baby's cot, consider removing it when the weather is hot, or cover it with several layers of tightly wrapped cotton sheets to absorb perspiration.

Don't forget to keep a careful eye on your baby if he falls asleep in his pram, as prams can be hot and airless, and never leave your baby sleeping in his car seat in the car. Even with the windows open, temperatures inside a parked car can rise frighteningly quickly.

When it's cold

Over the colder winter months, you may be concerned about keeping your baby warm enough during the night, especially if he starts to wriggle and kick off the bedclothes. Dress your baby in a sleepsuit as well as a vest and add sheets and blankets as necessary. If your baby does kick off bedclothes, you may prefer to use a baby sleeping bag.

Parents**Talk...**

"On a hot summers' night I put my baby to bed in just his nappy and vest, with a sheet over him. I also remove the waterproof undersheet, which makes him sweaty. If he has cooled down when I check on him I give him a blanket."
Claire, 33, mother of three

"On a hot day I make sure the curtains in the nursery are drawn and keep a window open to keep the room cool before bedtime."
Shelly, 35, first-time mum

"In cold weather, we make sure there's plenty of insulation around the windows to stop drafts."
Kelly, 29, first-time mum

"Dress your baby in a thermal vest if it's very cold, and put a microfibre blanket over him – and tuck him in properly to keep the warmth in!"
Mona, 38, mother of two

Development and play

KEY MILESTONES

✻ Can sit unsupported
✻ Rolls over ✻ Reaches for and
grabs objects

	1 month	2 months	3 months	4 months	5 months	6 months
SMILES AND LAUGHS						
IMITATES SPEECH SOUNDS						
HOLDS HEAD UP STEADILY						
BEARS WEIGHT ON LEGS						
MAY SIT WITHOUT SUPPORT						
ROLLS OVER						

How your baby develops

At six weeks, you may have been lucky enough to see your baby's first smile, and by six months she's probably sprouted her first tooth! In the intervening weeks, she has learned how to roll over, grasp objects, imitate sounds and maybe even said her first "da" or "ma".

Reaching milestones

What skills should you expect your baby to have mastered by the time she is six weeks, or six months, old? The answer is that every baby is different and your baby will meet her developmental milestones at her own individual pace.

may hold her head at a 45-degree angle. Head control is the basis for later movements, such as sitting and walking, and is a crucial milestone as babies are born with weak neck muscles. Generally, her movements become smoother.

Your increasingly responsive baby will be delighted whenever you give her the attention she loves and craves.

"Your baby may take a few days to learn to **sit up**, but be pleased and **surprised** when she gets there!"

Up to two months

At one to two months, your baby starts to watch moving objects and see black-and-white patterns. You may also be delighted to receive her first smile. She

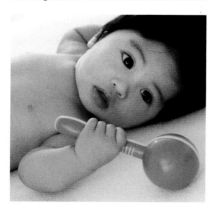

Three months and beyond

By three months, your baby recognises your face, voice and scent. She may squeal, gurgle and coo and also enjoy a new skill, mini-pushups: lifting her head and shoulders high, perhaps to get nearer to you or investigate a toy. This is the precursor to rolling over, so beware!

In the next few weeks, she'll bear weight on her legs and grasp larger objects, such as blocks. Learning to hold items is her introduction to the world of play. Being able to grasp objects is also the first step on the road to eating, reading and drawing.

The ability to grasp a favourite toy is an exciting step in your baby's development.

 Laidback mum

Each baby is unique and develops at her own pace.

"If there's one thing my first two children taught me, it's that babies grow up fast! You spend so much time looking forwards to the next milestone, or worrying that they haven't reached one, and before you know it, they're no longer babies. With Daniel, I'm making the most of his baby days. I won't push him to do things that he's not ready for. All babies develop differently, so I'm not worrying about how he compares to his siblings, or friends' babies. My health visitor is happy, and he's bright and content."

Welcome to parenthood!
0–6 weeks

Your growing baby
6 weeks to 6 months

Your older baby
6 months to one year

Baby healthcare
0–12 months

At around four months, your baby may start to master the exciting art of rolling over, propping herself up and then swinging her leg over.

Your baby's physical development

Over the next few months, your baby will start to change rapidly as he gradually develops the necessary skills that will enable him to become mobile and more independent.

Helping your baby's hand–eye coordination

Try the following to stimulate your baby's hand–eye coordination:

- Put toys or a colourful object slightly out of his reach and encourage him to grab them – but don't put something so far away that he can't get it, or he'll get frustrated.
- Give him a good supply of objects he can easily grasp, such as soft blocks, plastic rings and board books.
- Invest in a floor gym. Your baby can lie on a soft mat and swipe at fun objects hanging above him.
- Gently blow a few bubbles in his direction and let him reach out to catch or pop them (take care not to get the soapy bubbles in his eyes).

One to two months

Your baby's neck muscles are getting stronger all the time, allowing him to hold up his head for short periods. He's also becoming more aware of his body now, and is probably very interested in his hands and feet! Having learned to focus with both eyes, he can track a moving object, such as a rattle, passing in front of his face.

By two months, your baby's jerky newborn movements have given way to smoother, more circular motions. He is able to grab objects voluntarily, whereas before if he touched an object it was mostly involuntary and instinctive.

Three to four months

Your baby may be able to lift his head while on his front and hold it up for several minutes. He can also wave his arms and kick his legs.

Your baby may amaze you (and himself!) by rolling over from his back to his front, or vice versa. He is interested in reaching out and grabbing objects, and may try to put them in his mouth.

Some babies start teething as early as four months, but the first tooth usually doesn't surface until five to six months.

At five months

At around this time, your baby may sit momentarily without assistance, but you should stay nearby to provide support. If you hold him under the arms while letting him balance his feet on your thighs, he'll bounce up and down. He's easily capable of bringing an object to his mouth to taste and explore.

Six months

Your baby's hand control is developed enough that he can pull an object to him. By this age, most babies have learned to roll over in each direction, a milestone that will probably amuse you, and him. Some babies, though, never really roll – they skip that milestone and move on to sitting and crawling. Others adopt it as their primary mode of transportation. As long as your baby gains new skills and is interested in getting around, don't worry.

Senses and learning

Your baby's senses are becoming more refined, helping him to satisfy his curiosity about his surroundings.

One to two months

Your baby has been able to recognise you since he was a few days old, but by the end of his first month he may be able to show it: he may quieten down when you're close, make eye contact and hold your gaze for longer periods. He'll also enjoy music, so sing nursery rhymes or play some gentle music.

Between two and four months, colour differences become clearer, and your baby starts to distinguish between similar shades. He'll probably show a preference for bright primary colours and more detailed designs and shapes.

By now, he may gurgle, coo, grunt and hum to express his feelings. Coo and gurgle back, and talk to him face to face.

Three to six months

Verbal stimulation is particularly important for your baby, so reading to him, even at this age, pays off. Listening to your voice helps him develop an ear for the cadence of language, so try varying the pitch of your voice with different voices, accents and singing.

Your baby's sense of touch is more sensitive now. Touching, carrying and massaging relax him and may increase his alertness and attention span.

Researchers believe that by four months your baby understands all the basic sounds that make up his native language. Between four and six months, he develops the ability to make some vocal sounds, such as "ma" or "da." He doesn't yet connect those sounds with a parent, though. By now, he can also participate in back-and-forth imitation games: you say "boo", and he'll try to say it back. You can promote your baby's sense of communication by mirroring his faces and sounds.

By five months, your baby has added new sounds to his repertoire: his current favourites are probably making bubbles or blowing raspberries! His interaction with you, others and his surroundings is growing. He may drop objects to watch you pick them up, or to see how and where they fall. Soon, this will be accompanied by fits of giggles.

Your baby is better now at spotting small objects and tracking moving things. He may recognise an object after seeing part of it: the basis of hide–and–seek games you'll be playing soon.

By five months, your baby realises where sounds come from and turns towards a new sound. Five-month-olds recognise their own name, too: notice how he turns when you call him.

Squishy books that incorporate bright colours and different textures are a perfect first toy for your baby.

Fine and gross motor skills

A motor skill is an action that involves the movement of muscles in your body. Gross motor skills are larger movements that involve the arm, leg or feet muscles, or the entire body – for example, things like crawling, running and jumping are gross motor skills. Fine motor skills are those smaller actions, such as picking things up between the thumb and finger, using your toes to wriggle into sand, or your lips and tongue to taste and feel objects.

How motor skills develop

Gross motor skills and fine motor skills develop in tandem because many activities depend on the coordination of both sorts of skills. By three months, you may notice your baby bringing his hands together over his chest as he lies on his back (a gross motor skill) and then playing with his hands (a fine motor skill).

You can encourage your baby to develop his fine and gross motor skills by watching how he uses his fingers, arms and legs and then providing play opportunities for him to use his body in similar ways, perhaps with certain toys or by placing him in a different position.

Activities that stretch your baby just a little will also help your baby's development. Your baby will find developing new skills much more fun when he has a frequent change of position and activity. Let little and often be your motto.

Welcome to parenthood!
0–6 months

Your growing baby
6 weeks to 6 months

Your older baby
6 months to one year

Baby healthcare
0–12 months

Social and emotional development

Growing isn't only measured in metres and grams. Every day your baby is learning how to adapt and respond to people and developing important social skills along the way.

ParentsAsk...

My baby doesn't smile yet. What's wrong?

Smiling begins at different times for different babies. On average, most parents say they see their baby's first smile between six and eight weeks, though some are convinced that their baby smiles from four weeks and others that there is no hint of a grin from their baby until 12 weeks.

Babies almost always smile by accident the first time they do it, while exercising their facial muscles or passing wind. However, the reaction they get from you – enormous smiles, whoops of joy, big eyes and lots of talk – is so exciting that they try a smile again pretty soon. Once your baby sees that something gets your attention, she will use it again and again.

Until about six or seven months, babies smile at just about anyone and anything, although by four months they save their biggest smiles for the people they love the best. From about seven months, babies begin to realise that some of the people they see and some of the places they go to are not familiar, and they smile more warily, or not at all, at strangers, or in strange places – sometimes hiding their faces in their parent's shoulder, as though if they don't look at the unfamiliar person, that person won't be there.

In the highly unlikely event that your baby does not smile at all by the time she is three months old, talk to your doctor or health visitor.

Two months

You've been nappy changing, feeding, bathing, kissing and cuddling your baby since birth without much response. This month, all your efforts will be rewarded with beaming, toothless baby smiles (see p.68)! The first genuine smiles are certainly among parenting's most heartwarming milestones. This will probably delight you, even if you've just had your worst night to date.

Three months

By three months, and probably earlier, your baby will have formed an attachment to you and be familiar with your face. Most likely, she will still smile at strangers, especially when they coo or talk to her, but she's beginning to sort out who's who in her life and definitely prefers some people to others.

Your baby's parietal lobe, the part of the brain that governs hand–eye coordination and allows her to recognise objects, is developing rapidly now. Her temporal lobe, which assists with hearing, language and smell, is also more receptive. When your baby hears your voice, she may look directly at you and start gurgling. She will also use her smile to initiate interaction with you.

Four months

By now, your baby can amuse herself by playing with her hands and feet for a few minutes at a time. She may respond

Your baby imitates sounds and expressions in her bid to communicate with you and your partner.

Body language

Until your baby masters control of her voice, she'll use her body to communicate her needs and emotions.

Letting you know how she feels

At around five months, your baby starts to use her actions to express how she feels. For example, if she wants a cuddle, she may put her arms in the air. When you cuddle her, she may express her joy at being close to you with hugs and kisses. She'll also show her delight by

Your baby may not be able to talk yet, but she will have learnt how to use actions and expressions to indicate her needs to you.

laughing when you pull silly faces, and will kick her legs and wave her arms with excitement when you present her with a favourite toy.

Expressing her needs

Show her a breast or bottle when she's hungry and she may open and close her mouth in expectation or wave her arms. By four or five months, she may let you know she's interested in your food by watching your food from your plate to your mouth and reaching towards it. As she gets better at communicating, you may find her crying spells become shorter and less frequent.

---

to your presence, your voice and even your facial expressions by kicking and waving her arms.

About now, your baby, who up to this point probably bestowed smiles on everyone she met, may start to become more choosy about the company she keeps. In larger groups or with unfamiliar people, she may need time to feel more comfortable and secure. Her most enthusiastic reactions are towards the two of you.

Five months

Young babies can't express their emotions in the same complex way that adults are able to. While they are able to let you know when they're angry, bored or happy, they can't express love or humour during their first few months. Now, however, that's beginning to change. By five months, your baby displays a strong attachment to you by raising her arms when she wants to be picked up and crying whenever you leave the room. She may also give you hugs and kisses. She's also beginning to

get the joke – she'll laugh at funny expressions or positions and try to make you laugh, too.

Six months

Six-month-old babies are fairly indiscriminate, and many not only tolerate attention from others, they often initiate it. For some, though, "stranger anxiety" may be becoming apparent. However, although they may not be comfortable with everyone, on the whole, anyone who approaches your baby with raised eyebrows or a grin will probably delight her and become an instant friend. Don't worry though – she still needs and craves lots of attention from you!

Your baby is learning that her behaviours, both the ones you like and the ones you don't, engage you, so now (and for years to come) she'll do just about anything to get your attention. Right now, almost everything she does is endearing, but as she gets older, she's

Your baby conveys her emotions through facial expressions and gestures.

more likely to get into mischief and display negative behaviour to provoke a reaction, even if it's one of annoyance. Just don't forget to lavish attention on her when she meets with your approval.

One thing will become clear over this time: your baby is beginning to vary her attention-getting repertoire beyond crying, and now wriggles and makes noises and faces, too. Over the next three months, she'll develop a uniquely personal way of letting you know what she thinks, wants and needs.

Welcome to parenthood!
0–6 weeks

Your growing baby
6 weeks to 6 months

Your older baby
6 months to one year

Baby healthcare
0–12 months

Dad's Diary

Proud moments

"When friends with babies waxed lyrical about their little protégé's achievements, I could never quite appreciate their excitement, but since having my own son, I find that each milestone he reaches is a triumph. Sure, other five-month-olds can grasp a rattle and give it a good shake, but not with the same finesse as our Charlie. I'm almost certain that he can shake his rattle to the tune of whatever music I'm listening to on the radio!

I was lucky enough to see Charlie roll over from his back to his front for the first time today. He was reaching out to grab a toy that was nearby. He arched his back and finally realised that he needed to raise his leg over to swing himself around. I was so amazed at this achievement that I rolled him straight back over and coaxed him to perform the feat again so that I could film it for Gran and Grandad!"

Encouraging development

For your baby to move away and explore his world, he needs a secure attachment to you. Consistently give him love and support, and he'll build the confidence he needs to strike out on his own. Simple things, such as responding immediately to your baby's cries, feeding him when he's hungry, changing his nappy when it's dirty and smiling and talking to him, help build these crucial parent–child bonds. This, in turn, gives your baby the confidence he needs to feel free to explore his world, knowing you are always there for him.

Free to roam

You should also make sure that you've set up a safe environment for your baby at home. Babies need to test their limits and explore their surroundings to develop independence. Instead of running around saying "no" every time he touches something that could harm him, keep dangerous objects out of his reach and safe ones within it (see pp.213–15). That way your baby won't get frustrated when he wanders, and he'll be safe, too.

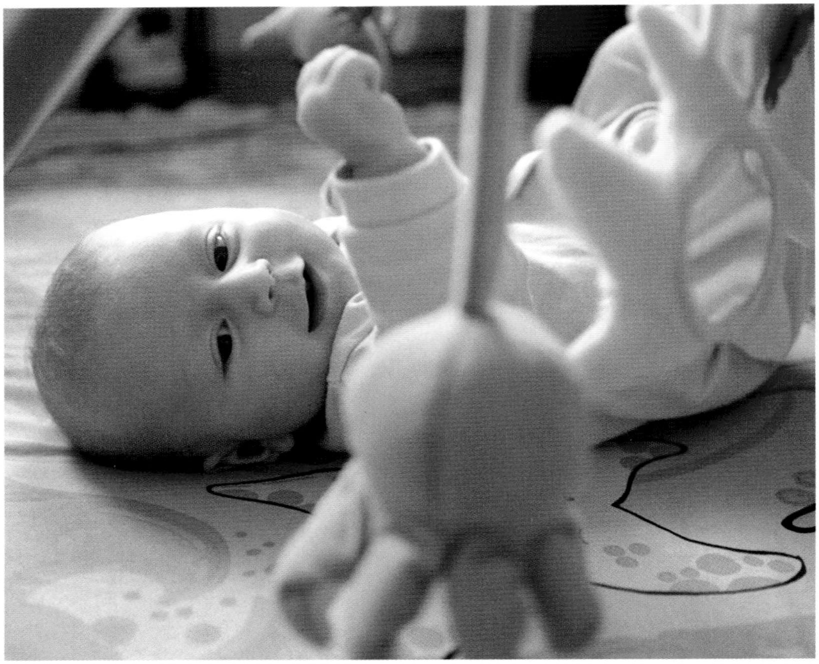

Your social baby

Every day your baby is learning how to adapt and respond to people, and developing important social skills along the way. Spend lots of face-to-face time with your baby. He'll love the attention and will enjoy making faces with you. Your baby will also love visitors, both young and old, especially when they're going ga-ga over him, so make a point of inviting over friends and relatives to help your baby's social development.

If your baby develops "stranger anxiety", don't be embarrassed. Babies may start to become nervous around unfamiliar people, at approximately six months. If your baby cries when you put him in a relative's arms, for example, take him back in your arms and try a slow desensitisation process. First, wait until he is comfortable in your arms while the other person is around. Then ask your relative to talk and play with your baby while you hold him. Next, hand him over to the other person for a short time, but stay close by. Finally, try to leave the room for a few minutes, and see how it goes. If your baby bawls at any point, take him back and comfort him, and try again another time – he should never feel pressurised into a situation that he doesn't feel comfortable with.

Giving your baby plenty of opportunites to stimulate his senses will help him to learn more each day about his world.

Development chart

Age	Mastered Skills (most children can do)	Emerging Skills (half of children can do)	Advanced Skills (a few children can do)
1 month	• Lifts head • Responds to sound • Stares at faces	• Follows objects • Ooohs and ahhs • Can see black-and-white patterns	• Smiles • Laughs • Holds head at 45-degree angle
2 months	• Vocalises sounds – gurgling and cooing • Follows objects • Holds head up for short periods	• Smiles, laughs • Holds head at 45-degree angle • Movements become smoother	• Holds head steady • Bears weight on legs • May lift head and shoulder (mini push-up)
3 months	• Laughs • Holds head steady • Recognises your face and scent	• Squeals, gurgles, coos • Recognises your voice • Does mini push-ups	• Turns towards loud sounds • Can bring hands together and may bat at toys • Can roll over
4 months	• Holds head up steadily • Can bear weight on legs • Coos when you talk to him	• Can grasp a toy • Reaches out for objects • Can roll over	• Imitates speech sounds; may say "ba" or "da" • May cut first tooth
5 months	• Can distinguish between bold colours • Can roll over • Amuses himself by playing with hands and feet	• Turns towards new sounds • Recognises own name	• May sit momentarily without support • Mouths objects • Stranger anxiety may begin • May be ready for solids
6 months	• Turns to sounds and voices • Imitates sounds, blows bubbles • Rolls in both directions	• Reaches for and mouths objects • Sits without support • Is ready for solids	• May lunge forwards or crawl • May jabber or combine syllables • May drag an object to himself

Welcome to parenthood! 0–6 weeks

Your growing baby 6 weeks to 6 months

Your older baby 6 months to one year

Baby healthcare 0–12 months

As your baby grows, he will start to "discover" his body and will love to spend time sucking his hands – and his feet!

At around four months, your baby will reach the exciting milestone of learning to grasp a toy – his world is opening up.

By six months, your baby may have gained sufficient coordination and strength to propel himself forwards to reach for a toy.

Playing and learning: 2–4 months

Enjoying simple games together is a wonderful way to develop your baby's motor skills and coordination and to teach her about human interaction. Games are great for building your relationship, too – there is nothing more rewarding than hearing your baby giggle with delight.

Physical games

Your baby probably won't learn to sit up for a few months, but as her back and neck grow stronger, she's ready to practise. You can help improve her gross motor skills by playing lots of simple, fun games together on the floor.

A new perspective
Try putting your baby on her back, propped up slightly with a pillow. Sit facing her and grasp her hands firmly. Gently pull her to a sitting position, letting her head follow her shoulders,

Your baby's head control is getting stronger all the time, enabling her to interact with her environment while on her tummy.

and enjoy her expression as she sees the world from this new angle. Gently lower her and, if she's having fun, repeat the action. As your baby gets used to this game, keep her sitting up a little longer. Sing a nursery rhyme, such as "Twinkle, twinkle little star" to capture her attention when she's upright, then lower her back down onto the pillow.

If your baby favours a certain position, for example lying on her back and looking up at a light, or at drifting clouds when you're outside, lie down next to her and watch together. She'll love the company and you'll experience the world from her perspective.

Roll over
By three months, your baby will be working hard to gain control over the way she moves. You can help her to explore her surroundings and get used to new positions with a simple rolling game. Sit on a large blanket and take off as many layers of your baby's clothing as the temperature permits (babies seem to feel freer to move around when they're wearing less) and lay your baby on her stomach or back. Then, with gentle support, let her roll herself over – and then roll her over again in the same direction so she's back in the same

Active mum
Your baby will appreciate you getting down to his level.

"I'm a fan of Pilates, but since having my son, I hadn't really managed to get back into it. However, recently my little one has been so happy to lie on the floor while attempting to roll over and reach for objects, that I've had no excuse not to get down there with him and do a workout. My baby seems to really enjoy watching mummy get into funny positions, and I think it encourages him to try out some new moves too!"

position. Continue rolling her in one direction until she reaches the edge of the blanket – to give her a sense that she is getting somewhere – then lift her back to the middle for her to start again. Keep repeating this game for as long as your baby enjoys it.

Encouraging coordination
Now that she's strong enough to hold her head steady, your baby is learning to control and manipulate her upper body in preparation for rolling over, and,

eventually, standing. To encourage full–body coordination, gently roll your baby on top of a beach ball or exercise ball. (This can also help her to relax before bedtime.) If you use a beach ball, blow it up most of the way, so it rolls, but has a soft spot. Hold her securely with your hands on either side of her ribcage, place her tummy-down on top of the ball and roll her back and forth and from side to side.

Backwards and forwards

In the next month, your baby may sit up unsupported. She'll love to practise for this by being propped up.

A gentle rowing routine will strengthen your baby's back muscles in preparation for sitting. This game involves rowing in time to "Row, row, row your boat". Sit on the floor with your legs in a "V" shape and sit your baby facing you with a sturdy pillow or cushion behind her. Grasp her hands and pull her gently so that she leans towards you while you lean back slightly, then reverse so that you lean forwards and she leans back. Sing the nursery rhyme with a slow, emphatic rhythm, so that you both move forwards and backwards in time to each key word; for example, the rhythm of the last line should be "*life* is *but* a *dream*". As your baby gradually gets used to this game, you can lean farther forwards and backwards, watching her giggle with anticipation each time.

Fact: Talking to your baby a lot of the time can boost his IQ levels later!

Recent research has linked higher intelligence levels to how many words a child hears during the first year of his or her life.

A gentle introduction to action nursery rhymes gives your baby a taste of the world from a new perspective.

ParentsTalk...

"My baby boy is learning the new skill of rolling onto his tummy, which he seems to be enjoying. I think he's finally getting fed up with lying around on his back all day!"
Harry, 31, father of two

"It gave us such delight when our four-month-old boy discovered his hands and feet – playing with them and putting them in his mouth gave him so much entertainment!"
Hannah, 24, first-time mum

"One day my little girl realised she could make noises other than laughing or crying – so began the babbling! I have no idea what's she's trying to say, but she seems to be having fun, so I talk back to her to get the conversation flowing!"
Brooke, 22, first-time mum

"When my baby started to notice the different expressions on my face it was the beginning of us being able to communicate and interact. Now, when I try to cheer her up by smiling and talking softly to her, she smiles back at me. She absolutely loves lying on her play mat staring up at this little smiley yellow face that has a flashing light and plays music – watching that keeps her amused for a good half an hour!"
Jess, 28, first-time mum

Welcome to parenthood!
0–6 weeks

Your growing baby
6 weeks to 6 months

Your older baby
6 months to one year

Baby healthcare
0–12 months

Sensory and learning games

While your baby's verbal skills are developing, he will constantly try to communicate with you with an ever-growing repertoire of sounds.

Over and out

You can play a fun game with two telephones, either toy ones or real ones switched off. Hold a receiver to your baby's ear. Use your phone to hold a one-sided conversation, speaking in a slow, exaggerated style. Leave long pauses; soon he'll make babbling and cooing responses. This helps him practise the rhythms of conversation.

A shadow display

Your baby is transfixed by moving shapes and patterns, and he may stare at the television when before he ignored it. Help him become an active audience member with a shape-making shadow game. Sit on the floor with your baby in your lap. Position a torch so it shines against a wall, and put your hands between the beam and the wall so that the wall is the screen. Start with actions, such as waving or holding up fingers. Then use your hands to make animal shapes, such as a dog or duck. Help your baby wave his hands and make shadows.

Noisy fun

Babies are born with an instinct to startle in response to loud noises. Over time, this turns into a love of surprising noises, especially rattling, crunching or squeaking sounds. Hearing a sound and seeing what made it helps your baby understand other types of connections.

Gather some household items that make a sound when crumpled up, such as waxed paper or cellophane. Toys that squeak, rattle or chime are good, too. Demonstrate each sound to your baby, varying the order so it surprises him. Put the objects in his hand and help him make the sounds himself. Repeat this over the coming months, watching to see if he looks at his hands or begins to realise he's making the sounds.

It's a thrill (for your baby, at least!) when he learns to clatter and bang. Realising that a thump of his fist makes a satisfying "whomp" is a powerful affirmation that actions get results. Make it fun by giving him a range of notes to aim for. Gather empty ice-cream tubs or containers with flexible cardboard or plastic lids and make them into "drums" using layers of cling film. Or use containers with drum-like lids, such as lunchboxes or food canisters. Tape the "drums" together to make a set. With your baby propped up between your legs and the drums in front of you, show him how to tap the drums with your palms, fingers and the heel of your hand.

"Pretend" conversations will captivate your baby. Ideally, use toy phones; if you use mobile ones, make sure they're turned off.

Touch and sound are a big part of your baby's world. Discovering that certain textures make a noise too will fascinate him.

When your baby has had enough playtime

In the uterus, everything was quiet, fluid and gentle. Your baby glided through a watery world of muted sounds and faint colours. By contrast, life outside the uterus can be pretty jarring with its bright lights, whirring machines and barking dogs.

Being sensitive to his needs

When you're socialising with your baby, be sensitive to any signs that he's had enough interaction, as too much stimulation can overload a baby's neural circuits, leaving him crying or unsettled. Your baby will often display signs, such as closing his eyes, turning away, tensing up, arching his back, avoiding your gaze and irritability, which all indicate that playtime is over and he needs a break. These signals are essentially your baby's way of communicating, "I've had all I can take right now."

Your baby is learning the art of anticipation and will squeal with delight as he waits for you to tickle him at the end of a nursery rhyme.

Encourage your baby's increasingly sociable nature with singing and plenty of animated talk.

Social play

As your baby becomes more aware of the world and people around him, it's great fun to play social games – things that involve recognition, singing and rhythm or imitation – and to teach him about turn-taking and interaction.

Words and rhymes
Once your baby is a few months old, play "This little piggy" or "Round and round the garden" with his feet or hands. Hold him on your lap and gently uncurl his toes or fingers as you sing. Repeat the song a couple of times until he giggles in excited anticipation of the tickle at the end. Simple, repetitive rhymes like these are great for improving your baby's memory skills.

Your baby is beginning to learn that certain words sound like their meaning. He'll love songs like "Pop! goes the weasel", where you can highlight the element of surprise with sound effects and actions. Clap your hands on the word "pop", or make a toy jump out at your baby. This is a great distraction during nappy changes and car rides.

Surprise, surprise!
When your baby is getting the hang of cause and effect, he'll be delighted whenever something unexpected pops into view. Hiding, then showing, your face will trigger giggles, but you can make it an even funnier surprise by using a range of silly expressions.

Sit your baby in his bouncy chair or car seat. Duck down out of sight, then pop up with an exaggerated smile or "surprised" face. Repeat this with other silly (and unscary!) expressions, varying where your head pops up from – behind, or either side of, the chair. This will also teach your baby object permanence: the realisation that objects and people exist when out of his sight (see p.146).

Systemised mum

Take a little time out from routines each day to enjoy some quality interactive time with your baby. This helps bonding and encourages her social skills.

"A lot of the time as a mum, I'm the one leading the interaction as I need to do so many things for my baby. I change her nappy, feed her, bath her and put her to bed. So, interspersed with our routine, I try to make sure there are things we do together so that we can interact on more equal terms. I find scheduled playtime is great for this. Singing, clapping games, rattle toys, swinging and bouncing her, looking at books, and having little 'conversations', are all ways we interact together. If she's clearly not enjoying something, I'll suggest something else, which gives her the chance to make decisions and discover for herself what she finds fun."

Welcome to parenthood!
0–6 months

Your growing baby
6 weeks to 6 months

Your older baby
6 months to one year

Baby healthcare
0–12 months

Playing and learning: 4–6 months

Your baby's motor skills are developing fast and she's getting the hang of "object permanence", the knowledge that just because she can't see something, it doesn't mean it doesn't exist (see p.146). Her new skills form the basis of fun hide-and-seek, language and sorting games.

Physical games

Your baby's gross motor skills are developing quickly now and her muscles are getting steadily stronger. With all this new-found strength and her newly acquired skills, your baby probably loves practising kicking her legs around, and bouncing up and down on your knees. As her hand–eye coordination improves, too, there are

As your baby's coordination improves, she will reach out to touch or grab objects.

plenty of opportunities to play fun games together to encourage her physical skills to develop further.

Motion games
Sit cross-legged with your baby in your lap facing away from you. With one hand holding her firmly and the other on the floor behind you for support, raise your legs, still crossed, with your baby resting on them. As she goes up, say, "Aeroplane taking off, up, up and away!"

Tips for encouraging physical development

Your baby develops at her own pace, but a little encouragement at the right time can help her consolidate her new skills.

Grasping
To stimulate her grasping reflex, put an easily held toy or bright object just out of reach and encourage her to grab it.

Head control
You don't have to do much to encourage head control, but you have to be careful. From three to six months, you can prop up your baby in a chair or on the bed (ensure she's not close to the edge and stay with her all the time), with pillows

for head and neck support. Or sit her on your lap with her head against your tummy.

Rolling over
Once your baby rolls, encourage her by wiggling a toy next to the side she favours. Applaud her: she may need reassurance as this new body flip can be alarming.

Sitting
Prepare her to sit by putting her tummy down and prompting her to look up at a toy or your face. This strengthens neck muscles and develops the head control needed for sitting. Using a bright or noisy toy ensures that her hearing and vision are on track, too.

Propping up your baby on some cushions or pillows helps him get used to this new perspective.

and, as you lower her down, "Aeroplane coming in for a landing!" Encourage your baby to raise her arms out to the sides and make aeroplane wings. Not only will this have both you and your baby giggling, but it will teach her about the sheer joy of being free and mobile.

If you're feeling adventurous and are confident of holding your baby firmly, try playing this bathtime game with you both sitting in a shallow bath. Using the same movement, you can lift your baby just clear of the water, then create a gentle splash as you lower her back in, announcing, "Rocket ship launching" and "Rocket ship splashdown!"

Finger games

Your baby loves small, shiny objects. Try collecting extra-large, colourful buttons (the biggest you can find – at least 5 centimetres/2 inches across, so they're not a choking hazard) and let your baby take them out and put them back into a small cloth pouch, over and again. This will help to satisfy her magpie instinct for gathering things, and also help to fine-tune her physical coordination.

It's also nice to sit your baby in your lap and spread the buttons out in front of her, helping her match them up or make a pattern of alternating colours, naming them as you go. The bag of buttons is perfect to keep in your bag to pull out when you're away from home and your baby is restless or bored.

In fact, your baby loves grabbing all kinds of things, not just buttons. Her coordination is improving and her hands are learning to do what her brain tells them to do: it's exciting for her to see something, reach for it and actually touch it. Blow bubbles gently in her direction so that she can reach out to pop them. Once she gets used to the way they pop, aim them to land on her legs, arms, hands, tummy and so on.

Name each body part as you go: "There's a bubble on your tummy!" "There's one on your hand!" This helps her sense of physical coordination and shows her the names of different body parts, even though she can't say them herself yet.

When she is older, this will be fun to play in the bath. An odd property of soap bubbles is that they attach to wet skin without bursting, giving your baby time to look at a bubble before popping it.

Old favourites

Help your baby's motor skills and appeal to her love of surprise with a game of "Humpty Dumpty". Lie down with your knees bent and sit her on your tummy. As you say the rhyme, sway from side to side; on the word "fall", roll over to one side, making sure she has a soft landing!

Dads often excel at physical play with babies. As your baby gets stronger, she will love action play that involves plenty of gentle movement and bouncing.

ParentsAsk...

Why does my baby seem bored with her toys?

You're probably reading a bit too much into your baby's behaviour. Three- to six-month-old babies are learning to focus on objects and to pick particular things out of everything they're seeing. Although she may favour some objects or toys over others, this doesn't necessarily mean that she is bored with any of them. If she's alone with her toys, maybe she doesn't enjoy the solitude. As she gets older and learns how to entertain herself, she'll become much more content to play on her own. In the meantime, remember that you're not responsible for keeping her busy and amused every moment of the day.

Welcome to parenthood!
0–6 weeks

Your growing baby
6 weeks to 6 months

Your older baby
6 months to one year

Baby healthcare
0–12 months

Sensory and learning games: 4–6 months

Your baby is grasping the concept of "object permanence": the knowledge that just because he can't see something it doesn't mean it's not there (see box, below). He also loves games with an element of surprise or silliness.

Hiding your baby under a blanket and then "discovering" him will amuse him endlessly and provoke peals of laughter.

Hide-and-seek games

Take one of your baby's favourite teddies and put it inside a small bag (not a plastic bag), then inside a box. Put the box into a larger box or bag, and so on, until the teddy is encased in at least five layers. Set the box-within-a-box-within-a-bag in front of your baby and ask, "Where's your teddy?" While he's watching you, open the first box or bag, take out the next layer, and ask, "Is your teddy in here?" as you open that one. Keep going until you open the last layer in front of your baby, exclaiming, "Here's your teddy!" Then let your baby make a grab for the teddy.

Visual stimulation

Nothing makes your baby giggle like the sight of you wearing something silly on your head, so round up a selection of "hats" – a tea cosy, a cardboard box, a plastic bowl, a pair of shorts, a wicker basket – and put each one on your head in turn, asking, "Do you like my hat?"

You could even sit your baby in front of a mirror and let him try the silly millinery on himself. If there are several of you present, pass the hats around in a line.

You've probably noticed that your baby loves watching people and movement, so you could take him to watch a ball game at a football pitch or a netball or tennis court. Sit him on your lap or park his buggy where he'll have a good, unobstructed view. Whether it's the colourful shirts of the players or the regular clunk of the ball hitting the court, your baby will be intrigued.

What comes next

Your baby loves surprises and learning to predict what might happen next. Try the old favourite "riding" game where you sit on a chair with your knees together and legs bent at a right angle. Sit your baby on your knees facing you, with his legs to either side. Place your hands on his waist to steady him and then bounce him gently up and down on your knees, saying, "This is the way the lady rides, tri-tree-tree-tree, tri-tree-tree-tree, this is the way the lady rides, tri-tree tri-tree tri-TREE". On the final "tree", part your legs so that he dips down, taking care, of course, to keep him well supported all the time and to ensure that he doesn't fall all the way down to the floor.

Object permanence

Wondering why peekaboo is such an exciting game for your baby? It's because it mimics what he is just coming to understand about the world around him: that objects and people still exist even when he can't see them. So he finds quick appearances and disappearances amusing (a jack-in-the-box is fun to play with right now).

A clearer understanding

Understanding this concept, also known as object permanence, is an important

milestone for your baby, and signals that he is making leaps in cognitive development – both his memory and his ability to think abstractly are growing. At around five months, your baby will also get better at spotting very small objects and tracking moving things. He may even recognise an object after seeing only part of it.

A jack-in-the-box is a perfect toy for your baby now, playing on his delight in surprising appearances.

Note: Your baby is becoming more responsive to language.

By three months, your baby's temporal lobe, which assists with hearing, language, and smell, has become more receptive and active. When he hears your voice, he may gurgle back.

Social play

As your baby becomes more social and responsive, you can enjoy increasingly interactive games together.

Name that part

Games involving body parts are more fun now that your baby's movements are more coordinated. Help your baby to link an arm, leg or belly button with its name with a bath game. When he is in his bath seat, or in the bath with you supporting him, saturate a sponge, then approach him with it submerged. Say, "I'm going to tickle your toes," and tickle them lightly with the sponge, pulling it out of reach if he tries to grab it. Approach from other directions, saying, "I'm tickling your knees, I'm tickling your back, I'm tickling your bottom," each time pulling away the sponge if he tries to grab it.

Tuning in

Your baby is learning to listen – or, as the experts say, "developing receptive language" – as fast as he's learning to communicate. Treat him to a surprise eavesdrop by turning his baby monitor into a listening device.

Lie him in his cot or safely on the floor. Give him the listening part of his monitor, then leave the room and spend a minute or so speaking gently into the talking part. Describe where you are, remark upon the weather and your plans for the day. (This works particularly well if you have a friend to join in.) When you reappear, your entrance will be met with pleased astonishment.

ParentsTalk...

"When I talk to and smile at my four-month baby, she stares at me, totally fascinated by how my face moves."
Fionnuala, 40, mother of two

"I've started having conversations with my baby. I'll say something and he'll gurgle in response. Sometimes, he gets animated and kicks his legs, so I respond in a lively way so he knows that I understand him (even though I'm not always sure I do!)."
Naomi, 37, first-time mum

"When my baby learnt to babble, she made the same noises over and over, sometimes changing the volume and bellowing. I chat and encourage her if she's sounding really enthusiastic!"
Becca, 26, first-time mum

"If we have visitors, my baby stares at them (which can be disconcerting for them!). If he's relaxed with them, he'll smile; if he's unsure, he'll hang on to me and turn away."
Victoria, 39, mother of three

Movement and colour will grab your baby's attention. A colourful windmill toy combines these elements perfectly (above).

Laughing with and talking to your baby at close quarters stimulates his listening and language skills (left).

Welcome to parenthood!
0–6 weeks

Your growing baby
6 weeks to 6 months

Your older baby
6 months to one year

Baby healthcare
0–12 months

Your baby's toys

Toys are a special part of your baby's childhood, so choosing the right ones is very important. At the very least, all of her toys must be safe and appropriate for her age and ability. Ideally, they will also help your baby to learn as she plays.

Choosing your baby's toys

Your baby's toys should be designed to be visually appealing and to enhance her cognitive, creative and social development skills, as well as her physical development.

Green mum

If a toy is cuddly, rattles, squeaks or moves, a baby will probably be interested in it. They won't care if it's wooden, homemade or from a toy library!"

"Most toys are made of synthetic materials and non-biodegradable plastic, so I've tried to buy mostly wooden toys. Charity shops are great, too, for good-as-new toys and books that cost hardly anything.

I'd recommend using your local toy library. You can borrow toys or drop in for play sessions. They're cheap, and have saved me from having to buy so many toys, as babies grow out of them so quickly. The toy library will be useful, too, as my baby gets older as there are larger toys, such as stationary baby walkers, climbing and ride-on toys, which we don't have room for on a permanent basis!"

Up to three months

In her first months, before she sits up, your baby will appreciate things she can look at and listen to. High-contrast patterns and bright colours (especially black, white and red) captivate her because they're the easiest for her to see. A mobile above her cot, especially one that plays music, will fascinate her. (Babies this age look to their right 80 per cent of the time, so hang a mobile to the right for maximum impact.)

Your baby will gradually become more intrigued by noises and music. As well as playing a variety of music – nothing too raucous – to entertain and soothe your baby, toys that make a noise will almost certainly be a hit. Soft toys

that tweet or squeak when pressed, and feet or wrist rattles will all entertain your baby and help her learn what her hands are doing. She may also love to listen to wind chimes in her room.

An unbreakable mirror is a good toy for your baby – choose one you can fasten to the side of her cot or hang near the changing table. She won't realise that it's herself she's seeing at this stage, but she'll find the reflection fascinating. By three months, she may smile at it.

Three to six months

As she gets older, your baby discovers how much fun her own hands can be now that they're no longer clenched in a fist. She can suck her fingers and grasp a toy that has been placed in her hands. She has begun to reach for toys and enjoys toys that she can pass back and forth between her hands. She'll rotate her wrist to inspect it from all sides, usually before popping it into her mouth!

Check labels to ensure that toys are safe for chewing! Never attach a toy to a cot or playpen with elastic or string, as this could strangle or entrap your baby.

Bold black and white patterns will capture your baby's attention in the early months as these are easy for her to focus on.

Keeping toys safe

Toys are childhood treasures, but they should be chosen with care. Check "age" labels to see if a toy is suited to your baby's level of ability and age. Parts should be bigger than her mouth to prevent choking, and buy only from shops and manufacturers you trust.

Beware of hazards

Watch out for toys that are heavy, or that could hurt your baby if dropped.

Make sure toys are well put-together too, with no loose bits, small parts, sharp edges or points. You should also avoid damaged or worn toys, or ones that have cords or leads, which pose a strangulation risk.

Always try to keep your baby's play area tidy, and supervise your baby at all times. Separate toys for different age groups, as younger children will always try to play with older children's toys.

At around this age, many babies form an attachment to a soft toy. It has to be soft and cuddly – you don't want a toy with wire ears or a tail that could poke through fabric. Look for soft dolls or cuddly animals with stitched-on features, but nothing that could pose a choking hazard, such as plastic eyes, bells, buttons, ribbons and threads.

Your baby may love a "play gym" or "activity centre" – a rack that comes with dangling toys. These are for babies who can't sit up, and they can make life more interesting while your baby is young. Your baby can bat at the toys, pull them, spin them and rattle them. She'll probably start to lose interest in her activity centre once she begins to roll.

By six months, your baby can probably sit up, giving her a new perspective and making her the centre of her own clanging, colourful world. Squeaky rubber toys – anything she can grab and squish – are popular now, and perfect for the bath. Expect to hear these squeaks, and your baby's happy squeals, often.

It's a great idea to start reading to your baby now: listening to your voice helps her develop an ear for language, and varying your pitch, using different accents, singing and making silly noises, will make reading together much more interesting for her. Colourful, durable board books will hold her interest, and they can withstand mouthing, drooling and most other forms of baby love.

Welcome to parenthood!
0–6 weeks

Your growing baby
6 weeks to 6 months

Your older baby
6 months to one year

Baby healthcare
0–12 months

Soft picture books with bright colours and different textures are cleverly designed to stimulate your baby's senses.

Your baby probably won't be aware that it's her in the mirror, but she will love the effect of the movement and shiny surface.

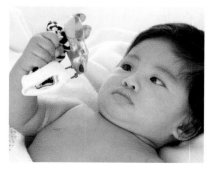

Toys that make a noise when held, shaken or squashed, will captivate your baby and help her understanding of cause and effect.

Playing together

Playing with your baby not only helps him learn and develop, but it's an important part of family bonding. Games are also a great way for dads to bond with their babies, and with a bit of gentle coaching, toddlers and older siblings make brilliant playmates, too.

Making time for older children and helping them to be involved will make them feel secure within the new family structure.

Single mum

Helping your baby develop other attachments benefits you both.

"Most of the time it's me and Ella. I love being with her, but I want her to know other people. Not many of my friends have kids, so she spends a lot of time with adults and enjoys the attention. My best friend is Ella's godmother, who babysits. I love the chance to get out and I think it's good for Ella, too.

I make sure that Ella spends time with other children, too. My sister has three kids so her house is pretty noisy; Ella loves it. She gets so excited, it can be hours before she calms down!"

Family time

All sorts of activities will stimulate even very young babies, helping them develop curiosity and confidence, as well as enhancing physical and emotional growth. Not only does interactive play stimulate your baby, but it also helps him to develop relationships with others. The more your baby shares activities with family members, the stronger family bonds will become.

Everyday play

Although it's important to build in some dedicated play time to your baby's day, your baby will nonetheless thrive simply by being a part of whatever you do. Even mundane tasks, such as housework or shopping, can seem like play to your baby if he is included – chatter with him while you're doing the dishes, scooping up water and pouring it into the sink, or get your partner to take him on the weekly shop.

As he gets older, let him play with the contents of safe kitchen cupboards (with plastic containers, measuring cups or pots and pans) or with other household items that are clean and harmless. It won't be tidy, but he'll enjoy exploring, learning and being part of the family's daily routine. You can also incorporate toys such as stacking boxes or blocks, balls, toys on wheels or mirrors. It will still be a while before he connects the idea of that fascinating baby in the mirror with himself, but encourage him with lots of smiles, upbeat words of praise and cuddles.

Playtime with dad

For dads, playtime is a great opportunity to get closer; babies love playtime with dads, and dads can find it easier to bond through games and activities. They are often inclined to try physical play, and as your baby develops more head control, he'll love to be lifted through the air like an aeroplane, or gently rolled over.

Although being physically playful is a great way to bond and to have fun, it's important to keep playtime gentle and never throw a baby into the air in play. The potential for a dangerous fall or neck injury isn't worth the risk.

Child's play

Older siblings can be the perfect entertainment for your baby. Not only will playing with, or entertaining, their new baby brother or sister help them to feel involved with the new addition to the family, but also your baby will be fascinated by them, watching them play their games. Older siblings might start

A big brother or sister can be the natural playmate for your baby, often displaying patience and interest in their sibling's activities when adult attention has begun to wane!

Welcome to parenthood!
0–6 weeks

Your growing baby
6 weeks to 6 months

Your older baby
6 months to one year

Baby healthcare
0–12 months

by showing him a book, reading aloud or repeating simple words and ideas ("This is your nose. This is Grandpa's nose. Your shirt is green. The grass is green."). Adults can grow weary repeating actions again and again to entertain their baby. Repetitive play, however, comes naturally to young children and toddlers, who won't tire of playing games such as peekaboo, or singing "Row, row, row your boat" to your baby, over and over again. Always supervise siblings with your baby.

An extended family

If you struggle to remember nursery rhymes, songs or games, parents, inlaws and older relatives can provide a wealth of information and are often more than happy to step in. This serves the dual purpose of letting them feel involved while giving your baby exposure to others. The sooner your baby trusts wider family members or friends, the more sociable and less prone to stranger anxiety he is likely to be. Developing his

relationships gives you a bit of space, and builds important bonds, which can be useful if you're planning to use family members to help look after him later on.

These days, the idea of "family" can stretch far beyond just your immediate family. With complicated relationships and physical distances between blood relations much more common, making the most of people you are close to (both figuratively and physically) will enrich your baby's life.

Dad's **Diary**

Playing the entertainer

"George's sense of humour is really starting to develop now that he's a bit older, and often it's the little things that make him smile or laugh. I'm always trying to find new ways to make him chuckle – and I have to say, it's really very easy. Just trying to teach him to say "da-da" results in a hearty chortling. His laugh is infectious, too – the more he laughs, the more I laugh, which makes him laugh even more.

The guaranteed way to make him giggle with absolute glee is to play our aeroplane take-off game. I lie him tummy-down on top of my legs while I'm sitting down, and then lift my legs up and down for take off and landing. I don't want to wish time away, but I can't wait until he's a bit older and I can "fly" him above my head. He'll love it!"

As your baby grows, he'll look forward to action play with dad.

Baby talk

Even though your baby only seems to gurgle, coo and cry at the moment, she is already getting to grips with human interaction and absorbing how you speak and respond to her. Over the coming months, there are many ways you can encourage her powers of communication.

Encouraging early speech

Babies are totally dependent on their parents, but they, like all small animals, have to communicate their needs somehow. While all baby animals cry when they are hungry, thirsty or cold, human babies also show a great deal of interest in speech and in those who talk to them. They move to the rhythm of human speech; for example, they turn towards anyone who is speaking to them and they carry out little "look, move and gurgle conversations" (see right) with anyone who is willing to engage in talk with them.

Your first conversations

Early "conversations" with your baby may go something like this: "How are you this morning, sweetheart?" You pause, your baby catches your eye and moves her mouth or gurgles as if to say, "I had a nice sleep." Then, like most parents, you will probably put what you think your baby is trying to say into words: "You had a nice sleep," and continue the conversation. "Are you ready for your breakfast?" When your baby gurgles again, you say, "You are ready, aren't you!"

This tendency to extend and second-guess what our children are trying to tell us forms the model for how we help them when they're older, too. In the future, when your baby starts to speak and says "Ca," you may clarify with, "It's a cat." If it's a car and not a cat she is telling you about, she might say, "No ca – CA." You'll probably reply, "Oh car, not cat." This is a language older babies encourage us to speak. If we say the "right" thing, they smile and gurgle or answer us back. If we get it wrong, they look away, cry or repeat

Interacting with your baby, whether through talking or looking at books, will help her to absorb words and expression.

Welcome to parenthood!
0–6 months

Your growing baby
6 weeks to 6 months

Your older baby
6 months to one year

Baby healthcare
0–12 months

Twins and language development

Twins seem slower to develop language skills than singleton babies. On average, they tend to be about six to eight months behind in their speech, but most catch up by school age.

Catching up

Around half of twins are born early, and some have a low birthweight, both of which affects speech development. Also, twins tend to have less speech directed at them individually. To help language development, talk to them separately whenever possible. Give them separate baths or bedtime stories occasionally, so that they get one-to-one attention.

Identifying problems

If your twins are late talkers they'll more than likely catch up with time. However, if you're concerned, talk to your doctor, who may refer them to a speech therapist to check that there isn't a particular problem, for example with hearing.

"Twin" speak

Sometimes, twins can create a shared language known as "idioglossia" or twin language. They may use their own, simpler words and use shorter sentence structures, which are difficult for adults to understand. If your twins use this language, don't worry, they will outgrow it. However, you might like to video their conversations, as you – and they – will find them fascinating to watch when they're older.

---

what they have just said to us. When your baby is older, she will pick out what works best for her and reward you with a smile when you do what she likes. This means that, if you're sensitive to her expressions of pleasure and displeasure, you will almost always make the best choices and will almost always be the perfect teacher for her.

Don't be afraid to use baby talk to communicate with your baby. If saying "moo-moo", "woof-woof" or "yum-yum" for "cow", "dog" and "food" hindered language development, then parents would have stopped using these words a long time ago! The doubling-up of sounds is found in almost all of a child's earliest words – Dada, Mama, Baba, puss-puss and so on – which suggests that this technique helps babies to produce the right sounds. You'll encourage her language development

by speaking to her simply, clearly and often. Many parents naturally adopt a pattern of speech known as "Motherese" which is the name that psychologists use for a particular way of talking to babies using simple phrases and a sing-song pitch.

Watching and learning

At two to three months, your baby's favourite activity is watching what goes on around her, and she understands now that you will soothe, feed and play with her when she needs you. Her first genuine smile pops up about this time, bringing you joy. She understands that this is one way to let you know she's satisfied. She'll also enjoy the response she elicits with her grin. By three months, she'll add some gurgling sounds to her smile, initiating a primitive form of conversation with you.

From four months, your baby will know her name and understand that you are calling her when you say it. She'll even respond by turning towards you. She will become more attuned to your tone of voice, too. When you sound friendly, she'll react joyfully, and if you speak to her sharply, she'll probably cry.

Always be guided by your baby. If what you do and say makes her happy, you can be pretty sure you are doing and saying the right thing.

Fact: All new babies have an innate ability to understand all languages.

They lose this at about eight months when they concentrate on the sounds they hear, which is why some sounds are particularly hard to say if you learn a language as an adult.

Meeting others

Those early weeks and months with your baby can feel isolating. Just getting out of the the house can be hard enough, and some days the thought of being sociable seems impossible. The great thing about meeting other new mums is that they know just how you feel.

Your baby's social network

The benefits of new friends for you and your baby can't be overstated, whether it's for moral support, stimulation for your baby or just the excuse to change out of your tracksuit and get out. You might not feel like emerging from the cocoon of your home right away, and there's no need to rush into booking up your social calendar. However, don't miss out on the fun of sharing your new discoveries about your baby with other new mums, and the reassurances that your baby's behaviour is normal. Whether or not your long-term friends have children, being part of a local antenatal or postnatal group has many benefits, not least that you meet other parents who are going through the same things as you at almost the same time. Almost all new mums have similar worries and a desire to confide; being part of a group means that you instantly have something in common.

There are endless reasons why socialising is good for your baby as well. Babies love new faces and thrive around different sights, sounds and smells. Your baby might start out just enjoying a cuddle with you while hearing the chatter of different voices. Eventually, though, he will happily take part in parallel play (playing alongside, rather than with, other babies). You can discover toys or activities he's interested in, and he will be introduced to concepts such as sharing early on.

Meeting others

Having a baby can be an isolating experience, but only if you let it. There are several approaches to finding out about your new social scene, and you can be as deeply or casually involved as you wish. Sign up for organised groups or arrange your own; for example, if you were involved with an antenatal class,

Making the effort to meet up with other mums offers welcome company and sets up a social network for your baby, too.

👟 **Active mum**

If staying at home all day drives you potty, there are plenty of ways to socialise with baby in tow.

"I can only tolerate a very small amount of daytime television. In my antenatal class, there was a group of four of us who got along really well. Once we had our babies though, we were all so busy that we didn't really get in contact with each other. I decided after a couple of months to arrange a meet-up at a local café. We all had a lovely time and try to do it at least once a fortnight now.

I've also joined a swimming class. My baby loves it and can't get enough of the water. We go to baby signing, too. We've made some great friends. In fact, I think I have a better social life now than I did before I had my baby."

Whether meeting up in the local park or arranging to meet for coffee, social engagements add structure to your day.

coordinate a coffee morning at your house or at a baby-friendly café. Coffee groups are quick to catch on, and particularly cohesive crowds stay in contact years beyond the baby phase. If you aren't already involved with an antenatal group, talk to your health visitor or check the internet for gatherings for parents with babies born within a few weeks of each other.

Your health visitor should know all about local activities for babies and how to connect with other parents in your area. Also, if you can't find information about baby activities through a quick online search or have an aversion to technology, you could always try the old-school mummy magnet, your local library. Most libraries put on free music or story groups for babies, although you're just as likely to meet a like-minded mum by turning up at any time. Many mothers are open to embarking on a conversation about parenthood, so don't be afraid to initiate a chat. You'll find that this ad hoc method of meeting

other parents works in most situations, including in parks, on public transport or in shops selling baby goods.

Most areas have a plethora of baby activities, from community centre and church playgroups to drop-in gatherings sponsored by local NHS trusts. You may find a community parenting publication with information about playgroups, and check less traditional venues, too. For example, many cinemas offer special screenings for parents and babies, enabling you to spend time with your baby while doing something for yourself.

To compare is to despair

New parents find friendships with other parents invaluable, but beware of falling into the comparison trap. Many parents, intentionally or not, measure their baby's progress against other babies, or are influenced by other people's opinions. Trust your instincts and remember that babies develop at different rates, and only your health visitor or doctor should be consulted about genuine concerns.

Parents Talk...

"Talking to the other mums I met actually made me quite worried. My little boy, Oliver, took his time learning to sit up and then walk. This didn't bother me initially, but when they started saying: 'Oh, is Oliver still not walking?', I felt like they were judging both me and my son. Ridiculously, I felt under pressure to get him on his feet. It wasn't until my partner sat me down and reassured me that Oliver would reach these milestones when he was ready, that I stopped letting their comments get to me."
Philippa, 34, first-time mum

"My little girl was a fast developer, but my sister's son took longer than most to reach his milestones. We could easily have become very competitive, but instead I supported her by reminding her as often as possible that all babies develop at different rates. I think it helped and our children are so close now in terms of ability."
Molly, 32, first-time mum

"It got to the point where I started to avoid seeing my friend because of the constant comparisons. The next time I saw her she was gloating over how quickly her baby had learnt to walk and wondering why mine was taking so long, so I asked her if she was trying to make me feel bad? She was embarrassed. She'd been so caught up in how her own baby was doing that she didn't realise the effect it had on others. She's been much better since."
Caroline, 29, first-time mum

Welcome to parenthood!
0–6 weeks

Your growing baby
6 weeks to 6 months

Your older baby
6 months to one year

Baby healthcare
0–12 months

Environment and everyday care

Your baby's environment

It won't be long before your baby starts crawling and exploring the world around her – and, inevitably trying to taste a lot of it, too! She may still be immobile at the moment, but it's never too early to begin baby-proofing your home, ready for her first expeditions.

Assessing your home

Parents worry endlessly about child abuse or abduction, but many overlook one of the biggest threats to their children's safety: their own home. In the UK, accidents involving babies and children in the home are common, with many resulting in hospital treatment.

So don't wait until disaster strikes. With careful planning, you'll be prepared when your baby is ready to explore.

As your baby approaches six months, she is becoming increasingly mobile. She can probably roll across a room by now, and may even be beginning to crawl. She's also getting better at grabbing objects that are within her reach and will automatically put everything into her mouth. If you haven't done so already, now is the time to ensure that your baby's environment is a safe one.

Many safety measures apply more to babies who have started to crawl and walk (see pp.213–15), but there are plenty of general measures that are important to implement as soon as you have a baby in the house.

Fire safety

Domestic fires pose one of the greatest risks to babies and children. If you have a fireplace, keep a fire extinguisher nearby, and have it serviced according to the manufacturer's instructions. It's a legal requirement to have a fireguard if you have children in the house.

Keep matches and lighters out of sight and reach. Extinguish and dispose of cigarettes properly. Plan an escape route, and practise it. Also fit smoke alarms that comply with British Standard, or BS, 54466 and test them regularly.

Around the home

Certain safety measures can be applied to every room in the house. For example, put safety covers in all unused electrical outlets and keep plug switches in the "off" position.

Hide appliance cords behind heavy furniture or conceal them with a special "flex holder" device. Tall lamps might topple over if your baby pulls on them, so anchor them behind furniture.

Keep scissors, letter openers, staplers and sharp instruments locked away. Be aware, too, of things that could pinch small fingers, such as door hinges and ironing boards – you may wish to consider buying hinge protectors.

Keep first-aid supplies in a locked cupboard and make sure you have poison-proofed your home to protect your baby from hazardous substances. Take a careful look around to make sure you don't have any hanging plants or plant pots on the floor that your baby could reach. Pebbles and soil in plant pots can be a choking hazard. The simplest solution is to move any plants up onto high-up shelves.

Despite the many childproofing gadgets on the market, the most important safety device is always going to be your supervision.

Safety checklist for young babies

Consult the list below to ensure your home is safe for your baby, both before and after she starts to move.

- Put safety plugs or outlet covers in unused sockets; hide electrical cords behind furniture and keep appliances unplugged and out of reach.
- Use doorstops to protect tiny fingers.
- Use the safety strap on changing tables and high chairs.
- Keep toiletries and medicines out of reach.
- Put safety locks on cupboards and fit window guards and safety gates.
- Install a fireguard; keep logs, matches, fireplace tools and gas fire keys out of reach.
- Place tall, unstable lamps out of reach behind furniture.
- Cut off/tie up curtain and blind cords.

Welcome to parenthood! 0–6 weeks

Your growing baby 6 weeks to 6 months

Your older baby 6 months to one year

Baby healthcare 0–12 months

Green mum

As a parent you will want to make sure your baby is safe. You may be worried about hidden toxins in and around the home, especially when scare stories hit the headlines so often.

"I sometimes feel that not a day goes by without a new piece of research telling me that something I thought safe might not be. I try not to panic about these stories: there are toxins all around us and you can't ignore them altogether. I'd like to buy everything organic, but that can be expensive and some products simply aren't available in an organic range. So instead I do what I can to find out how a product is made and what chemicals have been used before I buy it. I read the label, and if I'm concerned about something, I try to find an alternative. For example, I've avoided buying any pressed wood (MDF) furniture for my baby's room – it can release the gas formaldehyde when it's new. Instead, I've gone for solid wood or bought second-hand."

A safe environment

As well as ensuring that your home is fitted with all the necessary safety devices (see pp.213–15), especially once your baby is on the move, there are other general factors to take into consideration when assessing whether your baby has a safe environment, both in the home and when you're out and about or travelling with your baby.

Pushchair safety

When buying a new or second-hand pushchair, there are a number of safety issues to consider, and your pushchair should comply with British Standard or BS 7409. The brake on the pushchair should be easy to apply. As tyre wear can affect how well brakes work, check the tyres of your pushchair regularly.

Pushchairs should have two locking devices to hold them open securely when being used, and there should be no areas where a baby's fingers could get caught in the collapsing mechanism. Babies who can sit up or be propped up in a pram need a harness to prevent them tipping over the side, or toppling out when you steer the pram down a steep curb. Pushchairs should also be used with a safety harness that goes over the shoulders as well as around the waist and between the legs. The harness should be used with newborn babies as well as with older babies. Most pushchairs have their own safety harness built in, but if yours doesn't, you will need to buy one separately.

The buckles on the safety harness should be easy for you to clip together and undo, and the belt should fit snugly

A properly fitted car seat is a legal requirement when travelling with your baby, and ensures he travels as safely as possible.

round your baby's waist. All-terrain pushchairs need a five-point harness to keep your baby snug on rough ground.

Check the stability of a pushchair and see if it tips up easily. It's important to remember not to overload the back of the pushchair with shopping bags, as this will make it dangerously unstable.

In the car

Never use a rear-facing seat on a passenger seat fitted with an airbag: it's illegal to do so, unless the airbag has been deactivated. It's safest to install an infant carrier or car seat in a rear-facing position on the back seat; the safest spot is the middle of the back seat (if there is a suitable seatbelt). There's flexibility in the type of baby seat used; the safest restraint is a five-point harness.

Car seats in Britain are designed to allow a baby to sleep comfortably with his head and back supported. Two main advantages are being able to transport your baby safely by car, and being able to carry him in and out of the car and house undisturbed while he's asleep. However, being semi-upright for long periods can put a strain on the developing spine, so it's a good idea not to use seats for prolonged periods. Break up long journeys so that your baby can be taken out of his seat for breaks when awake.

There is also an increasing trend to leave babies in car seats when they are not in the car. However, babies with gastric reflux are more likely to vomit in this position and very premature babies could have breathing difficulties if sat in a baby seat for longer than necessary. Even full-term babies have been found to experience low levels of blood oxygen if left for long periods in car seats and buggies, particularly when asleep.

Playpens offer a safe environment when you're unable to watch your baby, but its best to use them just for short periods as they may restrict your baby's activities.

Overall, there is not a problem with healthy babies sleeping in car seats and buggies for a few hours at a time, but it's better to put your sleeping baby in a pram or cot whenever possible.

The pros and cons of playpens

Although a playpen gives you a safe space to contain your child while you answer the phone, do the ironing or just catch your breath and leaf through a magazine, some experts feel that playpens can restrict babies, and that in the past they were overused. However, sometimes the design of your house, or your circumstances at home, mean you need somewhere safe where your baby can be popped into for a short while. Then a playpen can be really useful.

Being prepared

Even the most cautious parent cannot be expected to foresee every eventuality. Children are adventurous and their curiosity can sometimes lead them to accidents, even in a baby-proofed home. Prepare yourself by learning first aid so that you can come to the rescue quickly and confidently in

an emergency, if a qualified health professional is not present. Make up a first aid kit to keep in the house and keep it somewhere accessible and safe.

A clean environment

Living in a spotless environment is not always the best thing for your child. He may pick up a few more colds than his peers who live in squeaky-clean homes, but he may also be less likely to suffer from asthma and allergies later in life.

Over the past few decades, there has been a leap in the number of children with allergies, particularly in developed countries. The *British Medical Journal* suggested that this rise might be due to falling family sizes and cleaner homes, which stop young children being exposed to as many germs.

This, in turn, may give children's still-developing immune systems less practice at fighting off intruders. The result is that the under-challenged immune system wants to be used, so it becomes primed to see otherwise harmless substances, such as dust and pollen, as dangerous invaders, leading to allergies and asthma.

Is it safe to have a PC in our baby's bedroom?

There should be minimal risk of any harmful emissions, but there are precautions you can take. Switch off the monitor after use, avoid operating it for long periods while your baby sleeps in the room and put the cot at a distance.

Can I leave my baby alone for five minutes while I shower?

If your baby is happy and safe in his cot then this is fine. If he hates to be left for even a few moments, put him in a baby seat in the bathroom. Put it where it won't be splashed, but be sure you can see him. Remove hazards such as a loo brush that can seem like a good toy!

Can I leave my toddler alone in a room with my baby?

Your baby needs to be protected, but not overly so, and enthusiastic cuddles from your toddler can be ignored if your baby comes to no harm. However, it's sensible to be nearby in the early months in case your baby is the subject of misplaced attention. If you're leaving the room for more than a few moments, encourage your toddler to come and help you, or distract him from the baby and involve him in an activity while you're absent. He wouldn't have malicious intent, but being alone and unchecked with a small, new object may excite his curiosity.

ParentsAsk...

Bear in mind that your baby's developing immune system is most likely to be influenced during the first few years of his life. His immune system was getting ready to do battle even before he was born, with the placenta acting as a filter that let through small amounts of harmless allergens and microbes. Babies, it seems, are born ready to have their immune systems challenged by germs.

Welcome to parenthood!
0–6 weeks

Your growing baby
6 weeks to 6 months

Your older baby
6 months to one year

Baby healthcare
0–12 months

Everyday care

Your baby's skin is delicate while she's so small, and skin problems are fairly common – but fortunately most of them are harmless and easy to treat. Have fun with bathtime and massages: you may find they become your baby's favourite part of the day.

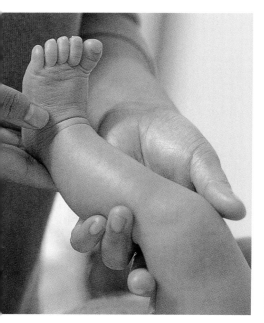

Skin care

Your baby has super-delicate skin that needs special care. Most problems can be avoided by changing her nappy frequently and using mild soaps and lotions when bathing her. Some skin problems, though, do need attention.

Keeping nappy rash at bay

If your baby has nappy rash, some of the skin covered by her nappy – the genital area, the thigh folds and her buttocks – will be red and inflamed. The area can be dry or moist, and may look pimply.

Your baby's skin, although incredibly soft, can suffer from dryness and sensitivity. Use just the gentlest of products on it.

The main cause of nappy rash is wetness, so keep your baby clean and dry by changing her nappy frequently. If your baby is not yet mobile, take her nappy off for a while to allow the air to speed up the healing process. If your baby is moving around, you might want to try this only if the weather is warm enough for her to go without a nappy outside, or if you have a floor that's fairly easy to clean.

When you're changing your baby's nappy, use just water and cotton wool or a very gentle cleanser to clean the nappy area. This will probably clear up any rash if it is allergy-based. You can use disposable or cloth nappies; there's

---

ParentsAsk...

I've heard that using water alone is best for bathing my baby – is this true?

Using water alone may not be enough to keep your baby clean. Apart from getting rid of general muckiness and grime, baby poo is unique in that it contains up to four per cent fats, which means that a mild cleanser is needed to remove the fatty deposits. Also, depending on where you live, water alone may not be as gentle as

you think on your baby's skin. For example, domestic tap water in hard water areas has been linked to a greater incidence of atopic eczema than in soft water areas. If you live in an area with very hard water, it may be kinder to clean your baby's skin using baby wipes with a moisturising cleansing lotion using purified water.

In general, to help keep your baby clean and to protect your baby's skin as she grows, follow these tips:

● Choose a mild soap or pH neutral cleanser, preferably with a proven safety profile for use with babies.
● Give your baby a bath when you think she needs one, but don't feel that you need to give a daily bath.
● At the first sign of dryness, use a gentle moisturiser on your baby's skin about every 12 hours, or as needed; preferably use a product without added perfumes, dyes or preservatives.

no proof that one type is better or preferable than the other for treating or preventing nappy rash.

A normal nappy rash should clear up after three or four days of at-home treatment with a barrier cream. If your baby's rash persists, spreads or otherwise worsens, talk to your doctor, who may prescribe a hydrocortisone or antifungal cream. If left, the rash can develop into something worse, such as an infection with thrush or another type of bacteria.

Preventing dryness

Dry skin can be another problem for babies and children, just as it is for adults. In fact, because young skin is more delicate, it's more susceptible to becoming dry.

Bathing can dry a baby's skin because it removes the skin's natural oils along with the dirt. So if your baby has a tendency to dry skin, instead of a 30-minute bath, cut bathtime down to about 10 minutes. Use warm, not hot, water, and soap up sparingly. Try a fragrance-free, soap-free cleanser, which is more gentle than regular soap. Applying an emollient cream before you put your baby into the bath acts as a seal to protect your baby's skin from the drying effects of the water.

Let your baby have her playtime in the tub before you wash her, so she won't be sitting in soapy water. Also, avoid adding bubble bath to each bath. You could limit bubble baths to special occasions only.

Once you take your baby out of the bath, quickly and lightly dry her with a towel, then apply a gentle moisturiser immediately to seal in the water that's still in her skin. As far as moisturisers are concerned, the general rule is the thicker the better. If your baby's skin is still dry even with daily moisturising, try switching from a thin lotion to a thicker

cream. You might also want to consider moisturising twice a day – once after bathing and once during the day. You could combine this with a soothing massage, which will also relax your baby and help her to sleep. See pages 164–67 to find out more about baby massage.

Dealing with eczema

If your baby has itchy red patches on her skin, it's possible she has eczema, also known as atopic dermatitis. The scratching caused by eczema breaks the skin, which means that the skin doesn't function as a protective barrier. This in turn makes your baby's skin more prone to infections and allergies.

Sometimes eczema will clear up over time with regular moisturising, so try an emollient lotion, cream or ointment to soothe your baby's skin. Also, keeping your baby's nails short helps to prevent her hurting herself through scratching. If the eczema patches don't get better, though, or your baby seems extremely itchy and uncomfortable, it's worth visiting your doctor for advice, who may prescribe a hydrocortisone cream.

Cradle cap

Cradle cap appears as a red area on your newborn's scalp, covered with greasy, yellow, scaly patches (see p.246). Over time, the scales become flaky and rub off easily. It's common in babies under eight months old, and can linger for weeks. The condition can look unsightly, but it's not itchy and won't cause discomfort. You can try gently removing the scales by regularly washing your baby's hair with a baby shampoo, then loosening the flakes with a soft brush. Or rub baby oil into the hair overnight to soften the scales and then shampoo it out. It's tempting to pick at the cradle cap, but doing so can leave sore patches that could become infected.

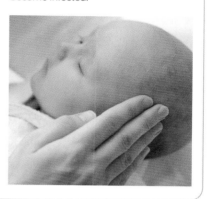

Green mum

Your baby's skin is so soft and sensitive – and so new! Using the most natural products is the gentlest way to treat her skin.

"I make my own baby wipes by using unbleached organic cotton wool or washable cloths, spritzed with some homemade cleansing lotion. It's easy to make: it's just camomile tea with a teaspoon of hemp oil poured into a glass or plastic bottle with a spray top. At bathtime, all I use is organic baby oil and water, or occasionally organic baby soap. Afterwards, I rub on a bit more baby oil to make her skin soft."

Welcome to parenthood!
0–6 weeks

Your growing baby
6 weeks to 6 months

Your older baby
6 months to one year

Baby healthcare
0–12 months

Bathtime

Many parents and babies love bathtime, but there is no evidence that suggests babies must have a daily bath. It's up to you and your baby. Washing his face frequently and thoroughly, cleaning his bottom and genital area after each nappy change, and cleaning off other obvious dirt, will be enough to keep him clean between baths (see p.38).

Where to bath your baby

Although your baby is growing rapidly, it's probably still possible to wash him in a plastic baby bath or in the kitchen sink. This also means that you don't have to kneel or lean awkwardly over your baby, giving you less control over his movements.

Alternatively you can get bath supports and chairs that fit into a bath. Bath supports are usually made of towelling type fabric or foam, whereas bath chairs are often made of plastic. Your baby reclines on the support so that he is not completely immersed in the water but can be washed easily.

A relatively new type of baby bath is actually a bucket shaped one. This enables a small baby to sit up with water up to his shoulders in a supported sitting or fetal position, leaving your hands free to wash him. These bucket-shaped baths are designed for babies up to six months old. Some models are transparent, enabling you to see your baby in the water.

Once your baby starts to sit up (or maybe even before), you might think about making the transition to the big

Bathtime checklist

It's wise to have everything you need to hand before you start running your baby's bath because you can't take your eyes off him, even for a second, when he's in the water. If the phone or doorbell rings and you really must answer it, wrap your baby in a towel and take him with you.

Consult the checklist below before you start to bath your baby to ensure that you have everything you need at the ready.

● A small plastic baby bath, or a baby seat for the family bath (plus a rubber mat and tap covers).
● A gentle cleanser or mild soap.
● Warm towels and blankets to wrap your baby in help retain your baby's body heat after his bath.
● A clean sponge or flannel for washing your little one.
● A small amount of cotton wool for cleaning his eyes and face.
● Mild moisturising lotion to rub in after his bath.
● A clean nappy and pyjamas ready for bed afterwards.

Until your baby is a very confident sitter, he will need to be constantly supported when he's in the bath.

Washing your baby's hair without giving him a bath at the same time can avoid a lot of unnecessary trauma and tears.

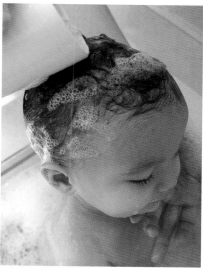

If hair washing is your baby's least favourite part of bathtime, perhaps limit these sessions to just once a week.

Dad's **Diary**

An aversion to baths
"Our daughter hated bathing with a passion from day one. She'd scream from the moment we put her into the water, until the moment we took her out. So I started to sponge bath her instead. She seemed to like that better. I started from her head and worked my way down to her feet and she really enjoyed this. When she was around six weeks old, we took it a step further and would finish off her sponge bath by dipping her feet and lower legs into the warm water in the basin. She didn't seem to mind that.

We continued with this "ritual" for a few weeks more and then I finally gave her a full bath. I started gently, dipping her feet in first and then slowly easing the rest of her body into the water. Surprisingly, once she was sitting in the baby bath she was completely fine.

She's been enjoying her bathtime ever since. Now she hates it when I get her dressed, but at least that's only a few moments of crying as opposed to the screaming we went through when she was tiny. That worked for us."

bath. There are a few things you can do to help ensure that the move into the big bath goes smoothly and that your baby is happy with the change.

If you're using the family bath, make it safer by putting a rubber bathmat in it (to make it less slippery) and covering the taps (so he doesn't burn himself).

Whatever kind of baby bath, bath chair or bath support you use, never, ever leave your baby unattended in the bath. Have everything you need for your bath ready in advance: towels, toiletries, clean nappy and pyjamas.

When running the bath, follow the guidelines on page 39. Also, for babies up to six months old, fill the bath with about 12.5 centimetres (5 inches) of water, or enough to allow your baby to recline in the water with his shoulders covered. Never fill the bath more than waist-high (in sitting position) for older babies.

Minimise body-heat loss after your baby's bath by keeping the room warm, wrapping him in a hooded towel and drying him immediately before putting

on his clean nappy. Once dressed, wrap your baby up in a dry, warm blanket. With any luck, your baby's bathtime will become one of the most enjoyable parts of your day together.

Cleaning products

Bubble baths suitable for babies are OK, but the overuse of strong cleansers and even tap water can damage the developing skin of young babies. Look for gentle pH neutral cleansers or mild soaps designed especially for babies, and use them sparingly in the first few months. You may wish to alternate baths using cleansers or bubbles with the occasional water-only bath.

Hair washing techniques

If your baby objects to having his hair washed during bathtime, there are other techniques you can try.

Hair washing doesn't have to be done every bathtime. You could wash your baby's hair just once or twice a week. This also avoids fights over hair

washing ruining an enjoyable routine. You might find it easier to wash your baby's hair outside of the bath. When he's small, you can wrap him up in a towel and hold him in a "football carry", his legs tucked under your armpit, his body supported with your arm and his head in your hand. You can then clean his hair by dipping a flannel into warm water and wiping it over his head. You can apply a mild shampoo and rinse using the sponge. Face shields are also available, to stop water or soap suds running down his face.

Try not to force the issue of hair washing. Using a sponge is fine until you're both ready to try again.

Welcome to parenthood! 0–6 weeks

Your growing baby 6 weeks to 6 months

Your older baby 6 months to one year

Baby healthcare 0–12 months

Baby massage

Massage is a great way to bond with your baby. Furthermore, apart from the clear benefits to you and your baby of feeling close, massage is also thought to help soothe common baby ailments, such as colic and dry skin. No wonder it's growing in popularity.

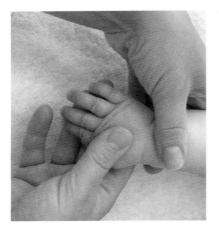

Massaging your baby is thought to have a multitude of benefits for your baby and is relaxing for you, too.

What are the benefits?

Babies love to be touched. In fact, they thrive on it. It's a critical part of their growth and development. Baby massage not only helps you and your baby bond, but it can comfort your baby when she's upset, and sometimes is even thought to ease the symptoms of colic (see p.245). Massage may also improve your baby's sleep patterns, which is always a top priority for new mums and dads.

Apart from the many benefits for your baby, massaging your baby is also a great way for you to relax and enjoy spending time together.

Before you begin

Find somewhere quiet and warm to massage your baby where you won't be disturbed. Use your bed, or your baby's cot, or even a mat on the floor, but make sure it's somewhere you'll both be comfortable. You might like to play some soothing music during the massage and burn some essential oils to relax you both – but never use essential oils on your baby's skin.

You can massage your baby any time of the day, but don't give her a massage just before or after a meal or when she needs a nap. If your baby is colicky, you could try to massage her an hour or two before her usual crying time.

Whenever you choose to massage her, make sure you're feeling relaxed and not hurried or stressed. Take a few moments before the massage to unwind yourself and ease the tension from your neck, shoulders, arms and hands.

Baby massage works best when your baby is naked so that you have direct contact with her skin and can put some baby oil, or vegetable oil, on your hands. However, if your baby prefers to be wrapped up, you can start by massaging her hands and feet, or you can gently massage her body through her clothes with dry, non-oiled hands.

Massage dos and don'ts

To ensure that both you and your baby have the best experience, follow a few simple guidelines.

Do
- Make sure the room and your hands are warm.
- Keep your hands well-oiled – your hands should glide over your baby and not drag her skin.
- Use baby oil or a vegetable oil.
- Ensure you're in a comfortable position while massaging.
- Use gentle strokes.
- Avoid the stomach area after feeding.
- Enjoy massaging your baby!

Don't
- Carry on if your baby isn't enjoying it.
- Use aromatherapy or nut-based oils.
- Massage if she's hungry or overtired.
- Massage your baby if she has a temperature, skin condition or seems otherwise unwell.
- Massage for 48 hours following an immunisation, and avoid the injection area for a week after an immunisation.
- Wake your baby for a massage.

Massaging the head and upper body

Try to look into your baby's eyes, and sing or talk to her as you do the massage. Pay attention to your baby's response: if she doesn't seem to be enjoying herself, try a lighter touch, or simply stop the massage.

Smooth strokes

Without putting oil on your baby's face, use your fingers to gently stroke from the centre of your baby's forehead to the tops of her ears. Gently stroke from the bridge of her nose, over to her cheeks. Make small circles around her cheeks, in the jaw area, with your fingertips. Make a smile on her upper lip with your thumbs. Do the same with her lower lip.

Now oil your hands and move on to her chest. Put your hands together in a prayer position over her heart. Then stroke your hands outwards and lightly flatten the palms down over her chest, and repeat this action several times.

Place one hand flat across the top of her chest without pressing down. Stroke it gently down to the top of her thighs. Repeat this massaging stroke several times, alternating your hands.

Take one of her arms in your hands and use a gentle milking motion from her armpit all the way to her wrist. Then, take her hand and gently rotate the wrist a few times in each direction. Switch arms and repeat.

Trace tiny circles all over the palm of each of your baby's hands with your thumbs. Gently take a finger between your thumb and forefinger and stroke up the finger, letting her finger slip through your grasp. Repeat on all 10 fingers.

Welcome to parenthood!
0–6 weeks

Your growing baby
6 weeks to 6 months

Your older baby
6 months to one year

Baby healthcare
0–12 months

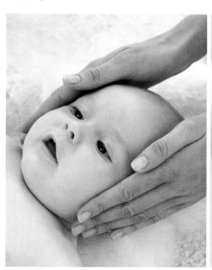

When massaging your baby's face, avoid using oil and use a gentle, stroking motion. Stroke the sides of your baby's head, and trace your fingers over her forehead, cheeks, nose, lips and chin.

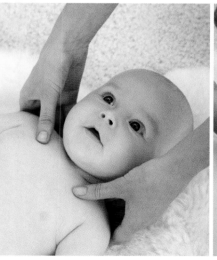

While your baby lies on her back, you can gently massage the backs of her shoulders. Then move your hands to your baby's chest; flatten your palms and massage in sweeping movements, being careful not to press down.

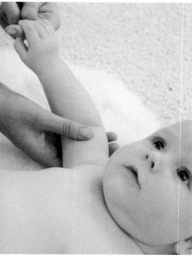

Holding your baby's hand to straighten out her arm, use your other hand to gently massage up her arm, from her armpit to her hand. Then gently stroke each of her fingers. Repeat on the other arm and hand.

Massaging the legs and abdomen

Giving your baby's legs a massage can help with muscle development, and if your baby has colic, a tummy massage may soothe the symptoms. However, the tummy is a sensitive area, so if your baby looks uncomfortable, stop. Massage in a clockwise, rather than anticlockwise, direction on the tummy.

Leg massage

Your baby's legs are a good place to begin a massage as they're less sensitive than other parts of the body. First, rub a little oil into your hands. Wrap your hands around one of your baby's thighs and pull down gently, one hand after the other, squeezing lightly, as if you're "milking" your baby's leg. Switch legs and repeat.

Next, take one foot and gently rotate it a few times in each direction; stroke the top of his foot from the ankle down to the toes. Repeat on the other foot.

Use your thumbs to trace circles over the bottom of each foot. To finish off, hold a toe between your forefinger and thumb and gently pull until your fingers slip off the end. Repeat for all 10 toes.

Tummy strokes

Although some babies enjoy having their tummy massaged, the tummy can be a sensitive area, so guage your baby's reaction and stop if he objects.

Try this soothing massage on your baby's tummy. While facing your baby, use two or three fingers to trace down the right side of his abdomen with firm

but gentle movements. Start under his ribs and go straight down to his hip joint, using some oil to smooth your way. Next, stroke from left to right across your baby's abdomen. Then stroke up from your baby's hipbone, on the left side of his tummy. Lastly, gently stroke your fingers along the top of your baby's tummy, and then stroke downwards on your baby's right side.

Note: Some studies show that baby massage reduces babies' stress levels.

It's thought to reduce levels of the stress hormones norepinephrine and epinephrine, and to release melatonin, linked with sleep.

"Baby massage is **relaxing** for you both, giving you and your baby **quiet time** together to **wind down**."

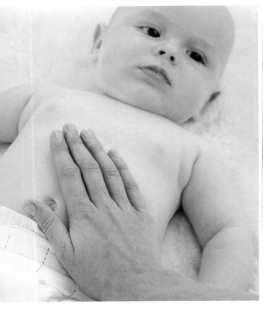

When massaging your baby's tummy, work in a clockwise direction and avoid massaging him straight after a feed (left). **Support your baby's foot** in one hand when massaging his leg and use your other

hand to work your way down his leg with a "milking" motion, from the top of the thigh down to the ankle (middle). **With your thumb**, gently massage your baby's foot and then stroke each toe (above).

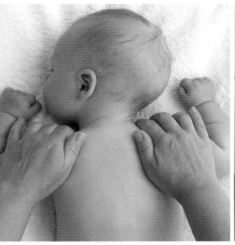

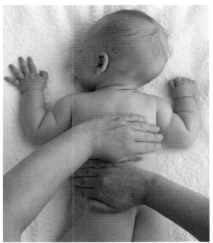

Once your baby is comfortable lying on his front, start off the back massage at the top of his back. Place your hands on either shoulder and gently massage across the tops of his arms.

With your palms flat, place your hands horizontally close to your baby's neck and then sweep them the length of his back down to his bottom. Alternate your palms so that you can maintain a constant motion.

End your baby's back massage with some single strokes from your baby's shoulders down his back to his bottom. Make the strokes gentle, but firm and talk to your baby throughout the massage.

Massaging the back

Once you've massaged your baby's front, and as long as he is still relaxed, you can turn him over onto his tummy to give him a soothing back massage. A back massage isn't advisable until around three months, when your baby has good head control and can hold his head up for a period of time, and support his weight on his forearms.

Long strokes

Gently turn your baby onto his tummy. If he doesn't seem comfortable in this position, try laying him tummy-down across your lap.

Using long, loving, gentle strokes run your hands down your baby's back from his neck to his bottom. Following the same direction, use your fingertips to very lightly massage the muscles on either side of his spine, tracing tiny circles as you go.

Finish the massage with some long, firm strokes from your baby's shoulders all the way down to his bottom. When you've finished the massage, put on a clean nappy, dress your baby and cuddle or breastfeed him. You'll probably find that he's so relaxed that he dozes straight off to sleep when you put him down.

Dad's **Diary**

Passing on skills

"Tanya has been going to baby massage classes and both she and Ellie enjoy it. Ellie seems to really chill out while she's being touched by her mum, and she's much more settled in the evenings when we put her to bed. I'd like to go along to classes, too, but they take place while I'm at work, so Tanya has been teaching me in the evenings. It's a great way for me to spend some quiet time with Ellie and I really feel that it's helping us to form a strong bond.

Tanya is breastfeeding Ellie, so they get plenty of time for skin-to-skin and eye-to-eye contact. Up until now, I haven't felt able to feel that sort of intimacy with Ellie, but learning baby massage has been a great way for me to feel closer to her.

While I'm massaging her, Ellie is very relaxed but also alert, watching me all the time while I talk to her. I think that massaging helps her get to know my smell, too, which apparently is very important to babies.

I feel more confident when I'm looking after Ellie on my own now. I know that I can comfort and soothe her, and that she knows her daddy is there for her."

Welcome to parenthood!
0–6 weeks

Your growing baby
6 weeks to 6 months

Your older baby
6 months to one year

Baby healthcare
0–12 months

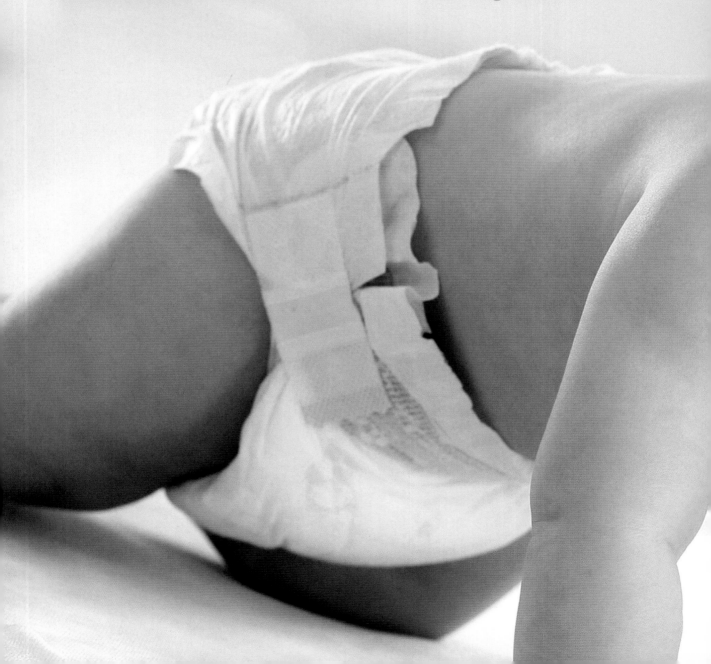

Your older baby

six months to one year

Feeding
your baby

Weaning

Weaning onto solids is a gradual process. Your baby still gets vital nutrition from her breast- or formula milk and, at first, introducing solids is about getting used to new tastes and textures. Weaning doesn't have to signal an end to breastfeeding: you can both still enjoy that closeness.

Getting started

The Department of Health recommends exclusive breastfeeding for the first six months of your baby's life to protect her against infections and diseases. After this, breastmilk alone doesn't provide enough nutrients. Some parents think that their baby is ready for solid foods earlier. If this is the case, talk to your health visitor. Solids shouldn't be started before 17 weeks, as the immune and digestive systems can't tolerate food before then.

Your baby may be ready for solids if she can hold her head upright and eat from a spoon. She should sit with support (you may have to help her initially) and be able to move food to the back of her mouth and swallow. She should be a healthy weight (double her birth weight) and may have a tooth or two. She will also show an interest in your food.

Once you start your baby on solids, you need to ensure that you practise strict kitchen hygiene (see p.177).

The first mouthful

How do you get started? First, offer her usual breastmilk or formula milk. When she's nearly full, give her one or two teaspoons of dry cereal with formula or breastmilk to make a soupy solution. Give this once a day on a soft, rubber-tipped spoon and finish with a milk feed. At first,

she may eat little. Be patient: it takes time to learn skills. As she develops a side-to-side grinding motion, add less liquid so the texture thickens. This lets her work on chewing (gumming) and swallowing.

Introducing new foods

Once she has two to three tablespoons of cereal a day, mix in a new food with her cereal, such as puréed vegetables or fruit (see p.172 for ideas). Try new foods one at a time so she gets used to tastes. This helps you to spot allergic reactions, too, such as diarrhoea, tummy ache or a rash.

Your baby's appetite will vary from one feed to the next, so watch for cues that she's full. If she refuses to open up for the next bite, turns away or starts playing with her food, she's probably full.

Nutritious milk

Your baby should have her usual breastmilk or formula milk, which provides vitamins, iron and protein in an easily digestible form. Solids will gradually replace some milk feeds, but breast or formula milk remain an important source of nutrition until she's a year old.

Broaden your baby's repertoire of foods gradually, but steadily, introducing new flavours one at a time.

Welcome to parenthood!
0–6 weeks

Your growing baby
6 weeks to 6 months

Your older baby
6 months to one year

Baby healthcare
0–12 months

Good first foods

One of the first things your baby has to learn when starting on solids is how to swallow "non fluids". So that he doesn't have to cope with new flavours as well as using different muscles, bland baby rice mixed with your baby's usual milk is the most common first food. Gluten-free baby cereals are good, too, such as iron-fortified baby rice or maize flour, mixed with your baby's usual milk.

Fruit and vegetables
However, there's no reason why you can't try vegetable or fruit purées first, introducing one food at a time. Or you may want to mix baby rice with, for example, apple or carrot purée.

Try purées of sweet vegetables, such as carrots, swede, parsnips, sweet potato, courgette or butternut squash; or purées of fruits, such as ripe cooked apple, pear, mango, papaya or mashed banana. Some experts advise beginning with green veggies, as babies can get fixed on the sweeter taste of fruits and yellow vegetables, and then may not give peas and beans a chance!

A wider range
Once your baby is happy eating from a spoon – use a rubber-tipped spoon to protect his gums – you can increase the range of foods you offer. Between six and seven months, you can try purées of lean meat or poultry, or purées of lentils or split peas. He may be ready to try purées with mixed vegetables with rice or potatoes or, if you haven't already tried one, a green vegetable purée, such as peas, cabbage, spinach or broccoli.

Try to limit the number of sweet or cereal purées your baby eats to one a day, and include a vegetable purée each day. Don't add salt or sugar, honey or other sweeteners to your baby's food.

Keep trying
As your baby gets used to his puréed dinners, his ability to join in with family meals increases enormously. You should offer him a wide range of foods to fulfil his nutrient requirements and to get him used to eating different flavours. If you get a negative reaction to a particular food from your baby, offer it again a few days later. He may always turn up his nose at some foods, but it doesn't hurt to continue offering them in the hope that they become more appealing.

If you are buying commercially produced food, the ranges normally go from four to seven months and seven months upwards. In fact, there's no nutritional reason why a baby of six months can't eat jars of food labelled seven months plus (although the consistency may need adjusting).

Systemised mum

When introducing new foods to your baby, he won't always like them straightaway – so be patient and try again later.

"Some foods and purées my baby loved immediately, others she just refused to eat! It is difficult when this happens, as I spend time preparing a new exciting blend of ingredients, or I try to hide a new flavour with something she loves in the hope that she will eat it. In the end, it's about her getting used to new textures and tastes, and being happy to eat them in her own time. If she takes a dislike to something, I wait a few days, then try it again, with something else on hand if she won't eat it again."

Don't be disheartened if your baby is less than enthusiastic about a new food! Leave it and try again in a week or so.

Tips for quick and easy purées

Giving your baby fresh, homemade food may sound challenging, but it needn't mean spending hours labouring in the kitchen. Uncooked ripe and sweet fruits, with their skins removed, make great instant purées for your baby.

● **Bananas** Mix in a little breastmilk or formula to make it less sticky.
● **Avocado** Add a little cream cheese and natural yoghurt (once your baby is seven months), and then mash together.
● **Mango** Try mixing this with a little ripe banana.
● **Papaya** Take some time to remove the black seeds before you purée it.
● **Peaches and nectarines.**
● **Pears** These work well mixed with nectarines or peaches.

Try to resist the urge to mop up constantly once your baby becomes more involved with his meals; instead, let him get on with the job at hand and clean up afterwards, rather than curb his enthusiasm mid-feed.

New tastes and textures

You may be keen to introduce all sorts of foods, but the advice on what to give when can be confusing. You may be bewildered by the "No egg, no nuts, no citrus fruits, no wheat, no raisins, no kiwi" advice. Sometimes, though, advice that applies to special circumstances, for example where there is a family history of allergies, becomes accepted as applying to all. If your family has a history of allergies, talk to your doctor to see if your baby needs to avoid certain foods for longer. Otherwise, introducing new tastes and textures regularly is an important part of the weaning process.

Expanding your baby's diet

As well as feeding your baby lean meat and poultry in purées, once he's six months old you can give him fish, too. Fresh fish, such as salmon, trout, cod and haddock, and canned fish, such as sardines and pilchards, as well as fish products, such as fish fingers, are nutritious foods for young children, and children and adults are recommended to eat at least two portions of fish a week. Avoid giving fish canned in brine to babies, though, as it is higher in salt than fish canned in oil. There are also certain fish you shouldn't give your baby: he shouldn't have swordfish, shark or marlin, which have high levels of mercury that could affect the development of his nervous system.

Between seven and nine months, you can give your baby a wider range of starchy foods, such as couscous, pasta, breadsticks, breakfast cereals and oats, as well as normal rice. You can also introduce well-cooked eggs; dairy products, such as cheese and yoghurt (although avoid cow's milk as a drink before one year) and citrus fruits, such as oranges and satsumas.

Gradually make his meals thicker in consistency, too, and start to include a few "lumpier" ingredients to help him get used to chewing and swallowing different textures of food.

Which foods to introduce, and when

It's usual to start your baby off on puréed foods and then gradually introduce lumpier consistencies.

● At six months, give vegetables and fruits, such as carrots, swede, potatoes, sweet potatoes, green vegetables, ripe cooked apples, pears, mangos and that old favourite, mashed banana. Also at six months, add purées of lean meats and fish; watch out for fish bones.

● At seven months, add mixed vegetables with potatoes or rice.

● At seven to nine months, include mashed or minced foods containing lumps. Starchy foods, such as bread and pasta, can be introduced. You can also try well-cooked eggs, citrus fruits, and dairy products, such as yoghurt and cheese.

● Finger foods are great once he can hold things, and give him some control. Try cooked green beans or carrots, cubes of cheese, slices of banana or soft pear.

ParentsAsk...

What is baby-led weaning?

Baby-led weaning means forgetting purées and weaning spoons and simply letting your baby feed himself. Many parents unconsciously choose baby-led weaning, particularly with a second or third baby. Babies love to copy older siblings and try to grab food from their plates, and are often happier if allowed to feed themselves. At family mealtimes, offer a selection of nutritious finger foods suitable for your baby's age and let him join in. Foods shaped like a chip, or that have a handle, such as cooked broccoli spears are great if he hasn't yet developed his pincer grip (see p.174).

Starting on finger foods

Between the age of seven and nine months, your baby will start to develop the skills necessary to eat finger foods. She'll probably start trying to pick up objects with her thumb and forefinger – a skill called the "pincer grasp". She'll also continue to put everything she can into her mouth, another sign that she's ready to expand her diet.

If your baby starts reaching for food on other people's plates, she's not being rude, she's just trying to mimic you. She'll start to imitate chewing patterns as well now, moving her jaw from side to side. She still doesn't have enough teeth to chew properly yet, but it's important that she gradually gets used to swallowing lumpier foods.

When your baby starts to display all of the above behaviour and skills, it's time to start offering her finger foods, such as sticks of well-cooked carrot, chunks of banana or unsalted breadsticks and mini rice cakes, so that she can practise feeding herself.

Other good finger foods include cheese and peeled apple chunks. Slices of bread or toast are good (as long as you avoid granary or multigrain breads for now because the hard pieces may increase the risk of choking). Pressing the bread with a rolling pin before toasting or cutting into fingers can help to avoid crumbs or lumps of the bread falling off. Your baby may also like tiny, finger-friendly sandwiches with a fruit or savoury filling.

Try to avoid sweet biscuits and rusks so your baby doesn't get into the habit of expecting sweet snacks.

It's best to avoid small foods, such as raisins, which present a choking hazard, until your baby is able to chew them well. Always stay with your baby when she is feeding herself.

Larger chunks of food, such as a slice of watermelon (seeds removed), are easier for a baby to grasp and ideal first finger foods.

Bananas are the perfect portable baby food, easy to carry around and peel for an instant meal when you're out and about.

Easily held foods, such as steamed broccoli spears, provide nutritious snacks and enhance your baby's chewing skills.

Parents**Talk...**

"My little girl had a sweet tooth when I started introducing solids. I started her on cereal or rice mixed with breastmilk, but she wasn't interested, no matter how many aeroplane noises I made. When I mashed up parsnips, swede and carrots though, she couldn't get enough."
Megan, 28, first-time mum

"Once my daughter became used to the cereal mixed in with her breastmilk, I started to include chunkier, soft lumps. We then moved on to mashed foods and finger foods. I cut bread, bananas, melon, carrots and cooked potatoes into bite-sized pieces and she loved gumming them. I think getting her used to finger foods really helped her hand–eye coordination and the development of her motor skills. It was also a great way to get her used to a variety of different foods and avoid fussy eating. Finger foods are easily digested, too."
Sal, 33, mother of two

Combining breastfeeding and solids

Even after the introduction of solids, your baby's milk, whether breast or formula, is her most important nutritional source for the first year. It's fine to continue breastfeeding after the first year. As long as you are giving your baby breastfeeds, even if it's just once or twice a day, your body will continue to supply breastmilk.

Winding down breastfeeding

If you decide to reduce breastfeeds, or move to formula, experts recommend that you stop gradually. Stopping abruptly can be upsetting for your baby and may be painful for you, leaving you with engorged breasts or mastitis (see p.112). Some experts recommend following your baby's signals as to when to start winding down breastfeeding. When you do wind down breastfeeding, it can require patience and time, depending on how quickly your baby adjusts. Some mums say it takes only a few weeks, especially if their baby is becoming more interested in all the exciting foods now on offer. Others say it can take anything up to six months.

At first, offer the breast only when your baby indicates she wants it. If she's uninterested or distracted when you feed her, she may be signalling that it's a good time to wean her off the breast. Drop a feed and offer a bottle of milk instead; you can use your own pumped milk, or infant milk formula.

Your baby's daily needs

By seven months, your baby should be eating semi-solids three times a day. A typical day's intake may be her usual milk feeds; iron-fortified cereal; vegetables; small amounts of meats, poultry or fish; yoghurt; hard-boiled egg; well-cooked lentils and cheese and fruit.

Continuing closeness

Weaning your baby off the breast needn't signal an end to the intimacy you and she have established through breastfeeding. It just means you have to replace breastfeeding with other nurturing activities. If you often fed your baby to comfort her, find other ways to soothe her. Read a book or sing her a song, or enjoy some dedicated playtime.

Breastmilk continues to give your baby essential nutrients throughout her first year of life, even once she's started on solids.

ParentsAsk...

What drinks should my baby have?

There are flavoured or plain waters that are marketed solely for babies, but these can be expensive and aren't necessary. Cooled boiled tap water is sufficient; if your baby gets used to water rather than juice, she'll be less likely to have tooth decay in the future. If you do give juice, dilute it with water and give it with food.

A baby who is enjoying infant formula at six months can continue to use it up to and beyond one year of age.

If you've been breastfeeding, you may want to continue with this for as long as you both wish. You may want to consider introducing a soft spout or lidded beaker containing cooled, boiled water before one year.

It's important to wait until your baby is one year old before you introduce cow's milk because it doesn't contain sufficient iron for your baby before then, although small amounts of cow's milk can be used in cooking from six months.

Lidded beakers with easy-to-suck spouts are good first cups and let your baby supplement milk feeds with water.

Which foods to avoid in the first year

While you want to introduce your baby to as many tastes and textures as you can, there are some foods that you should avoid giving to her in the first year of her life.

● Don't introduce your baby to salt, sugar, honey (which can contain bacteria that can cause botulism in babies) or artificial sweeteners. Try sweetening desserts with mashed banana or a purée

of stewed dried fruit, or use expressed breastmilk or formula milk.

● Don't feed your baby foods that carry a risk of food poisoning, such as soft mould-ripened cheeses (camembert, brie), liver pâté and soft-boiled or raw eggs.

● Don't give your baby low-fat spreads, yoghurts or reduced-fat cheeses. Always offer your little one the full-fat versions because she needs the calories.

Welcome to parenthood!
0–6 months

Your growing baby
6 weeks to 6 months

Your older baby
6 months to one year

Baby healthcare
0–12 months

Lightly steaming fresh vegetables ensures that essential vitamins and minerals aren't lost in the cooking process (above).
Mini electric food blenders, or hand-held electric blenders, are useful kitchen implements, enabling you to blend your baby's food to the right consistency (middle).
Storage trays allow you to make up batches of purées and freeze them in individual meal-sized portions for your baby (right).

Systemised mum

Being well equipped will help you and your baby to concentrate on the important thing – his food.

"My baby, Joe, was six months old before starting solids, and first I made sure that I had everything I needed. Before buying a highchair, I did lots of research on websites and asked friends for recommendations.

The feeding items that I found really useful were plastic weaning spoons that change colour if your baby's food is too hot, and plastic bowls with lids that can also go into the freezer. I'd definitely recommend getting as many bibs as possible – you can never have too many!

I wanted Joe to have home-cooked food, so I invested in a kitchen device that is an all-in one blender and steamer that even defrosts food. It saves a lot on washing up and means it's easy to prepare small amounts of food at a time."

Feeding equipment

As with many aspects of babycare, there are a few essential items you need to invest in before starting your baby on solids. Getting equipped will help you to organise your baby's meals and ensure that he has the equipment he needs to help him tackle solids successfully.

The basics

When you first start your baby on solids, it's good to have a range of small plastic containers with lids. Make sure they are suitable for the microwave, freezer and dishwasher. If your little one develops a habit of throwing his dinner on the floor, try bowls with suction cups underneath.

The spoon you use to feed your baby should have a soft rubber tip, a shallow bowl and a long handle to reach into jars. Some spoons are heat sensitive and change colour to show you when food is too hot. Your baby will want to try holding his own spoon from around six months, and this is an important step towards him feeding himself.

Trainer cups

When it comes to cups, there are two things to think about: ease of sipping and lack of leaking. Cups with sipper spouts are easy for a baby to drink from, but they can dribble. Cups with vacuum valves in the top won't leak, but babies have to work harder to get a drink. The latter tend to be better for older babies who are able to suck harder. Have a trainer cup at the ready before your baby gives up his bottle.

Seating arrangements

Once your baby can sit up on his own unsupported, you'll need a highchair for feeding. Most parents opt for either an old-fashioned wooden chair or a modern metal/plastic highchair, but a special booster seat may do if space is tight. Bibs are important, too. Small, basic cloth bibs are all your baby needs to begin with, but you may find that you need something more substantial as he gets older – and messier.

Food hygienes

Once your baby starts solid foods, you'll need to think carefully about hygiene as babies' tummies are particularly susceptible to bugs and infections.

Taking precautions

Wash your hands before preparing your baby's meals. Food prepared in advance should be cooled and stored in the fridge, and you should freeze anything that won't be used within 24 hours. Defrost food thoroughly before you cook it (unless the label says otherwise).

When reheating food, make sure it's piping hot throughout (you should see steam coming out) and let it cool down before you give it to your baby: test a bit on the inside of your wrist to see if it's a comfortable temperature. Don't reheat anything more than once. You can reheat food in a microwave, but stir it well to avoid hotspots and let the food cool down before giving it to your baby.

If your baby leaves any food in his bowl after a meal, always throw it away. Food that has been in contact with saliva (from your baby's mouth or a feeding spoon) will contain bacteria that will multiply if kept.

Take particular care when cooking certain foods. Cook eggs until the yolk and white are solid and cook meats until they are no longer pink in the middle.

Check best-before and use-by dates. Also, if you're using prepared baby foods and you have any uneaten baby food in a jar (that hasn't been heated up or been in contact with your baby's mouth) you can keep it in the fridge for 24 hours after it's been opened.

A clean eating area

Wash highchairs, bibs and eating areas in hot soapy water, or give them a good wipe with an antibacterial cleaner. Change kitchen cloths and tea towels frequently. Keep the kitchen as clean as you can, especially the floor, where babies love to crawl.

If your baby eats finger foods or eats with his hands, remember to wash his hands before he eats his meals.

Working mum

Preparing and freezing batches of puréed food can set you up for the week ahead.

"I'm about to return to work and the timing isn't great because I've only just started weaning my baby onto solids. I've been a demon in the kitchen recently! I've been puréeing parsnips, broccoli, carrots, potatoes and pears. My daughter loves them all, although I must say she prefers the sweetness of a banana to green beans. Don't we all? The kitchen has been a bit of a mess at times, as you can imagine.

I do like to know she's eating only the best, so I've been spending most of my Sunday evenings with my trusty blender. I make enough purées for the whole week and store them in the freezer. Her childminder gives her one for lunch, and when I get home I just defrost another one. The last thing I feel like doing is mashing vegetables after work, so it really has made life so much easier."

Dad's **Diary**

Being involved

"Starting Lola on solids has been great fun – and a challenge at times! Katrina breastfed her exclusively for six months, which left me out in the cold somewhat when it came to feeding (not that I minded at two in the morning). However, now she's having solids, I'm enjoying being involved. It hasn't always been easy. The first time I fed her – a bowl of my finest puréed apple and pear – more of it ended up around her face. I managed to get some into her mouth – it was getting it to stay in that proved more of a challenge!

Two months on, Lola really adores her food. As a bit of a foodie myself, I love to see her react to all the new tastes and textures. However, she can be choosy at times; she's not a fan of cauliflower and definitely favours fruity desserts over savoury starters (just like her mum), but on the whole she's a good eater.

She loves to hold the spoon now herself, too. The only problem with letting her feed herself is that she's unable to find her mouth, so she ends up with food on her eyes, nose, ears and chin. Everywhere, in fact, except in her mouth."

Your baby will become more independent, as she becomes more confident about feeding.

Welcome to parenthood!
0–6 weeks

Your growing baby
6 weeks to 6 months

Your older baby
6 months to one year

Baby healthcare
0–12 months

Sleep and your baby

Your baby's sleep

Sleep is essential for your baby's growth and development, but don't panic if she suddenly starts waking again in the night, or sleeps lightly at times. Babies' sleep can be affected by many things, including growth spurts and new-found physical skills, such as sitting up.

What your baby needs

When your baby is between six months and a year old, she will gradually sleep more during the night and less in the day. Most babies are physically capable of sleeping through the night from the age of six months, although may still continue to wake after this age.

A colourful mobile suspended over your baby's cot creates an enjoyable and welcoming sleeping environment.

80%
of a premature baby's sleep is REM sleep.

Experts say premature babies spend most of their sleep in REM "dream" sleep. This drops to 50 per cent for full-term babies, 33 per cent by three years and 25 per cent by 10 to 14 years.

Six to nine months

Between the ages of six and nine months, your baby needs around 14 hours of sleep every day. By now, she is capable of sleeping for as long as seven hours at a time. If your baby sleeps for longer periods than this, she is probably waking up briefly, but has figured out how to settle herself back to sleep – a sign that she's becoming a good sleeper. She's probably having a couple of hour-and-a-half to two-hour naps each day now: one in the morning and one during the afternoon. Keeping consistent times for bedtime and daytime naps will help to regulate her sleep patterns.

Nine to twelve months

Between the ages of nine and 12 months, your baby will probably sleep for around 10 to 12 hours during the night and nap twice a day for an hour and a half to two hours at a time. Make sure that she's getting about this amount of sleep, because it is crucial to her development, which is rapid at this time. Try to stick to a consistent daytime nap routine, too. If that slips, you may find that you have more trouble getting her to sleep at night, and she may start waking up more often.

 Systemised mum

Identifying why your baby is waking at night is the first step to resolving the issue.

"When Esme was born I suppose I should have expected she'd be a light sleeper – after all, I wake up if the dog sneezes downstairs! But at around 10 months she started waking every couple of hours in the night and it really hit us hard. This went on for a few weeks. At first, I breastfed her when she woke, but she would just comfort suck for a minute or two and then go back to sleep. I found that all she wanted was a cuddle. So instead of picking her up, we experimented with just rubbing her cheek or kissing her so that she'd know we were there, and then leaving it longer and longer before going back in to her.

It was hard to hear her crying and I felt like the cruellest mum in the world, but by the third night, she was going off to sleep by herself and sleeping really well. Now we put her to bed every night at about 7–7.30pm and she generally sleeps through until around 6am. Occasionally, she does wake in the night, but we simply rub her cheek and hush her and she falls back to sleep in no time."

Welcome to parenthood!
0–6 weeks

Your growing baby
6 weeks to 6 months

Your older baby
6 months to one year

Baby healthcare
0–12 months

Routines for your older baby

While you've probably already set up a bedtime routine, at this age your baby will really begin to participate and you may find you take longer over all of his favourite rituals. Whether you include a warm bath, a quiet game, extending his story time, singing a lullaby, or all of those things, carry out the routine in the same order and at the same time every night, just as you did before.

Resisting bedtime

It's not unusual for older babies to resist being put to bed, especially when there's a lot going on and he wants to be part of the action. You could try creating a regular pre-bedtime ritual.

Let him say goodnight to each family member, to each of his teddies, even to family photos. If he still won't settle, it might help to potter quietly in his room, tidying up and putting away clothes until he calms down and falls asleep.

Night-lights

Many parents wonder if their baby needs a night-light. They can be a source of comfort for toddlers and older children who are afraid of the dark, but they're not necessary for babies. Night-time anxiety doesn't develop until children are two or three years old, when their cognitive development enables them to understand the concept of fear

and they're capable of imagining scary things. In the meantime, your baby will sleep better in a dark room.

Early waking in older babies

Many parents complain that their baby wakes up too early. As your baby gets older, he may be able to amuse himself for a while when he wakes. You can place a couple of familiar soft toys in his cot in the night. If you're in the habit of bringing your baby into your bed when he wakes up, but you'd rather he slept longer on his own, be consistent about keeping him in his cot. You'll have a week or so of tired mornings, but you'll solve the issue in the long run.

Your baby's comfort object

Allowing your baby to adopt a favourite "comfort" object can help him to deal with separation from you.

Bedtime buddy

From six months onwards, you might notice that your baby has adopted a special comfort object, such as a blanket, a teddy bear or a muslin cloth. These soft, cuddly objects are usually held close to the mouth and nose and offer him familiarity and a sense of security, especially when he's away from you. These comforters can be an enormous help at bedtime, especially if you're trying to help him self-soothe – after all, he may be forced to leave you behind, but no one can stop him from taking his "blankie" with him. If your baby doesn't already have a comfort object, it may be a good idea to introduce one now.

As your baby develops, so will his capacity to enjoy a more extended bedtime routine. He'll adore looking at picture books with mum or dad, and you'll probably find that you both look forward to this special part of the day.

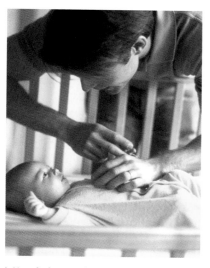

Your baby may be sleeping blissfully, but noises and snuffles in the night can be mutually disturbing.

Welcome to parenthood
0–6 weeks

Your growing baby
6 weeks to 6 months

Your older baby
6 months to one year

Baby healthcare
0–12 months

Parents**Talk...**

"My eight-month-old still wakes me up a couple of times a night. I check he's not hungry and that his nappy is clean, but it seems all he wants is a cuddle. I stay with him briefly just to comfort and reassure him."
Robyn, 33, first-time mum

"My baby has started teething and I don't think I've ever been this tired! I'm struggling to comfort her. I've tried rubbing a finger and cold spoon on her gums and teething rings. I keep telling myself it's just a phase."
Allanah, 29, first-time mum

"Each time my baby's dummy drops out, he wakes up screaming. I have to go into his nursery just to pop it back in his mouth. I rue the day we ever went down the dummy route!"
Bernadette, 25, first-time mum

"We live in a semi-detached house, and our neighbour's music kept waking our baby. We went round there to talk to him about it and it's been so much better since. If you stay calm and polite, you can solve problems like this."
Jennifer, 24, first-time mum

Your baby's room

Still haven't put the finishing touches on the nursery? Don't fret. Experts advise keeping your baby in your room for the first six months, and even after he settles into his room he won't notice that the lampshade clashes. What he may notice, though, is that after spending his whole life with you there, you're suddenly … not. Or, he may be fine, while you might be longing to see him, or panicking at how quiet he seems.

Making the move

Your baby can't stay in your room forever, even if you and your partner agree on co-sleeping or a family bed. So whenever he does make the swap to a room without a view (of you), take steps to prepare her, or you, or whoever is most troubled by the change. You can start by considering the reasons why it's important to disrupt what may have seemed the perfect arrangement.

First of all, what does your partner think? While some dads are as anxious about every slight pause or murmur from their baby, many are not nearly as tuned into his breathing as the baby's mother. What your partner may have thought about in the past few months, though, is the presence of your baby in what has always been the private space you share together. If you feel ready to get your sex life back on track, the best boost will be moving your baby out.

Of course, the decision to relocate your baby to his own room shouldn't revolve solely around your desire for intimacy, but should be reached with everyone's best interests considered. Perhaps one or both of you find your sleep disturbed by your baby's noises. Or maybe he wakes when you come in the room, especially now he's older, which can lead to problems later if he can only fall asleep with you next to him.

Chances are, your baby won't be too troubled by the move – or at least not for long. After all, he'll have the familiarity of his own bed, and you will still be on hand if he wakes. He may, however, pick up on your anxiety, so try not to make a big deal out of the move. A baby monitor may help to ease your worries.

Putting a baby monitor in the nursery can allay your fears of neglecting your baby during the night once he's in his own room.

Settling and sleep training your older baby

Between six months and a year, babies who have never had sleep problems may suddenly start waking up at night or have difficulty falling asleep. Why? Sleep disturbances often come hand-in-hand with separation anxiety, when she wakes in the night, misses you and worries you won't return. Night waking in older babies is also linked to new developmental stages.

You are not alone if you're having difficulty getting your baby to sleep at night. About a quarter of children under five in the UK have sleep problems, particularly refusing to go to bed or waking in the night, and the two often go together. As your baby grows, it's important to sort out sleep difficulties, because it can put pressure on relationships between you and your partner, and between you and your baby.

Sleep and development

Disrupted sleep may be linked with your baby reaching major developmental milestones. She is learning to sit up, roll over, crawl and possibly even pull herself up to a standing position – an impressive list of achievements! Not surprisingly, she probably won't want to stop practising her new skills at bedtime and may get so excited that she'll wake up to try them one more time.

However, if she gets too energetic – or worse, if she stands up and can't get back down – she won't be able to go back to sleep right away. If that's the case, she'll soon start crying for you. You

will need to teach her how to lie down if she's stuck in an upright position, but how you help her soothe herself back to sleep is up to you.

Your baby's sudden burst in development isn't the same as a growth spurt, so feeding her during the night won't help her sleep better. In fact, it may prolong the problem and make it worse, because she may learn to depend on a feed to fall asleep.

After nine months, if your baby is still waking in the night, you could try moving her afternoon nap to an earlier time and making it shorter. When you do put her down in the evenings, try leaving the door to your baby's room ajar so she can hear you and be reassured that you're nearby.

What the experts say

Most experts say it's fine to go in and check on your baby if she starts waking again in the night, but after that the advice varies from staying with her until she settles, perhaps cuddling and rocking her, to settling her without picking her up (see pp.128–29).

As your baby gets older, you may consider letting her cry for progressively longer intervals of time during the night before you go to her. If you do decide on this approach, start by leaving your baby for five minutes, and then increase this to 10 minutes the next time, and so on. Between intervals, you can spend two to three minutes with your baby, reassuring her by talking to her and possibly patting her on the back. Don't pick her up or rock her or give her a dummy – she'll only learn to depend on these conditions to fall asleep.

A reassuring word and soothing stroke may be all that is needed to help your baby settle herself back to sleep.

ParentsAsk...

My baby hates her cot. What should I do?

Parents who have a baby who doesn't sleep well often report that she hates her cot. However, it's unclear whether a baby hates it, or simply doesn't want to go there to sleep on her own. For some babies, being put to bed in a cot means adjusting to a new way of falling asleep. Instead of being fed or rocked to sleep, as she may have been accustomed to, being put down in a cot means she has to fall asleep by herself.

Before making a drastic change in your baby's bedtime routine, work with her on making the cot a place where she wants to be. Put some favourite toys in the cot during the day when she isn't sleepy. Make a game out of reaching in and getting them out. Then step it up to putting her down in the cot so that she can get the toy. Eventually, she'll think of her cot as a good place and hopefully will no longer resist being put down.

When you hear your baby wake at night, another method to try is to give him a few minutes to settle himself before going to him (see p.124)

Conversely, some parents and experts don't agree with letting babies "cry it out", even when they're older.

An appropriate response

With developmental milestones coming thick and fast, many babies this age wake at night because they're just too excited to sleep. If you think this might be the reason why your baby wakes, some experts think you should let him find his own way back to sleep with self-comforting techniques, such as thumb sucking. When he wakes up, don't feed him or go to him at his first cry.

Another approach encourages flexibility. Don't let your baby cry it out, but instead try to find the source of his wakefulness, such as a full nappy, hunger, upset routines during the day, a stuffy nose, or even irritating pyjamas.

Your older baby may start to develop some self-soothing techniques, such as thumb sucking, to settle back to sleep.

Increase his daytime attachment to you (breastfeeding, playing and cuddling) and let dad play the role of night-time co-comforter so both parents can help their baby fall back to sleep.

There's no "right" way to help your baby to settle or sleep through, so choose an approach that works for you all.

Letting dad comfort your baby in the night encourages your baby to settle back to sleep without a breastfeed.

Dad's **Diary**

A regular bedtime

"Now that Tracy is back at work full-time, we take it in turns to put James to bed. I've always been involved in bedtime, especially when Tracy was on maternity leave, so he's happy for me to put him to bed. I bath him in the evenings while Tracy cooks dinner. He doesn't need a bath every day, but it helps to settle him down for the evening, and he associates it with bedtime now. Once he's in his pyjamas, I sit in his nursery with the nightlight on and read him a story. He often falls asleep while I'm reading, although we've been trying to let him fall asleep on his own. Being at work all day, it's tempting to keep him up later in the evening, but we resist as he really benefits from the regular bedtime."

Welcome to parenthood!
0–6 weeks

Your growing baby
6 weeks to 6 months

Your older baby
6 months to one year

Baby healthcare
0–12 months

Development and play

Your baby's development

With every month that passes now, your baby develops new skills. Those magical milestones, such as rolling over, crawling and, eventually, walking, are big moments for proud parents, but don't worry if your baby seems slower or faster than others: all babies develop at their own pace.

What your baby can do now

Your baby is expending a lot of energy now in developing new skills. You can help by being patient and encouraging.

On the move

At around six months (sometimes later), your baby's hand control is developed enough that he can grab a toy; soon, he'll practise moving it from one hand to the other. He may also discover that dropping objects is lots of fun. It's too soon to tell whether he is left- or right-handed.

By this age, most babies can roll over in each direction, so keep a hand on him during nappy changes, and always watch him on a bed or a raised surface.

A greater awareness

Towards the end of his first year, your baby may begin to seem anti-social, crying when you leave his side or anxious when held by someone other than you or your partner. Many babies go through separation anxiety, which starts at six to seven months and peaks between 10 and 18 months. Your baby will prefer you to the exclusion of others and may be distressed when you're not around. Only your presence will calm him.

Early conversations

By six months, your baby sees and hears almost as well as you do. Now, his communication skills are expanding rapidly, with squeals, bubbling sounds, operatic octave changes and possibly babbling. At this age, about half of all babies babble, repeating one syllable, such as "ba", "ma" or "ga", and some may soon start to use two-syllable sounds. Your baby can also recognise different tones and inflections by now, and may cry if you speak to him harshly.

Remember, each baby meets both physical and mental milestones at his or her own pace. These milestones are simply a guide to what your baby has the potential to accomplish – if not right now, then shortly.

ParentsAsk...

Can I help my son's development?
What works best when you learn something: instruction or exploring on your own? Probably a bit of both! It's the same for babies: structured and free-play contribute, in different ways, to his development.

Structured, parent-led activities introduce new ideas. Showing your baby how to stack toys, for example rings, teaches the concept of "bigger and smaller", as well as ideas about patterns. To truly master the ideas, your baby needs to explore what happens when he tries stacking. He'll benefit from both observing you and by exploring himself.

More important in the long run is that he gets lots of opportunities for play and that adults don't over-manage it. Demonstrating new ideas is fun, but he should decide what he wants to do with the information. For example, those stacking rings can also be loaded into a dump truck. Babies use play to help them understand concepts and ideas. They are the best judges of how to play, and will learn naturally in the process.

Welcome to parenthood!
0–6 months

Your growing baby
6 weeks to 6 months

Your older baby
6 months to one year

Baby healthcare
0–12 months

Your baby's physical development

The days of your baby spending most of her time lying on her back are fast receding. Over the next few months, your baby's muscles will develop, greatly increasing her strength, and her balance will improve as she masters the skills of sitting up, crawling and, eventually, walking.

Seven months

Your baby can now support some of her weight on her legs, and she loves to bounce. She may be able to get into a sitting position from lying on her stomach, by pushing up on her arms.

She's probably able to sit unsupported (which frees her hands for exploring), and will turn when sitting to reach a desired object. By now she can probably scoop things up with just one hand and transfer them to the other hand fairly easily. She may also be able to clasp her hands together and, with your help, sip from a two-handled cup.

Eight months

Once she's eight months old, your baby will probably be able to sit confidently without support and may be crawling (or starting to crawl) or moving about by bottom-shuffling. She may also be starting to pull herself up to a standing position while holding onto furniture.

At around this time, your baby may look for dropped objects, and use her index finger to point at them. She can use her fingers to scoop up a piece of food and hold it with her fist closed, and can open her hand and fingers at will to drop objects. She may be beginning to master the pincer grasp, too: the delicate manoeuvre that lets her pick up small objects with her thumb and forefinger.

Your baby's vision is now almost adult-like in its clarity and depth perception. Her short-range sight is still better than her long-range vision, but it's good enough to recognise people and objects from across a room.

Nine months

At nine months, your baby may be close to fully fledged walking (although this may be several months away). She may be able to crawl upstairs and "cruise" – which means moving around upright while holding onto furniture. Your baby is also learning how to bend her knees and how to sit after standing, which is harder than you might think!

"By **eight months**, your baby may be **mobile** at last, **crawling**, or **bottom-shuffling** her way around."

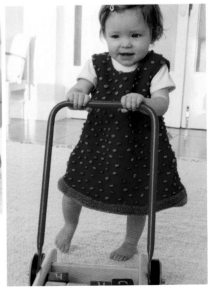

Once your baby has sufficient strength in both her arms and legs, she may lift herself off the ground and start to crawl (above)!
Your baby's centre of balance will continue to improve, eventually enabling her to sit confidently without any other support (middle).
A push-along baby walker helps your baby to practise the art of being upright before she takes her first solo wobbly steps (right).

You can help your baby when she's upright by kneeling in front of her and holding out your hands encouragingly; by holding both her hands and walking her towards you; or by buying a baby walker your baby can hold onto and push.

Ten months

By the time they're 10 months old, most babies are usually able to crawl well on their hands and knees, with their limbs straight and their trunk parallel to the floor. Many babies start trying to crawl before 10 months, but only master the skill properly now.

At this age, your baby can also sit confidently and may even walk while holding onto furniture with just one hand, possibly letting go momentarily and standing without support. Those magical first steps towards your baby becoming more independent are just around the corner.

Your baby's fingers are becoming more agile all the time. She's intrigued by tiny things and is still likely to taste-test everything she picks up; this is fine as long as objects are not so small that she could choke on them.

Eleven months

Your baby is no longer that helpless infant who couldn't do anything without your help. She still needs plenty of care and support from you, but her growing independence is becoming apparent. She may walk while gripping your hand, and she'll hold out her arm or leg to help

Note: Left- and right-handedness is thought to be a familial trait.

If both you and your partner are left-handed, your child has approximately a 45 to 50 per cent chance of being left-handed as well.

Your baby's coordination is becoming ever more finessed, allowing her to increase her interaction and play repertoire.

you dress her. She may soon be able to grip a cup and drink from it independently, and may be able to hand-feed herself an entire meal.

Twelve months

That major rite of passage is almost here – at some point during this month, your baby may take her first wobbly steps alone (although she may not do this for several more weeks or months yet, so don't worry if your baby doesn't become a toddler during this month). Most babies make those early strides on their tiptoes with their feet turned outwards. Also, at around this time, your baby may begin showing more of an interest in feeding herself with a spoon, although she may frequently miss her mouth!

Your baby probably thinks it's great fun to push, throw and knock down everything these days. She's also becoming more interactive, for example she'll give you a toy as well as take one, and she likes games where she can put things such as blocks into containers and then dump them out again. This also works with kitchen pots and pans where she can put the smaller ones

Systemised mum

A safe environment allows your baby to explore without constant reprimand from you.

"Jasper started crawling when he was just seven months; then there was no stopping him. He was off exploring at every chance he got, using chairs in the living room to haul himself up to a standing position. So instead of leaving things to chance, I decided to arrange the room to make a safe 'journey' for him from corner to corner, with furniture to grab on to (but not low enough to climb).

First, I removed anything that might topple over, such as our reading lamp, and moved an armchair in front of the TV. I put the sofa in front of the bookcase and removed the tablecloth, in case he tugged it down with everything on it! I attached corner guards, fitted socket covers and put childproof locks on all but one of the cupboards. In this, I kept some toys to 'reward' him for getting there under his own steam.

It took a few minutes to Jasper-proof the room each morning, and of course I always stayed with him in case he toppled over. But within no time he was confidently negotiating the room and he was walking by the time he was 11 months."

inside the bigger ones, as well as enjoy the loud sounds they make when banged together!

Around now, your baby's play repertoire will probably start expanding. As well as practising mastering her fine motor skills (she's got that thumb and forefinger grasp down to pat) she will also become interested in exercising her larger arm and leg muscles.

Welcome to parenthood! 0–6 weeks

Your growing baby 6 weeks to 6 months

Your older baby 6 months to one year

Baby healthcare 0–12 months

Senses and learning

From six months, your baby's brain develops rapidly, enhancing his abilty to process information. His learning and memory skills grow constantly and he needs plenty of stimulation.

Six months

By this age, your baby uses all of his senses to explore his environment. He will delight in squishing a soft rubber ball, gnawing a teething ring or hearing a bell sound inside a stuffed animal.

Six-month-old babies love turn-taking games, especially ones that involve sounds and language. A good way to teach your child – and make him laugh at the same time – is to make animal noises and encourage him to copy them.

Seven months

Your baby is starting to understand object permanence (see p.146) and loves games in which people or things appear and disappear. Try hiding an object under a blanket for him to discover.

He's also beginning to understand how objects relate to one another in three-dimensional space. He may be able to sort toys, grouping items such as blocks by size. At this age, babies also form attachments to certain toys.

Eight months

At around eight months, babies start to examine and explore objects more by shaking them, banging them, dropping them, throwing them and tasting them. Your baby understands more about how objects relate to one another, too. For example, he realises that smaller objects fit inside bigger ones.

Over the next few months, your baby will start to use objects for their intended functions; for example, he will use a toy brush to brush his, or his teddy's, hair, drink from a cup and will babble on his toy telephone.

Nine months

Your baby can now put objects in a container and remove them. If you take a toy away, your increasingly assertive baby is likely to object. He's really starting to be able to make his needs and wants known.

Fact: By eight months, your baby's vision is now almost adult-like in its clarity and depth perception. Though your baby's short-range sight is still better than his long-range sight, his vision is improving all the time and he can now identify people or objects within a room.

Learning that an object still exists even if he can't see it is an important development in your baby's understanding of the world.

ParentsTalk...

"I bought my son a bucket and spade and he can't get enough of it. We have a sandpit in the garden and he spends hours filling and emptying. I can't see the appeal, but it keeps him entertained!"
Hazel, 32, first-time mum

"My daughter loved watching me talk on my mobile and would often imitate me, so I bought her a toy phone. She holds the receiver, pushes the buttons and babbles. It's a great way to keep her entertained while I'm having a conversation."
Cheryl, 27, first-time mum

"My baby loves ball play. At first, he just pushed balls around, but now he can stand, the game has reached a new level. He's bouncing them on the floor and chasing them around. He's a little wobbly so I have to play "the fetcher" a fair bit. I don't mind. It's great he's having such a good time."
Mary, 34, mother of two

"My son loves shape sorters. He enjoys figuring out why the square block won't go into the round hole. He never gets annoyed, just determined. I have to resist helping him because I don't want to ruin the game."
Frankie, 36, mother of three

Everyday household items can be excellent toys for babies, allowing them to explore textures, shapes and sounds.

Your baby's babbling is probably starting to sound more like real words. Although he still comprehends more from your tone than from your actual words, he may respond to his name by looking around to see who called.

Ten months

At 10 months, your baby is beginning to understand many simple words and phrases. When he rattles off a sentence of gibberish, respond with, "Oh, really? How interesting." He'll probably smile and keep chattering away to you. Soon, you may notice some words you actually understand, as well as other forms of communication, such as pointing and grunting.

Eleven months

Words and word-like sounds are now spilling out of your baby – words he's able to use meaningfully. As the frontal lobes of his brain gradually develop, coinciding with the arrival of reasoning and speech, you can encourage his interest in language by avidly listening and responding to his babbling. This will help to teach him about two-way communication.

Your baby can probably imitate word sounds and inflections as well as actions by now. He may also be able to follow simple directions, such as "Please bring me the ball."

Twelve months

Though at this point their vocabulary usually consists of just a few words, many one-year-olds can babble short, fully inflected sentences that sound like they're speaking a foreign language.

By now, your baby may be able to respond to simple questions, especially if you give him clues with hand gestures. For example, ask, "Where's your mouth?" and point to it. Your baby may even answer you in his own way, using his own gestures, such as shaking his head for "No".

Dad's **Diary**

Increasingly mobile

"Amy is getting more and more mobile every day. She hasn't quite mastered the art of crawling, but she can bottom shuffle across the room in less than a minute. She's growing more and more inquisitive, examining everything in her path and trying to open cupboards. I can see I'm going to need eyes in the back of my head soon.

I've been upgrading our baby-proofing system. We've got a fireguard in place, and socket covers plugged in. All houseplants and ornaments have been moved out of her reach. We've got two stairgates in boxes in the spare room that I'll be putting up very soon.

She's already started terrorising the cat. Luckily, he stays out of her way most of the time, but you've got to keep an eye on her all the time.

We've invested in some new toys to keep her busy. Her building blocks are my favourite. I've been showing her how to stack them up and then knock them over. She loves it, although seems much more adept at demolishing than building at the moment. She's pretty good at passing her little football, too. I'm hoping that rolling it around the room will encourage her to start crawling after it."

Stacking toys present a new challenge, helping develop skills of logic.

Welcome to parenthood!
0–6 months

Your growing baby
6 weeks to 6 months

Your older baby
6 months to one year

Baby healthcare
0–12 months

Your baby may display shyness with less familiar people, but she'll be delighted, as always, by your undivided attention.

Laidback mum

Giving your baby reassurance when she needs it can help her grow in confidence.

"At around eight months, Nancy was quite clingy. She'd never been hugely sociable, but she hadn't minded being in a group, but I noticed a change at that age. If we went to mum-and-baby groups she'd be fine if she sat on my lap, but if I put her down she got upset. I stopped going for a bit as it seemed pointless. If she wanted to sit quietly and have a cuddle I was happy to do that at home.

I know there were a few (mostly older) members of my family who thought I spoilt her by giving her so much attention, but I didn't see it that way. Babies aren't calculating, they ask for what they need, and she needed a lot of cuddles. It felt absolutely like the right thing to do. She's 18 months now, and can still have clingy moments, but has come through that phase."

Social and emotional development

Your baby's understanding of language grows rapidly now as does her ability to communicate, enabling her to express more clearly how she feels.

Six months
Your baby may be starting to become wary of strangers, but she still loves attention and will be delighted with anyone who gives her a smile. She is also learning that her behaviour attracts your attention, and will enjoy wiggling and making noises to provoke a reaction.

Seven months
At about seven months, your baby develops greater self-awareness and begins to realise she is independent of you, whereas before she saw herself as an extension of you. This is an amazing development. Unfortunately, this new understanding of separateness makes her anxious. When you leave her, even for just a minute, she may cry. She doesn't yet realise you will always come back.

Your baby may seem more willful now, testing your authority by refusing to follow your directions. However, she's not being disobedient – just curious.

Eight months
At eight months, your baby's emotions are more obvious and she may start to perform tricks, such as throwing a kiss. Over the next few months, she may learn to assess and imitate moods and show the first stirrings of empathy. If she sees someone crying, she may cry, too.

When unsure of new situations, your baby may "nestle in" to mum for some comfort and reassurance.

Your baby may become shy around strangers, especially when she's tired or irritable, and when you're out of sight, she'll become upset. It's hard to see your baby distressed, but it's important to let her experience this. When you leave your baby and return, proving that you always come back, you're helping her develop trust and the ability to form attachments to other people.

Nine months
Now, and for the next few months, is when separation anxiety is at its peak. Although it's normal for a nine-month-old to show an extreme attachment to you, and fear of everyone else, it can be difficult for doting grandparents and other relatives and friends. Encourage people to approach slowly and let your baby make the first move.

Ten months
Your baby's personality is probably really emerging now. She may be very sociable, granting smiles to everyone she meets, or a little more reticent, shyly hiding her face from well-meaning

strangers. She'll repeat sounds, gesture for your attention and may even wave goodbye. She's also developing a mind of her own, and may protest at being put in her pushchair or car seat.

There will be times when your baby is scared of things that didn't bother her before, such as a ringing doorbell or the telephone. When this happens, comfort and reassure her.

Eleven months

Your baby may engage now in parallel play – playing alongside, but not with, another child. She may have designated a favourite toy as a security object.

Twelve months

Your baby probably has bouts of separation anxiety still. To ease departures, ask your babysitter to arrive early so your baby has time to adjust. Be matter-of-fact when you leave, and don't prolong the agony with extended goodbyes; make it quick, with just one goodnight kiss. Your baby's tears will subside soon after you're out of sight.

You can help her independence to grow by not hovering over her all the time. If she toddles to another room, wait a couple of minutes before following her.

Common concerns

A baby's development depends on many factors, such as genetics, environment and attachments. All babies develop differently; milestones simply act as a guide to what your baby might be doing at a certain age. If you do have concerns, talk to your doctor or health visitor.

Your baby's mobility

Some babies develop certain skills more quickly than others, but if your baby hasn't shown an interest in getting mobile by some means (whether it's creeping, crawling, rolling or scooting), worked out how to move her arms and legs together in a coordinated motion, or learned to use both arms and both legs equally by the time she's one, bring it up at your next doctor's appointment. Keep in mind that premature babies may reach this and other milestones several months later than their peers.

Talking

Babies with hearing problems stop babbling at about six months. If your baby isn't making sounds (or trying to) or eye contact with you when you talk to her, consult your doctor. Some babies form words at about nine months, but many wait until they're 13 or 14 months. If your baby isn't saying any words by

15 months, or you still can't understand a word she's saying, talk to your doctor or health visitor for reassurance.

Hearing

While the vast majority of babies have excellent hearing, a few have problems, especially if they were either very premature, or were deprived of oxygen or had a severe infection at birth. Babies with a family history of hearing loss are also more likely to have impaired hearing.

When your baby is awake and alert and not suffering from a cold or ear infection, which may temporarily affect her hearing, she should startle at loud, sudden noises. Then she'll calm and turn to you when she hears your voice, and react normally to other sounds.

All newborns are offered a hearing test after birth, either in hospital, at a community clinic or at home. If you have concerns later, you can ask your doctor or health visitor to check her hearing.

Sight

Babies should be screened for vision problems regularly, starting at birth and continuing at every check-up. Most eye deficiencies can be corrected if spotted early enough; the older she gets, the harder it will be to fix problems. If she

can't focus on or track an object (or your face) with both eyes by three or four months, tell her doctor. Premature babies have a higher risk of developing eye problems, such as astigmatism, eye misalignment (strabismus) and myopia, so more attention should be paid to their sight. Inform your health visitor if your baby has trouble moving one or both of her eyes in all directions; her eyes are crossed most of the time; or one or both of her eyes tend to turn outwards.

Parents**Ask...**

My baby was born 10 weeks early. Is there anything I can do to help her development?
There is a lot you can do, but above all try not to worry. Most premature babies with no other health problems catch up with their peers by two years of age.

Premature babies usually do best when they're given as normal a routine as possible. The most important thing is to interact closely: talk to her, make eye contact, sing to her and play with her gently. Skin-to-skin contact is also good.

Be reassured that if you are interacting with her when she's awake, and giving her plenty of time to rest, you're doing the best you can.

Welcome to parenthood!
0–6 weeks

Your growing baby
6 weeks to 6 months

Your older baby
6 months to one year

Baby healthcare
0–12 months

Development chart

Child's age	Mastered skills (most children can do)	Emerging skills (Half of children can do)	Advanced skills (A few children can do)
7 months	• Sits without support • Reaches for toys that are placed close by with a sweeping motion • Imitates speech sounds (babbles) • Is able to drag an object towards self	• Combines syllables into wordlike sounds • Begins to crawl or lunges forward • Starts to experience stranger anxiety	• Stands while holding onto something • Waves goodbye • Bangs objects together • Begins to understand object permanence
8 months	• Says "dada" and "mama" to both parents (isn't specific) • Begins to crawl • Passes object from hand to hand	• Stands while holding onto something • Crawls well • Points at objects • Searches for hidden object	• Pulls self to standing position, cruises around furniture while holding on • Picks things up with thumb–forefinger "pincer" grasp • Indicates wants with gestures
9 months	• Combines syllables into wordlike sounds • Stands while holding onto something, such as furniture, for support • Understands object permanence – the concept that objects exist even when she can't see them	• Uses pincer grasp to pick up objects • Cruises while holding onto furniture • Bangs objects together • Eats with fingers	• Plays pat-a-cake and peekaboo • Says "dada" and "mama" to the right parent (is specific) • Begins to understand the word "no"

By seven months, your baby will probably sit confidently without support and has learnt to reach out and grab at objects.

At around eight months, your baby's arms will be considerably stronger and she may lift herself up and even begin to crawl.

Your increasingly inquisitive baby loves to discover "hidden" objects. He may actively seek out toys hidden from his view.

Development chart

Child's age	Mastered skills (most children can do)	Emerging skills (Half of children can do)	Advanced skills (A few children can do)
10 months	• Waves goodbye • Picks things up with pincer grasp • Crawls well • Cruises • Understands more from tone of voice rather than words	• Says "dada" and "mama" to the right parent (is specific) • Responds to name and understands "no" • Indicates wants with gestures • Picks up small objects in a thumb–forefinger pincer grasp	• Drinks from a cup • Stands alone for a couple of seconds • Puts objects into a container • Jabbers word-like sounds
11 months	• Says "dada" and "mama" to the right parent (is specific) • Plays pat-a-cake and peekaboo • Stands alone for a couple of seconds • Repeats sounds and gestures for your attention	• Imitates others' activities • Puts objects into a container • Understands "no" and simple instructions • Jabbers word-like sounds • Looks at books and leafs through pages	• Drinks from a cup • Says one word besides "mama" and "dada" • Stoops from standing position
12 months	• Imitates others' activities and expressions • Jabbers wordlike sounds • Indicates his wants with gestures • Is able to pick up and hold small objects with a thumb–forefinger pincer grasp	• Says one word besides "mama" and "dada" • Takes a few steps • Understands and responds to simple instructions • Bangs objects together • Takes a few steps alone	• Scribbles with a crayon • Walks well • Says two words besides "mama" and "dada" • Begins feeding himself with a spoon, though frequently misses his mouth

Welcome to parenthood!
0–6 weeks

Your growing baby
6 weeks to 6 months

Your older baby
6 months to one year

Baby healthcare
0–12 months

As your baby becomes a more confident feeder, he may start to display an interest in holding his spoon and feeding himself.

Around 12 months, your baby's fine motor skills have advanced considerably and he may manage his first crude scribbles.

By her first birthday, your baby will have developed from a tiny, helpless newborn to a soon-to-be-walking toddler.

Your baby's playtime

As development experts say, play is a baby's work. Hiding, rolling, moving and throwing all help your baby learn cause and effect, spatial awareness and object permanence. Social games teach her about interaction and language. What's more, playing happens to be fun.

Development through play

Allowing your baby to make a mess and explore her environment is crucial to her development, both physical and mental.

Play is crucial for your baby's social, emotional, physical and cognitive growth. It's the perfect way for her to learn about her body and the world, and she'll use all five senses to do this, especially in her first year. "What does this feel like when I touch it?" "What does this sound like when I squeeze it?" "What will happen if I push this or pull that? Or what will this taste like?"

Exploration is the heart of play, and in your baby's mind any experiment counts – even hurling a bowl of cereal off the highchair tray. Development experts are fond of saying that play is the work of babies – and cleaning up after play seems to be the work of parents!

Age-appropriate play

The type of play best suited to your baby depends on her developmental stage. Play is the tool she uses to learn about the world, so the skills she's working on now are your biggest clues to choosing activities. A three-month-old baby who is learning how to grab enjoys large soft toys, while a 12-month-old exploring cause and effect will love a simple game of hide-and-seek under tables and chairs.

More than just toys

Interaction is important throughout the first year of your baby's life. Infants like to smile, look and laugh. Older babies will enjoy interactive games such as

Parents Talk...

"My toddler is so pleased that her little brother can now play with her. I found them opening cupboards the other day. The best I could get out of my toddler was that they needed 'something' for a game."
Carole, 36, mother of two

"I've just started playing "hide the object" with my baby. I'll take one of his cuddly toys and hide it in the room somewhere. He loves looking around to try and find it."
Rhian, 24, first-time mum

"Now my little boy is an accomplished crawler, he loves exploring our garden. It's not big, but he always manages to find something to interest him. It's sweet watching him pick at flowers and chase insects – he never gets close!"
Donna, 35, mother of two

"My daughter has taken her first steps. The other day I left the room briefly. When I returned, she was gone. I found her in the lounge opening a cabinet! She's certainly curious."
Mel, 29, first-time mum

As your baby's curiosity about the world grows, he'll be eager to find out the consequences of actions, such as what happens when he drops a toy on the floor.

peekaboo and "Incey wincey spider" where, after a while, they will giggle in anticipation of what's coming next.

You are your baby's ultimate play thing, and any activity is more fun if she shares it with you. Talking to her while she plays boosts her language skills, too. Think of playtime as more than just toy time. Playing is any enjoyable activity that involves people, movement or objects. Anything from blowing bubbles to singing songs or splashing in the tub qualifies. If you've seen a 12-month-old enthralled with a box, you'll understand how wide the parameters are.

Exploring her world
Babies do like to explore objects, too. When your baby is aged between about four and 10 months, she will enjoy touching, banging, mouthing, throwing, pushing and otherwise experimenting with things to see how they feel, taste, smell and land on the floor!

At around 12 months and beyond, when your baby's imagination starts to blossom, she'll begin playing with familiar objects in an appropriate way – pushing a toy lawn mower over the grass, for example, or tending to Grandma's hair with a hairbrush.

Following her lead
Introduce activities when your baby is happy and rested, as she's more likely to enjoy and learn from them. Give her a chance to play alone and with others – both types of play are beneficial. Also, let her choose activities and control the direction of her play. You can present new options, but let her be the boss. After all, play is about fun, and if there's one thing your baby is an expert at already, it's having a good time.

Stop when she's had enough. Babies have different thresholds for stimulation. When she seems bored, fussy or tired, it's time for a break.

The benefits of repetition

Older babies and young toddlers love repetition because that's the way they learn best. Hearing something many times helps babies to remember information for longer periods of time.

Knowing what comes next
Once your baby has learned something, she'll enjoy repetition because she can anticipate what comes next. This is why simple songs and nursery rhymes have such an impact on older babies. Singing songs such as, "Row, row, row your boat" and "Humpty Dumpty" nine times over helps her link words and actions, even though she is too young to sing along.

Older babies repeat activities for the same reason: the sheer joy of mastering something. Once she can stack two bricks or pass a toy to you (for you to pass it back to her), she may want to do it over and over to enjoy her new skill. Repetition is her way of reminding herself of what she can do and enjoying that excitement of completion all over again.

Action nursery rhymes are fun and teach the art of repetition and prediction.

Welcome to parenthood! 0–6 weeks

Your growing baby 6 weeks to 6 months

Your older baby 6 months to one year

Baby healthcare 0–12 months

Playing and learning: 6–9 months

What better way to teach your baby new social and physical skills than by playing games? From tickling, rhyming and clapping games to lively activities that incorporate his mealtimes and bathtimes, the next few months will bring unlimited scope for giggly fun.

Systemised mum

Age-appropriate activities help your baby to develop skills.

"I started playing tickle songs with Freddy when he was tiny. He enjoyed 'This little piggy' and 'Round and round the garden'. Before long he'd giggle before the tickle at the end, so I knew it was developing his memory. When he was about four months, my mum bought him a baby gym, which he really enjoyed. The different toys tied to it really helped his hand–eye coordination as he tried to grab each object in turn. Another favourite was the bubble-blower; he would be entranced watching the bubbles and trying to pop them.

By seven months, he was becoming more mobile and exploring further, so I made a homemade obstacle course. I stacked cushions and encouraged him to climb over them to get to a special toy. I'm sure it built up his physical strength and balance and helped him when he was learning to walk later.

Towards his first birthday I noticed that he copied me if I started to dance. So I bought a CD with fun songs and silly actions. He imitated me, putting his hands in the air, touching his nose and so on."

Physical games

Your baby's motor skills are coming along all the time: his arms and legs are stronger and more coordinated, and he's gaining finer control over his hands and fingers. You can encourage this burst of exciting development with some fun physical games involving clapping, stomping, bouncing, kicking and pulling.

Clapping games

There comes a moment, around the six-month mark, when your baby discovers he can spontaneously bring his hands together. Once he has mastered this skill, clapping games are great fun, and these games also give your baby a chance to interact with you face-to-face and to mimic your actions.

"Pat-a-cake" is an old favourite, and encourages two–hand coordination. This version is a bit more challenging. Sit your baby on the floor facing you – prop a pillow behind him if necesary. Then sing this song (to any tune), acting out the commands: "Clap, clap, clap your hands, clap your tiny hands. Clap, clap, clap your hands, clap your tiny hands."

Additional verses could be, "Stomp, stomp, stomp your feet …" (and so on); "Pat, pat, pat your head … "; or "Rub, rub,

Encouraging your baby to mimic your actions helps him to build on and develop new skills.

Games to encourage hand–eye coordination

Learning how to hold and pick things up launches babies into the world of play and toys and is the first step on the road to eating, reading, writing, drawing and self-care. Help him in a few simple ways:

● To stimulate his grasping reflex, put a colourful toy slightly out of his reach and encourage him to grab it, but not so far away that he can't get it.

● If he hasn't discovered clapping yet, he will soon! Encourage him by clapping to a song and doing simple rhythms.

● Give your baby plenty of objects that he can grasp easily, such as soft blocks, plastic rings and board books. Also, encourage your baby's pincer grasp by offering him finger foods, such as carrots and rice cakes.

Shape-sorting toys help your baby to discover how shapes work in relation to each other and what fits where.

Colourful, textured soft books help your baby to explore the world of touch, and introduce the concept of turning "pages".

rub your tummy ... ". Help your baby make the movements himself. You can invent sillier and sillier verses (wiggle your eyebrows; stick out your tongue) as long as he continues to giggle.

Mealtime fun

It can be hard to keep your baby's attention focused on food for long enough to get him to eat, but if you think how tricky it is for him to get even a spoonful of food near his mouth, it's easy to see why he loses interest and

"Your baby's **coordination** is becoming **increasingly** refined."

sends it all over the floor. Turning mealtimes into fun occasions for practising his coordination and feeding techniques may help. Try giving him lots of different utensils (that are safe for him to eat with) such as wooden spoons,

measuring spoons and rubber spatulas. He may spill food, but he probably does that with his normal spoon anyway!

Kicking out

Getting ready to crawl, stand or walk is a big challenge – all sorts of muscles need to develop in those little legs. Help your baby develop his gross-motor coordination with this fun kicking game.

Sitting cross-legged on the floor, hold your baby in front of you (and facing away from you), placing one arm around

his chest and the other hand supporting his bottom so that his legs stick out in front of you both. Place a ball directly in front of him and "help" his feet kick the ball; then move forwards so that he can propel the ball across the floor, like a

mini footballer. Cheer encouragingly every time your baby's foot makes contact with the ball, and point out how far he's "kicked" it.

Holding tight

You may have noticed how your baby absolutely will not let go of something when you try to take it away. It's as if he's instinctively protecting his territory, and in a way, he is. (He's finally learned to hold on to things, and he's going to hold on tight!) Go along with his new doggedness by starting a game of tug-of-war. Let your baby grab hold of a tea towel or other soft, strong object. Then grab the other end of it and pull gently, testing his strength. This game is not only fun, but it also builds upper body strength. Think of it as your baby's first weight-lifting routine.

If your baby gets tired or loses interest, it's time to have a break from games. He'll learn best – and have more fun – when you go at his pace.

Welcome to parenthood!
0–6 weeks

Your growing baby
6 weeks to 6 months

Your older baby
6 months to one year

Baby healthcare
0–12 months

Sensory and learning games

As your baby gets used to the notion of cause and effect, she'll be fascinated with light switches, television remotes and other objects that seem like agents of change. Cater to her interest by showing her how actions bring results.

Cause and effect

Start with simple changes: open and close a cupboard door, then flick a light switch on and off to demonstrate light versus dark. Then branch out into more active scenarios, such as rolling a ball

Fact: Your baby's mouth has more nerve endings than anywhere.

If she wants to find out what something feels like, she puts it in her mouth. Don't leave items in reach if you don't want them in her mouth.

across the floor or putting a cuddly toy at the edge of the table, then pushing it off onto a chair.

Mealtimes are a good time for your baby to learn that actions have results. If she seems bored and resists eating, enlist help from a favourite teddy. Bring the toy to the table and explain that a special friend is serving dinner tonight. Hold the spoon in the toy's paw, and get the "dinner guest" to feed your baby. Teddy's coaxing is almost guaranteed to get the result you're looking for.

Hide and seek

Another way to liven up mealtimes, and develop your baby's sense of object permanence (see p.146), is to show her a snack, then cover it with a tea towel. Let your baby lift the veil and discover that her treat is still there, even though she couldn't see it before.

In fact, your baby's increasingly fine motor skills provide lots of opportunities to play new finding games. At the beach or in a sandpit, show your baby a brightly coloured object, such as a rubber ball, a plastic dinosaur or anything else that stands out. With your baby watching, bury it under a small mound of sand. With a perplexed look, say, "Now where did that ball go?" Then put your baby's hand on the mound of sand and help her brush the sand away until the object is uncovered. Once she gets the hang of the search, she'll do the digging without any help from you.

Homemade stories

Is your baby unimpressed by her usual night-time routine? Make bedtimes more entertaining, and boost her verbal and hearing skills by introducing your own hand-animated story.

Try making your own "story" shapes out of felt squares. (Avoid shop-bought felt shapes because these have small parts that are unsuitable for babies.) A good place to start is to make a cut-out doll that is the same gender as your baby, then cut out a simple wardrobe or some props that let you make it day or night, winter or summer. Then you can add a dog, cat or rabbit and a house and car, and spin a tale that reflects your baby's life.

Sit facing your baby with a felt board propped up on your knees so that it is clearly visible to her. Then tell her a simple story, illustrating it with the felt shapes. You might start, "Once upon a time there was a little girl", (lay out the felt figure) "who lived in a tiny house" (lay out the house). When your baby is a bit older, it will be fun to get her to tell you her own felt-board bedtime story.

Benefits of music

Many experts believe that playing classical music to a baby can boost their IQ. Whether or not this is true, music does have other more immediate advantages! Here are a few of the benefits of playing your baby a gentle lullaby or piece of classical music.

Lulling notes

Many parents find that a CD of soothing lullabies can help their baby to fall asleep – it may be something to do with the gentle rhythms that can help "rock" your baby into a peaceful slumber. So if your baby consistently refuses to settle when you put her to bed, try playing some gentle music to her, and leave it on until she's in a deep sleep.

Calming tunes

Some calming Bach or Mozart may assist in relaxing your irritated or upset baby. The music, along with soothing cuddles and kisses, may create the right ambience to help your baby calm down.

Playing tranquil music during feeding times may keep your baby feeling settled – therefore an attempt to spoon in a new flavour of purée may be a little easier!

Toys with
built-in lullabies can be soothing and reassuring, helping to settle your baby.

As your baby grows, hide-and-seek games will continue to amuse her, and she will start to interact more, perhaps "hiding" herself.

A bowl full of water and accompanying toys will provide endless fun for your baby, but always supervise your baby near water.

Interactive games, such as rolling a ball to your baby and encouraging her to roll it back, help her physical development, too.

Social play

You and your baby will enjoy games that involve interaction – not only will they have you both giggling, but they're great for teaching her about turn-taking and language. Roll a ball and encourage her to roll it back, or sing nursery rhymes accompanied by silly actions.

Learning to read expressions

Make your own "peekaboo" picture-based lift-up flap books. On sturdy bits of paper or cardboard, draw sketches of people with a happy, sad or grumpy expression, or cut out pictures from a magazine. Cut rectangular pieces of cloth a little taller than each figure. Glue the cloth above each picture, creating a lift-up flap and show your baby how to raise the flaps. Make up a simple story about the person, and end it with your baby "finding" the face. This builds on her fascination with expressions, which she's been noticing more lately.

A hidden noise

Your baby loves to be surprised by unexpected sounds, so introduce some squeaky toys to a traditional game of peekaboo. Show your baby a toy, give it a good noisy squeeze, then cover it with a tea towel and let her uncover it. Then cover it again and make it squeak while it's invisible. Next use a toy that rattles, then one that makes a crunching noise or other sound (you can make your own with a ball of waxed paper). For the final act, throw a cloth over a radio, then push the button (through the tea towel) to make it play. This game will help to improve your baby's understanding of object permanence, and encourage her hand–eye coordination, too.

Water play

Make some fun bath blocks for your baby by cutting sponges or foam into a variety of interesting shapes and sizes. Cut at least one larger flat shape to use as a base for the others. Then take it in turns with your baby to press the blocks against the sides of the bath, squeeze the water out of them, push them down to the bottom of the tub and let them pop back up again, and stack them up. Sponge blocks are soft enough to safely throw against the wall or into the water for a resounding splash.

Dad's **Diary**

Bathtime games

"Bathtime is a great time for dad–baby playtime. You can't get messy, so it's a good way to hone Josh's filling and pouring skills (great for his hand–eye coordination and spatial awareness). We give him a couple of plastic beakers to play with and a funnel and a toy teapot. He looks so engrossed as he's pouring the water from one beaker into another.

Josh has a tub of foam animals, which he sticks to the sides of the bath. Playing with them is helping him become more dexterous, and I try to teach him the colours of each of them.

Now Josh can sit up, hairwashing has become much easier and I like to give him a Mohican! He doesn't appreciate it yet, but I do! He likes it when I blow bubbles – the bigger the better!"

Welcome to parenthood!
0–6 weeks

Your growing baby
6 weeks to 6 months

Your older baby
6 months to one year

Baby healthcare
0–12 months

Playing and learning: 9–12 months

Your baby can clap his hands together now, and will love making big noises with pots and spoons. He's becoming more coordinated every week and, although he might not be walking yet, you can show him the joy of movement with some fun bouncing and "cruising" activities.

Toys for your older baby

Tailor toys to suit your baby's developmental stage, so that he can explore and consolidate his latest skills.

- Push-along toys help babies exercise their new walking skills. Choose one that is heavily weighted so your baby can safely lean on it.
- Shape-sorters are good early problem-solvers. They fascinate, and occasionally frustrate, babies this age.
- He's encountered them before, but balls get even more thrilling once you're standing and can actually bounce them off the floor.
- Toy telephones are great as babies love to imitate their parents. Even if he can't say much, he'll hold the receiver and push buttons.
- At this age, babies are intrigued by books with flaps that open, or with textures that can be rubbed or stroked.
- Blocks help babies practise the art of stacking. He may stack three or four, and will enjoy the subsequent crash.
- Bucket and spades come in handy when your baby's all-time favourite activity is filling and emptying. Buy a little sandpit for the garden or take him to the one in the park, and he'll stay contented and busy for some time.

Physical games

Your baby is going through some major developmental changes at this time. There is no better way to encourage and nurture your baby's emerging skills than with some fun, noisy games that are aimed to help him improve his hand-eye coordination, strengthen his leg and arm muscles and teach him about spatial awareness – not necessarily all at the same time though!

Making contact

Once your baby has learnt the art of bringing his hands together, nothing will amuse him more than consolidating this skill. He looks from one hand to the other, moves each one, and then suddenly they're touching and he's clapping away. Try giving your baby a wooden stick or spoon to hold in each hand and show him how to clack them together.

Your baby's world opens up as he learns new skills and concepts such as empying and filling. Indulge him with some messy water play and plenty of plastic containers!

At first he'll miss as often as he hits, but soon he'll get a rhythm going, and the satisfaction of each noisy contact will keep him happy through many a nappy change. This simple game will also help to improve his hand–eye coordination.

Cruising along

Walking is one skill you can't rush with your baby: he'll walk when he's good and ready. However, as he gets closer to taking his first steps, it's fun to sneak preview the joys of getting around.

Line up a row of chairs against a wall (preferably in a carpeted room). Help your baby stand up and hold onto a chair at one end of the row, then show him how to use the chairs to "cruise" – that is move himself slowly along from one to another. If he needs an extra incentive, take a favourite toy and place it on the farthest chair, and when he reaches the toy, help him get it, then clap and give him a big hug. Put another toy at the opposite end and send him back in the other direction. You can keep this up as long as he's having fun and is still steady on his feet.

Measuring and pouring

Pouring activities are a great way to explore concepts like "full" and "empty", and help your little one develop his sense of dexterity and spatial awareness. The following is messy, so try this activity outside, or in the kitchen or bathroom with a bath mat or towel on the floor. Fill a large plastic tub about

$Fact$: At 13 months, three quarters of toddlers have mastered the art of walking.

However, they may be somewhat unsteady still. Some children don't walk until 16 or 17 months or even later, which is fine, too.

Bouncing games not only are enormous fun, but also help your baby to balance.

halfway with water, and set out various pouring implements – plastic cups, bowls and lids – next to it. Show your baby how to scoop water out of the bucket and pour it back in. When he has grasped this technique, show him how to transfer water into a larger cup or bowl using a smaller one as a tool. Funnels and measuring cups with spouts also make for great water play.

Jump for joy

It's no secret that kids love to jump on beds. Actually, babies do, too, and it's a perfect way for little ones to build lower-body strength and learn to control their wobbly legs.

Stand your baby upright in the middle of your bed, carefully supporting him with your hands holding him on both sides. Help him bounce up and down, lifting him off the bed, then land him in a standing position. If your baby is already walking, you may be able just to hold his hands once he gets used to the springy motion of the bed. Make sure you never leave your baby unattended on a bed.

 Laidback mum

You may love to encourage your baby to develop new skills, but remember, he will do something only when he is ready.

"Harvey was a big baby and only really started crawling when he was past nine months. So I knew there wasn't a chance he would be walking by his first birthday. He could pull himself up and cruise along furniture, but would only do this if he had to. He definitely wasn't one of those babies who, once they learn a trick, do it all the time.

It honestly didn't bother me. Sometimes I felt sorry for him when he found himself stranded, hanging on to the sofa, while my friend's more agile baby was scrambling around the room. If they both went for the same toy, my friend's baby would always get there first, but other than that it wasn't a problem. I knew he would walk when he was good and ready and sure enough he did. He was nearly 15 months when he finally took his first step, and it was well worth the wait."

Your baby may spend a lot of time "cruising" before taking her first steps – rest assured that she'll get there in the end.

Welcome to parenthood!
0–6 weeks

Your growing baby
6 weeks to 6 months

Your older baby
6 months to one year

Baby healthcare
0–12 months

Chunky shapes and toys will fascinate your baby and help develop her dexterity.

Systemised mum

Encourage development by choosing age-appropriate toys and puzzles for your baby.

"I gave Mai her first simple puzzle. It was a plastic box with primary-coloured triangle, circle and square shapes to post through the holes. The pieces were exactly the right size for Mai's little hands as they were chunky enough for her to pick up and hold easily. It also helped her learn her shapes, which I'm told is a good pre-reading skill.

Next, she moved onto a wooden jigsaw puzzle. It had six pieces, in the shape of farmyard animals, so we could talk about them, too. Once I'd shown her what to do, I tried not to help, unless she got really frustrated, then I'd suggest turning the piece round or trying another slot. If this didn't work, I would get out her first puzzle, which she could do easily by now, to boost her confidence again. Her hand–eye coordination really came on in a few short weeks."

Sensory and learning games

Your baby's motor skills are developing quickly, which means the scope for game-playing grows every month, too. She'll appreciate building blocks (and knocking them down) and shape-sorters soon, and as she approaches her first birthday, you can get her started on her first chunky jigsaw puzzles.

First scribbles

As your baby becomes more dexterous, she may be ready to hold a chunky pencil while you encourage her to scribble on paper. If that doesn't appeal,

how about some outdoor water "colouring" to improve her hand–eye coordination? In the garden, fill a small plastic container with water and give your baby several real paintbrushes. Set her up so she's sitting in front of a wall or low piece of outdoor furniture, such as a bench, then show her how to "paint" it with water. Don't worry if the water goes everywhere but on the paper; your baby may stay engrossed for a surprising amount of time – developing all the fine motor skills of painting (without the mess).

Blowing bubbles

Your baby probably loves bath toys – they're a great way to liven up bathtime and can be incorporated into any number of silly, interactive games. However, you don't need any toys for this "now you see it, now you don't game", just a bottle of bubbles.

Safely settle your baby in a bath seat or the bath tub. (If she's not enclosed in a seat, make clear that a rule of this game is that she can't stand up in the water.) Duck down, then blow clouds of bubbles, letting them cascade down on her. Pause inbetween blows to come up and check your baby, then duck down and blow some more bubbles. Each surprise shower will elicit fits of giggles from your baby – somehow, not being able to see you, but knowing you're there producing the bubbles is endlessly funny. Remember though, do not take your eyes off her for more than a moment while she's in the bath.

Fact: The part of the brain that controls memory develops still after birth.

The hippocampus in the brain is about 40 per cent mature at birth, 50 per cent mature at six weeks and fully mature at 18 months.

Parallel play

Babies and young toddlers don't really need to "play" with other children. They may be interested in observing other babies and even touching, grabbing, or hitting them, but they don't engage in continued playful and interactive activity with other children until well into toddlerhood. However, your baby is likely to enjoy the stimulation of having other babies around her, although no one knows whether being around other babies and children will make a significant difference in her development.

Playing side by side

Children between one and two years will engage in "parallel play," which means they'll play side by side with another child, but not interact (other than to grab a toy). True playing, where children engage in an activity with another child (such as playing families or a game of chase) doesn't start until about two years, and until three years, don't expect your child to have a deep understanding of sharing. In other words, you'll have to do a lot of refereeing until then.

Babies may play side by side, but their activities remain quite separate for now.

Social play

Your baby is increasingly sociable. Alongside her first words and nonsense words, she's becoming more aware of people and their emotions, and the power of human interaction. You can encourage her early language development by engaging her in conversation as often as you can, and maybe even teaching her some simple baby signing (see pp.206–07 for how to do baby signing).

Sing along

As your baby starts to take more of an interest in the world, one natural way to develop her memory and concentration is to concentrate on moments that are likely to be memorable for her. This also provides a comforting way to bring the day to a close. Try singing a little song called "What shall we do when we all go out?", which lends itself well to personalisation. It can be sung to the tune of "Here we go round the mulberry bush," and the lyrics are very simple and repetitive, "What shall we do when we

all go out, all go out, all go out. What shall we do when we all go out, when we all go out to play?"

Sing more verses to reflect what she is going to do tomorrow, such as, "Swing on the swings when we all go out" and "Slide down the slide when we all go out." Follow with verses about special people: "Visit Uncle John" or "Play with Emily." She'll fall asleep thinking happily of loved ones and happy occasions.

Puppet play

Another sociable game your baby will love is a puppet show. If you don't have finger puppets, it's easy to make simple finger puppets from cut-off gloves, giving them ears, eyes and a mouth with glued-on felt. Show your baby how to make them sing, dance, tickle and kiss! She'll love watching them come alive, and pretending that the puppets are real will help develop her imagination.

Parents**Talk...**

"Alfie learnt to wave and he doesn't stop! He even waves at the check-out ladies in the supermarket."
Rachel, 30, first-time mum

"I've been trying to teach Daniel to say hello. It's a bit of a mouthful for him, but I keep encouraging him, especially if we bump into friends."
Shona, 39, mother of three

"Daisy says "Bye bye" now. She puts her hand up in the air and moves it to and fro! It's so cute."
Heidi, 31, mother of two

"I always say please and thank you to Freddie. He hasn't said his first word, but I believe in teaching politeness from the start."
Jo, 27, mother of two

Welcome to parenthood! 0–6 weeks

Your growing baby 6 weeks to 6 months

Your older baby 6 months to one year

Baby healthcare 0–12 months

Communication

When it comes to communicating, babies are fast learners. Research shows that they start listening to their parents' voices in the uterus. Once born, they soon begin tuning into your words and sentence patterns to figure out what you're saying.

Language and understanding

As well as language development, babies also use their powers of observation to learn about more complicated things, such as love and trust, and cause and effect.

Words and meaning

By the age of three, your little one will have a vocabulary of several hundred words and a good sense of the more complicated aspects of everyday life, such as food shopping and cleaning the house. But there are many more stages of language acquisition before then.

Between four and seven months, your baby learns his name, knows that you're calling him when you say it, and starts to respond by turning towards you. He's become more attuned to your tone of voice, too. When you sound friendly, he may react joyfully, and if you speak to him sharply, he may start to cry.

Your baby's first books

It's never too early to start reading to your baby; start with colourful board books. While he won't understand

Interacting with your baby is an important precursor to her speech and understanding.

Systemised mum

Chatting helps familiarise your baby with words and speech.

"Millie always noticed the way I responded to the things she did, even at nine months. If she dropped her spoon onto the floor and I said, 'No', she'd shake her head back.

I decided to give her a commentary on whatever we happened to be doing, so she'd get used to the sounds of different words. For example, if I was making her lunch, I'd talk about the colours of the fruits and vegetables. If we were out in the car or her buggy, I'd point to dogs, traffic lights or whatever we saw. I named her clothes as I dressed her and described what was happening in picture books."

everything you're saying, it helps him to become familiar with the rhythm and intonation of speech. It's helpful to vary the pace, pitch and tone of your voice, perhaps giving different "voices" to different characters. You can point out and name pictures, too.

Whatever else, your baby will love the cuddles he gets when you read to him – and, you never know, this may help to instil a lifelong love of reading.

Checking your reactions

At eight to 12 months, your baby begins to understand simple requests. Say "No" when he tries to touch a socket, for example and he'll pause and look at your face, and maybe even shake his head "no" in return. He's also testing out your responses to his behaviour. He'll throw food on the floor just to see what you'll do, and will remember your response. Later, he'll test the waters again to see if you react the same way when he does the same thing.

Words, expressions and taking turns

Encourage your baby's language learning by talking to him simply, clearly and often. He won't always understand you, but he'll enjoy having "look, move and gurgle" conversations whereby he watches you talking, moves his mouth to make a noise and gurgles in response. Help him to develop his vocabulary by saying in words what he shows in signs and expressions; for example, "You're not very happy about going in your buggy today, are you?" It's good to extend and second-guess what you think your baby might be trying to communicate. If you ask him whether he enjoyed his breakfast and he gurgles in response, say, "You did enjoy that, didn't you?" If he shows interest in an object, say what it is: "That's a red car".

Encouraging speech

You baby is born with an innate desire to communicate with you, and for you to communicate with him. Although it's still early days, your baby will want to try to talk to you, even if it does sound like a babble! Here are a few top tips to encourage your baby's early vocal interaction with you during this first important year and beyond.

Talk all the time

Talk constantly to your baby. Babies move to the rhythm of human speech. They may not understand what is being said, but they turn towards anyone who is speaking and carry out little "look, move and gurgle conversations" with anyone willing to engage with them (see opposite).

Baby talk

If you double words like "woof-woof" or add "y" or "a" sounds on the end of words then this is fine! It may actually help your baby to talk, as "dada", "mama" and vowel sounds are found in your baby's earliest words and noises.

Words and pictures

Read picture books with your baby from six months. This will help him to put objects and words together, so even if he can't say the words yet, he will at least understand them.

Reading to your baby and sharing books together from an early age will stimulate his interest in language.

Talk for him

Express in words what your baby communicates to you. So if he's smiling and laughing, say something like, "You're happy today!" This way he will start to connect your words with his feelings.

Giving him a clue

Help your baby respond to simple questions and commands by giving him clues with hand gestures. For example, "Where's the cat?" and point to it. Your baby may start to use gestures such as shaking his head for "no".

Learning to take turns in conversation is a vital part of learning to talk. Turn-taking is best developed in the simple conversations we have with our children and in the games we play with them. Peekaboo, tickling games and simple action games like "This is the way the lady rides" (see p.146) all have an element of turn-taking. As he waits to be tickled he will almost certainly communicate with you by way of giggles, squirms or looks that show he knows what is coming next. Let him know you understand.

Be guided by your baby. If what you do and say makes him happy, you can be pretty sure you are doing and saying the right thing.

Welcome to parenthood!
0–6 weeks

Your growing baby
6 weeks to 6 months

Your older baby
6 months to one year

Baby healthcare
0–12 months

Baby signing

It's not surprising that babies can learn how to use signs. Both their understanding of language and their motor skills develop much faster than their ability to speak. Also, babies love to mimic the actions of others. Most babies discover how to wave and point long before they are able to say "Bye bye" or "Look at that!"

The origins of baby signing

The idea of teaching babies a vocabulary of signs was inspired by Dr Joseph Garcia, an American child-development expert. Having discovered how easily babies with normal hearing who had deaf parents learned sign language, he then made the observation that these babies appeared less demanding than non-signing babies because they could express their thoughts and needs more easily. So he wondered whether families where both parents and babies had normal hearing could enjoy the benefits of signing, too?

While baby signing doesn't promise to cut out tears or tantrums, babies as young as six months old have been

Teaching your baby signs for words such as "play" can open a channel of communication between you.

Getting started

If you've decided to try baby signing, think about your approach and how to ensure that your baby benefits.

● Start at around nine or 10 months, when your baby starts to develop a real desire to to communicate – she is more sociable and starts to babble and use noises and facial expressions to get your attention.

● Go at your baby's pace and keep it fun. She will learn much more easily if she enjoys herself.

● Begin with a sign for something she's interested in or very familiar with, such as "food" or "sleep".

● Every time you use the word, show your baby the sign, too. Always use the same sign for something, repeat it often, and always say the word at the same time as making the sign.

● Elaborate on the sign with words, too, so her verbal vocabulary grows at the same time.

● Have a look for baby-signing classes in your area, or check out the books and DVDs available in your library.

● Be patient! Don't expect your baby to get the hang of signing straight away and don't prompt her to use signs. It may take a few weeks for your baby to start signing back to you.

Welcome to parenthood!
0–6 weeks

Your growing baby
6 weeks to 6 months

Your older baby
6 months to one year

Baby healthcare
0–12 months

First signs

Your baby may not be able to talk yet, but she still tries to communicate with you if she wants a drink, or a second helping of lunch. However, you may not always be sure what she's trying to tell you! Baby signing, based on sign language, allows your baby to express her needs in a way that both of you can understand. The signs are simple to learn and easy for little to hands to use. To start you off, here are three signs your baby will enjoy learning.

The sign for bed is an easy and obvious one for your baby to learn. Place your palms together and rest your head sideways on your hands to indicate bedtime.

Teaching signs for animals and objects may help observational skills. For a cat, put thumb and forefinger together, drawing them back and forth across your face to indicate whiskers.

A useful sign for your baby is the one for "drink". Hold one curled hand up to your mouth and tilt your head back, as though drinking from a cup.

taught to "sign" successfully and therefore communicate their needs more easily. Baby signing is now becoming increasingly popular in the UK as well as in the US, and several organisations run baby-signing classes all over the country.

Although you need lots of patience, teaching your baby to sign isn't too hard. Even learning just a few easy signs such as "drink" (thumb to the mouth, tilting up) can make a difference, reducing the levels of frustration your little one feels when she tries to tell you something.

For and against

Opinion is divided as to the value of baby signing. While many see it as a tool to help babies communicate before they can speak, others worry that it could have a detrimental affect on normal speech development as parents may ignore early vocalisations. Some experts argue, too, that parents and babies find their own ways to communicate anyway. Supporters say it improves language and vocabulary as it's about enhancing, not replacing, language. Also, because you need to ensure your baby is looking at you, it means she's concentrating on what you're saying, as well as on what you're doing. It's vital to use signing alongside speech so your baby links the gesture and the word.

Once your baby starts to sign back to you, communication becomes two-way. If, for example she tells you she can hear a plane, you can respond, "You heard an aeroplane? Yes, I can see it. Look, it's over there. Isn't it loud?" In this way, you will probably spend even more time than usual talking to your baby, which is one of the best ways to help her speech and language develop.

When is your baby ready?

The best time to start signing is when your baby starts trying to communicate, usually around nine or 10 months. You'll notice she's more sociable, starts to babble and uses noises and facial expressions to get your attention.

Start with a sign for something she is interested in. Lots of babies pick up the sign for "more!" Every time you use the word, show her the sign. Use repetition and emphasise the key word, so she can see and hear the connection, "Do you want some more? You'd like some more, would you? OK, let's get some more!"

Your baby's behaviour

Your baby won't benefit from being disciplined just yet – he's too young to understand. However, now is about the right time to start setting boundaries and to let your baby know gently when it's not OK to do something. Often this is for his own safety.

Learning boundaries

Your baby is becoming more and more curious about exploring the world. His new-found crawling or walking skills enable him to reach and touch, taste, pull or poke at the things that interest him, which in earlier months he was probably unable to reach or pick up. He's not being naughty when he picks up something that he shouldn't, just inquisitive, but there are a few simple things you can do now to start setting boundaries for when he's older.

Your baby looks to you for reassurance. She'll pick up on your tone of voice and use this as a measure of your approval.

A new understanding

Your baby is beginning to understand simple requests now. So if you say "No" when he tries to touch an electric socket, for example, he'll pause and look at your face – and maybe even shake his head to say "No" in return. He's also testing out your responses to his behaviour. One of his favourite ways to do this is to throw food or toys on the floor from his highchair just to see what you'll do, and then file your response in his memory bank. Later he'll test the waters again to see whether you react in the same way.

Setting limits

As your baby becomes increasingly independent, this is about the right time to start setting limits. Your baby probably understands simple instructions and may purposely choose to ignore you when you say no. (To help the word carry a little more weight, make sure you reserve its use for things that are truly dangerous.)

You're not being mean if you don't let your baby devour a second cake: you're setting limits. If he pulls the cat's tail, move his hand, look him in the eye, and say, "No, that hurts the cat." Then guide your little one's hand to pet the animal

Your baby will be delighted when you praise her "good" behaviour and may imitate your gestures and expressions.

gently. His desire to explore is stronger than his desire to listen to your warnings, so it's up to you to protect and teach him. What seems to be defiance of your authority isn't really; it's just his natural curiosity to see how the world around him works.

Keeping him safe

Your job right now is to keep your baby safe, secure and stimulated. A crawling baby may be old enough to make mischief, but he's not old enough to learn the difference between right and wrong. It's too early to discipline your child. Real discipline – the kind that teaches lessons and changes behaviours – will have to wait.

You can head off many problems by ensuring that your baby has a safe place to explore. Babyproofing your home – covering up sockets, storing dangerous items well out of reach, blocking "off-limit" places with baby gates, and so on (see pp.213–15) – is the best way to ensure good behaviour as the chances to get into trouble will be limited. Instead of looking for discipline

opportunities at this point, give your baby scope to explore, and enjoy and appreciate his fascination.

Although it's too early for your baby to grasp discipline, this is an ideal time to start practising techniques that will work in the months and years to come. When your baby pulls on a lamp flex, firmly tell him "No", explain why and quickly redirect him to a safer activity. With your baby's short attention span, he'll quickly forget about causing trouble. When he does obey your request, be sure to reinforce his good behaviour with plenty of praise and a big cuddle (see p.211).

No matter what your baby does, smacking, swatting and yelling are never appropriate responses. Harsh discipline will only scare him and can even cause an injury. You'll already be aware that shaking a baby can cause lifelong brain damage or even death, so if you feel that anger is getting the better of you, take a few breaths, put your baby down in a safe place, such as his cot or playpen, leave the room and give yourself a short break to calm down.

ParentsAsk...

If I lavish love and attention on my baby, will I spoil him?
No. Young babies are completely spoil-proof. Your baby needs all the care and attention you can give. Ignore the advice of well-meaning relatives who think that babies need to learn independence. Instead, listen to your parental instinct – that inner voice that tells you to soothe and comfort your baby whenever he cries out.

Your baby is too young to manipulate or annoy you purposefully. He cries to communicate his needs, whether he wants a snack, a clean nappy or a little cuddle with mum or dad. When you respond quickly to your baby, you're building his sense of self-worth. You're also establishing a foundation of trust that can last for years to come.

By the time your baby is six to eight months old, he'll be paying close attention to cause and effect – noticing, for example that his bowl falls when he drops it from the highchair. He'll also start to see a direct link between his actions and your responses. At this point, it's OK to set some limits. If your baby starts crying to get something he doesn't need, hold your ground and give him a hug when he calms down. Similarly, give hugs and praise for good behaviour and gently redirect him when he's doing something hazardous.

Paying attention

Remember that your baby can't yet communicate everything that he might want to say. This can also be frustrating for a young baby who is trying to communicate something to you, so always show him that you're listening to him, and try to expand on his words and babbling with simple and clear questions, such as "Are you feeling tired? Is that why you're feeling grizzly? Shall we have a nap?"

Welcome to parenthood!
0–6 weeks

Your growing baby
6 weeks to 6 months

Your older baby
6 months to one year

Baby healthcare
0–12 months

Encouraging good behaviour

Encouraging your baby to behave well doesn't mean disciplining him, but simply giving him as much love and attention as possible to help him grow into a well-adjusted person.

The trust you're building up now means that, in the future, your child will feel more secure and less anxious, knowing that you take his wants and needs seriously. He'll have confidence in you later, when it's time to set boundaries and lay down rules, and understand that you love him even when you correct his behaviour.

This doesn't mean your baby won't infuriate you with some of his behaviour over the coming months. While your baby didn't really have a "temper" before (he cried because he needed to be fed, held or changed, or because he was tired or in pain), as he gets older, around six months and beyond, new emotions emerge, including frustration. Although he probably isn't feeling angry in the way adults feel anger, it's easy to interpret his mood as such.

Too soon for tantrums

Thankfully, your baby isn't emotionally or developmentally capable of a true toddler-style tantrum yet, and it's likely that his bad moods can be diffused fairly easily. However, looking now at when and why your baby becomes temperamental, and trying to avoid it, is good practice for the years to come.

You may find that if your baby's sleeping or eating patterns are disrupted, this can make him cranky. One way to avoid cross or frustrated moments and to help your baby to feel calmer is to stick to a consistent routine so that he knows what to expect at certain times throughout the day. Look out for the late-afternoon "witching hours", too, when many babies become especially fussy and overtired. This may be the result of overstimulation from a busy day of running errands and having

(see pp.213–15)

ParentsAsk...

When will my baby understand when I ask him not to do something?

While some babies start to understand what "no" means and respond to this at around six months of age, most babies won't stop what they're doing in response to the word until they're somewhere between 12 and 18 months.

However, if you feel as though "no" is becoming the word you say most often to your baby, try changing your tactic and instead start to use words that explain exactly why you don't want your baby to do whatever it is he is doing. For example, when your baby tries to eat a piece of dog food, say "Yucky!" Or when your baby gets too close to the oven, say "Hot!" and so on. Even though you haven't said "no", the stern tone of your voice and the firm expression on your face will help to express your wishes and deliver the most important part of your message across to him.

It's also important to have places at home where your baby can play safely so you don't have to be the "no" police all the time. Your baby is too young to understand that certain areas are "no go areas". Instead, work at making his environment safe (see pp.213–15) so that you can both relax more.

If your baby is unsettled, a new toy or activity may distract and soothe him. However, take care not to over-stimulate him and be aware of when he needs some "down" time.

Positive reinforcement

Tiredness and overstimulation can cause frustration and tears, although your baby is too young for a proper tantrum!

The best way to encourage good behaviour in your baby at this early stage in his life is to reward the behaviour that you like. It's easy to fall into the trap of lavishing the most attention on your baby when he's doing something you don't want him to, such as throwing his food on the floor, or pulling all the books off the shelf ... again. If he learns that this is the best way to get your attention, then that's what he'll do.

Rewarding "good" actions

Unless what he is doing is dangerous, try to ignore it. You'll often find that it's not the activity itself that's interesting to him, but your reaction to it. Instead, try to pay him lots of attention when he is doing the things that you want him to be doing. When he's quietly playing, looking at a book, or happily eating his lunch, encourage him with praise; rub his back; or kiss his head. That way he'll learn what behaviour brings rewards, and what just isn't worth bothering with.

Encouraging good behaviour

As well as praising his good behaviour, as your baby gets older, he can be taught – even with small day-to-day lessons – how satisfying it is to help others. From as early as 10 months, you can teach your baby the satisfaction of give and take. If you give him a bite of your banana, let him do the same by feeding you a piece. Show him how happy his gesture makes you feel. These small moments can nourish a sensibility towards sharing and caring for others.

company, or of simply not getting enough rest during the course of the day. Frustration is also likely to occur when your baby is using additional energy trying to reach a certain developmental milestone, such as sitting up or crawling.

Diversion tatics

Now is the golden age of distraction. If your baby becomes frustrated with a particular toy, swap it for another one. If he is annoyed because you won't let him play with your mobile phone, hold him up to the window to see what's outside. If your baby is grabbing for something dangerous, take the object away or physically move him – and then give him a safe alternative.

Remember, too, that like the rest of us, babies learn by doing things repeatedly. When he throws his bowl of peas off the highchair, he's not being naughty because he wants to upset you

or mess up the kitchen floor. He's simply curious to see what will happen when he does certain things. Bearing this in mind may help you to keep your cool even when your baby has ignored your "No" for the fourth time.

Explain your actions

Talking to your baby and explaining to him why you're doing something can help to diffuse his frustration. Although he may be too young to understand you at the moment, this is a good habit to develop. Eventually, for example he'll associate "tidying up toys" time with winding down before bedtime. Also, if you pick up your baby and move him away from something, or confiscate a sharp object, explain what you're doing, even if he's still too young to understand. You're teaching a fundamental lesson – that some behaviours aren't acceptable, and that you're in charge here.

Fact: At around nine months, your baby is becoming more assertive.

If you take a toy away from him, he is likely to make his objection clear. By now, he is really starting to find more ways to express himself to make his needs and wants known.

Babies have an amazing, and often aggravating, ability to make demands. However, your baby needs to know that you care about his feelings, even when he expresses them by screaming or flailing his fists. It may look like he's throwing a fit, but he's really seeking reassurance. As long as you stick with your original decision – for example, that he can't play with the remote control – then it's fine to sit down for a cuddle with him, and no one can accuse you of "giving in". Pay attention to his cues and try to anticipate his desires and needs.

Welcome to parenthood! 0–6 weeks

Your growing baby 6 weeks to 6 months

Your older baby 6 months to one year

Baby healthcare 0–12 months

Environment and everyday care

Welcome to parenthood!
0–6 weeks

Your growing baby
6 weeks to 6 months

Your older baby
6 months to one year

Baby healthcare
0–12 months

Your baby's environment

As soon as your baby is on the move, your job as a parent steps up a gear. For a curious, active baby, a staircase is an exciting mountain to climb, kitchen cupboards are treasure chests and electrical switches have magical powers. Suddenly you see potential dangers everywhere!

A safe haven

The term "childproofing" is actually a bit of a misnomer. It suggests it's possible to achieve 100 per cent safety, but you can't cocoon your baby from every risk in life and you wouldn't want to. Minor accidents are part of a child's normal experience. Your baby needs to learn how to cope with everyday hazards and discover the consequences of his actions to find out how the world works. At the same time, you want to make his environment as safe as possible.

Reassessing your home

To spot likely hazards and control them, it's best to check out the territory before your baby is fully mobile. Get down on your hands and knees for a baby's eye view of your home. What's within reach? What looks tempting? Where would you go if you could crawl, toddle or walk? This helps you identify the cupboards, drawers and other spaces your baby might get into. As he starts walking and climbing, you'll have to repeat this exercise, looking higher each time.

Eliminating hazards

Lock up or stow away potential poisons or hazards. Safety gates are useful to limit your baby's access to potentially dangerous areas of your home. Keep an eye out for any tiny objects that your baby could choke on, and be vigilant when you have visitors – an open handbag on the floor, for example, may contain paracetamol, pens, make-up and other items that could be harmful.

Most importantly, the best way to prevent injuries, in the home and out, is to supervise your baby at all times.

 Systemised mum

Babies are naturally curious, so keep one eye on him and the other on the things around him.

"I've done my best to childproof my home, particularly now that my baby can crawl. I keep surfaces clear and make sure there's nothing on the floor that wouldn't be safe for her to come into contact with, so no muddy shoes or laptop bags left lying around! I also keep rooms as clutter-free as possible, and I've put rubber pads on sharp table edges and safety gates in the entrance to the kitchen and at the bottom of the stairs. I feel fairly confident that my house is safe; I'm extra vigilant, though, when we visit other peoples' homes."

Safety check list

One of the biggest threats to your baby is his home environment. Consult the checklist below to ensure that you have taken all the measures necessary to keep your baby as safe as possible.

- put socket covers on electrical sockets
- put protectors on sharp corners
- fix locks to low-level cupboards
- keep sharp objects, matches and lighters well out of reach
- fit a fireguard
- fit smoke detectors (to BS54466) near the kitchen, on landings and in bedrooms
- avoid curtains and blinds with cords
- keep furniture and other potential climbing structures away from windows
- put non-slip pads under rugs and mats
- fit safety gates (to BS4125) to stairs
- anchor tall lamps behind furniture to prevent them being toppled over
- be aware of hinges that could pinch
- keep medicines in a locked cupboard
- lock away poisonous substances
- take care with hot drinks

Safety measures

It's well worth investing a little time and money on childproofing your home properly, especially once your baby starts to move around and crawl (and is more likely to have accidents).

Cordoning off

Safety gates will make life easier for you – and safer for your baby. They can be fitted at the top or bottom of the stairs or across doorways, giving you more control over which parts of the house your little one can visit.

Check that the gate fits the space you need it for, or that it is extendable. Some gates come with extension kits in case you need them to fit a wider gap, and some have pressure gauges so that you can tell whether or not they are safely fitted. Adults climbing over stairgates can lead to accidents, so it's a good idea to choose gates that have an opening section in the middle.

Safety fixtures and fittings

If you don't have one already, now's the time to invest in smoke alarms (see p.213). Be sure to test the batteries on a regular basis.

Other good safety gadgets are corner protectors for furniture to prevent heads being bumped, and door-slam protectors to look after fingers. Glass safety film is also useful; this sticks onto large sheets of glass to prevent them from shattering into little pieces if broken. Temporary window locks can be lifesavers, allowing windows to be opened only a little way.

From hot cookers and sharp knives to cleaning cupboards, the kitchen can be dangerous for your baby. It's wise to fit cupboard, drawer, oven and fridge locks. A cooker guard – a narrow strip of clear plastic that fits across the front of a hob – stops your baby getting hold of hot pans. If you don't have a guard, turn pan handles towards the back of your stove. Also, if you have leads hanging down, you can buy a device that shortens them and keeps them out of harm's way.

Electrical sockets are often just the right height to attract crawling babies and curious toddlers, so insert socket covers, preferably before your baby starts crawling. If you have electrical leads lying around, you can buy plastic tubing that gathers them together and hides them away from little hands.

Your baby's role model

Babies eight months and older focus on what adults are doing – and want to play with the items they see you using. So scissors, stereos, DVDs, cookware and tools all have enormous appeal! It's a good idea to give your baby child-safe, toy versions of household objects, and keep appliances, sharp objects and tools safely out of reach.

Easy-to-fit safety catches give peace of mind, allowing you to relax as your baby explores every nook and cranny.

As your baby becomes more mobile outside spaces are particularly enticing, but can present a whole new range of hazards.

Outside hazards

Once your baby is crawling around, or perhaps beginning to cruise or even walk, your garden becomes a wonderful new world for her to explore. However, you do need to be aware that many garden, and household, plants can be potentially poisonous.

A safe garden
Take steps to find out which of your plants are poisonous, and then keep your baby well away. If you need help identifying a particular plant, take a clipping to your local nursery or garden centre for assistance.

Put patio plant pots out of your baby's reach if possible, or supervise her around them, so that she doesn't choke on any pebbles or try to eat the soil.

Constant supervision
You may find that you need to supervise your baby all the while she is playing outdoors until she is old enough to learn that she must not touch or eat the plants. Many parents find that it's possible to fence off a safe area of the garden near the house for their baby to play in. Some flexible playpen systems are suitable for use outside as well.

"Find out which **garden plants** are **poisonous** and **dig them up** before your baby starts **toddling**."

Pets and the older baby

Many pets are tolerant of young babies, however, it's still important to be aware of potential dangers and take precautions to avoid situations where your baby could be harmed. This especially applies once your baby starts to crawl around and walk.

Living together
Dogs need to be supervised at all times when babies and young children are around. Even the most tolerant of dogs can be unwell or bad tempered sometimes, and this can make them unpredictable around babies and children who may handle them inappropriately. Most cats will simply escape if a child is teasing or hurting them, but some will scratch and bite.

You may find it very helpful to use a safety gate to keep your pets and your children apart, at least some of the time. These gadgets can also help keep your baby away from animal foods and litter trays.

Curious babies have been known to use a cat flap to escape into the garden, so you may need to keep it locked while your baby is around!

Health hazards from pets
Double check with your vet that your pets have been adequately wormed, and never leave worming tablets or other pet medications in a place where your baby can reach them. If your pet has free range of the garden, you may need to check it over and use a pooper scooper before letting your baby play outside. You could also fence the garden in such a way that there is a safe baby area and a separate pet area.

Welcome to parenthood!
0–6 weeks

Your growing baby
6 weeks to 6 months

Your older baby
6 months to one year

Baby healthcare
0–12 months

Sometimes it's best to relax a bit about the mess and mayhem and let your baby do what comes naturally.

A world to explore

New parents often ask, "How can we stop our crawling baby touching everything?" The simple answer is that you can't. Children have a natural curiosity and learn about the world by exploring and touching things. This inquisitiveness is essential for their development – it's not "naughty", and constantly discouraging your baby will cause both of you a lot of stress.

The best approach is to remove dangerous or precious things from your baby's reach. This allows him to explore his environment safely, and avoids his becoming frustrated as you constantly snatch away tempting objects. It lowers your stress levels, too!

A stimulating environment

Once you've dealt with obvious household hazards, keep one cupboard easily accessible for your baby. Fill it with age-appropriate toys and books and rotate them regularly to keep up his interest and make it worth the effort of exploring. You could also put in some everyday household objects, such as a plastic lunchbox full of old wooden dolly pegs that he can empty out and fill up again (rather than the contents of your handbag or the cat's feeding bowl!). Or fill a string bag with scraps of clean fabrics, such as velvet or fake fur – babies are sensual creatures and love discovering "fun-to-feel" materials. Remember, though, that babies put things in their mouths well into their second year, so avoid any objects that you don't want to end up in his mouth.

Don't fret about the mess: remind yourself it's good for his development. The tactile experience of handling shapes and textures stimulates his senses and helps him develop hand–eye coordination and fine motor skills.

Ever watchful

Finally, stay alert – your watchful eyes and speedy actions are the best tools to keep your baby safe. Anticipate the next skill he'll learn and plan for it – he'll surprise you constantly.

Laid-back mum

Babies can't help making a mess, so there's no point getting stressed about it.

"When I brought my baby home, the chaos started and it hasn't stopped. I don't think there's been a day when I've looked around my home and felt satisfied that it's tidy. I'm not letting it worry me, though. I need to make purées while I'm weaning my son, so the kitchen is bound to be a mess at least once a day. I need to let my son explore his surroundings, so it's inevitable he's going to be pulling things out of cupboards and chucking toys around. Also, until my baby is potty trained, I'll have a constant stream of cloth nappies waiting to be washed or drying on the radiators.

I've just decided to go with the flow for the time being. I do try to make sure that the house is clean though. I make an effort to give the kitchen surfaces a wipe down several times a day, not to mention my son's highchair. The bathroom is cleaned once a week, too. My friends and family know I don't have enough hours in the day to pick up every dropped sock, so they don't judge me when they come round. They're there to see me and my family anyway, not inspect my home."

Tip: Making a mess is a natural stage in your baby's development.

You may be frustrated by the mess your baby makes, but his motor skills aren't up to being neat and tidy yet, so let him get messy, especially while he's learning to feed himself.

Containing the chaos

Before your baby was mobile, you probably didn't think twice about those delicate ornaments tidily arranged on your low-slung coffee table, and didn't notice how easily that free-standing lamp in the living room could topple over. Now your baby's on the move, though, each room looks like a potential war zone, and even the most innocuous household items suddenly seem to present a danger. There are ways and means to control the chaos, however.

Of course, the stairs are an obvious place to install a safety gate to keep the area "out of bounds", but they are also useful for blocking your baby's access to multi-hazard rooms, such as the kitchen or the downstairs loo. However, you should still make these rooms as safe as possible for your baby, just in case there is one occasion when the gate is not fastened properly.

Satisfying his curiosity

While you'll want to keep family heirlooms and dangerous objects out of your baby's reach, it's a good idea to encourage his natural curiosity by placing interesting items where he can access them without too much difficulty. For example, if he's just starting to pull himself up to standing using furniture, place one of his favourite toys on a sturdy chair at the opposite side of the room. It will be an incentive for him to crawl or shuffle over to it and practise his latest skills!

It's not too early to set boundaries for your baby. By now he understands simple instructions and may purposely choose to ignore you when you say "no" (to help it carry more weight, reserve its use for things that are truly dangerous). It's not defiance, rather his natural curiosity to see how the world works.

When to tidy

Babies create no end of mess as they play, and you may be tempted to "tidy up as you go along", but this approach is more than likely doomed to fail. The minute your baby sees you put something away, his interest is immediately drawn to it and he'll want to play with it again. Instead of creating constant work for yourself, try to relax and let your baby enjoy himself. If you really can't bear your living room being untidy, designate a "messy area" in your home – perhaps your baby's bedroom – where the toy boxes can stay out 24/7, or at least during the daytime while your baby is playing.

When playtime is over, make it clear to him that it's time to tidy up. Praise him when he puts things away tidily – it's a good habit to acquire early on. Most of all, make it fun!

Welcome to parenthood!
0–6 weeks

Your growing baby
6 weeks to 6 months

Your older baby
6 months to one year

Baby healthcare
0–12 months

Parents**Talk...**

"When our baby was about six months and old enough to sit up to play, my partner and I started making a little game of tidying up all the toys before bed each night, which she loved to join in with. We'd sit on the floor next to her with all the toys and throw them into the box. Sometimes she refused to part with something, or was more interested in taking toys out of the box than putting them in, but as she's got older she's got the hang of it. I'm looking forward to the day when we can leave the pre-bedtime tidying up session to her while we put our feet up!"
Maeve, 31, mother of three

"Now that our baby is nine months, he's starting to understand what I'm doing when I tidy his toys away at the end of each day. I give him some things to put in the toy box, and whenever he puts a toy in, I encourage him, saying 'Well done!' He feels proud to have done something to please mummy."
Lorna, 38, first-time mum

"I made up a silly song about tidying the toys away that I sing while dancing around picking them up. I look and sound daft, but my baby giggles and hands things to me to put in the box. When he's talking, he can join in!"
Bernadette, 41, mother of two

Making a game out of tidying up at the end of the day is a great way to introduce your baby to the concept of clearing up.

Safe play equipment

Toys are childhood treasures, especially when they have been chosen with care. However, before you buy a toy, it's important always to assess if it's appropriate for your baby's age. Remind grandparents and other family members to bear this in mind, too.

Beware of baby walkers

If you're thinking of buying your baby a baby walker, be vigilant. Data suggests that more accidents happen with these than with any other form of baby equipment. This is because baby walkers give babies extra speed (a baby can reach up to one metre per second in one zoom), extra height and access to multiple hazards.

Most baby walker injuries are caused by falls when the baby walker tips and the baby is thrown downstairs or crashes into furniture, heaters or ovens. There's also an increased risk of your baby being burnt by previously inaccessible objects, such as candles and hot cups of tea, or finding household poisons, such as perfume or mouthwash.

A common misconception is that when a baby is occupied in her little "wagon", she is safe and can be left unsupervised for short periods. In reality, extra vigilance is needed when your baby is in a walker. She is actually safer left on the floor in a hazard-free room.

Toy checks

Other toys and equipment can pose safety risks, too. Always check the "recommended age" label on new toys, and be realistic about your baby's level of ability and maturity. Also, younger children play with older children's toys, if left lying around. Until your child is three, toy parts should be bigger than her mouth to prevent choking.

Avoid toys with strings or cords, or ensure they're no longer than 30 centimetres (12 inches). A cord can be wrapped around a baby's neck, risking strangulation. Once your baby can climb up on her hands and knees, remove cot gyms or hanging mobiles from her cot. Also, be wary of older toys. For example, the five-year-old model of a popular play kitchen may have a phone attached with a potentially deadly cord, while the latest model of the same kitchen has the more current and safer cordless phone. Always try to follow the warnings and instructions provided on toys.

With outdoor equipment, such as garden swings and slides, check that they're robust, safely assembled and don't pose a risk of strangulation.

In general, it's safer to keep your baby's play area relatively tidy and supervise her while she's playing.

Potential hazards in play things

Keep these safety guidelines in mind when choosing toys for your baby, and always be sure to supervise play.

- Is the toy too heavy? Could your baby be hurt if it fell on her?
- Look for toys that are well put together. Check for small parts, sharp edges and points.
- Is the toy in good condition? Check for wear and discard damaged toys.
- Is there a string or cord on the toy longer than 30cm (12in) that could be a strangulation risk?
- Make sure the toy is suitable for your baby. Is the age range suited to your baby's level of ability?
- Think big: parts should be bigger than your baby's mouth up to the age of three to avoid the risk of choking.
- Check garden swings and slides. Are they robust and safely fixed?
- Buy toys only from outlets you trust. Always look for the official European Community (CE) symbol on toys.

Keep toys age-appropriate. Push-along toys are perfect once your baby has taken her first few wobbly steps.

Chunky toys with large pieces are safe and stimulating for babies under a year, enabling them to learn about different shapes.

Away from home

It's one thing making your home environment a safe haven for your baby, but what about when you visit other peoples' homes? You want to relax and enjoy your host's company, but all you can think about is what unknown dangers are lurking around the corner for your precious baby. You need to think safety first.

Quick adjustments

Your easiest option is to make the room that you're in as safe as possible and to stay put! For example, in a living room where there are no gates to keep your baby from roaming, suggest that you move a sturdy armchair against the door. Remove any long, hanging tablecloths that your baby may pull down – with everything else on top of it. The same goes for trailing electrical wires and table lamps – if possible, unplug appliances or rearrange the furniture to put hazards out of bounds. Do a quick scan of the floor for choking hazards, such as small coins or glass beads, or sharp objects such as paper clips, and tie blind or curtain cords up, well out of the reach of your baby.

If you're sitting in the kitchen, check that the dishwasher is empty (a determined baby could easily open it and reach inside for a knife). Turn pot handles to the back of the cooker, and remove any small fridge magnets. Put the rubbish bin and any pet food bowls outside, and move any potential poison hazards, such as cleaning products, from cupboards that your baby can open.

Longer visits

If you're staying overnight or longer, check the bathroom and put any medicines and cleaning fluids (and the toilet brush) out of reach. For a longer visit, it's worth buying some cupboard locks and plug safety covers. If you regularly stay at someone's house, for example with grandparents or other relatives, consider asking them to install some child gates or stairguards – it's worth the investment for peace of mind.

Visits to grandparents or friends will be more relaxed if you're reassured that your baby is in a safe, secure environment.

 ### Systemised mum

Knowing your baby is safe away from home gives peace of mind.

"Joshua spends one day a week at my mum's house while I work. My mum thinks I'm fussing, but I was surprised that she'd left cleaning products under the kitchen sink. I moved them to a high cupboard as soon as I saw them. Joshua isn't crawling yet, but it won't be long before he's all over the place.

I childproofed our house before Joshua arrived and I bought a double set of cupboard locks so that I could give some to my mum. I'm also going to make sure that there are safety gates up there as soon as Josh is crawling.

I find it relaxing with my antenatal group; our babies are the same age so we don't worry about older children getting in the way or unsuitable objects getting into babies' mouths!

I know things will get easier as Josh gets older, but for now I prefer to go to places where Josh can play safely and I can breathe easy."

 # Parents**Talk...**

"By far the best safety device we found is the slide cabinet-door lock. We're also installing window guards in the upstairs bedrooms."
Karen, 39, first-time mum

"Some catalogues sell foam tubes for dangerous edges. A friend said that they're no more than foam insulation tubes you get at DIY shops. Slit one lengthwise and voila! A cheap way to protect your baby from sharp edges."
John, 34, first-time dad

"I give my son soft toys only (cloth books or stuffed animals) to play with in the car. I also put all purchases in the boot to avoid something knocking into him!"
Nikki, 29, mother of two

"I keep all medicines in a locked box. It might be inconvenient, but at least I don't have to worry about my children getting hold of anything that could harm them."
Deanna, 38, mother of three

Welcome to parenthood!
0–6 weeks

Your growing baby
6 weeks to 6 months

Your older baby
6 months to one year

Baby healthcare
0–12 months

Everyday care

It's amazing how your baby becomes a little more independent every day. He may be able to feed himself with a spoon, or hold his arms out helpfully while you dress him ... and he may also start developing his own ideas about what's fun (and what isn't).

Dressing your older baby

Once your baby starts to move around, whether crawling or walking, he will need clothes that are both comfortable and durable enough to cope with being washed again and again! Your older baby will be climbing, crawling, getting mucky and splashing in puddles whenever he can. He therefore needs clothes that allow him to explore, keep his knees protected as much as possible and allow some air to circulate around the nappy area.

Layers of clothing are the answer, so that you can remove or add items to your baby's clothing, depending on the weather or the time of day.

Practical clothing

You may be tempted to buy clothes that your baby can "grow into", but make sure they're not so big that your baby trips over the hem of a dress or trouser legs. Clothes need to be functional so that explorations and movements aren't inhibited. Dresses are fine once your baby can walk, but they will only frustrate a crawling baby.

 Systemised mum

Second-hand baby clothes are often in excellent condition. So you don't have to run your bank account dry buying brand new clothes every month or two.

"As my baby grows so fast, I don't see much point in buying expensive clothes. I go to my supermarket or the cheaper high street shops for most things – the quality isn't bad, and when he's grown out of them I sell them or give them to a charity shop. I regularly buy second-hand clothes, too – that's where I get my baby's stylish designer clothes from! They're usually in great condition (probably from a baby with so many babygros he's barely worn any!), and a third of the price, if not cheaper, than when new. I do my best to look after them so I can pass them on again."

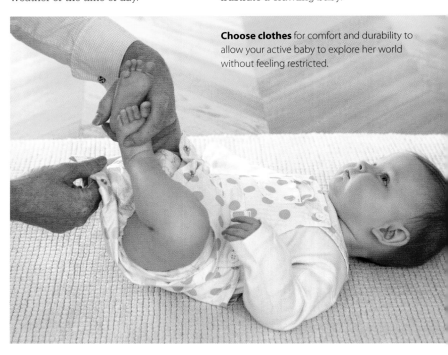

Choose clothes for comfort and durability to allow your active baby to explore her world without feeling restricted.

Beware of too many fastenings. Clothes that are loaded with buttons and poppers are awkward to put on a wriggling baby. Go for natural fabrics, such as cotton jersey, and slip-on styles that come off easily for nappy changes. Separate tops and bottoms with elasticated waists are also good choices. Make sure that any

A machine-washable coat with a drawstring hood is the most practical type of winter coat for your baby. Choose a coat with large buttons or loops and toggle buttons, so that eventually your child will be able to manage these by himself. Also, make sure that the coat is not so bulky that he

information through their feet, and shoes may be restricting at this age. Also, feet have natural "non-skid" surfaces, and toes can grasp and help your baby balance as he pulls himself up. At this age, shoes are more for warmth or protection, for example wearing wellies in wet weather.

"A **cheerful, light-hearted** commentary while **dressing** your baby keeps him **distracted**. A colourful mobile or toy sometimes helps, too."

jumpers or sweatshirts that you buy have a decent sized neck-hole so that they slip quickly and easily over your baby's head. Or better still, opt for tops that have a buttoned-up or zipped style around the neck or the back. For night-time, look for sleepsuits or pyjamas made with pure cotton fibres because these have natural thermal qualities that help to keep your baby warm when it's cold, and also keep him cool when it's warm.

can't move freely in it. Sometimes, a few thinner layers may be more comfortable and just as warm as a coat, but without the added bulk.

For babies this age, whole-hand mittens are warmer than gloves. Buy two pairs in the same style, since it's likely that at least one mitten will get lost! You don't need to buy shoes for your baby before he can walk (see box, below). In fact, babies are better off barefoot, since they get a lot of sensory

Baby's first shoes

Once your baby can walk confidently, it's time to protect his feet when outside with shoes made of flexible, lightweight and natural materials such as soft leather, with flexible soles and non-skid bottoms.

A good fit

Make sure these first shoes (and future ones) are fitted by a children's shoe fitter, as your baby requires a specific width (D to H, with F and G the most common) and length of shoe (babies' shoes start at size 3). Aim for lots of room and width in the toe area, a secure fastening, such as Velcro or laces, and a supportive heel cup.

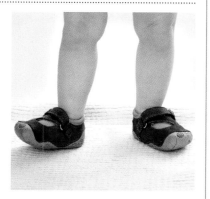

Buying your baby's first shoes is a significant parenting milestone. Look for a soft, lightweight style with flexibility.

ParentsTalk...

"Attempting to dress a baby who keeps trying to crawl or wriggle away can be frustrating! The only way I can entice her to stay still is to let her play with the television remote or her toy mobile phone that makes noises when you press the buttons. It keeps her still and amused for ages. I'm waiting for the moment she decides she's bored of that activity and I have to find another distraction."
Chris, 27, first-time mum

"I end up dressing my baby in stages if she's in a lively mood. She's 11 months and has started walking, and also crawls at high-speed. I end up with her half dressed, with me on stand-by with the next item of clothing ready to make a move when she's stopped. When I'm in a rush, I do have to be a mean mummy and hold her still. She makes a fuss, but once they're on it's forgotten!"
Sian, 33, first-time mum

Welcome to parenthood!
0–6 weeks

Your growing baby
6 weeks to 6 months

Your older baby
6 months to one year

Baby healthcare
0–12 months

Dad's **Diary**

An easier bathtime

"It's much easier bathing Ellie now that she's a bit older and can sit up well unsupported. I've still got to supervise her at all times, of course, but she's quite happy to sit and play with her bath toys. In fact, I often put her in the bath with me – it saves time and it's much more fun (although the water's a bit cooler than I'd like it).

I like to hide her rubber duck under the water at the bottom of the bath – it never fails to make her squeal when I let go of it and it pops out of the water with a splash! For her, washing seems to be an incidental inconvenience that daddy inflicts on her while we're playing. So we bought a washcloth puppet to make it more fun. She even has a couple of waterproof books to leaf through while we're in the bath."

Keeping your baby clean

It's a fact of life that active babies are dirtier babies! Where once you could get away with giving your little one a quick top-and-tail, you may now find that a bath is essential to remove the day's mess and grime.

Bathtime for older babies

For older babies, a bedtime bath is often part of a well established routine, along with pyjamas, a story and a goodnight cuddle. Others may be less keen on getting wet. The key to making bathtime more enjoyable is first for you to relax – babies can pick up if you seem stressed or anxious.

Although your baby can sit up now, this doesn't mean that you shouldn't supervise her at all times – you should be constantly at the ready in case she slips. Also, once she starts to pull herself up, you will have to teach her that it is not safe for her to stand up in the bath.

Even though your baby is older, the detergents in bubble baths and shampoos can still irritate her sensitive skin, so use a mild soap, and wash and shampoo her at the end of her bath so that she isn't sitting in soapy water for too long. If she enjoys bathtime, you might want to start extending the length of time she spends in the bath now. Otherwise, continue to keep it brief. In time, it will become more enjoyable for your baby.

Eczema and bathing

If your baby suffers from eczema (see p.267), you'll need to protect her skin. Talk with your doctor about how often to bathe her. Some experts believe that daily bathing can be helpful for babies with eczema. Just don't make the water too warm, because very warm water dries out the skin faster and can make skin itchy. Use an emollient rather than soap or a detergent, as this helps protect skin from the drying effects of water. As soon as you get your baby out of the bath, pat her dry (don't rub), then promptly apply a liberal amount of moisturiser to "seal in" the body's own moisture.

You could also try changing the washing powder you use. Use a mild, fragrance-free, non-biological detergent and avoid using fabric softeners.

Constant vigilance is essential at bathtime. Even when your baby can sit unsupported, keep an eye on him at all times.

Hair care

Some babies are born with a luscious thatch of hair, while others are past their first birthday before any hair detangling is necessary. Untangling unruly hair can prove to be a challenge.

Tangle-free hair

To attempt your first detangle, pick a time when your baby isn't feeling tired or hungry. Before you start combing, distract her with a toy or game to help her cooperate. Use a wide-tooth comb and one of the detangling sprays that are widely available for babies. Don't spend too long at first; if she starts to object, don't persevere, just try again another time. If she is happy for you to continue, make a big fuss of her. Get a hand mirror and compliment her on how beautiful she looks! If you use this positive reinforcement after each hair wash, it will help make grooming easier! With proper hair care, you can eliminate those tangles and make combing easy.

Start cleaning your baby's teeth as soon as the first one appears. Use a soft, "first" toothbrush, or simply wipe her teeth and gums with a clean cloth.

Your baby's first teeth

Your baby's first tooth is likely to be a bottom front one, emerging at around six months to one year. As soon as you see a tooth emerging, start cleaning it at least once a day (see below).

NHS dental treatment is free to under-18s. Check with your dentist when to book your baby's first appointment. Dentists start checks at around six months, or whenever the teeth start to come through.

Early brushing

Your baby's gums will feel tender while teething, so don't be too vigorous with the brushing. At first, you may find it easier to use a piece of clean gauze or muslin wrapped around your finger. Use small, gentle circular movements, concentrating on the area where the teeth and gums meet, and clean one section at a time. Your dentist will be happy to show you how to clean her teeth if you need more guidance.

Your baby's first toothbrush should have soft bristles and a small head that allows it to reach all parts of her mouth easily and comfortably. Check the age range on the packaging.

Her first toothpaste

Until your baby's permanent teeth appear, normally at around six years of age, use a low-fluoride baby toothpaste, containing about 1,000 ppm (parts per million) fluoride. These toothpastes are safe in areas where the water is fluoridated, and won't cause harm if a tiny bit is swallowed. Only use a pea-sized amount of toothpaste.

As your baby grows, encourage her to spit out the toothpaste and rinse after brushing, as swallowing large amounts of fluoride can damage teeth, and may cause vomiting and diarrhoea. Some parents avoid toothpastes with tasty, fruity flavours, so that their children understand that toothpastes aren't food.

Dealing with teething

While some babies sprout their first teeth with no problems, for others it's painful. Signs of teething include red, swollen gums, ear rubbing on the affected side and heavy drooling. Your baby may feed inconsistently, sleep badly and seem unsettled and cranky.

Comforting sore gums

Giving your baby something cool to bite on, such as a teething ring, can ease discomfort. Or you could let her chew on breadsticks, non-sweetened rusks or oven-hardened bread. Some parents use frozen bread for a cool chew, and fresh and frozen fruit and vegetables, such as cucumber or frozen bananas, make good chewable soothers. Watch your baby and avoid vegetables such as raw carrots, which she may bite lumps off and choke on. Chilled water in a bottle or feeding cup can be soothing. If she's been weaned, try cold apple purée or plain yoghurt. If she rejects everything, try a cuddle.

Medical treatments

Teething gels usually contain a local anaesthetic and an antiseptic, which together ease pain and prevent infection. A small amount rubbed on with a clean finger numbs the gum for about 20 minutes. Don't use gels more than six times a day.

Thumb sucking

Does your baby suck her thumb for prolonged periods? The British Dental Health Foundation advises parents to discourage thumb-sucking, as it can cause problems as teeth develop, especially when permanent ones come through at six years. Until then, it's unlikely to cause a serious problem.

Lycra sun suits and Legionnaire-style hats protect your baby's delicate skin from the damaging rays of the sun.

Weather protection

The link between sunlight and skin cancer is proven. So even in Britain, babies should not go outside without sun protection from the middle of April to the end of September.

Sun safety

Try to get your baby used to wearing a hat. Baseball caps may look cute, but they don't provide enough protection. Look for a "legionnaire" style hat instead, with a brim at the front and a flap to shield the back of his neck.

Between 11am and 3pm on sunny days, T-shirts are essential, as shoulders are particularly vulnerable. If you go to the seaside, encourage your child to keep a T-shirt on, even while splashing around in water, and pack a spare one for when he comes out.

Alternatively, try a Lycra sun-protection suit. These block out more than 80 per cent of the harmful UVA rays, dry quickly and can be worn in or out of the water.

Sunglasses for children may seem like a luxury, but they do protect eyes, and children should be encouraged to wear them from six months upwards. Make sure they protect against both UVA and UVB rays and conform to the safety standard BSEN 1836/1997. Cheaper versions may actually harm your baby's eyes.

Sunscreen creams

When buying sunscreen, look for products labelled "broad-spectrum", which means the cream protects against both UVA and UVB rays. Choose a water-resistant sunscreen with a sun-protection factor (SPF) of 15 or higher, and four stars or more. The stars measure UVA protection: five is the maximum.

Which factor?

There's not a lot of extra protection to be gained by going for an SPF higher than 30, because the difference becomes smaller the higher you go (so double the SPF doesn't mean double the protection). For example, SPF 30 will provide 96 per cent protection, and SPF 60 will provide 98 per cent. You don't need to use expensive brands, the cheaper brands are just as effective if used properly.

It's important never to use sunscreen to spend longer in the sun; it should be used only to increase your protection. Also, no sunscreen offers 100 per cent protection against the sun.

Choose a sun protection cream that is suitable for babies, and check that it offers adequate protection from both UVA and UVB rays.

It's best to keep babies out of direct sunlight altogether, but if they're exposed to sun, look out for creams or sprays specially formulated for a baby's sensitive skin, and choose one with a sun-protection factor (SPF) of at least 15. Some companies make coloured sun creams for children, so you can check for full coverage.

Canopies and cabanas

Canopies and parasols fit onto your buggy and shade your baby from the sun. Or, elasticated UV sun covers made of a dark, synthetic mesh cover the whole seat area of the buggy. Beach sun tents, or cabanas, pop-up shelters made of nylon stretched on a frame, screen out up to 97 per cent of UV rays, and provide somewhere for your baby to sleep, eat his lunch or take a break from the sun.

When it's cold outside

For trips outdoors during winter, look for clothing with a layer of insulation, such as a fleece or flannel, and a water-repellent exterior fabric. If your baby doesn't have an all-in-one snowsuit, dress him in warm, layered clothing, and wrap him up in a light blanket, topped off with another, heavier blanket made of wool or fleece. Put a hat (preferably wool) on him before going out in the winter. Dress him in mittens and warm socks or booties, too.

Once you're indoors – even if it's just for a stop at the supermarket – take at least one layer off your baby so that he doesn't sweat, otherwise the dampness will make him even colder when you get back out in the cold air. If you've covered your baby with a blanket in the car at the start of a journey, stop and take it off once the car warms up.

Bear in mind that while you're working up a sweat pushing his buggy, your baby is just sitting still in the cold. If he's happy to be out at first, but starts fussing after a while, he may be trying to tell you that he's feeling too cold now. Check his little fingers, toes, ears and face regularly, and go inside before he gets uncomfortable.

It's important to be aware that even the weaker winter sun can damage your baby's skin, so dab a little protective sunscreen on whenever he might be exposed to sunlight.

Ensure your baby stays snug in the colder months with layers of clothing and a cosy hat to keep the warmth in.

"Dressing your baby in **layers** means you can **adjust** his clothing throughout the day as **necessary**."

Fact: Your baby can get burned by the sun even on a cloudy or cool day.

Sunburn isn't a risk in hot weather only. This is because it's not the visible light or the sun's heat that burns, but the invisible UV light.

ParentsAsk...

How do I treat heat rash, sun burn or wind-lashed skin?

Your baby's skin is delicate and vulnerable to seasonal problems as the weather changes. Fortunately, there are plenty of things you can do to soothe his skin if he develops a rash or flare up.

If your baby is suffering with heat rash, you can relieve his discomfort by moving him into an airy room or a shady spot and encouraging some quiet time to help reduce his sweating. Dress your baby in light cotton clothes and dab the rash with cold, wet flannels. Calamine lotion is also soothing, but avoid ointments and other lotions, which may make the rash worse by trapping in moisture. Most heat rashes will clear within a few days.

Sunburn can be more serious than it appears in babies; if your baby has sunburn, keep him out of the sun and call your doctor or NHS Direct (see pp.312–13). Give him plenty of fluids to prevent dehydration. Soak a flannel in cool water, wring it out and gently place it on the sunburned area for 10 to 15 minutes a few times a day. You could also apply a water-based moisturising lotion or calamine lotion to his skin.

In the winter, the wind outside and dry heat indoors can sap moisture from your baby's delicate skin, so try to keep it moisturised. There are many lotions and creams made especially for babies.

Welcome to parenthood!
0–6 weeks

Your growing baby
6 weeks to 6 months

Your older baby
6 months to one year

Baby healthcare
0–12 months

Twin care

When you have young twins, it can sometimes feel as though you barely have time to brush your teeth – let alone get on with all the bigger jobs in life! If at all possible, try to get your twins into some sort of routine, if just to make your life a little easier.

Establishing a sleeping routine with twins can be key to managing the extra workload of two babies.

This is never a quick or simple process, though. Unlike mums of "singles", you can't rely on the nature of your baby to help you establish a pattern ("Oh, she's a really good sleeper"), because it's likely that if one of your twins sleeps well through the night, the other doesn't. For this reason, parents of twins often find that more rigid routines tend to work better, helping them synchronise two lots of sleeping and waking patterns.

Where there's a will ...

At first, it will go against your gut instinct to wake two quietly sleeping twins from their nap just because the routine says it's "time". You'll think it's madness! After a while, though, you will know that if you don't try to synchronise them in the day, they won't sleep at the same time in the night. One day – and it will happen – your twins will develop complementary sleeping patterns.

Routines need an iron will to get going, but they do give you some certainty of how the day will pan out: when you can get dressed, for example and whether you might get to eat a meal with your partner again in the evening. Also, once it starts working, you will finally start to get some much-needed sleep.

Sleeping arrangements

While it's fine (and may even be beneficial) to have your twins sleeping in the same cot when they're tiny, as your babies grow there will be less room for them to be comfortable in one cot. Their waking patterns may begin to differ too (unless you've managed to synchronise them), and eventually it will be simpler to separate them. It's also important to give your twins more individual attention and to view them as separate personalities who may appreciate their own personal area. However, once they're in their own

Dad's **Diary**

Team work

"Everyone asks us how we cope with twins, but for us two babies is just normal and we cope because we're a team. We parent the girls equally – not just because there's two of them, but because I want to be as involved as my partner is in looking after them. If we want to go out, we plan around the girls' routine and aim to leave the house immediately after they have been fed. This gives us a couple of hours until they need to be changed and fed again. The girls have a side-by-side double buggy and we can get into most shops, but we still have to think before we go out about which shops we need to visit and plan accordingly.

There are other places where we encounter problems, too. Taking the girls to the doctors is a bit of a challenge because our surgery doesn't allow buggies inside. If we both go, we can carry the girls in a sling each, but if one of us is on our own and we need to take the buggy, we warn the receptionists in advance. They are generally pretty helpful and keep an eye on one baby while I get the other baby out of the buggy, but this isn't ideal.

A lot of shops don't have space for a double buggy either once you're actually inside, so we have to plan our shopping trips carefully. We often split up while we're out shopping so that one of us can run some errands, while the other entertains the babies, and then we may do a swap."

Fathers of twins are likely to feel an essential part of the "team" as they muck in and help with baby duties.

With time and inevitable experience, you'll develop the confidence and know-how to deal with two babies at once.

Welcome to parenthood!
0–6 weeks

Your growing baby
6 weeks to 6 months

Your older baby
6 months to one year

Baby healthcare
0–12 months

Systemised mum

When you're a mum of twins, getting into a routine is essential

"I've got the twins into a really good routine now, but I do have to be ultra organised to keep it going. I use the babies' nap times to make up batches of baby food for the following day, sterilise bottles and feeding equipment, sort out washing and try to do a bit of tidying up.

I'm lucky that we can afford a cleaner. She comes once a fortnight and it really helps. I now do all of my shopping online, too – going to the supermarket with twins is just not a fun experience!

When I was pregnant, I asked at my local further education college if any childcare students wanted a family placement. Helen comes to help out two afternoons a week. It's definitely worth finding out about placements: not many people know about them and, importantly, they're free!"

room, they may well enjoy having their cots close together so that they can communicate in their own special way.

A supportive network

You'll need plenty of support from others. Your local twins club may be a fantastic source of advice and new friends, and you'll meet other mums who understand what you're going through. Your family and friends will probably be keen to spend some time with your babies, so take advantage and accept offers of help.

Dads of twins tend to be more involved in their babies' care. Even if you're breastfeeding, there's plenty your partner can do to help with the babies and looking after you, too.

If you can afford it, you could consider hiring a nanny or au pair (see p.309), or someone to help with housework. Whether you do this through a private advertisement or through an agency, ask for, and check, references carefully before employing anyone in your home.

Families with twins or more have no statutory entitlement to help in the home, but it's worth asking your health

ParentsTalk...

"I joined my local twins club when my boys were a couple of weeks old and it was the best thing I did as I really didn't have a clue about some things! It was great to get advice from mums of older twins who'd been through synchronised breastfeeding and nappy-changing sessions. As my twins have grown, there's been advice on everything from which double buggy to buy to the art of spoon feeding two babies at the same time."
Ruth, 33, mother of twins

"My twins group has been brilliant since the start. I joined when I was pregnant, and my girls are now 10 months, so the mums have been through the whole process together. The best thing about it is the feeling that you're part of a special breed of super mums who can feed, dress, change and play with two babies simultaneously."
Anna, 35, mother of three

visitor or local Social Services department if any help can be arranged, particularly if you have other children.

Other sources of help include the family support charity Home Start, which has trained volunteers who help families with pre-school age children for a couple of hours a week. Or you can contact your local further education college to find out if they train nursery nurses or nannies. They may be looking for work placements for students, although you'll need to organise this well in advance. Also, bear in mind that students on placement can't be left in sole charge of babies or children.

Holidays and festivities

Traditions and festivities

Whether you're celebrating birthdays, Christmas, Hanukkah, Diwali or Eid, family festivals take on a magical meaning when you have a baby. Although your baby might not appreciate the merrymaking, his relatives will definitely appreciate him! Make the most of special occasions.

Celebrating with your baby

Christmas, birthdays and other special dates on your family calendar will help to give your baby a sense of security and belonging. You'll want to make the most of these special family occasions now that your baby has arrived. The following pages offer a helpful guide to celebrating birthdays, the festive season and other family traditions and times of celebration with your baby.

Family traditions

When it comes to traditional religious holidays, such as Christmas, Eid or Hanukkah, every family has their own particular style of celebrating. As well as getting the family together at these times, exchanging gifts and feasting, once you have a baby you may remember or resurrect special holiday rituals from your own childhood, such as making festive decorations or celebratory dishes. Having a new baby in the family is also the perfect time to create some new traditions! Whether old or new, your little one will grow up with the excitement of anticipating and enjoying these special family traditions each year. Whichever way you celebrate, crackling wrapping paper, bright colours, sparkling lights, seasonal music and the comings and goings of visitors at these times of year are all wonderful forms of stimulation for your baby.

Keeping on the case

A word of caution, though. However much fun you're having, remember to keep your baby safe. With all the hustle and bustle, it's easy to forget that festive decorations and unwrapped gifts are irresistible to little fingers, while foods such as small sweets, fruits and nuts are choking hazards.

Also, don't worry if your baby doesn't seem to be enjoying the celebrations as much as you had hoped. Too many new faces, sights and sounds at once can overstimulate a young baby. So don't neglect your baby's routine – put him down for a daytime nap or to bed at the usual times when you see the telltale signs of sleepiness.

Tips: During festivities, try to keep roughly to your baby's usual routine. Your baby won't know that everyone else is busy celebrating and will need his meals and naps at the usual times. If he gets too out of his routine, you will probably end up with a grumpy and overtired baby on your hands.

ParentsTalk...

"Now my husband and I have started a family, we really want to carry on the Christmas traditions we both had as children. Even though our baby is too young to understand at the moment, we're starting as we mean to go on. My husband had a tradition of getting a stocking and I always got to open one present on Christmas Eve – so our baby is going to be thoroughly spoilt!"
Jenna, 30, first-time mum

"Passover, Mothers' Day, Fathers' Day... these special days that have always been part of our lives seem like something new to celebrate now we've got a baby. Particularly Mothers' and Fathers' Day – now we're parents we won't allow these events to be forgotten!"
Rachel, 32, first-time mum

"Christmas has always been fun, even as an adult, but since having a baby, I've recaptured some of the magic it held when I was little. I'm looking forward to creating our own traditions as our brood grows."
Helen, 25, first-time mum

Welcome to parenthood! 0–6 weeks

Your growing baby 6 weeks to 6 months

Your older baby 6 months to one year

Baby healthcare 0–12 months

Your baby's first birthday

A baby's life is made up firsts – the first bath, first smile, first word, first step – but her first birthday is an especially significant milestone. It's a time for the whole family to celebrate your baby turning from a helpless newborn into a sturdy toddler, thanks to your loving care. That's why her first birthday will always be a red-letter day (even if she's too young to remember it herself!).

Your baby's first party

You may wish to celebrate the day with a small gathering of family and friends, but don't feel pressurised into going over the top. Your baby won't appreciate extravagance and small is definitely beautiful at this age. You don't have to spend lots of money to make it special. If you have a spring or summer-born baby, you could invite family and friends down to the park for a celebratory picnic and a game of rounders. Tie some bunting to a tree to create a party atmosphere. The birthday girl or boy can enjoy the proceedings from a blanket in the shade. Otherwise, hold the party at home where your baby feels secure. She'll appreciate a few decorations or, if you want something more adventurous, you could buy a baby ball pool.

At this closely-attached-to-Mum stage, the best way to make this a special day for your baby is by offering her undiluted attention. Her social network will be small and intimate, and that's how she likes it. She won't thank you for a house full of strangers, so stick to close friends and relatives.

First birthday dos and don'ts

However you decide to mark the occasion, check out the tips below to ensure celebrations run smoothly.

- Do get the timing right – after nap time works well (check out the nap times of any other babies).
- Don't invite too many people.
- Do plan some simple musical activities – dancing or nursery rhymes.
- Don't go on for too long – an hour is long enough.
- Do keep pets out of the way.
- Don't go overboard with catering – finger foods are ideal.
- Do provide somewhere clean and well-equipped for guests to do nappy changing.
- Don't let your baby near the cake candle – she'll want to grab it.
- Do ensure stair gates and fireguards are in place.
- Do relax – let your baby and her guests set the pace.
- Do offer a variety of toys on a large, safe floor space.
- Do recruit a volunteer to take plenty of photos – you'll be too busy!

A few sweet treats and a plate of sandwiches will delight your baby – and her guests.

The secret to a first birthday party is to keep it simple. Opening presents and enjoying a birthday tea will be more than enough entertainment for her big day.

Parents**Ask...**

How can we make big festivities as stress-free as possible?

The festive season is different when you're a parent. The lights and decorations can seem like a disaster waiting to happen in small hands, and there's so much pressure to give everyone the perfect day. It's no wonder stress levels rise.

Fortunately, it's possible to preserve your sanity and still enjoy yourself, just don't try to do everything yourself. Recruit family to help with the cooking, and invite your guests to bring nibbles or desserts instead to reduce your load.

Very young children may appreciate the attention that comes with gift giving, but they probably don't need as many presents as you think. Your baby will value the time you spend playing with her just as much (if not more) than any expensive toy.

If there are tensions in your family, don't feel you have to resolve them all in time for the big day. It's a good idea to declare a truce during the holiday season and focus on having a good time together instead.

If you do find your fuse running short, take a deep breath, hold it for a moment and exhale slowly. Try to find a moment for yourself when you can relax. Young children are very sensitive to a parent's mood, so do whatever makes you feel refreshed – swimming, having coffee with a friend, reading a book or taking a bubble bath. You may find yourself having a wonderful time.

Systemised mum

Sticking to routines can help your baby to enjoy the festivities as much as possible.

"I always try to stick to Lucy's routine whenever possible, even when it comes to things like birthdays and parties. I know it can seem a bit inflexible, but I think it makes life easier. For example, I decided to hold Lucy's first birthday party in the morning, after her nap, rather than during the afternoon. It worked really well and none of the children were tired and cranky.

If I'm going round to a friend's or relative's house for lunch, I let people know that Lucy has her lunch at 12 o'clock and that I'm happy to bring food for her, rather than waiting for lunch to start. Likewise, this Christmas I will feed her first, and then I can put her down for a nap while I tuck into my turkey at a leisurely pace!"

Family festivities

The festive season takes on a whole new meaning when you have a baby. The world is supposed to be full of peace and goodwill, but all too often the celebrations end in tears and tiredness (and that's just the parents!).

However, if you bear in mind a few simple things and view the holiday season through your baby's eyes, it can be a magical time for all of you.

Focus on her needs

When your baby is little, everyone wants to hold her, give her treats to eat and see her play with the toy they've lovingly chosen. Although they mean well, it's easy to end up with an overstimulated, grumpy baby – and that's no good for anyone (least of all her).

Stick to her usual routine, if you can. Your baby won't appreciate that everyone else is busy celebrating; she will still need her meals and naps at the usual times. Keep visitors busy while your baby is asleep so they don't keep checking if she has woken up. They can always do the washing up!

Separation anxiety (see p.190) can set in anywhere between nine and 18 months. Once, your baby would go to anyone, now she cries when other people come in the room. This can be disappointing for grandparents, who would love to play with her. Explain that it's a phase, and encourage relatives to sit nearby and just talk to you both.

A sensual delight

Your baby's developing senses will feast on the sounds and sights of the season. She's too young to understand what all the fuss is about, but it's never too early to start your own family traditions, whether that means lighting the Hanukkah candles, preparing a feast for Eid or decorating a Christmas tree.

A new baby lends an added significance to family celebrations, helping you to appreciate anew old-time traditions.

Welcome to parenthood!
0–6 weeks

Your growing baby
6 weeks to 6 months

Your older baby
6 months to one year

Baby healthcare
0–12 months

Travel and holidays

The thought of travelling with a small baby is daunting for many new parents, but going on holiday – even overseas – doesn't need to be a huge upheaval. Babies are more adaptable than people think, and with some careful planning, a holiday can be wonderful for all of you.

Your older baby is likely to be more awake and aware on journeys and may therefore need more "entertainment" while she travels.

Long journeys

By the time your baby is around eight months old, he's become more used to his surroundings and familiar faces. Travel may now start to disrupt his sense of security and routine, which is also well established now, especially when visiting an unfamiliar place or meeting lots of strangers. Furthermore, if your baby has to eat, sleep, and play in a way that he's not used to, he may become grizzly and difficult and who can blame him?

Everything you need

As always, you'll need to be prepared before embarking on a long journey. As well as nappy-changing equipment and a first-aid kit, you may want to take some infant medicine and, if you need them, colic treatment, saline nose drops for stuffy noses and a teething gel.

Your baby should still always travel in a rear-facing car seat, preferably in the back of the car, and never in a front seat with an airbag.

As your baby is now on solids, as well as any bottle-feeding equipment you need, you may have to pack tins, jars and packets of baby food. Plastic bibs are useful, saving changes of clothes.

On a long journey, you may need to distract or entertain your baby. Bring some of his favourite toys, plus a couple of new ones, plus teething rings and some of his favourite CDs for the drive.

When to leave

Plan your departure time around your baby's routine. You could leave when he's awake and alert in the morning (and likely to drift off as the journey wears on), or in the evening when he's ready to sleep. Time it right, and you might have an easy journey with a peacefully snoozing baby.

Parents**Talk...**

"If we're planning a long journey, we set off when our baby is most likely to sleep. We sometimes leave at five in the morning when he's sluggish and we get a good two or three hours before he wakes up. Or we go after lunch while he naps. When we drive to France next month, we're going to drive through the night, so hopefully it will be a peaceful journey."
Emma, 36, first-time mum

"Once on a long journey we stopped so I could feed our baby, but we didn't stop for long enough because as soon as we moved, she was sick everywhere! My advice is to allow plenty of time for stops, and have plenty of plastic bags and tissues!"
Louise, 27, first-time mum

"Bring plenty of distractions. Our baby loves clapping along to a CD, and often my husband or I sit in the back and chat to her or play peek-a-boo. Sometimes though she just stares out of the window at the scenery, which holds her fascination for a good hour before she drops off."
Claire, 33, first-time mum

Welcome to parenthood!
0–6 weeks

Your growing baby
6 weeks to 6 months

Your older baby
6 months to one year

Baby healthcare
0–12 months

Laid-back mum

It's perfectly possible to travel with a baby without working to strict schedules or routines.

"We took our baby on our first family holiday abroad when he was eight months old. Lots of people told us we were brave to take him away when he was so young, but it was absolutely fine. We're lucky that Eddie is quite a relaxed baby. It really didn't bother him when we stayed out later than his usual bedtime in restaurants.; he just slept in his buggy if he was tired.

As he's breastfed, I didn't have to take bottles and sterilising equipment. We did take some jars of baby food with us, but he refused to eat it! He loved the local fresh bread, fruit and vegetables. It's definitely worth trying to introduce your baby to new tastes while you're away. We discovered that he enjoyed all sorts of food that we would never have tried at home."

Going abroad

Travelling abroad with your baby may not be as difficult as it sounds. Young babies sleep a lot and are often easier to travel with than toddlers, who can get bored and fidgety. If you're still giving breastfeeds instead of bottle-feeds, you won't need to carry lots of feeding equipment around with you, so you can travel fairly lightly.

Advance preparations

An overseas holiday with your baby still needs lots of careful planning, though. Before you go anywhere, your baby will need a passport. Your local post office has the application forms you need, and the passport can take three or four weeks to come through.

The passport photo will need to be of your baby against a plain, off-white, cream or light grey background. It's possible to take your baby's photo in a booth, but it's not easy. He must be on his own in the picture, so you'd have to support him at the right height without your body appearing! Or you can go to a high-street photographer. Here, your baby will be placed on a white sheet or beanbag for his big moment.

Before you go

Your method of travel may affect your plans. Whether you're going by plane, train or boat, it's a good idea to phone ahead and check what facilities are offered for families with young children. Again, if you're breastfeeding, this will reduce your baggage significantly. If you're flying, feeding your baby on take-off and landing is also a good way to soothe any ear pain he might feel.

For bottle-fed babies, the best solution is to buy ready-to-feed formula, available in handy cartons or disposable bottles. Most airlines will warm babies' bottles, but you may like to double-check this with them or your tour operator before you fly.

Take a well-stocked baby bag with your hand luggage so that you are equipped during the flight and any delays.

Parents**Ask...**

How can we take the stress out of flying with a baby?

Flying with your baby needn't be as stressful as it sounds. It's a good idea to look for flights that won't upset your baby's routine. Night flights are good for long-haul journeys.

When you book, explain that you have a young baby. You may be able to sit in the "bulkhead" seats at the front of the plane, where there is more legroom. Keep a note of all your reference numbers and the name of the person you spoke to, and then phone 24 hours before departure and check your requests are on the computer.

If, when you board the plane, you notice that it isn't full, see whether you can be moved to a spare row of seats.

Be prepared for delays. Have extra food and a change of clothes and nappies in your hand luggage. It's also wise to prepare individual nappy sacks with a nappy and wipes, so you don't have to haul your entire hand luggage to the loo when your baby needs changing!

Avoid giving your baby sedatives: they can have the reverse effect. Cooled camomile tea in a sucky cup is a good natural alternative. You can soothe any ear discomfort your baby may feel during take-off and landing by feeding him.

If you have to change planes, ask for a courtesy cart between gates. Look out for play areas or family-friendly spaces in airport lounges.

Low-key, hassle-free beach holidays can be perfect when you have a young family in tow.

Systemised mum

There are so many things to think about when planning a holiday, and it's so easy to forget essential things – careful planning will make life easier.

"When planning our first holiday with our five-month-old baby, I started by making lists. First, I made a pre-holiday "to do" list, which involved making sure we had passports, medical insurance, travel insurance and necessary vaccinations. Next were the packing checklists, one for my baby, one for me and one for my husband. It was particularly important that we made sure we had everything for our baby – there was so much to remember, and we didn't want to risk forgetting something and then not being able to buy the same or a similar product abroad. I started making lists a few weeks in advance so that I could keep adding things on as I went along, and I could do any shopping well in advance. I didn't want a situation where I'd forgotten something that the airport shop had just run out of!"

Family holidays

A weekend away or a summer holiday should be a chance to chill out and relax. However, if you have a baby or toddler in tow, you might think it would be a lot easier to stay at home. Where will you pack all that baby gear, and how will you cope if your baby starts to scream in the hotel dining room?

However, with the right preparations, your baby's first holiday will be child's play. Bon voyage!

New priorities

When baby makes three you may need to rethink the type of holiday you book. While staying in a hotel relieves you of the tedium of cooking and cleaning, it can be quite restrictive. Unless you've booked a suite, your baby will probably be sleeping in the same room as you. You will need to check what facilities are provided, such as a kettle in the room (handy for making up bottles), or if there is a highchair and travel cot that you can book in advance. Some hotels also have a "no children in the dining room after 7pm" policy.

Many families opt for a self-catering holiday, which gives them more privacy than a hotel and more space and flexibility to fit in with their children's routines. Holiday-rental cottages, villas and apartments are usually situated near a beach or in a rural location, so there's no shortage of things to see and do, but the self-catering facilities can vary enormously. More upmarket villas will have dishwashers, TVs with satellite channels and good-quality furniture, others are more basic.

Designed for families

Other family-friendly options are holiday parks and campsites. A chalet, mobile home or tent in a traffic-free setting, with plenty of play areas, child-friendly activities and a fun pool can take the stress out of holidays. Fixed campsites in France and Spain are popular choices with families, as the tents are up, the beds assembled and the barbecues are ready to be lit on your arrival. Again, facilities vary – check to see what's available and what can be pre-booked. Some of the camping sites offer a babysitting service, so you can even have some time off to yourselves.

Festival fun

Talking of camping, you don't have to miss out on summer music festivals now you're parents. Many festivals have family fields and activities safely away from the melée of the mosh pit! Invest in a pair of ear defenders for your baby and pack some disposable nappies – unless you don't mind the smell of a nappy bucket in the confines of your tent...

Keeping it simple

Don't be too ambitious when taking a baby or toddler on holiday. The novelty of the experience can play havoc with their regular routines (particularly if you've crossed time zones), so try not to get too stressed about this. You may decide it's simpler to follow the continental approach of putting your baby to bed later in the evening and letting her wake up later, which is no bad thing on holiday!

Keep each day as simple as possible. If you can find somewhere to stay within walking distance of a beach, it will save you the hassle of rounding up everyone into the car and finding somewhere to park each morning.

Unless you're travelling to a particularly far-flung place, formula milk, baby food and nappies should all be available at your destination, so don't over pack.

Check your family travel insurance is up to date and covers any medical costs while abroad. Pharmacies in Europe are very helpful for dealing with minor ailments, otherwise you can get free emergency treatment in EU countries upon presentation of a European Health Insurance Card (EHIC).

If you're travelling to somewhere with a hot climate, it's probably best to travel off peak, when airports are quieter, crowds are dispersed and the heat is less intense. Once there, protect your baby's skin at all times (see pp.224–25) as young skin is extremely delicate and can burn easily in just 10 to 15 minutes. Dehydration is another concern (see p.242), so offer your baby plenty of fluids. If you are travelling anywhere where mosquitoes are a problem, pack a baby mosquito net that fits over a cot.

Your first holiday with your baby can be a precious one as you share in her delight at novel experiences and new places.

Active mum

You don't have to wait until your baby is older before you start to enjoy family holidays.

"We went on our first holiday with our daughter when she was just four months old. I was a bit daunted at first taking her abroad when she was so young, but it was surprisingly easy. She was still sleeping a lot at that stage, so she missed most of the waiting around at the airport and being on the plane. When we arrived in Italy, it was easy for us all to enjoy the sights thanks to the baby carrier we took with us – our little one loves being so close to her daddy. We got lots of attention in restaurants, too, as staff loved coming over to serve us so that they could coo over her. It was really wonderful being on our first family holiday.

What you'll need

Babies sleep a good deal of the time when travelling. Even so, you'll need a remarkable amount of gear to help them stay comfortable and happy. Consult the checklist below to ensure you have everything you might need.

- a baby bag with a waterproof lining and a shoulder strap
- nappies, baby wipes, changing mat or 60cm (24in) square plastic sheet
- nappy rash cream and nappy bags for stashing dirty nappies, clothes and bibs
- baby bath and lotion
- tissues
- extra dummies
- at least one baby blanket for warmth, comfort or shade
- one or two outfits per day

- a sun hat and sun shade for a buggy
- sun screen, at least factor 15
- food, formula, water and/or juice – bring extras in case of travel delays
- washable bibs
- sterilising equipment, bottles and beakers
- breast pump
- nightlight for night-time feeds and nappy changes
- baby sling
- travel cot, unless you've reserved one, or your baby sleeps with you
- baby car seat (for car, plane, train or bus) – doubles as a baby seat, too
- collapsible buggy from six months
- extra clothes for yourself in case of accidents

Welcome to parenthood!
0–6 weeks

Your growing baby
6 weeks to 6 months

Your older baby
6 months to one year

Baby healthcare
0–12 months

Water safety

A major worry when going on holiday is how to keep your baby safe around water. Once he is mobile, you'll need to watch him at all times near water.

Swimming tips

You may want to wait until your baby can hold his head up well on his own (usually by four or five months) before you take him into a pool when you're on holiday. Make sure the water is warm enough, preferably between 28 and 30°C (84 and 86°F). If necessary, the swimming pool attendants can check it for you. As soon as your baby starts to shiver, get him out of the pool and wrap him up warmly.

Pool water should be properly chlorinated, and natural bodies of water should be unpolluted and safe for wading. Don't put a baby less than six months old under the water. Although babies naturally hold their breath under water, they continue to swallow. If you decide to take your own paddling pool with you on holiday, never leave your baby unattended, and drain it and store it in an upright position after each use.

Don't keep your baby in water for too long. Once he's out of the water, wrap him up snugly in a towel.

Holiday safety

Travelling and staying in holiday accommodation with your baby introduces a whole new range of safety issues to consider and deal with.

Safety first

Before you travel, find out if the hotel will childproof the room. If they won't, bring your own childproofing kit, including things such as electric socket covers (although some destinations have different sockets to UK ones) and electrical cord holders. Ask your holiday company or travel agent if you need to bring along a stairgate and, if there's a balcony, check that it's safe for babies.

When you arrive, find out where the fire escapes are and who to contact in emergencies. Bring a first aid kit, too, to deal with minor medical problems.

Air safety

If you're travelling by air, the safest way for your baby to travel is secured in a car seat strapped into the airline seat. Bear in mind you may have to pay for an extra seat to do this. Alternatively, your baby can sit on your lap with an extra seatbelt around him.

Avoiding sunburn

The same sun-safety advice (see pp.224–25) you follow at home applies on holiday, although you may need to be even more vigilant. If you can't always keep your baby in the shade, the best way to protect him is by dressing him routinely in a hat, lightweight trousers and a baggy T-shirt. Apply water-resistant sunscreen with an SPF of 15 or higher to remaining exposed areas, such as his

When you're away from home, your constant vigilance is, as always, the most effective way to keep your baby safe and secure.

ParentsTalk...

"I got a sun tent for my nine-month-old to protect her from the sun and for her to nap in during the day when my husband and I are sunning ourselves on the beach. It's also big enough for her to play and crawl around in safely."
Sarah, 29, mother of two

"We recently went to France with our seven-month-old, and we took some long-lasting food with us such as rice cakes. As we were self catering, we also brought a little blender with us and made baby meals from scratch using fresh ingredients. This meant she ate more or less what she was used to at home, and so we didn't risk her

turning her nose up at the local ready-made baby food."
Su, 26, first-time mum

"My eleven-month-old boy had just started walking when we took a weeks' break in Spain. To keep him safe on the beach I got some little jelly shoes, and a swim suit with built-in floats for the sea or pool. I bought lots of baby-safe beach toys, too, such as a bucket and spade and a beach ball."
Hannah, 34, first-time mum

"I prefer my baby to sleep somewhere he's used to, as he's unsettled for the first few days somewhere new, so when we go on holiday we take his travel cot and bedding, which he also often naps

Keeping your baby well covered on the beach is a basic safety requirement.

in when visiting friends or family for the day. Then we know that he's sleeping somewhere safe, comfortable and clean!"
Mel, 40, mother of three

---

face and the backs of his hands. Reapply sunscreen at least every two hours and after your baby has played in water, even if it's waterproof.

You'll also need to make sure your baby drinks more than usual to avoid dehydration (see p.242).

medium resealable plastic bags in your hand luggage as they are handy for holding messy items, such as dirty bibs.

Boiled tap water in most of Europe and North America is safe for making a baby's feed. However, a change in the water can cause tummy upsets due to

sterilise your feeding equipment as usual. Large bottles of mineral water should be stored in a fridge after opening. Rather than taking your bottle sterilising unit abroad, it's easier to take a large, clean container with a lid and use handy cold water sterilising tablets.

"You may worry that your **first family holiday** might be stressful, but with extra **planning** beforehand, you should find that your trip runs really **smoothly**."

Safe eating and drinking

If your baby is eating solids but you're not sure about the hygiene of the local water, it's best to opt for foods that you have to boil or peel first. Don't rely on restaurants and cafés to have baby feeding equipment – pack spoons, bowls and bibs, too. Stash some

different mineral contents and purifying chemicals. Outside Europe and North America, it's safer to use still bottled water. Choose low-sodium varieties: no more than 200 milligrams per litre.

When using bottled water to make up a feed, make sure the seal is intact. Boil the water in a kettle and wash and

Alternatively, if you know you'll have a microwave, a compact microwave steam steriliser with a clip-on lid is perfect for travelling. If you don't have much access to sterilising equipment, or indeed a microwave, it may be best to use disposable, pre-sterilised bottle liners and sterile packs of teats.

Welcome to parenthood!
0–6 weeks

Your growing baby
6 weeks to 6 months

Your older baby
6 months to one year

Baby healthcare
0–12 months

Baby healthcare

0–12 months

Newborn health

Health concerns in newborns

It's frightening when your newborn baby gets poorly – he seems so small and vulnerable. Young babies seem to go downhill very rapidly, but they also tend to recover quickly with the right treatment, so check your baby's condition with your doctor.

When your baby is unwell

Your newborn's immune system isn't fully developed at birth, so he's vulnerable to infection. He has some antibodies from you, passed on via the placenta in the last months of pregnancy, which help him to fight some bacteria and viruses for a few weeks or months after the birth. If he was premature, he'll be more vulnerable to infection because he'll have received fewer antibodies.

If you're breastfeeding, your baby receives antibodies via your breastmilk, particularly from the colostrum that makes up his first feeds. Breastfeeding makes it less likely that he'll get some common infections that cause earaches, tummy upsets and other problems, but it won't protect him totally from illness.

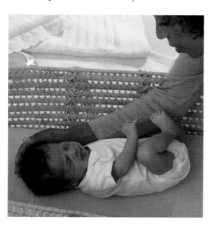

Seeing your baby in distress can be alarming, so don't hesitate to seek reassurance from your doctor.

Reading the signs

As a new parent, you may feel out of your depth when your baby becomes ill for the first time. With certain conditions it can be hard even to tell when your baby is unwell. He can't tell you if he's got a tummy ache or his ear is hurting. Instead, you have to look, listen and feel for signs that something is wrong.

Sometimes it's obvious that your baby is unwell, for example when he's runny-nosed, red-faced and grizzling. At other times, the signs of illness are subtle. You know your baby best, and are best placed to notice any change from the normal: crying more, being unresponsive when he's usually alert or being clingier. These are all signs that your baby may be unwell and not his usual self.

When he needs a doctor

If you think your baby is unwell, you have to decide what to do. A cough or cold may be eased with baby medicine to bring down his temperature (consult your doctor if your baby is under three months before medicating), and lots of rest. Stay close to keep an eye on him.

Be aware of the warning signs of a serious problem (see p.254) and get your baby checked if you have any concerns. Visit your doctor if there's a worrying rash or you're concerned that an illness is worsening, or go to Accident and Emergency if you think he needs immediate attention. Don't worry about wasting your doctor's time. She would rather you brought your baby in than miss the early signs of a major problem.

Parents**Ask...**

How will I know when my baby is unwell?

Trust your instincts. Often you'll be able to tell that he is poorly just by looking at him. He may seem grizzly and unsettled, or he may be clingy. Or he may be tired and fall asleep earlier than usual.

A high temperature (see p.256) can be a sign that your baby is fighting off an infection. You can take his temperature with a thermometer, but often you can just tell by touching his forehead. His cheeks may be flushed, too. He may also have a rash, or be sick or have diarrhoea.

If your baby is unresponsive when he would usually be alert, or if you have any concerns, it's best to be safe and take him to your doctor straightaway.

Welcome to parenthood!
0–6 weeks

Your growing baby
6 weeks to 6 months

Your older baby
6 months to one year

Baby healthcare
0–12 months

Common concerns

Newborns often have spots, marks, lumps on their heads and other conditions that are quite normal for new babies, but can be alarming for you as a first-time parent. During the birth, your baby may have scratched herself, or her head might have been squashed during contractions or from an assisted birth. These marks and swellings usually clear up on their own over the next days or weeks, but your baby may feel achy and sore, and need gentle handling.

Initial worries

Jaundice is common in the first two weeks after birth, giving your baby a yellow tinge to her skin and eyes (see p.247). This usually passes without the need for any treatment.

If you notice that one or both of your baby's eyes are "sticky", it could be a sign that the tear ducts are blocked. These usually clear as your baby grows, but the stickiness could indicate an eye infection that needs medical attention.

Once the jaundice has faded, you'll probably have a couple of clear weeks to admire your baby before she breaks out in a new skin condition! An early dose of acne is common and is caused by hormones that she received from you via the placenta. The spots will clear up without treatment as the hormones leave her body. You may also notice some little white milk spots called milia on your baby's face. These are also harmless and will clear up on their own.

Another common problem is thrush (see p.265). Your baby may catch this from you during the birth, or you may pass it back and forth between you. It can cause a white coating inside your baby's mouth and can make her sore, and breastfeeding painful for you if you get thrush on your nipples. Thrush is a fungal infection that needs to be treated. See your doctor if you think your baby has thrush and you are breastfeeding as you will both need treatment.

Concerns about birthmarks

Birthmarks and large moles can be a cause for concern depending on the type, size and location of them (see p.17). Some are not present at birth, but start to grow after a few days. Birthmarks, such as stork marks or angel kisses, usually at the back of your baby's neck, on her forehead or near her eyes, are very common. Most birthmarks disappear over the course of a few years. Port-wine stains, however, are permanent, but can be removed with lasers when your baby is older.

Avoiding infections

While your baby's immune system is developing, an infection that would cause you no problems can make your baby very unwell and can be difficult for her to fight off. In the early weeks, it's best to protect her from infections as much as you can. Ask people to wash their hands before handling her. Avoiding infections can be hard if you've got older children bringing home illnesses picked up at preschool or school. Be prepared for your newborn to have coughs, colds, ear infections, tummy bugs and rashes, and keep your doctor's surgery and out-of-hours phone numbers to hand.

Possible complications

Most of the time when your baby is unwell, you'll be able to look after her at home without needing to visit your doctor, but be aware that what starts out as a simple cold or tummy bug can rapidly turn into a more complicated condition. The most common complications to look out for are breathing problems and dehydration (see opposite). Babies often sound snuffly because the air passages through their nose are small. However, wheezing and rapid, shallow breathing can be signs of bronchiolitis, a highly infectious respiratory infection, which will need checking by your doctor. A feverish baby will need lots of fluid, so keep offering feeds, whether you're bottle- or breastfeeding. Plenty of wet nappies will show that your baby is well hydrated.

The stress of colic
One of the hardest challenges of the newborn months that many parents face is dealing with colic (see p.245).

Although your doctor will reassure you that there is nothing actually physically wrong with your baby, the hours of inconsolable crying that characterise colic can make this hard for you to believe. Finding ways for you to cope with the crying, while it lasts, is extremely important to help you get through this particularly stressful time.

Common problems in newborn babies

Illness	Symptoms	What to do
Umbilical stump infection (see p.244)	Fever and lethargy, stump becomes swollen or smelly, navel becomes swollen or red.	Keep the umbilical stump clean to prevent infection. Call your doctor if symptoms of infection appear.
Jaundice (see p.247)	A yellow tinge to eyes and skin, starting on the head and face then spreading to chest and stomach; poor sucking/feeding, sleepiness.	Check it out with your midwife or doctor. They may suggest giving plenty of breast milk or formula, and they may do blood tests to see if the jaundice is increasing. If this is the case, your baby may need to spend some time under phototherapy lights.
Colic (see p.245)	Uncontrollable and often unexplained crying in an otherwise healthy baby.	Try swaddling or carrying in a sling, keeping her in motion, burping, baby massage and taking her for a walk. If your baby has severe wind, your midwife may suggest an antispasmodic medication.
Cradle cap (see p.246)	Greasy, scaly, yellow patches on your baby's scalp. Patches become flaky and rub off.	Wash your baby's hair with a baby shampoo, then loosen the flakes with a soft brush. Rub mild baby oil or olive oil into her scalp, leave it for a while (even overnight if you want) then brush off the flakes.
Nappy rash (see p.246)	Red and inflamed skin around the genital area, the folds of the thighs and the buttocks.	Keep your baby clean and dry by changing her nappy often. Remove her nappy to let air speed up the healing process. If it doesn't clear, check with your doctor in case it's thrush, which needs a specific cream.
Spitting up/mild reflux (see p.281)	Regurgitating a little milk after a feed or during a bout of hiccups, or coughing up milk that has gone down the wrong way.	This is normal; as long as your baby is well, don't worry. Try holding your baby upright for 20 minutes after a feed. Speak to your doctor if reflux happens regularly more than five times a day, if your baby cries excessively after feeds or if there is regular vomiting or coughing.
Watery eyes (see p.255)	Watery eyes due to a blocked tear duct. Babies are often born with a duct that is not fully open, so the tears are unable to drain away.	See your doctor who may prescribe antibiotic drops if there is an infection. He may also show you how to massage the lacrimal sac, which is part of the eye's drainage system; you will need to do this on a regular basis.

Welcome to parenthood! 0–6 weeks

Your growing baby 6 weeks to 6 months

Your older baby 6 months to one year

Baby healthcare 0–12 months

Use a clean piece of cotton wool dipped in cooled boiled water and some mild soap to clean the area around the cord stump.

ParentsAsk...

How do we prevent an infection in the stump?

Your baby's umbilical stump must be kept clean (see opposite) and dry to prevent infection. Harmful bacteria that live naturally on skin can travel up the cord stump, so it's important to wash your hands well before handling your baby's cord stump, and before and after each nappy change.

Avoid getting urine or poo on the stump by folding your baby's nappy down and away from it, leaving the stump exposed to the air. If urine or poo does get on the stump, wash these off with clean water and a mild soap, because a higher percentage of fatty deposits in baby poo can make it difficult to remove with just water.

While waiting for the cord stump to fall off and heal, it is perfectly safe to bath your newborn if you want to. Many families enjoy giving their newborn a bath, although your baby doesn't need a daily bath to keep clean. Provided you wash off any obvious muck, your baby will be clean enough.

Stump problems

When your baby was in the uterus, he received nourishment and oxygen through the placenta, which was connected to the inner wall of your uterus by the umbilical cord through an opening in your baby's tummy (where his belly button is now). After your baby was born, the cord was clamped and cut by the doctor or midwife in a painless procedure, leaving a 2 to 3 centimetre (5 to 7 inch) umbilical stump.

Keeping the stump clean

At some point between five and 15 days after the birth, the stump will dry up, turn black, and drop off, leaving a small wound that may take a few days to heal.

In the meantime, it's usually fine just to wash your baby's stump with water

Fold the front of the nappy down so that the area is not covered. Fresh air will help with the healing.

The healing process

After the cord stump falls off, it usually takes around seven to 10 days for the area to heal over completely. When the stump falls off, you may see a little blood on your baby's nappy, which is normal. Sometimes, when the umbilical stump takes a slightly longer time to heal, bits of lumpy flesh (a type of connective tissue) appear in the wound. These lumps are not a cause for concern and will soon disappear.

In the meantime, you should always consult your midwife if your baby develops a fever, becomes lethargic,

> "Use **water** to clean around the stump and be **vigilant** for signs of **infection** such as redness."

and mild soap. In the past, cord stumps were cleaned routinely with antiseptic tissues or sprinkled with an antiseptic powder. The use of antiseptics or antibiotics may still be relevant today in less industrialised societies, where umbilical cord infections continue to cause many infant deaths, but in most Western countries, where standards of cleanliness are high, this is not necessary. Studies of the healing process of the umbilical cord have found no advantage to using antiseptics over simply keeping your baby's cord clean, unless your baby was born prematurely or is in intensive care. Antiseptics also cause the cord to take longer to fall off.

starts to feed poorly or generally appears unwell, in case any of these are signs of an infection in the umbilical area. You should also tell her if the navel and the surrounding area become swollen or red, or if your baby's cord stump becomes swollen or smelly, as these are clearer signs of an infection that needs to be treated promptly.

It is normal for your baby's cord stump to look a bit "mucky", or appear to have pus at the base as it dries up and gradually heals, but this does not mean that it is infected. Ask your midwife to check your baby's cord stump if you are at all worried about its appearance or smell.

Colic

About 20 per cent of all babies develop colic, a catch-all phrase for uncontrollable crying in an otherwise healthy baby. A baby with colic cries or fusses for more than three hours a day, for more than three days a week. Colic usually occurs between 6pm and midnight, although it can occur around the clock, generally becoming worse during the evening.

While all babies cry sometimes (the average baby cries for about two and a half hours a day), a colicky baby looks truly uncomfortable while crying. She may alternately extend or pull up her legs and pass wind.

The causes

For more than 50 years, scientists have tried to determine what causes colic. It's often blamed on the immature digestive system of the baby, as a newborn's digestive tract contains few enzymes or digestive juices to break down food substances. Others believe a baby's still-developing nervous system simply tenses up, while some think that when a baby is tired or overstimulated, colic is a way of blocking everything out so she can sleep. Babies who are exposed to smoke are more likely to develop colic.

It's thought that, occasionally, breastfed babies become colicky due to something in their mother's diet, although there's no firm evidence for this. Some mums find that if they stop having cow's milk and other dairy products, things improve. Try cutting out dairy products for a few days to see if that makes a difference.

Some breastfeeding mums swear that eating spicy foods, wheat products, oranges or cruciferous vegetables, such as cabbage, broccoli, cauliflower and brussels sprouts, affects their baby. If

you think this is the case, you could try avoiding these foods, plus maybe garlic, caffeine and alcohol, for a few days. If your baby seems better, try reintroducing foods one at a time, allowing a few days between reintroductions. It should be easy then to pinpoint which one, if any, might be causing problems. You may find you'll have to abstain from it until your baby outgrows her sensitivity, but that's a small price to pay for a happy baby.

If your baby is bottlefed, try changing teats in case your baby was swallowing too much air during the feed. Make sure that you burp her during and after feeds because this helps to relieve the pressure that builds up when she swallows air.

How you'll cope

It's hard to know who finds colic harder: you or your baby. A colicky baby is obviously in distress, uncomfortable and unable to soothe herself. However, listening to her crying for hours on end is enough to drive you to tears, too.

If you start feeling tense, it's important to put your baby down for a while somewhere safe so that you can calm yourself. Taking a break will help you both. Or take her for a walk so both of you can get some fresh air. If possible, ask a friend to babysit for an hour or take turns with your partner soothing your baby. A break will help you feel calmer and better able to deal with your baby.

When colic goes

Generally, babies recover from colic by about three months. In the meantime, try not to become too distressed. There will come a time when your baby stops crying every day and the memory of this difficult time will fade.

What you can do

Colic isn't a really serious condition – apart from the household tension it creates. Try swaddling your baby or carrying her close in a sling. Or she may settle next to continuous noise that blocks out other stimulation, perhaps when she's near a humming washing machine. You could also try massaging her (see pp.164–67).

If nothing seems to work, you may start to think that your own negative feelings are affecting your baby. Take heart, though: parental anxiety doesn't cause colic. If you feel tense, put her down somewhere safe for a while so that you can destress. Better still, ask a friend to babysit for a short time. Take a relaxing bath, or lie down in a quiet room. Soon you'll have the energy to go back to your baby.

When to see the doctor

If your baby seems to be crying uncontrollably a lot of the time, it's good to get her checked by the doctor, just to rule out any other medical problems.

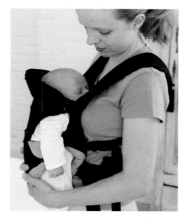

The motion and closeness your baby feels when in a sling may soothe her and give you a break from her crying.

Welcome to parenthood! 0–6 weeks

Your growing baby 6 weeks to 6 months

Your older baby 6 months to one year

Baby healthcare 0–12 months

Cradle cap

This is a condition that looks like a bad case of dandruff. It shows up as a red area on your newborn's scalp that is covered with greasy, yellow, scaly patches. Over time, these scales start to become flaky so that they rub off easily, a bit like dandruff. However, in the case of cradle cap, unlike dandruff, there will often be bits of your baby's hair attached to the flakes that fall off.

Sometimes cradle cap can become fairly extensive. It can cover the whole of your baby's scalp, and it can also appear on your baby's face, around the nappy area, the armpits and the nose. When it appears in places other than the scalp, it's called seborrhoeic eczema (dermatitis) rather than cradle cap.

Causes

The condition is thought to be a result of hormones left in your baby's body from pregnancy. These stimulate secretions from the oil glands in the skin, making the skin cells on your baby's head stick to the scalp. The secretions reduce in the months after the birth, which is why it tends to clear up of its own accord.

A harmless condition

Cradle cap is common in babies under the age of eight months, but it can also occur in older babies and in toddlers. Although the condition can look a bit unsightly, it's not itchy and won't cause your baby any discomfort or pain. It's harmless and is nothing to worry about.

What you can do

Cradle cap usually disappears on its own within a few months of the birth. In the meantime, you can wash your baby's hair with a baby shampoo, then loosen the flakes using a soft brush. You could also try rubbing baby oil or olive oil into your baby's scalp, leaving it for a while, then gently brushing off the flakes and shampooing with mild baby shampoo.

It's tempting to pick at cradle cap, but try to resist as you may leave sore patches that could become infected.

When to see the doctor

Cradle cap will eventually go away on its own, but talk to your doctor if the condition persists, worsens, or spreads to your baby's face or neck.

Nappy rash

If your baby has nappy rash, some of the skin covered by her nappy – probably the genital area, the folds of the thighs and the buttocks – will appear red and inflamed. The affected areas can be dry or moist, and sometimes look pimply.

Causes

The main cause is wetness. Newborns urinate often and have frequent, loose bowel movements. Diarrhoea can also lead to nappy rash. A baby left in a dirty nappy for too long is more likely to develop nappy rash; however, it can also strike the bottoms of babies with particularly sensitive skin, even if their parents are frequent nappy changers.

The best defence against nappy rash is a dry bottom. It's important to change your baby's nappy as soon as possible after it becomes wet or soiled. Clean her genital area thoroughly after each bowel movement and allow it to air dry. Nappies, wraps and clothing should be loose enough to let your baby's bottom breathe, so don't fasten nappies so tightly that there's no room for air to circulate within them.

Coat your baby's bottom with a thin layer of protective ointment or barrier cream after each nappy change, but don't use talcum powder, because this can be inhaled into your baby's lungs.

Allergic reactions

Sometimes, nappy rash can be caused by allergies. So when your baby starts on solid foods, introduce only one new item at a time, and wait a few days between each new food. That way, it will be easier to determine if nappy rash is due to a food allergy.

What you can do

If your baby has nappy rash, keep her clean and dry by changing her nappy frequently. Just use water and cotton wool to clean her – this should help clear up any nappy rashes that are caused by allergies.

You can use disposable or cloth nappies; neither one is better than the other for treating or preventing nappy rash. If possible, let your baby go nappy-less for a while so the air can speed up the healing process.

When to see the doctor

A normal nappy rash should clear up after three or four days of at-home treatment. If your baby's rash persists, spreads or worsens, talk to your doctor – she may prescribe a cream. It's important to get it treated, as it may turn into an infection.

Jaundice

About half of all normal, healthy babies develop a yellowish tinge to their skin in the first few days of life. Jaundice develops in a healthy baby when the blood contains an excess of bilirubin – a chemical produced during the normal breakdown of old red blood cells.

Newborn babies have extra oxygen-carrying red blood cells and their young livers sometimes can't metabolise the excess bilirubin. As bilirubin levels rise above normal, the yellowness of jaundice that this causes moves downwards from the head to the neck, then to the chest, until, in severe cases, it finally reaches the toes. This so-called physiological jaundice (unlike a rare, more serious version caused by liver disease or rhesus disease) usually causes no damage in otherwise healthy, full-term infants.

If your baby is breastfed, you should breastfeed her frequently, as this will help to clear the jaundice. You may need to wake your baby to feed her if she is very sleepy.

Recognising jaundice

Experts recommend the following quick home test to check for jaundice in your baby. In a well-lit room, apply gentle pressure to your baby's nose or forehead; if you notice a yellow tinge to the skin as the pressure is released, consult your doctor or the midwife.

This technique works best for fair-skinned children; if your baby has dark skin, check for yellowness in the whites of her eyes, in the gums, her palms, and soles of the feet. If your baby has developed jaundice, you may also notice that she has very pale coloured stools.

Breastmilk jaundice

Some otherwise healthy breastfed babies remain jaundiced for several weeks after they're born, although experts are unsure why this happens. If your baby has breastmilk jaundice, she may be feeding well and gaining weight, having normal bowel movements and passing clear urine, yet her skin will still appear to have a yellow hue. Her blood levels will be normal, except for a raised total bilirubin. This "breastmilk" jaundice will not harm your baby and will gradually disappear.

If you suspect jaundice, consult your doctor or midwife if they haven't already noted the condition. If your baby has breastmilk jaundice, your doctor may want to measure her bilirubin level weekly to make sure it's returning to normal. If you're breastfeeding your baby, it's usually fine to continue even if she has mild symptoms of jaundice.

What might be done

If your baby is otherwise healthy, but has a yellowish tinge to her skin, this is probably nothing to worry about, but do mention it to your midwife or health visitor if they haven't already noted it. If your baby has dark skin, you are more likely to notice a yellow tinge to the white of her eyes, on the palms of her hands, or the soles of her feet.

If your baby appears very jaundiced or is unwell, your doctor may measure her bilirubin levels with a blood test and may investigate what's causing the jaundice. Some babies need treatment in hospital, usually phototherapy, whereby an ultraviolet light over the bed helps break down excess bilirubin so that the baby's liver can process it.

Be reassured that jaundice is very common and usually has no long-term effects. You can always ask your doctor or midwife for advice if you are concerned.

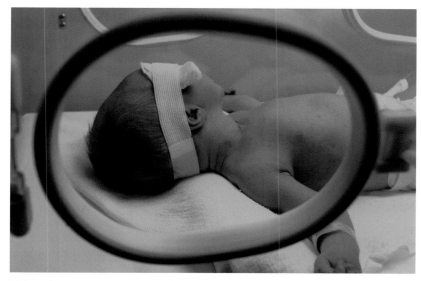

Phototherapy treatment is given for severe cases of jaundice; the ultraviolet light helps to break down the bilirubin in the baby's body.

Welcome to parenthood!
0–6 weeks

Your growing baby
6 weeks to 6 months

Your older baby
6 months to one year

Baby healthcare
0–12 months

"Clicky" hips

"Clicky" hips is a commonly used term to describe a condition that includes both congenital dislocation of the hips (CDH) and developmental dysplasia of the hips (DDH). The hip is a "ball-and-socket" joint, and various problems can affect this joint as it develops. Sometimes, the ball doesn't lie properly in the socket and is displaced. Sometimes, although the ball is in the socket, it can slip in and out of place, or the socket is too shallow so that the hip can dislocate easily.

Diagnosis

Straight after the birth, your doctor or midwife will check the stability of your baby's hip joints with movements that include opening his legs wide and then bending and unbending them. A "clunk"

sound indicates that both the thigh bones are moving in or out of their sockets in the pelvis, which is known as clinical hip instability.

If any instability is detected in the hips, further investigations, such as an ultrasound scan, will be done. An X-ray can be used, but this is usually for older babies (young babies have soft bones that are difficult to see properly on an X-ray). Tests will be repeated at your baby's six-week and eight-month checks.

Babies born with clicky hips do not feel any pain or discomfort, and often grow out of the problem without any particular treatment.

Development problems

Some babies have hips that appear normal in initial tests, but then do not develop properly. Later on, you may notice that one leg looks slightly shorter, and there may be extra skin creases on one thigh or buttock. Or, when changing a nappy, you may notice that one of the hips does not open as much as the other. Very occasionally, dislocated hips are not noticed until a baby starts to walk, when he develops a limp and may walk on his tip toes on the affected side.

If you notice any of these signs, contact your doctor. The earlier clicky hips are diagnosed, the easier and more effective is any necessary treatment.

Treatment

If clicky hips are recognised early, they can usually be treated by giving your baby a splint to wear for six to 12 weeks. The splint keeps his hips in the correct position so that they'll develop properly.

If a problem isn't detected until your baby begins to walk, treatment can be more difficult. Sometimes, the hip is put

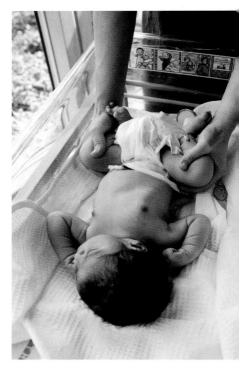

Soon after the birth, your baby's hips will be checked for signs of dislocation by rotating and bending his legs.

in a plaster cast to hold the thigh in the socket. Alternatively, your baby might need to stay in hospital for about three weeks for traction, where weights or gravity are used to encourage the hip into the socket.

Occasionally, the doctor may release some tendons in the groin by making a small incision. On some occasions, it may be necessary for your baby to have an operation to put the hip safely back into its socket. After the operation, it is usual to put the child in a plaster cast to help set the hip in place.

Children with either CDH or DDH are monitored for a long time to ensure their hips grow properly during childhood.

Risk factors

There are several factors that make clicky hips more likely. Girls are more likely to have clicky hips than boys because their ligaments are generally more lax; so are breech babies; babies who had little room for kicking around in the uterus (such as larger babies or twins); babies who were born very late (and were a little squashed in the uterus); or those who have a family history of clicky hips. In many cases, though, the cause of a baby's hip dislocation is not properly understood.

If your baby has been diagnosed with clicky hips, it doesn't always follow that he also has CDH or DDH (see above and right), however, he may need to have further investigations. The sooner clicky hips are spotted and treated, the more effective the treatment is likely to be.

Immunisations

The human body's natural defence against infection is called immunity. When we get an infection, our bodies produce chemicals called antibodies to fight it. After an infection, we are usually immune to that virus or bacterium and the immunity may last for life.

Thanks to medical advances, immunisations, or vaccinations, allow us to stimulate immunity without having the full-blown disease or infection. Immunisations are given by injection or by mouth. They work by introducing a very dilute version of the disease into the body, so that the body creates antibodies to it.

In the UK, vaccinations have been used since the 1940s, and their impact is clear to see. For example, in 1915 there were approximately 60,000 known cases of the disease diphtheria. A vaccination for this disease was introduced in 1942, when there were 41,404 known cases and 1,827 deaths. By 1946, the death rate had dropped dramatically to just 472. In 2006, there were only 10 reported cases of diphtheria in England and Wales and one death.

While it's clear that immunisations have a profound effect on the number of cases of a disease, sometimes there is debate about their side effects. A link was suggested between the measles, mumps and rubella (MMR) vaccination and autism, for example, and between the whooping cough vaccination and asthma and disorders of the nervous system. However, with both of these, undisputable evidence has been given to disprove these claims.

Your baby may not enjoy vaccinations, but the benefits of undergoing an immunisation programme are evident.

Your baby's immunisations

There are childhood immunisations for 12 infectious diseases. The BCG (Bacille Calmette-Guérin), which protects against tuberculosis, and hepatitis B immunisations are offered to babies considered at a higher risk. The other 10 are offered routinely to every baby.

Your baby will have a combined injection at eight, 12 and 16 weeks, of the diphtheria, tetanus, whooping cough (DTaP), polio (IPV) and haemophilus influenza type b (Hib) vaccines. In a separate injection, but also at 12 and 16 weeks, he will be offered a meningitis C (MenC) immunisation to protect against the bacterium that causes one form of meningitis and septicaemia (blood poisoning). This is given again at around 12 months in an injection that also contains Hib. At eight and 16 weeks, with a booster at 13 months, your baby will be given the pneumococcal vaccine (PCV), which protects against the bacterium that causes the illnesses meningitis, septicaemia and pneumonia.

Your baby will be offered the MMR vaccination for measles, mumps and rubella at around 13 months.

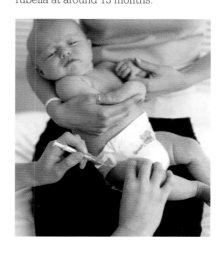

Immunisations during the first year

Below is a timetable of vaccinations offered to your baby in the UK during the first year of his life, and then up until the age of five years. You will be informed when these vaccinations are due. Babies usually receive injections into the top of their thigh, while for older children, the injection site is usually in the arm.

Eight weeks
- Diphtheria, tetanus, whooping cough, polio and haemophilus influenza type b immunisations in one injection (DTaP/IPV/Hib)
- Injection to protect against pneumococcal infection (PCV)

12 weeks
- DTaP/IPV/Hib
- Immunisation against meningitis C in a separate injection (MenC)

16 weeks
- Another DTaP/IPV/Hib
- Another MenC
- Another PCV

Around 12 months
- Another DTaP/IPV/Hib plus MenC, in one injection

Around 13 months
- Vaccination for measles, mumps and rubella in one injection (MMR)
- Another PCV

Between three years and four months, and five years
- Another immunisation for diphtheria, tetanus, whooping cough and polio in one injection (DTaP/IPV)
- Another MMR.

Welcome to parenthood!
0–6 weeks

Your growing baby
6 weeks to 6 months

Your older baby
6 months to one year

Baby healthcare
0–12 months

Getting help

It's tough deciding what to do when your baby has a never-ending run of coughs, sniffles and rashes. You don't like to fuss, but nor do you want your baby to suffer. However, doctors are used to seeing young babies frequently, so always make an appointment if you're worried.

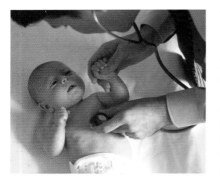

It's always wise to err on the side of caution and take your baby to the doctor, rather than risk neglecting a problem.

ParentsTalk...

"When my son was a few weeks old, he was crying all the time and nothing I did seemed to help. We went to see the doctor. She reassured me that I had done everything right and that my baby was just a touch colicky."
Phoebe, 29, first-time mum

"My six-week-old daughter had awful nappy rash; I felt so guilty as I thought I should have prevented it. The doctor was really kind and told me how common it is and that it could be easily treated."
Lorraine, 23, first-time mum

When to see the doctor

If you've got a new baby, you should get used to trips to the doctor's surgery; chances are you'll be doing this a lot over the next few years, as your baby's immature immune system means she's more prone to minor illnesses, such as coughs, colds and tummy upsets, than older children and adults.

Who you should contact

Doctors are used to seeing families with babies and young children, but it can be hard to decide when to see your doctor, or when to seek help elsewhere.

If your baby has a minor problem, such as possetting or wind, for example, your health visitor will be able to help. She can also help with worries about your baby's wellbeing, and can advise on breastfeeding, solids, immunisations, development issues, sleep and on minor health problems, such as colic and nappy rash. Your pharmacist is another good port of call; he can help with queries about minor ailments, or about any medications your baby is taking. He can also advise you on which over-the-counter medicines are suitable.

Some health problems need to be checked out immediately. See a doctor as soon as you can if your baby has diarrhoea or vomiting for more than 12 hours; has a very high fever (see p.256) (especially if accompanied by a rash); or has blood-streaked vomit or poo. Burns, bad coughs, dehydration, or objects lodged in a nose, ear, mouth or vagina also mean you should see a doctor quickly.

If your baby is unusually irritable for more than 24 hours for no apparent reason, it's worth making a doctor's appointment for the following day. Also, make an appointment if your baby has an eye infection; a discharge from the ears, navel, penis or vagina; or if she loses her appetite and misses more than two feeds in succession.

When you call your doctor's surgery, explain the problem to the receptionist. If the doctor is already seeing patients, the receptionist will pass on information that will help the doctor to prioritise. Give as much information as you can. Many doctors prioritise seeing young children and will be able to fit them in.

Getting reassurance

More often than not, you'll be looking for advice or reassurance. If you can't get an appointment with your doctor, or you need guidance, try NHS Direct, a 24-hour health line run by nurses (see pp.312–13). They can advise you on whether or not your baby needs to see a doctor.

Going to hospital

If you think that your baby is very unwell and needs immediate medical help, the best place to take her is to your nearest Accident and Emergency department. In babies, coughs and colds can rapidly develop into more complicated illnesses that need urgent treatment. You need to be aware of the signs of meningitis (see p.274), breathing problems, fits or severe allergic reactions.

Accidents happen, too, especially when babies start rolling, crawling or walking, or when older siblings play rough or feed babies something that they shouldn't! Bumps to the head, burns, scalds, severe cuts and poisoning can also all mean a hospital trip. If your baby choked on something and you had to use chest thrusts to clear the blockage, take her to hospital afterwards so that a doctor can check her.

If your baby has an illness that is worsening, or has a persistent health problem, contact your doctor before going to hospital. Most doctor's surgeries are helpful with babies and you may get an appointment immediately, or at least talk to a doctor on the phone through the receptionist or an out-of-hours service. If you have problems contacting your doctor and you're very worried, take your baby to accident and emergency.

If your baby is having severe breathing difficulties and you're far from the hospital, call an ambulance. The paramedics will be able to give your baby treatment as soon as they arrive and then get her to hospital quickly.

Getting to hospital

Some babies are referred to hospital by a midwife or doctor. You may be able to take your baby yourself or, if immediate attention is needed, travel with her by ambulance. A midwife will go with your newborn to care for her en route if she is transported in an incubator. Make sure you know which hospital your baby is being taken to and the ward name, if possible, so that, if only one of you can go in the ambulance, the other can be with your baby without delay.

Staying at hospital

It's best for you and your baby if you can stay with her, particularly if you're breastfeeding. It can be hard if your baby is in intensive care or a ward where you can't stay (although this is rare). Some hospitals have transitional units where you can stay if your baby isn't seriously ill, but needs monitoring. Staff understand your needs, and will help you to care for your baby while they're treating her.

What you might need

If your baby has to go into hospital, take the following items with you:
- clothes for your baby
- nappies; wipes, or small bowl and cotton wool, for nappy changing; and nappy bags
- muslin squares
- toys to attach on her cot
- Formula milk and bottles if needed
- snacks for you and money for parking and/or the telephone

Parents**Ask...**

What will happen in hospital?

When you arrive at accident and emergency, a receptionist will ask for your name and contact details, and a brief outline of why you've brought your baby in. Most units have a separate area where doctors and nurses see babies and children.

The staff will assess how urgently your baby needs to be seen. A triage nurse will probably see your baby first, who will take down notes and examine your baby. If the nurse thinks your baby needs immediate attention, a doctor will be called at once.

When you see the doctor, don't be surprised if you're asked to explain why you're there all over again. If your baby is ill, the doctor will examine her, take her temperature and make other observations. He may ask you questions about the illness, such as when it started, whether you've given your baby medication and when your baby last fed. Depending on the problem, he will either give immediate treatment, send you home with advice and perhaps medication, or admit your baby onto a ward for tests or treatment.

If your baby has had an accident or swallowed something, the doctor may order an X-ray. You'll have to wait to see the doctor again after the X-ray so he can decide what to do, based on what it shows.

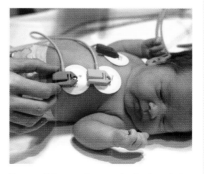

Some of the equipment in the hospital can be frightening, but try to stay focused and calm, which will reassure your baby.

Welcome to parenthood! 0–6 weeks

Your growing baby 6 weeks to 6 months

Your older baby 6 months to one year

Baby healthcare 0–12 months

General health

Health concerns in the first year

Recognising when your baby is ill and deciding what action to take is a challenging part of parenthood. This section details both common and not so usual conditions, and how you should deal with them.

Common concerns

It's usual to feel like your baby is always going down with or recovering from an illness in the first year. Coughs, colds, ear infections, allergies, skin problems and childhood diseases, such as chickenpox, are common. On the plus side, his immune system will grow stronger after each illness as he builds up antibodies.

A plan of action

Make sure you know how to get hold of your doctor out of hours, and where are the nearest walk-in surgeries. If you have older children or other dependants, have back-up arrangements with friends or neighbours so that if you have to rush to hospital you can do so.

Knowing the basics

Knowing the symptoms and signs of common illnesses before your baby goes down with them helps you feel more prepared and able to cope. It's wise to have some first-aid knowledge (see pp.288–293) and keep a first-aid kit with medicines appropriate for a baby.

Common illnesses in the first year and what you can do to help

Illness	What to do
Coughs and colds (see p.259)	Offer fluids (breastfeeds, if breastfeeding); tilt the mattress using a pillow or folded blanket under the head end to ease breathing; ask the doctor or pharmacist about using saline drops to clear a stuffy nose; take your baby to the doctor if a cold persists or you're worried.
Bronchiolitis (see p.261)	Offer plenty of fluids (breastfeeds, if breastfeeding); give smaller, more frequent feeds; take your baby to the doctor. Go straight to accident and emergency (A&E) if breathing difficulties are severe.
Ear infection (see p.262)	Take your baby to the doctor to confirm there is a problem and for advice on medications.
Febrile seizure (fit) (see p.257)	Stay calm; lie your baby on his side; remove his dummy if using one; call your doctor – you may need to take your baby to accident and emergency.
Fever (see pp.256–57)	Offer plenty of fluids (breastfeeds, if breastfeeding); keep the room cool; take your baby to the doctor or call him if his temperature is 39°C (102.2°F) or more (or 38°C/100.4°F if under three months). Consult the doctor before giving infant paracetamol to a baby under three months.
Vomiting and diarrhoea (see p.278 and p.282)	Offer plenty of fluids (breastfeeds, if breastfeeding); take your baby to see the doctor, who may prescribe an oral rehydration solution.
Thrush (see p.265)	Talk to your doctor about treatment with antifungal medicine for you and your baby.

Welcome to parenthood! 0–6 weeks

Your growing baby 6 weeks to 6 months

Your older baby 6 months to one year

Baby healthcare 0–12 months

When your baby is unwell

As a parent, it's a dreadful feeling when your baby gets poorly. Even though you instinctively know she's strong and sturdy, at times you are reminded how vulnerable she can be.

Much as parents would like to shield their children from harm, all children get ill once in a while. Don't give yourself a hard time if your baby does get a bug or a cough or a rash. Also, try not to worry unnecessarily – you'll know when something is really wrong. Your knowledge of your baby's usual patterns of feeding, sleeping, fussing and responding to you is critical in judging her overall state of health.

Signs of illness

When your baby is off-colour, check whether her temperament is different. If she has a slight fever (see p.256) or the sniffles, but still seems her usual sunny self and is feeding well, she's probably not seriously ill. This doesn't mean that you shouldn't make an appointment to see your doctor if you're worried, but a baby who has a runny nose and a big smile is probably not as sick as a baby who has a runny nose and is lethargic.

Look out for unusual crying patterns. If your baby suddenly starts crying more than usual and you can't comfort her in the usual ways, or if her cry is weak or unusually high-pitched, take her to the doctor at once. Likewise, if your baby seems unhappy and doesn't cry, but is unusually inactive and difficult to wake from sleep, get help straightaway.

Appetite is another good indicator of how well or unwell your baby is. A baby who tires easily from sucking or loses interest in feeding is probably unwell. Also, if you notice your baby regurgitating her food more than usual, or if the spit is greenish in colour, she may be unwell.

Parents**Talk...**

"My baby had an ear infection when she was just a few weeks old. It was horrible to see her so uncomfortable. She would tug at her ear and was generally out of sorts. Our doctor prescribed antibiotics and advised me on how much infant paracetamol I could give her to ease the pain."
Craig, 34, father of two

"My son was eight months old when he had his first tummy upset. He was vomiting a lot and it was pretty scary. I called the doctor and he advised me to make sure he wasn't becoming dehydrated. So whenever he stopped being sick, I gave him sips of an oral rehydration solution regularly to replace lost fluids. I also kept offering the breast so that he could feed when he wanted to."
Joanne, 39, mother of two

"My daughter has sensitive skin and developed a bad nappy rash. The area became inflamed and I could tell she was uncomfortable. I left her without a nappy on as much as possible to let the skin breathe, and used just water and cotton wool to clean her. The rash was gone in days."
Holly, 31, first-time mum

If you're unsure how to judge your baby's condition, a chat with the doctor can help decide your course of action.

Young babies, especially breastfed ones, may typically have very soft bowel movements. However, if your baby has diarrhoea (persistently watery stools), her tummy may be upset. Monitor her bowel movements thoughout the day to see if the diarrhoea continues. Make sure she drinks plenty of fluids so she doesn't get dehydrated. She should wet at least six nappies a day.

Getting help

If your baby seems very sleepy and begins to have small, hard or dry bowel movements, or if you notice that her stools are streaked with blood or mucus, or they have the consistency of jelly, consult your doctor. Similarly, if your baby's breathing becomes laboured or if she's having trouble breathing at all, get help immediately.

Does your baby have a high fever (see p.256)? Although the presence of fever in a baby is a sign that she is unwell, the fever alone is usually not a reason to be worried. Sometimes, a baby can have a low-grade fever and yet be seriously ill, or she may have a high fever and be only mildly ill. However, if a baby under three months of age has a fever higher than 38°C (100.4°F), she should be examined by a doctor.

If you are ever in any doubt as to your baby's condition or wellbeing, make an appointment with your doctor. It's important to have peace of mind, and doctors do expect to see tiny babies quite often. They know that young babies can become ill and deteriorate very quickly, but they will also be able to reassure you most of the time that your baby will get better quickly, too.

Your baby is likely to be lethargic and need plenty of rest and sleep when she's feeling off colour.

Welcome to parenthood!
0–6 weeks

Your growing baby
6 weeks to 6 months

Your older baby
6 months to one year

Baby healthcare
0–12 months

Understanding your baby's symptoms

Seeing your baby suffer through any type of illness is a heart-wrenching (and sometimes scary) experience. It's a good idea to arm yourself with information on common conditions such as allergies, infections, flu, constipation, and skin conditions and rashes. Check the symptoms chart below to identify the possible reasons for your baby's condition.

Runny or stuffy nose	Most likely to be a cold or flu, but could also be an allergy or an object lodged in the nose.	**Fever**	Could be cold, flu, overheating, ear infection, croup, urinary tract infection, bronchiolitis, roseola or other infection.
Breathing difficulties	Most likely a cold or flu, but could be asthma, bronchiolitis or environmental or food allergies. Call 999 if your baby is struggling to breathe.	**Vomiting**	Possible causes are overfeeding, reflux, tummy bug or gastroenteritis, urinary tract infection, ear infection, flu, colic or excessive crying.
Diarrhoea	Could be due to milk intolerance or allergy, flu, gastroenteritis, ear infection, parasitic infection, or the effects of medication such as antibiotics.	**Sore throat**	Could be a cold, flu, thrush, or viral or bacterial throat infection.
Rash	Could be eczema, heat rash, ringworm, newborn acne, psoriasis, scabies, measles, hives, chickenpox, roseola, slapped cheek disease or nappy rash.	**Ear pain**	Possible causes are ear infection, cold, flu, teething, swimmer's ear, object lodged in ear.
Cough	Possible causes are cold, flu, croup, bronchiolitis, allergies, asthma, reflux or whooping cough.	**Sore, watery eyes**	Possible causes are blocked tear duct, bacterial conjunctivitis, or allergic conjunctivitis.

Your baby's temperature

Normal body temperature is 36–37°C (96–98°F), but this can vary a few points of a degree from child to child. A fever is anything that is high for your child. If your baby has a fever, is crying and his temperature is soaring, it's hard not to worry, but actually a fever in itself rarely does harm. It's simply the elevation of the body's temperature above normal, and is a defence against infection.

Macrophages, the "clean-up" cells of the body, are constantly on patrol. When they find something that doesn't belong in the body, such as a virus, bacterium or fungus, they mop up as much as they can. At the same time, they call for help, signalling to the brain to raise the body's temperature. The heat kills some types of bacteria directly. It also speeds up the body's production of white blood cells and chemicals that kill germs.

When to be concerned

Fevers are usually not dangerous, but they are more serious in a young baby under six months. This is because it's relatively unusual for young babies to develop a fever, and their temperature control mechanism is not as effective. For this reason it's really important to contact a doctor straightaway if your baby is under three months and has a temperature of 38°C (100.4°F) or more, or is under six months and has a temperature of 39°C (102.2°F) or higher. There are a small number of children who do get very poorly very quickly, so it's good to be safe and get reassurance.

For older babies, their actual temperature or duration of fever does not give any clues as to how unwell they are. In all cases, your instinct that your baby has a fever or is off-colour is

Taking your baby's temperature

To take your baby's temperature, you'll need a digital thermometer, available from pharmacies. These are easy to use, easy to read and most give accurate readings in 10 seconds to two minutes. Old-fashioned glass thermometers can shatter and leak dangerous mercury.

Some thermometers are used under the arm. Strip thermometers can be used on the forehead. Digital ear thermometers are more expensive and can only be used in the ear. Don't take your baby's temperature orally until he's much older and can hold the thermometer in his mouth safely.

Wait at least 20 minutes after your baby has bathed before taking his temperature for an accurate reading.

Digital under-the-arm thermometers are easy to use and non-invasive, allowing you to take your baby's temperature without fuss.

Forehead strip thermometers are thought to be less accurate, but some find them useful for giving a quick assessment.

often just as reliable as measuring her temperature, although it can be useful to use a thermometer to be aware of what is normal for your child.

Causes

Babies and children get feverish for plenty of reasons and often the actual cause is unknown. Common reasons for a feverish illness include colds, flu, sore throats, ear infections, respiratory illnesses, croup, viral or bacterial infections and urinary tract infections. Babies often develop a fever after receiving immunisations, too. Your doctor or practice nurse will give you advice on what to look out for after your baby has had his vaccinations.

Recognising a fever

You will usually be able to tell if your baby has a fever just by touching him. You can feel his brow, or for a younger baby, feel his chest or back to see if he is hot to the touch.

If you want to, you can use a thermometer to give you a better idea about his temperature (see box, opposite). You don't need to buy an expensive thermometer; most are easy to use with clear instructions. Digital underarm thermometers are reasonably accurate and beep when they are ready. Ear thermometers can be accurate but can also be expensive and difficult to use correctly. Forehead strips are less accurate, but can be useful as they are quick and easy to use.

Treating a fever

To treat your baby's fever, offer him plenty of drinks to make sure he is well hydrated. Regularly offer him whatever he usually drinks, that is breastmilk for breastfed babies and formula or some cooled boiled water if he usually has formula milk.

Let him rest if he wants to, but he doesn't need to stay in bed. You don't need to take off layers of your baby's clothes, either, or add extra clothing. You can also let him eat if he feels like it. He will need energy and plenty of fluids to help him get better.

You might want to offer your baby infant paracetamol suspension if he seems uncomfortable or upset. Follow the directions on the packet. Don't give both at the same time, but if you have offered one and it hasn't helped, you could think about giving the other one later on instead. Never exceed the stated dose.

With a fever, your baby will usually get better by himself and he is best cared for at home. However, if you are at all worried, or if your baby seems to be getting worse, seek advice from your doctor. Be particularly cautious with a young baby (under six months) in whom a feverish illness is quite unusual.

Febrile seizures

Febrile seizures are fits that sometimes happen in young children with a raised temperature. They are frightening, however, they rarely harm a child. Symptoms include a brief loss of consciousness, twitching or spasms, stiffness, noisy breathing and frothing at the mouth. They usually continue for about 20 seconds, and rarely for more than two minutes.

What to do

If your baby has a seizure, seek medical advice immediately. If a fit lasts for more than four minutes, call an ambulance. Don't restrain him, just loosen tight clothing and carefully remove anything in his mouth, such as a dummy or food. Parents often worry that their baby will swallow his tongue if they do this, but that won't happen.

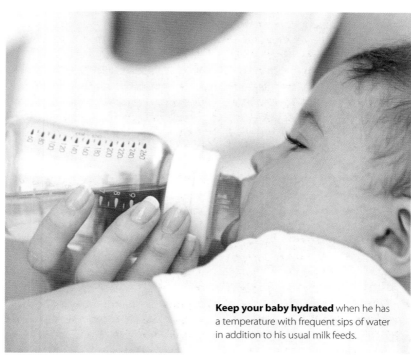

Keep your baby hydrated when he has a temperature with frequent sips of water in addition to his usual milk feeds.

Welcome to parenthood! 0–6 weeks

Your growing baby 6 weeks to 6 months

Your older baby 6 months to one year

Baby healthcare 0–12 months

Giving your baby medicine

Most medicines for babies, such as infant paracetamol, are sweet syrups that taste nice. Young babies find it hard to use spoons, so you can use a syringe. Read the label to ensure you give the right dose for her age and weight. If you're unsure, check with the pharmacist or your doctor.

Using a syringe

Fill the syringe with medicine, hold your baby upright in the crook of your arm and squirt the medicine down one side of her mouth. Babies can wriggle so you may need another adult to help, one of you to hold your baby and one to administer the medicine.

Other methods

You can also buy drops for colic, pain relief and vitamins. Take up the right amount of liquid into the dropper. Place the mouthpiece just inside the mouth and let the medicine trickle in.

If your baby is prescribed a suppository, for constipation for example, wash your hands, then push it gently into the back passage. Try to keep her still for a minute or two.

Giving medicine via a syringe may meet less resistance than other methods.

Medicines and remedies

Babies are more sensitive to medications than adults. If given in the wrong dose or at the wrong time, even the most benign over-the-counter medicines can be at best ineffective or, in the worst case scenario, harmful to your baby. Careful preparation will help you give your baby medicine with confidence.

Getting advice

Talk to a pharmacist or doctor about your baby's medicine. If it's prescribed, ask what it's for and what side effects might occur. Will it interact with other medications, what should you do if you miss a dose and should it be refrigerated? Check that over-the-counter medicines are suitable for babies and consult your doctor before giving medicine to babies under three months. Ask about side effects and tell the doctor or pharmacist about any allergies your baby has.

The correct dose

If you make a mistake and give your baby too much medicine, it's not likely to do any lasting harm, but talk to your doctor or pharmacist. If your baby can't or won't take her medicine, perhaps because she's vomiting or doesn't like the taste, let her doctor know. She may choose another method, by injection or suppository, for example to make sure your baby gets the treatment she needs.

Timing is everything when giving your baby medicine. Carefully read labels to find out how often you should be giving a particular medicine. If it says "four times a day", for example, give it four times during your baby's waking hours. If it says "every six hours", ask the doctor or pharmacist whether you'll have to wake your baby to give her the medicine. Follow the directions about whether medication should be given with meals or on an empty tummy, and whether there are foods you should avoid or partner with the medication. If you notice unexpected side effects, call the doctor.

What to avoid

Never give your baby aspirin. This is because in babies and children it can cause a serious, but rare, illness called Reye's syndrome that babies can get while recovering from a viral infection. Also, never give your baby another child's prescribed medicine.

A guide to over-the-counter medicines

Some medicines suitable for babies are available over the counter. Talk to your doctor or the pharmacist about correct doses. Don't diagnose your baby's condition yourself. Also, cough and cold medicines that can be purchased over the counter are not recommended for babies. The following is a guide to over-the-counter medications:
- infant paracetamol/ibuprofen suspension for pain relief and fever, including fever following immunisation.
- infant teething gels (never use mouth ulcer treatments aimed at adults)
- colic drops to reduce tummy gas or help your baby to digest lactose
- oral rehydration solutions to treat dehydration resulting from diarrhoea or vomiting
- some prescription medicines, for example steroid and emollient creams for eczema, are available over the counter

Infections

Babies' immune systems are immature, so they are more prone to viral infections. Experts estimate that babies get between eight and 10 colds in their first two years alone! It's hard seeing your baby suffer, but most infections aren't serious and your baby will recover quickly.

Colds

Colds are upper respiratory tract infections caused by one of many different viruses. They're commonly spread when someone sneezes or coughs and unleashes a cold virus into the air to be inhaled by someone else. They can also be transmitted through hand-to-hand contact, so wash your hands after blowing your nose. Babies tend to get lots of colds because they're born with immune systems that function at about 60 per cent of capacity.

Symptoms

It's difficult to watch your baby suffer with her first cold. She may have a fever (up to 38°C/100.4°F), a cough, reddened eyes, a sore throat and runny nose. She may be irritable, too, and lose her appetite. Babies under six months can't breathe through their noses when they're stuffed up, so have trouble breathing while eating. Your baby will probably wake several times in the night due to her discomfort and difficulty breathing.

Symptoms generally abate after three to 10 days, though in very young babies they may last up to two weeks. Most babies who have some exposure to older children experience six to 10 colds in their first year; it may seem as if her nose is runny all winter long.

Protecting your baby

Breastfeeding is one of the best ways to protect your baby's health, as your baby gets your antibodies and natural immunities. It won't guarantee she won't get ill, but when breastfed babies become ill, their cold symptoms are usually mild.

You can try to protect your baby, too, by keeping her away from people who are ill and asking sick family members to wash their hands before handling your baby or her things. If you or your partner smoke, try to give up, and avoid taking your baby to smoky places. Children who live with cigarette smokers have more colds and their colds last longer than those of peers not exposed to smoke.

Parents**Ask...**

Why won't my doctor prescribe antibiotics for my baby's cold?
A cold is caused by a virus. Antibiotics treat diseases caused by bacteria, not by viruses. Children stay healthier when a viral illness is allowed to run its course.

Antibiotics can do more harm if taken when not needed. We carry bacteria in our nasal passages and digestive tracts. When a baby takes an antibiotic, these normal, often protective, bacteria are killed, and new, more resistant bacteria grow. If a baby is over-treated with antibiotics, she can then develop resistant organisms and need stronger antibiotics when she really needs them. Antibiotics can also cause diarrhoea and allergic reactions.

What you can do

There's little you can do except help your baby to get plenty of rest and liquids. If she's feverish, you can give paracetamol suspension under a doctor's direction. Don't give her any cold remedies without consulting your doctor.

You can help your baby breathe more easily by wiping her nose. If she is having trouble breastfeeding with a stuffy nose, your doctor may prescribe saline drops to apply 15 minutes before a feed.

When to see the doctor
If your baby is under three months old, it's good to see the doctor at the first sign of illness. In an older baby, call your doctor if a cold persists for more than five days; if your baby's temperature climbs above 39°C (102.2°F); or if she seems to have an earache, has breathing problems, wheezing, a persistent cough, or a persistent, thick, green mucus running from her nose.

Welcome to parenthood!
0–6 weeks

Your growing baby
6 weeks to 6 months

Your older baby
6 months to one year

Baby healthcare
0–12 months

What you can do

Babies need sleep and fluids. For an older baby on solids, clear soup may ease congestion. For fever, give children's paracetamol. He should start feeling better in three to five days.

When to see the doctor

Call at the first sign of illness in a baby less than three months. In an older baby, call if any of the following apply:
- symptoms lasting over five days
- a temperature over 39°C (102.2°F)
- earache, breathing problems, a lingering cough, wheezing, or persistent, thick green nasal mucus

Antibiotics may be needed if there's a secondary bacterial infection, such as an ear infection, pneumonia or bronchitis.

Flu

Flu is caused by a specific bug – the influenza virus. It can be especially dangerous to young babies.

Symptoms

In young babies, flu symptoms resemble those of other illnesses, such as colds. That said, your baby is more likely to be suffering with flu if he experiences a sudden onset of fever, typically 38°C (100.4°F) or higher. Other symptoms of flu can include fatigue, chills, runny nose, dry cough, diarrhoea and vomiting. Some young children have a cough and body aches for two weeks or more.

A bout of flu can come on suddenly in your baby, and his temperature may soar.

If congestion or coughing shows up before the onset of a fever, your baby probably has caught a cold rather than flu. He may be irritable and have a poor appetite, as well as having a sore throat and swollen glands.

Croup

Croup, a common childhood virus that affects the larynx and trachea, is well-known for causing the sudden onset of a bark-like cough in babies and young children. In adults, we would call the illness laryngitis (in fact, two of the conditions that are associated with croup are laryngotracheitis and laryngotracheobronchitis – two long words for viral respiratory inflammations), but in babies and children, the inflammation can swell the windpipe, making it difficult to breathe.

Croup usually affects babies and children aged between six months and three years old, although it can occur in older children. It most often occurs during the autumn and winter. Typically, the condition is due to a mild upper respiratory-tract infection caused by a variety of viruses.

Symptoms

If your baby has croup, he will develop a cough that sounds like a dog barking, or a sea lion. Although alarming, the cough sounds worse than it actually is.

Croup typically makes its first appearance in the middle of the night. You may discover that the slight cold your baby went to sleep with has turned into the unmistakable bark. Don't hesitate to respond: you'll probably find your baby awake, sitting up, coughing and very frightened. It's best to treat croup right away (see box, opposite), especially if your baby is crying, which only exacerbates the symptoms.

Your baby may have croup for four to six days, peaking on the second or third night. Once you both get used to the nasty cough, it usually runs its course and leaves your baby a bit tired, but well.

What you can do

Encourage your baby to take extra milk or water to keep him hydrated. For babies on solids, juice and warm soup may taste good if they have lost their appetite. Give your baby liquid paracetamol if he has a fever or seems in pain. Read the dosage information, or check with your doctor if you're unsure how much to give.

Sit him upright on your lap, or hold him upright over your shoulder to help him to relax and breathe more easily.

When to see the doctor

It's best to take your baby to the doctor as soon as you can, even if he has had a bout of croup before. The doctor may give your baby a single dose of a steroid called dexamethasone, which works by reducing the swelling in his airways.

Bronchiolitis

Bronchiolitis is a variation of the common cold. It's a disease that causes the smallest airways of the lungs to swell and fill with mucus, which in turn blocks the flow of air.

In adults and older children, bronchiolitis behaves like an upper respiratory tract infection, sometimes causing a sore throat or cough. However, when it strikes a baby under one year old, it can develop into serious lower respiratory tract problems affecting the lungs. The most severe cases occur in infants under six months old.

Symptoms

The warning signals for bronchiolitis in your baby are mild cold symptoms, such as a runny nose, a minor cough and a fever (see pp.256–57), which then develop into a more pronounced cough and laboured breathing a couple of days on.

Also, watch carefully for signs that your baby has respiratory problems, such as flaring nostrils, grunting, wheezing and whistling, or tightening his abdominal muscles when he breathes. In addition, he may have a cough and struggle to feed well.

Treatment

Colds are viral, so antibiotics won't work (see p.259), but secondary infections, such as pneumonia, can often be treated, so monitor your baby closely and call the doctor if you're worried.

What you can do

There's no simple antidote for bronchiolitis. Keep your baby as comfortable as possible by offering plenty of fluids to flush the virus from his system. If he's breastfeeding, feed him as often as he'll take the breast.

Slightly elevate the head of his bed or cot with towels under the mattress (don't use pillows). Raising his head helps him to breathe through a stuffy nose.

When to see the doctor

See your doctor if your baby is under three months. Call your doctor if your baby has signs of respiratory problems (see left), or if you're not sure if he has a common cold or bronchiolitis. Go to A&E if your baby is struggling to breathe.

Pneumonia

Pneumonia is a general term for an infection of the lungs. There are two types of pneumonia: viral and bacterial. Viral pneumonia typically starts like a cold and slowly, but steadily, gets worse. In babies, pneumonia can be a very serious condition.

Symptoms

Your baby may have a fever of 38.6°C (101.5°F) or higher, a worsening cough and rapid breathing. With bacterial pneumonia, there is a sudden onset of symptoms, including a fever up to 39°C (102.2°F), rapid breathing and coughing. He won't eat and will seem very ill.

Diagnosis and treatment

Your doctor will listen to your baby's lungs with a stethoscope, looking out for decreased breathing sounds or other abnormal sounds. If your baby has pneumonia, he will usually be admitted to hospital, where a chest X-ray will be ordered. It's likely that he'll have more tests there to determine the cause of pneumonia, and then appropriate treatment. These tests might include doing a nasal or throat culture, or taking some blood to see whether the infection is viral or bacterial.

Treatment depends on what kind of infection it is, how ill your baby is and how old he is. Viral pneumonia, like all other viral infections, doesn't respond to antibiotics, so treatment may be limited to rest and fluids. Your doctor may also provide your baby with supplemental oxygen through a tube or mask to make breathing easier. Bacterial pneumonia will be treated with antibiotics, which may be given via a drip.

What you can do

There are several things you can do to decrease your baby's risk of getting pneumonia. Keep him up to date with his immunisations and practise good personal hygiene. It's not a good idea to smoke, as studies have shown that children who live around cigarette smoke become ill more often and are more susceptible to illnesses such as pneumonia, upper respiratory infections, asthma and ear infections.

When to see the doctor

Since a fever and a cough are pneumonia's main symptoms, it can be hard to tell if your baby has pneumonia. If your baby has a cold that seems to get suddenly worse after a few days or doesn't seem to be getting any better after about two weeks, call your doctor.

Welcome to parenthood!
0–6 weeks

Your growing baby
6 weeks to 6 months

Your older baby
6 months to one year

Baby healthcare
0–12 months

Ear infections

Infections of the middle ear are very common in young children, especially during the winter months. It's often hard to tell, but if your baby has a cough or runny nose and then suddenly develops a fever about three to five days later, it may be caused by an ear infection. She may also tug at her ear. If she is toddling, she may have balance problems and be more clumsy than normal.

Causes

The problem starts in the Eustachian tube, which connects the middle ear to the back of the nose and throat, and transports bacteria of viruses from there to the middle ear whenever you yawn or swallow. That's fine as long as the tube is in working order; a healthy Eustachian tube lets fluid in the ears drain back out. If the tube is swollen due to an allergy or sinus infection, the fluid can become trapped in the middle ear.

At this point, any bacteria or viruses living in the fluid have a warm, wet environment in which to flourish; pus develops, and pressure on the eardrum causes it to bulge and become inflamed, a condition known as "acute otitis media" (or glue ear). As your baby's body attempts to fight the infection, she may get a fever.

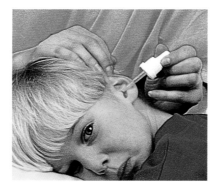

Another reason babies are susceptible to ear infections is that their Eustachian tubes are short and horizontal. As your baby grows up, the tube will triple in length. It will also become more vertical, reducing the likelihood of infection.

Several factors increase the risk of ear infections, including your baby drinking from a bottle lying down; using formula rather than breastmilk; using a dummy; exposure to cigarette smoke; and going to nurseries when less than a year old, where there's greater exposure to viruses.

Complications

Rarely, a severe or untreated infection breaks the eardrum and floods the ear canal, causing a discharge of pus. The eardrum heals, but may be scarred. This doesn't happen often, but it's important to ask your doctor to examine your baby's ear if you think she has an infection or if the symptoms have not improved, with or without treatment, within three days.

Repeated infections can cause scarring that can lead to some degree of hearing loss. This happens in a relatively small number of cases, but it's important to stop repeated mild ear infections developing into severe infections to prevent possible long-term damage.

While your baby is in the throes of an infection, you may have broken nights, trips to the doctor and to the pharmacist and worry over whether repeated infections will affect her hearing, all of which is stressful. Most ear infections clear without complications, but it's important to get treatment promptly.

If your doctor suspects an ear infection, she may prescribe antibiotic ear drops to fight bacteria that gather within trapped fluid in the middle ear.

Ringworm

Ringworm, or tinea, is a contagious fungal skin infection (the same fungus that causes athlete's foot) that has nothing to do with worms. It's called ringworm because the infection appears in a round shape. It can be itchy, but isn't painful or dangerous. It's common in children and can also affect babies. It usually affects only the torso or scalp.

Symptoms

If your baby has ringworm on her torso, she'll have a rash of one or several red rings on her chest, stomach, back and sometimes thighs. The rings are usually crusty or scaly on the outside and smooth in the middle. As the fungus grows, the rings enlarge, ranging in size from a few millimetres to a few centimetres. Sometimes several rings develop near each other and merge.

When the fungus affects the scalp, it can appear as dandruff or bald spots and can be dry and crusty, or moist and filled with pus. It's easy to confuse scalp ringworm with dandruff or cradle cap. If you're unsure, consult your doctor.

Causes

The ringworm fungus gets into the body through broken skin, such as a cut or scratch or a patch of eczema. Your baby probably got it from an infected person or pet, or possibly from soil.

Scalp ringworm is much more likely to have been passed from person to person, such as from sharing a hairbrush or a hat, or from bedclothes or towels. Shared public facilities, such as swimming-pool showers, are also potential sources of ringworm infection.

Complications

In healthy babies, complications are usually minor, such as the infection spreading, slight scarring or hair loss from a scalp infection. Sometimes, a secondary bacterial or fungal infection can set in, but the risks are still small.

You can often treat ringworm with an over-the-counter cream (see box, right). Wash your hands after touching the area, and avoid washing or scrubbing the area too often as this can break the skin and lead to further infection.

What you can do

In most cases, ringworm clears up if you treat it with an over-the-counter antifungal cream, like the kind adults use for athlete's foot. Look for products with one or two per cent clotrimazole or miconazole. Some babies are sensitive to these creams, so test a bit first to see how the skin reacts.

If a rash develops in response to the cream, talk to your doctor about alternatives. Otherwise, smooth a small amount of the cream over and a little bit beyond the infected area twice a day. Carry on treating it for a further one to two weeks once the rash has cleared. Wash your hands thoroughly afterwards.

When to see the doctor

Ringworm of the scalp can be more difficult to treat using a cream, so it's best to see your doctor, who will probably prescribe an oral antifungal medicine and a medicated shampoo.

Ringworm should get better with treatment within about four weeks. If not, take your baby to the doctor.

Welcome to parenthood! 0–6 weeks

Your growing baby 6 weeks to 6 months

Your older baby 6 months to one year

Baby healthcare 0–12 months

Molluscum contagiosum

Molluscum contagiosum is a type of viral skin infection that appears as small, round, shiny, pearly white or pinkish spots. There are usually no more than 20, and each spot has either a dimple in the middle or a tiny pus-filled head. They range in size from one to 10 millimetres in diameter and can grow over a period of several weeks.

How is the body affected?

In babies, the pimples most commonly appear on the trunk or on the inside of the joints, such as on the inner elbows and behind the knees, as well as around the bottom and genitals. However, the spots can break out almost anywhere on the body, including on the mouth and eyelids, although this is rare. If the spots become infected or red they can hurt, but they're mostly painless.

Molluscum contagiosum usually clears up within around 18 months without any form of treatment. The good news is that once a bout has completely cleared up, it's rare for it to return.

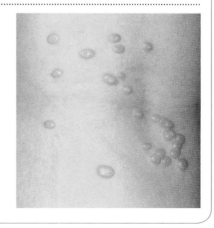

Conjunctivitis

If your baby's eyes are inflamed or very pink, he may have conjunctivitis. This means that there is inflammation of the conjunctiva, the membrane that lines the eyelids and covers the white part of the eye. Conjunctivitis can be caused by infection, allergy or irritation. It can be very itchy and sore, but is rarely serious.

Causes

Infectious conjunctivitis is often caused by bacteria, passed between people. It can also develop when your baby has a cold or chest infection. He may wake up with his eyelids stuck together and it may spread from one eye to the other.

Allergic conjunctivitis often affects both eyes and is more likely to be itchy. The allergen may be obvious, for example eye swelling or redness just after your baby strokes a cat. Young babies don't often get hayfever, but this can happen. Treatment is by antihistamine, but ask your doctor or pharmacist for advice before giving babies antihistamines.

Irritant conjunctivitis is not common in babies. Probably the most common irritant is cigarette smoke. However, it can also develop if, for example a chemical is splashed near the eyes. In this case, take your baby to a hospital accident and emergency department.

Urinary-tract infections

Normally, urine drains easily from your baby's kidneys and passes down tubes called ureters into the bladder where it's cleared through the urethra and into his nappy. However, bacteria from the genital area can get into the urethra, or from the blood moving through the kidneys, causing a urinary-tract infection (UTI).

Symptoms

It can be hard to tell if a baby has a UTI. Some symptoms are general, such as fever, vomiting, tiredness and irritability, but if your baby needs to urinate often and is in pain when he does, then he may have a UTI. His urine may also smell unpleasant or have blood in it.

It's important to contact your doctor if you suspect a UTI. If an infection is left untreated for a while, it can move to the kidneys and possibly cause permanent damage. Babies under two years are more likely to suffer serious damage.

Diagnosis

If your baby has signs of a UTI, the doctor may need a sterile urine sample to identify the bacteria. You may be given an absorbent pad to put in a nappy and urine is sucked out of the pad with a syringe. This can be done by you at home, at the doctor's or occasionally at hospital.

Thrush

This is an infection caused by the *candida albicans* fungus. If your baby has white patches on the inside of his cheeks, it could be a thrush yeast infection.

Causes and symptoms

Thrush is most common in babies aged two months and younger, but can appear in older babies. It resembles cottage cheese or milk curds on the sides and roof of the mouth and sometimes the tongue. Everyone has yeast in their bodies, but if there's an imbalance, infection can set in. Factors that can tip the balance include hormonal changes and antibiotics.

If you notice a white coating on your baby's tongue but nowhere else, it's probably just milk residue. Thrush can be found on the tongue, but is most often on the sides of the mouth, causing soreness. You may first suspect it if your baby cries when breastfeeding, or when sucking on a dummy or a bottle. If you think your baby has thrush, look for the characteristic white patches. Gently touch a patch with a gauze-covered finger. It probably won't come off easily, but if it does, you'll find a raw, red area underneath that may bleed.

Prevention

There's not much you can do to prevent your baby getting thrush, especially if he picked up the bacteria during the birth. Some think it can also be caused by prolonged sucking on a bottle or dummy; others think poor hygiene of bottle teats is to blame; still others blame a dummy or bottle teat that's too large. However, babies who exclusively breastfeed and don't use dummies can also get it.

Take care if your baby is put on antibiotics, or if you're breastfeeding and take them to treat an infection. They can kill off infection-fighting bacteria as well as bad bacteria (see p.259): either can trigger a case of thrush in your baby.

Complications and treatment

Thrush isn't dangerous to your baby. The biggest problem is if his mouth is too sore to suck, as he may get dehydrated. Your doctor may prescribe an oral antifungal drop solution. Alert your doctor if the infection doesn't clear up with treatment, or if your baby has a fever over 39°C (102.2°F) (or 38°C/100.4°F under three months), which could indicate a different type of infection.

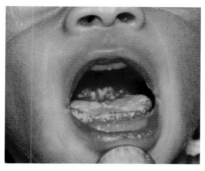

Thrush infection in babies typically produces a white, curd-like coating on the tongue, which can make it difficult to suck.

What you can do

If you're breastfeeding, you will need to apply an antifungal treatment (see below) to your nipples so that you and your baby don't pass the infection back and forth to each other. Breastfeeding mothers are also advised to let their nipples air dry between feedings to prevent thrush; this is also especially important if you do have thrush, because damp nipples are a good breeding ground for yeast.

Some experts recommend giving your baby sterilised water to drink after breast- or bottle-feeding to rinse the milk residue away. Cleaning and sterilising dummies may also help.

When to see the doctor

If you suspect your baby has thrush, consult your doctor. She may prescribe an antifungal gel called miconazole, which can take about a week to clear the infection.

Give your baby all the comfort he needs and follow your doctor's instructions for pain relief and medication. Although a bout of thrush can be very trying for all of you, it should soon pass.

ParentsAsk...

Do I need treatment too?

If your baby has thrush or a fungal infection, the chances are that you have it too, if you're breastfeeding. You'll need treatment just as much as he does, and at the same time, or you may pass the infection back and forth.

Common signs of thrush in mums include loss of colour in the nipple or areola; pink or red, shiny areola, often evenly distributed around the base of the nipple; cracked nipples; white plaques on the folds of the nipple or areola; itchy nipples that may be sensitive to any touch, even to clothing; burning sensation and pain in the nipples.

Can I still breastfeed?

Yes. Thrush shouldn't affect breastfeeding and you can continue while being treated. But if you store expressed milk while you or your baby have thrush, it might be best not to use it as it might cause re-infection.

Allergies and allergic conditions

Industrialisation, energy-efficient homes and the eradication of many childhood illnesses may be to blame for the rise in allergies and allergic conditions. If your baby develops an allergy, it's important to learn to manage and control it, allowing her to lead a healthy, normal life.

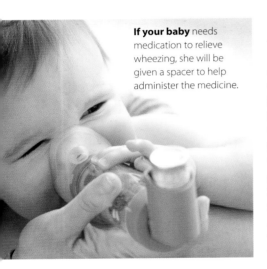

If your baby needs medication to relieve wheezing, she will be given a spacer to help administer the medicine.

Asthma

Asthma is an allergic condition that causes the airways to constrict and mucus to build up, making it hard to breathe. Asthma is often a reaction to a trigger, usually tobacco smoke, pet fur, mould spores, dust mites or pollen. As with other allergies, the trigger stimulates antibodies to produce histamine and other chemical mediators. Chemicals released by the antibodies swell the lung's lining and tighten the muscles of the airway, and they also start producing mucus.

Diagnosis

Babies' airways are so small that they can wheeze when they have an upper respiratory-tract infection or are suffering with a cold. This can be alarming and you may think that your baby has asthma, but asthma is actually very rare in young babies.

If your baby regularly wheezes in the absence of a cold, though, tell your doctor. Doctors only make a firm diagnosis of asthma when they see a pattern of symptoms emerging over a period of time.

Managing asthma

Asthma is a chronic condition, and there is no known cure. However, it can be successfully managed over time with medicines, and by reducing the exposure to the trigger for the asthma when possible. Talk to your doctor about the best treatments, both to help prevent your baby from having an asthma attack and how to deal with one if it occurs. Your doctor may refer your baby to a specialist.

If your child is diagnosed with asthma, it shouldn't prevent her from taking exercise and leading a healthy, active lifestyle as she grows up. Many children outgrow asthma, or find the severity lessens.

What you can do

If you think your baby is having an asthma attack, call for medical help immediately. Drugs called relievers can stop an attack quickly. These drugs relieve the spasm in the airway, which in turn eases breathing. A spacer is needed to help babies inhale the medicine.

If your child has been given another type of drug, known as a controller, which helps prevent attacks, ensure that she takes this as prescribed. These prevent allergic reactions occurring in the first place, so avoiding wheezing. Controllers include anti-inflammatories.

An increased risk

Genetics are thought to play a role in asthma. Children whose parents have asthma are more likely to develop it and at a faster rate.

Environmental factors

A baby who has a parent who smokes is four times more likely to wheeze. Even if you don't smoke near your baby, particles cling to clothes and she's at risk from second-hand smoke.

Poor housing and living in a large town make asthma more likely, too.

Eczema

This is a dry, itchy skin condition that affects somewhere between 15 to 20 per cent of children at some point. It usually appears for the first time before the age of two. The skin gets dry, itchy, red and cracked, and can sometimes ooze fluid and bleed. The areas most affected in babies are the hands, face, neck, elbows and backs of the knees.

Causes

Eczema means that the skin's barrier doesn't work as well as it should. This can mean your baby's skin is more easily prone to infections and allergies, which can make the condition worse.

Eczema affects the skin in "flares" or "flare-ups". Your baby's skin may have red and itchy patches most of the time, but during flare-ups these areas worsen and may need more intensive treatment.

Flare-ups can be triggered by skin irritation caused by chemicals, such as the detergents in bubble baths, shampoos, washing powders and fabric softeners. Use bath emollient rather than soaps and detergents in the bath. You could also try changing your washing powder (use a non-biological one) to see if this improves your baby's skin.

Eczema can be very distressing in babies because they find it very difficult not to scratch. In some cases, eczema can disturb your baby's sleep.

Treatment

The treatment of eczema depends on its severity. If your baby has only a few red, itchy areas, you may simply need to use an emollient lotion, cream or ointment, sometimes with a short course of a low-strength steroid cream. Putting scratch mittens or socks on your baby's hands at night can stop her scratching.

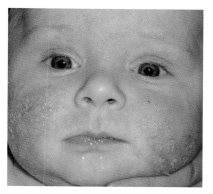

Eczema in young babies is a distressing and frustrating condition. Learning to manage it can help reduce its severity.

Dryness makes eczema worse, so moisturising the skin is crucial. Liberal quantities of an emollient applied several times a day can stop skin drying out.

The good news is that most children grow out of the condition once in their teens. Eczema can't be cured, but it can be controlled with the right treatments.

What you can do

There are many moisturisers and emollients and you may have to try several to find one that suits your baby. These are available as creams, ointments, lotions and bath additives. You may have to use large quantities on a regular basis and your doctor should give repeat prescriptions once you know which one works. Keep your baby's nails short to help prevent skin irritation from scratching.

When to see the doctor

If eczema is persistent, it's worth consulting your doctor. Doctors often recommend using steroid creams from time to time. Many parents worry about side effects from overuse of steroids and are reluctant to use them. However, steroids are safe if used appropriately. Their main side effect is thinning of the skin if they are used for long periods of time, but there is no evidence that this is permanent.

Parents**Talk...**

"My baby had quite mild eczema – just a few red and itchy areas on his elbows and legs. I tried applying plenty of moisturiser, but it didn't seem to clear it up, so our doctor prescribed a short course of low-strength steroid cream. That managed to do the trick!"
Emma, 27, first-time mum

"We thought our little one's eczema might be caused by the everyday chemicals we were using in our home. So we changed our washing powder and baby shampoo and started using bath emollient rather than bubble bath. It certainly improved things."
Vicky, 35, first-time mum

"My son had very severe eczema and was clearly uncomfortable. We tried lots of things to no avail, but after our third visit to the doctor we were told about a technique called wrapping. Bandages are soaked in emollient or steroid cream and applied to the area, then dry bandages are wrapped on top. It worked wonders!"
John, 33, father of two

Welcome to parenthood!
0–6 weeks

Your growing baby
6 weeks to 6 months

Your older baby
6 months to one year

Baby healthcare
0–12 months

What you can do

You can make your baby more comfortable by rubbing calamine lotion into his skin to soothe the itching. Dress him in cotton clothes to minimise irritation, and keep his nails short so he doesn't damage his skin when scratching.

When to see the doctor

Hives usually go away naturally, but if treatment is needed, your doctor may recommend antihistamine medicine to reduce the itching and swelling. Occasionally, with severe hives that don't respond to antihistamines, doctors will prescribe steroids.

If hives are accompanied by other serious symptoms, they can be a sign of anaphylactic shock. If your baby develops additional symptoms (see box, below) call 999 immediately. If your baby has a history of severe allergic reactions, you may need to carry injectable adrenaline around with you at all times.

Urticaria (hives)

Hives are raised, swollen, itchy areas on the skin. They can appear on any part of the body, and may come and go in anything from a few hours to a few days. They're also known as wheals, nettle rash and, by the medical term, urticaria. A typical rash has small, raised areas (1–2 centimetres/2½–5 inches) that develop quickly. Wheals are red or white, itchy and surrounded by a red area. They can join so the rash looks extensive.

Hives are common, especially in young children and women; one in six people develops them at some point.

Causes

The most common cause of hives in young children is a viral infection, such as a cold or flu. They can also result from an environmental or food allergy.

Generally, the most common food allergens are milk, eggs, peanuts, tree nuts, shellfish, seafood, wheat and soya. A reaction to cow's milk is more common in babies under six months.

Hives can also be caused by irritants, such as nettles and plants. Toddlers who develop an allergy to cats may break out in hives when stroking a pet. Although rare, antibiotics and non-steroidal anti-inflammatory drugs (NSAIDs), such as ibuprofen, can cause a reaction. If your baby has an allergy to penicillin, he may get hives when taking certain antibiotics. This may happen about a week after starting medication for the first time or during a subsequent course.

Hives can be caused by insect bites and stings, for example from bees or red ants. Another cause can be heat: some children first develop hives after a sweaty play session or on a very hot day.

Help your doctor to work out what has caused the hives by making a note of when they started, how long they lasted and any possible triggers. In about half of all cases, the cause isn't identified.

Although itchy and very uncomfortable, hives usually go away on their own after a few hours or days.

Anaphylactic shock

Anaphylaxis is a severe allergic reaction to a food or substance and is life-threatening. It occurs when the immune system overreacts to an allergen, triggering the release of massive amounts of histamine and other chemicals, which can cause the body to go into anaphylactic shock.

Symptoms

Onset of symptoms is rapid and serious and includes hives; swelling of the skin, lips or face; wheezing and breathing problems; a rapid pulse; sweating; dizziness; fainting; nausea; vomiting; abdominal cramps; diarrhoea; very pale skin; and possible loss of consciousness.

Prompt action

If your baby experiences a severe reaction, it's important to act swiftly. Call 999 immediately and try to keep your baby calm by talking to him reassuringly and staying calm yourself. When the paramedics arrive, they'll probably treat your baby on the spot with an injection of adrenaline. It works in minutes by raising your baby's blood pressure, relieving his breathing difficulties and reducing swelling.

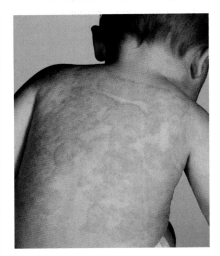

If your baby has a severe allergic reaction, he may develop an extensive hives rash that covers much of his body.

Food intolerances and allergies

Food allergies and food intolerances are different, but they are often confused. Food allergies happen when our immune systems react to a protein in food that is normally considered harmless. Food intolerance doesn't involve the immune system. Your baby has an intolerance if he has difficulty digesting a certain food. Milk is the most common food allergy in babies. It's estimated that between two and seven per cent of babies are allergic to it.

Allergic reactions

If your baby has a food allergy, he will probably have an itchy or runny nose, a sore throat, itchy, watery eyes, rashes (hives) and swelling. These symptoms usually come on fairly quickly after eating the food. It is estimated that between six and eight per cent of children have a food allergy.

The most common food allergies in babies and young children are to milk, eggs, peanuts and tree nuts.

More severe reactions, involving wheezing, breathing difficulties and/or a drop in blood pressure, may be life-threatening and are known as anaphylaxis (see box, opposite). Fortunately, severe reactions are rare in babies and in young children. If you suspect that your baby is having a severe allergic reaction, call an ambulance immediately.

A delayed reaction

When your baby reacts quickly to an allergen, it's usually easy to spot. However, delayed allergic reactions to foods are becoming more common. Your child's body may take longer to react as different parts of his immune system are affected. Symptoms to look out for include reflux; colic; diarrhoea; eczema (common in babies with a milk allergy); and constipation. Do remember, though, that all these symptoms are common in early childhood and an allergy is only one possible explanation.

Your baby may grow out of his allergy, but it depends on what he's allergic to. Up to 90 per cent of children will outgrow cow's milk and egg allergies, for example whereas only about 10 to 20 per cent outgrow nut allergies. Some children may go on to develop other allergy-related, or atopic, conditions, such as asthma, eczema or hayfever, later in life.

If your baby has a food allergy, it's essential that he is checked often by a specialist, and retested at intervals to see if he has outgrown his allergy.

Recognising intolerance

If your baby is suffering with a food intolerance, he might have tummy pain; colic; bloating; wind; diarrhoea and vomiting. The most common intolerance in babies is milk, known as lactose intolerance. This usually occurs after a tummy upset and may last a few weeks.

If you suspect that your baby has a food intolerance, talk to your doctor. Never try to diagnose your baby yourself, since there are other conditions that cause similar symptoms. Your doctor may refer him to a dietitian, who will put him on an exclusion diet, where suspect foods are removed from his meals then slowly reintroduced. This helps to identify which foods are causing the problem.

What you can do

If you think your baby is allergic to a food, ask your doctor for a referral to an allergy specialist. Don't be tempted to buy do-it-yourself testing kits. He may have a skin-prick test to diagnose allergies, and possibly blood tests.

If an allergy is diagnosed, follow the doctor's advice about avoiding foods. A baby with a mild allergy, for example to eggs, may tolerate them in baked goods, whereas one with a severe allergy should avoid all traces of it. Take any medication with you on a trip out.

Coeliac disease

This is a bowel condition caused by a life-long intolerance to gluten and foods containing it. Gluten is a protein found in wheat, rye, barley and, possibly, oats.

Symptoms

These are usually first seen in babies between nine and 18 months. They include diarrhoea; weight loss or poor weight gain; malnutrition; poor appetite and tummy bloating; and anaemia. Your baby may be unsettled.

Prevention

The Department of Health advises that gluten shouldn't be given to babies under six months, and never as a first weaning food if there's a family history of allergy or coeliac disease. Waiting until six months to introduce solids may minimise the risk of a baby developing adverse reactions or an allergy to foods, including coeliac disease. If you feel your baby needs to start solids before six months, discuss it with your health visitor; avoid gluten-containing foods until your baby is six months old.

Welcome to parenthood! 0–6 weeks

Your growing baby 6 weeks to 6 months

Your older baby 6 months to one year

Baby healthcare 0–12 months

Infectious diseases

Thanks to advances in immunisations, we've all but wiped out infectious diseases such as mumps and measles in the UK. To protect your baby, make sure she's up to date with her vaccinations and learn to identify telltale symptoms of illnesses she's still likely to catch.

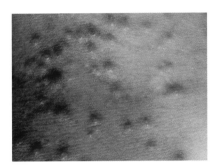

The chickenpox rash is recognisable as clusters of red spots topped with blisters.

What you can do

There's no specific treatment for chickenpox, but recent research using anti-viral drugs in the early stages of the illness has shown a slight benefit.

Paracetamol may relieve fever and aches and pains; use a suitable infant paracetamol. Don't give aspirin as this can be dangerous in babies (see p.258).

You may also be able to soothe your baby's itching by rubbing calamine lotion onto her spots, or by using a solution of sodium bicarbonate (use ordinary baking soda and dissolve it in a small quantity of water). Keep her nails short, too, so she doesn't damage her skin if she scratches a lot.

Some homeopaths suggest the homeopathic remedy Sulphur to help boost your baby's immune system.

Chickenpox

This is a highly infectious disease caused by one of the herpes viruses. All the viruses in this group share one feature, which is that they lie dormant after the initial infection and can reactivate much later.

The chickenpox virus is transmitted via droplet spread, for example by sneezing, and by close contact with an infected person. Most children contract chickenpox when they're young and it's usually mild in children. The incubation period (the time from when the disease is first caught until the symptoms appear) is 14–21 days. The child is infectious from about two days before the rash appears until all the spots have dried up, which can take up to 10 days.

Symptoms

Some babies with chickenpox have a high temperature while others are just a bit off-colour. The rash starts as little red spots, which develop tiny blisters on the top within a few hours. They usually start on the face and trunk and spread to other parts of the body, appearing in crops. There may be so many spots that they appear to run into one another. They are particularly sore on the scalp, in the mouth and throat and, in girls, around the vulval area.

Complications

These are rare. The most common complication in children under five is a bacterial infection of the blisters.

ParentsAsk...

Should my baby be isolated?
Your baby should be kept away from pregnant women who haven't had the virus as it can cause problems for the unborn baby. People whose immune systems are deficient, such as those having chemotherapy or with HIV or AIDS, are also more at risk from the chickenpox virus. If you think that you or your baby has been exposed to the virus, you may not be able to visit friends or relatives in hospital. Call the ward to check first.

How can I stop it spreading?
Chickenpox can be spread through contact with items that have been infected with the virus, such as toys and clothes. You can halt its spread by wiping objects or surfaces with a sterilising solution, and by washing infected clothes, bedding and towels.

Measles

Measles is an infection caused by the rubeola virus. When someone who has the virus sneezes or coughs, droplets containing the virus spray into the air. The droplets stay active for two hours in the air or on a surface. A child who breathes in these droplets or comes into contact with them can become infected.

Nowadays, it's rare for children in the UK to come down with measles. However, the incidence of measles has increased in recent years due to fears about the measles, mumps, and rubella (MMR) vaccine, which have stopped some parents immunising their children. If a baby doesn't receive the MMR vaccine, given at 13 months, she has a chance of catching this nasty viral illness. This vaccine is not given to babies under six months of age.

Your baby has a 90 per cent chance of contracting the virus if she's had contact with someone who is infected with it before she's immunised. It usually takes around six to 21 days for a child exposed to the virus to become ill. A person with measles is contagious for two to four days before developing the telltale rash and about five days after.

Symptoms

If your baby has measles, her first symptoms are likely to be a fever, a runny nose, a cough, and sore, red, swollen eyes. A few days afterwards, she may develop small white spots in her mouth, called Koplik's spots, particularly on the mucous membranes that line her cheeks. A couple of days after these appear, a measles rash will develop on her face and neck, and spread down her body. The rash starts out as flat red patches, but eventually develops some bumps. As the rash appears, the fever usually climbs, sometimes reaching as high as 40.6°C (105°F). The rash may be itchy.

Your baby may feel sick and tired, and may be experiencing aches and pains. Her cough may become troublesome, and she will also be irritable. The measles rash usually lasts about five days. As it fades, it turns a brownish colour. It will fade in the order it appeared on your child's body and will leave her skin dry and flaky.

Prevention

If your baby has been exposed to measles before having the MMR vaccine, the course of action will depend on her age. If she is younger than six months and you've had measles in the past, your antibodies will have passed to your baby in the uterus and your baby should be immune. If you've never had measles, your baby may be given an injection of human normal immuniglobin (HNIG). HNIG is a concentration of antibodies that can give short-term, but immediate protection against measles.

If your baby is older than six months and has been exposed to the measles virus, she will usually be given a dose of the MMR vaccine straightaway to prevent the virus from developing.

Complications

Most otherwise healthy children recover from measles without problems. In 20 to 30 per cent of cases, though, an affected child will develop some kind of complication, such as diarrhoea or an ear infection. Other less likely but possible difficulties include pneumonia, meningitis, encephalitis (inflammation of the brain) and, very rarely, other serious brain complications.

What you can do

If your baby is unwell with a temperature, you can give her the recommended dose of infant paracetamol for fever and aches and pains if she is three months old, or infant ibuprofen if she is at least three months old and weighs 5kg or more. If your baby is younger than three months old, check with her doctor before giving her any form of medication. Do not give your baby aspirin as this is potentially dangerous in babies and children (see p.258).

When to see the doctor

If you suspect that your baby has contracted measles, contact your doctor straightaway.

Antibiotics (see p.259) aren't useful for treating measles, but they may be needed to treat any secondary infections that your baby develops, such as an ear infection.

Try to make your baby as comfortable as possible, and keep her isolated from other children to avoid spreading the infection around. Make sure she gets plenty of rest and fluids.

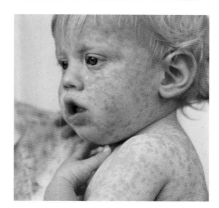

A red rash that may become bumpy over time and is sometimes itchy is a sign that your baby has the measles infection.

Welcome to parenthood!
0–6 weeks

Your growing baby
6 weeks to 6 months

Your older baby
6 months to one year

Baby healthcare
0–12 months

Slapped cheek disease

Also known as "fifth disease", slapped cheek disease is caused by the parvovirus B19. The virus got its name because it was the fifth red-rash disease of its ilk. The other four are scarlet fever, measles, rubella and roseola. Despite all these scary sounding names, it's actually a relatively mild illness. The virus is most common in school-aged children, but babies can get it, too.

Symptoms

Your baby's cheeks will be red and look as if they've actually been slapped. A red, lacy-like rash may appear on his body and limbs. Your baby may have a slight fever and feel achy and flu-like, or he may have no other symptoms at all. Another non-rash symptom, which is much more common in adults, is joint pain. Sometimes the rash can reappear months later in response to exposure to sunlight or heat, after a hot bath or exercise for example. Don't worry if this happens to your baby as it is not a recurrence of the infection and should soon settle down.

Causes

Like other viruses, slapped cheek disease can be spread through oral secretions. The incubation period for the infection is around 10 to 14 days, and your baby is most contagious the week before the symptoms appear. Once the rash appears, however, he's minimally contagious. Nonetheless, keep him away from other children, not only to prevent the virus from spreading, but also to prevent him from picking up other infections at the same time.

The virus that causes the disease can also trigger an asymptomatic infection or a mild respiratory infection in adults.

Risks to others

People with certain kinds of deficiencies, such as sickle-cell anaemia, can actually become seriously ill and end up being hospitalised if they contract this particular virus as adults, so where possible you should avoid your baby coming into contact with people who are immune deficient.

Pregnant woman are at a small risk of this virus if they haven't had it as a child, although at least 50 per cent of women are immune. There is a blood test to check immunity, but it's not 100 per cent reliable. If you're pregnant and have been exposed to slapped cheek disease, check with your doctor. In rare cases, the virus can cause miscarriage in early pregnancy.

Prevention

There's no vaccine for slapped cheek disease, but if you're immune to it, your baby will also have some immunity from the antibodies he received from you during the birth.

As a person with the disease is contagious well before the rash actually develops, you can't completely protect your baby from fifth disease, especially if it's making the rounds at your baby's nursery. However, you can reduce your baby's chances of catching it by washing his hands – and yours – often.

$Fact$: 60% of people in the UK have been infected with parovirus B19.

Over half the population of the UK have had the slapped cheek virus. It most commonly affects children aged between four and 12.

What you can do

Treat the virus as you would a cold, with fluids and rest. Like most viruses, slapped cheek disease just needs to run its course. By the time your baby has the rash, he'll probably no longer be uncomfortable, but early on you may want to give him infant paracetamol or ibuprofen for fever or other discomfort.

When to see the doctor

When in doubt, see your doctor. Although the virus will run its course, if a fever lasts longer than a few days or reaches high temperatures, a different infection may be the cause. It's not uncommon for the rash to linger for up to a month. In an otherwise healthy baby, slapped cheek is usually a mild illness. However, if your baby has a form of chronic anaemia or a weakened immune system, fifth disease will put him at risk for other serious complications.

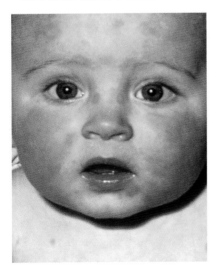

The bright red cheeks typical of slapped cheek may look alarming, but the condition is usually a mild one.

Rubella

This is a relatively mild viral infection caused by the togavirus group. It is commonly referred to as German measles, or three-day measles, but it's actually not the same disease as measles (see p.271), which is caused by a different virus.

As most preschool children in the UK now receive the measles, mumps and rubella (MMR) vaccine, rubella is now an extremely rare illness here. In 2008, there were just 27 confirmed cases throughout England and Wales.

Risks during pregnancy

Rubella isn't dangerous to young children, but it can be devastating to unborn babies during the first trimester. In fact, the rubella vaccine was developed primarily to protect women around childbearing age before they become pregnant.

A woman infected with rubella during her first trimester has an 85 per cent chance of having a baby with congenital rubella syndrome (CRS), which can lead to miscarriage, stillbirth, or severe birth defects, including deafness, blindness, and heart and brain defects. Fortunately in the UK, the majority of women in their childbearing years are immune to the disease, either because they were vaccinated against it as a child or because they have already had the illness.

How rubella is spread

While rubella isn't as contagious as other infectious illnesses, such as measles or chickenpox, an unimmunised preschooler could become infected with the virus by inhaling droplets of saliva or mucus when an infected person sneezes or coughs nearby.

A baby with the rubella virus is considered to be contagious from a week before the rash actually appears to a week after it goes away, although he's most contagious while he has the rash. If you're pregnant and were never immunised against rubella, it's important to stay away from an infected child until at least a week after his rash has disappeared.

Symptoms

The infection can cause a pinkish-red rash that first appears on the face and later spreads elsewhere on the body. Other symptoms include a low fever (38°C/100.4°F) that lasts about 24 hours; a stuffy or runny nose; red, inflamed eyes; and enlarged lymph nodes at the base of your baby's skull, behind the ears, and at the back of the neck.

The virus runs its course in about three days, but up to half of people don't get any symptoms so they won't know that they've had it.

Most babies with rubella recover quickly and completely. Call the doctor, though, if your baby's fever rises above 39°C (102.2°F), (or 38°F/100.4°F for a baby under three months of age), or if your baby has symptoms other than the fever and rubella rash.

Prevention

Once your baby is over a year, make sure he receives the MMR vaccine. This is usually given at 13 months of age – and again between three and five years of age – as part of his scheduled immunisations. If your child is behind on any of his vaccinations, check with your doctor or practice nurse about a make-up schedule to bring your baby fully up to date.

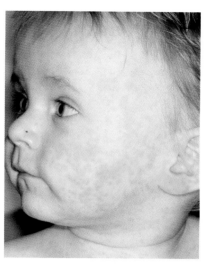

The red rubella rash usually first appears across the face and then gradually spreads over the rest of the body.

What you can do

In the unlikely instance that your baby contracts rubella, you won't need to do much because it's usually a mild illness. Antibiotics won't work because it's caused by a virus, not bacteria. You may want to give your baby some infant paracetamol if the fever is making him uncomfortable.

When to see the doctor

If you think your baby has rubella, you should inform your doctor. As well as checking your baby's wellbeing with the doctor, in the UK, rubella is a notifiable disease, which means the Department of Health is recording the number of cases of it (to keep track so that they can react quickly to outbreaks and epidemics).

Plus, rubella is easily confused with other illnesses, such as measles and scarlet fever, so the doctor may want to examine your baby and take blood samples to confirm the diagnosis.

Welcome to parenthood!
0–6 weeks

Your growing baby
6 weeks to 6 months

Your older baby
6 months to one year

Baby healthcare
0–12 months

Meningitis

This is an inflammation of the meninges, the membranes covering the brain and spinal cord. Meningitis can develop rapidly and can be very serious.

There are many different types of meningitis. The two main forms of meningitis are viral and bacterial. The most common type is viral meningitis, which can be a relatively mild illness. Some sufferers are not even aware that they have an infection. The bacterial form of meningitis is a rare illness, however, it is life-threatening and requires prompt treatment.

Bacterial meningitis also comes in many forms (meningococcal and pneumococcal are the two main types). It is always a serious and severe illness, but rapidly developing complications can make it even more dangerous.

Immediate treatment of bacterial meningitis is vital. Septicaemia (blood poisoning) is a complication of meningitis caused by bacteria entering the bloodstream and multiplying rapidly. The septicaemic form of meningitis is the most dangerous.

Symptoms

There's no textbook pattern to the disease. Symptoms can occur in any order or may not appear at all. In young children, it's important to look out for unusual high-pitched crying or moaning; grunting or rapid breathing; and being fretful or irritable when touched. Your baby may vomit; refuse food; have pale or blotchy skin; and be floppy, listless or unresponsive. She may also be drowsy or difficult to wake, have a fever but with cold hands and feet, and her fontanelle (the soft spot at the top of your baby's head) may bulge.

There may be a rash caused by septicaemia, which appears under the skin as a cluster of tiny spots (see box, below). If a rash develops, do the glass test described in the box below.

See your doctor immediately if you suspect she has meningitis. If no rash develops, but her condition is deteriorating rapidly, take her to hospital.

Many of the symptoms that are commonly associated with meningitis only appear when the disease is already

What you can do

If you suspect meningitis, you need to contact a doctor immediately. The earlier antibiotics are given in the case of bacterial meningitis, the greater the chance that your baby will survive without complications. Always trust your instincts.

Diagnosis is by lumbar puncture – the doctor removes a sample of fluid from the spinal cord with a needle, and examines it. If he suspects bacterial meningitis he will give your baby antibiotics as soon as possible.

Bacterial meningitis needs immediate treatment in intensive care so bodily functions can be supported while the antibiotics take effect. Viral meningitis doesn't respond to antibiotics, so treatment is based on rest and nursing care. It often clears up quickly, although headaches and tiredness can persist. In rare cases, viral meningitis causes encephalitis (inflammation of the brain) and antiviral treatment may be needed.

The "glass" test

If your baby has meningitis, there may be a rash caused by septicaemia, which appears under the skin as tiny spots. They look like pinpricks and can start anywhere on the body. If untreated, they develop a bruise-like appearance, followed by purple skin damage and discolouration. They're harder to see on dark skin, so check paler areas.

Identifying a meningitis rash

You can use the "glass" test to check suspicious rashes on your baby. To do

this, press the side of a clear drinking glass on to the spots. A meningitis rash doesn't usually fade when pressure is put on it. Ocasionally, though, the rash may fade at first, so keep checking.

If there's any doubt in your mind as to whether or not your baby has meningitis, call for medical help immediately or take your baby straight to the nearest accident and emergency department. This is because the rash is one of the later signs of sepsis (blood poisoning), after which your child's condition can become critical.

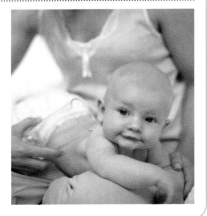

advanced. Lots of the symptoms are also common for other childhood illnesses, such as flu. The important thing to remember is that if you are worried you should seek urgent medical advice. Don't wait.

The spread of meningitis

Most cases of bacterial meningitis are isolated, but clusters of meningococcal meningitis occasionally appear. People who've been in close contact (usually defined as sharing a house) with someone with bacterial meningitis or meningococcal septicaemia are offered precautionary antibiotics. Infection is spread by sneezing or, in adults, intimate kissing. The bacteria that cause the problem are extremely common, living naturally in the back of the nose and throat, and many people carry them without becoming ill.

Viral meningitis is spread, just like other viruses, from person to person, sometimes by coughing and sneezing and other times by poor hygiene, for example, by not washing your hands after going to the toilet. Viral meningitis used to be a complication of other childhood illnesses, such as measles and mumps, but the introduction of the MMR vaccination has virtually eliminated this threat.

Roseola

Roseola is one of those harmless, but uncomfortable, childhood diseases. Characterised by a fever and a rash, it commonly strikes babies aged between nine and 21 months.

What you can do

As a precaution, it's a good idea to call your doctor if you think your baby has roseola. Your doctor will ask about your baby's symptoms and may tell you to look for the typical roseola rash after a few days.

If the fever persists or if the rash looks different than described, check back with your doctor.

There is no treatment for the virus itself. Instead, you can try to ease your baby's symptoms by keeping her cool and comfortable during the fever stage. Offer plenty of drinks to prevent dehydration and lower the fever, and remove layers of clothing or bedclothes if the room is warm.

If your baby is old enough, give her infant paracetamol to reduce the high temperature and aches and pains. If she's under three months, consult your doctor before medicating.

Causes

Roseola is caused by a herpes virus known as the human herpes virus type 6 (HHV-6), and is passed on through saliva (think of all those toys going from hand to mouth). It's often difficult to identify the actual source of the infection, as roseola is infectious before the rash is visible and has an incubation period of around five to 15 days.

Symptoms

The first few days of roseola will seem like nothing worse than a mild virus. Your child will also have a sudden fever of up to 40°C (104°F), which lasts for three to four days, before suddenly disappearing. Other symptoms of the virus include listlessness, irritability, a runny nose, cough, mild diarrhoea or a decreased appetite.

Once the fever subsides, your baby will have a pinkish-red, spotty rash starting on her trunk, which may spread to the neck and extremities. This fades within a few hours to two days.

It's the sudden onset and disappearance of the fever, followed by the rash just when your baby seems to be better, that are the telltale signs of roseola infection.

Complications

Although most babies and children will recover quickly and well from roseola, there are a few complications to watch out for. Occasionally, the high temperature can cause a febrile (fever) seizure (fit), which can be alarming to watch but doesn't usually cause any harm (see p.257).

It's very rare, but the fever stage of the disease can also sometimes lead to meningitis or, in even rarer cases, encephalitis (inflammation of the brain). That's why it's very important to call the doctor if you are at all concerned about your baby's symptoms.

In most cases, though, and as with most viruses, roseola just needs to run its course. Most children recover without any problems.

Adults aren't usually in danger of catching roseola, either. Most children have antibodies to roseola by the time they're four, whether or not they had the virus. In certain cases, for example in an adult with a weak immune system, such as someone receiving chemotherapy, the virus could reactivate, taking a form similar to shingles. Because almost all adults are immune, there is no known risk if you are pregnant.

Welcome to parenthood!
0–6 weeks

Your growing baby
6 weeks to 6 months

Your older baby
6 months to one year

Baby healthcare
0–12 months

What you can do

Give your doctor a call as soon as you suspect that your baby has gastroenteritis. Call too if your baby has been vomiting for more than 12 hours, has blood in his stools, if he is excessively fussy, if he has a fever, or if he seems dehydrated. Dehydration can be a serious problem in babies (see p.242), so keep him as well hydrated as possible.

If a blood or stool test reveals that your baby has a parasitic or bacterial infection, he may be given a course of antibiotics. He'll probably be back to normal in a few days. Viral gastroenteritis has to run its course. If he has a fever and is uncomfortable, ask your doctor about giving infant paracetamol.

Gastroenteritis

Stomach flu, or gastroenteritis, is an inflammation of the lining of the digestive tract. Despite the name, it's not caused by the influenza virus. The most common culprit is one of a number of other viruses, including rotavirus, adenovirus, calicivirus and astrovirus.

However, gastroenteritis can also be caused by a potentially more serious bacterial infection, such as salmonella, shigella, staphylococcus, campylobacter or E. coli. Still other cases are caused by parasites such as giardia.

Symptoms

If your baby has gastroenteritis, he may have symptoms such as diarrhoea, vomiting, abdominal pain, fever, chills and achiness. His symptoms may be mild or severe, and they may last for just a few hours or continue for days, depending on the culprit.

How it's contracted

Viral gastroenteritis is very contagious. Your baby may have eaten something contaminated with the virus or shared a cup or utensils with someone who has it. If bacteria or a parasite is to blame, your baby may have ingested contaminated food or drinking water. Or your baby may have picked up the illness by coming into contact with infected fecal matter and putting his hands in his mouth. This does happen a lot, especially in nursery situations. Germs are microscopic, so even if hands look clean, they may carry bacteria.

What you can do

Don't give a cough suppressant unless your doctor recommends it. Coughing is the body's natural reaction when it needs to clear the lungs of mucus.

When to see the doctor

If you think your baby has whooping cough, take him to the doctor. If he has trouble breathing, call 999. The doctor will listen to his cough, and may swab his nose to test for bacteria. If he suspects whooping cough, he'll immediately give an antibiotic. This relieves symptoms if given early. If given later, it may not shorten the illness, but can remove the bacteria from his secretions so he doesn't spread the infection. Beyond that, you can't do much but wait for the cough to subside, which takes six to 10 weeks.

Whooping cough

Also known as pertussis, whooping cough is a bacterial infection that inflames the lungs and airways. It brings on a persistent, violent cough.

The name comes from the "whooping" sounds that people typically make when they try to take a deep breath between coughs. Babies are routinely vaccinated against whooping cough at two, three and four months.

Symptoms

Whooping cough often starts with cold or flu-like symptoms: sneezing, runny nose and a mild cough, which may last up to two weeks before more severe coughing begins. Your baby may have diarrhoea or a fever. A baby will typically cough for 20 or 30 seconds non-stop and then struggle to breathe before the next coughing spell starts. During coughing episodes, which may happen more at night, his lips and nails may turn bluish from lack of oxygen. His cough may produce thick mucus and he may vomit.

Complications

Whooping cough can be dangerous for babies under a year, who are susceptible to complications such as pneumonia, convulsions, brain damage and even death. If you think your baby may have whooping cough, take him to your doctor at once as it's important to watch him closely in case his breathing stops. If your baby has trouble breathing, call 999. Take him to accident and emergency if he has accompanying symptoms, such as persistent vomiting, seizures or signs of dehydration.

Scarlet fever

This is an infection caused by the type A streptococcal bacteria that produces a red rash on the body and flu-like symptoms. It's most likely to occur among children, particularly four to eight year olds. It's quite rare in the UK and very uncommon for children under the age of two to get scarlet fever, but it's possible. However, although scarlet fever used to be one of the most serious diseases of childhood, today it's treatable with antibiotics.

Symptoms

The initial symptoms of scarlet fever include a sore throat, headache, fever and nausea or vomiting.

Obviously, some of these symptoms won't be obvious in a baby, but you should contact your doctor if your baby has a fever or you're concerned. Later symptoms include a red rash with a sandpapery texture that normally develops 12 to 48 hours after initial symptoms. The rash starts in one place, and then spreads over the body. It is unlikely to spread to the face, but his cheeks may become flushed, with the skin around his mouth remaining pale. Always use the "glass test" to check suspicious rashes (see p.274).

Other symptoms may include a loss of appetite, abdominal pain, swollen neck glands, pastia lines (broken blood vessels in skin folds, such as in the armpit) and a white coating on the tongue.

There is a milder form of scarlet fever, often known as scarletina. If your baby has a rash, but no other symptoms, he may have scarletina.

How it's spread and complications

Scarlet fever is passed on by bacteria from an infected person, spread through airborne droplets from coughs and sneezes, or by touching drinking glasses, plates, utensils and other items an infected person has used, and then touching the mouth, nose or eyes. It can also come from contaminated foodstuffs, or through contact with the broken skin of an infected person.

Most cases have no complications and once your baby has had scarlet fever he's unlikely to catch it again.

Occasionally, though, scarlet fever can lead to other infections, such as throat abscesses, ear infections, sinusitis, pneumonia, kidney inflammation or rheumatic fever. In rare cases, it can lead to meningitis (see p.274), kidney failure, septicaemia (blood poisoning), bronchopneumonia or osteomyelitis (infection of the bone and bone marrow). It's important to contact your doctor for advice if your baby's symptoms don't subside 24 hours after starting antibiotic treatment, or if new symptoms develop.

If your baby has scarlet fever, keep him away from others until he has been on antibiotics for at least five days. Wash kitchen utensils, bed linen or clothes he has used and dispose of tissues. Wash your hands after touching them.

Fact: Group A streptococcus is found on the skin and the throat.

In many people, the bacteria doesn't cause symptoms. As well as scarlet fever, it can cause sore throat and skin infections such as impetigo.

One to two days after initial symptoms have developed, a red, rough-feeling rash may appear and spread over the body.

What you can do

Once diagnosed, you can help your baby to recover by giving plenty of cool fluids, keeping his bedroom cool and giving infant paracetamol to bring down his temperature and to relieve possible aches and pains. If he is under three months, check with your doctor before giving medication.

When to see the doctor

If you think your baby has scarlet fever, tell the doctor. In some cases, she may take a throat swab to confirm the diagnosis. Your child may also need a blood test to check for other infections. If he has scarlet fever, your doctor will prescribe antibiotics to speed his recovery and prevent any complications.

Once your baby has started antibiotics, his fever should disappear within 12 to 24 hours. The rest of his symptoms will go in a few days. Make sure that he finishes the whole course of treatment to ensure the infection clears fully.

Welcome to parenthood! 0–6 weeks

Your growing baby 6 weeks to 6 months

Your older baby 6 months to one year

Baby healthcare 0–12 months

Gastrointestinal illnesses

Gastrointestinal illnesses are the messy ones – not pleasant at all! It can also be frightening to see your baby repeatedly vomiting or having diarrhoea. Read up on the symptoms and treatments, and make sure your baby doesn't get dehydrated. If in doubt, always call the doctor.

Chronic diarrhoea

Newborns have frequent bowel movements, so it's common for parents to think that their baby has diarrhoea. You'll soon get to know what's normal for your baby, though. The bowel movements of newborn breastfed babies are usually yellowish, on the soft or liquid side and may occur up to five times daily. Within a month, though, most breastfed babies have just one or two bowel movements a day. The bowel movements of formula-fed babies tend to be less frequent, occurring about once a day and are fairly firm and smelly.

Occasional loose stools are normal, but if your baby begins frequently passing smelly, watery, mucus-streaked stools, or has a fever or appears to be losing weight, it may be diarrhoea, so consult your doctor.

Causes

The most common cause of diarrhoea is rotavirus. Nearly all children catch this by the age of five. Rotavirus causes gastroenteritis, an infection of the gut that damages the inner lining of the intestine. The injured lining leaks fluid and allows food to pass through without absorbing any nutrients.

Diarrhoea in babies can also be caused by formula feeds not being made up properly, colds, antibiotics, food poisoning, allergies or intolerances or, more rarely, enzyme deficiencies.

Looking after your baby

If your baby gets diarrhoea, ensure she gets plenty of fluids to ease her symptoms and prevent her from becoming dehydrated. If she is drinking her formula or breastmilk well, stick with these feeds. In addition, your doctor may recommend giving your baby an oral rehydration solution a few times an hour, in addition to water and the usual milk feeds.

Avoid other drinks, such as fruit juices or glucose drinks, as unabsorbed sugar draws water into the intestine and can increase diarrhoea. Don't give anti-diarrhoeal medicine to children under 12 years old, as it could have serious side effects.

To prevent your baby passing on her diarrhoea, keep her away from childcare or nursery until at least 48 hours after her last episode, and don't take her swimming for two weeks afterwards.

If your baby is on solids, unless she is vomiting frequently, you can still give her solids. If she is six months or older, you could try foods like bananas, rice, apple purée and dry toast. For an older baby or toddler, try small amounts of chicken and starchy foods, such as mashed potatoes and pasta. Don't worry, though, if she isn't hungry; it's more important that she drinks plenty.

Proper hygiene helps reduce the risk of diarrhoea spreading as it prevents the hand-to-mouth transfer of the micro-organisms that cause it. Wash your hands with soap after handling soiled nappies or using the toilet.

What you can do

Diarrhoea can be worrying, but it usually clears up on its own. The main concern is dehydration. Cuddle and comfort your baby and keep her dry. Use care when changing nappies, as it's easy for her bottom to become irritated; barrier cream may help.

When to see the doctor

Call the doctor if your baby has dry skin or lips, listlessness, tearless crying, a sunken fontanelle, discoloured hands and feet, strong yellow urine or fewer wet nappies than usual. Call, too, if she refuses drink; has a fever, diarrhoea or vomiting for more than 12 hours; has blood in her stools or a swollen tummy.

Constipation

Constipation is rare in younger babies, especially breastfed ones. Although breastfed babies may go from having several bowel movements a day in the first few weeks of life to only having one or two in an entire week, they are unlikely to become constipated. Even when it's soft or liquid, all babies sometimes have to strain to pass a stool. In fact, before long, you'll recognise your baby's particular grimaces and grunts as she works on her bowel movements.

Bottle-fed babies tend to have one firm bowel movement a day, though some may only have a bowel movement once every three or four days. This isn't considered abnormal unless the stool is hard and pellet-like. True constipation occurs when a stool in the lower intestine is pinched by the tightening of muscles, which can stall it, and the longer it remains there, the firmer and drier it becomes.

Symptoms

Although it's normal for some babies to grunt and strain with every movement, if your baby cries or looks uncomfortable when she passes a stool, check with your health visitor or doctor.

For older babies who've started on solids, constipation is a more common problem. Symptoms of constipation include irritability, gastric discomfort, a hard abdomen, abdominal pain, especially if it decreases after a bowel movement, blood-streaked stools (usually due to rectal fissures caused by passing hard stools) and hard-to-pass, pellet-like stools.

Your baby's diet

If your baby seems constipated, give her plenty to drink. Talk to your health visitor or doctor before trying home treatments. If your baby is formula-fed, give her extra water between feeds, but don't dilute her fomula.

If your baby is on solids, give her fruits (not bananas, see box, below) and vegetables (in small bits, of course) so that she gets adequate fibre, and ensure that she gets plenty to drink, including plain water. Some babies become constipated simply because they aren't getting enough fluids.

If the problem persists, it's important to arrange for your baby to have a check-up; your doctor may want to rule out illness or anal fissures.

Once your baby has started on solids, ensure that she has a sufficient intake of fluids to help prevent constipation.

Parents**Talk...**

"Now my baby is on solids, getting constipated is a more common occurrence as she gets used to new foods. When this happens, I find that puréeing fruits and adding some bran flakes to her cereal makes her regular again – and also relieves the strain when she's doing a poo!"
Nicola, 29, first-time mum

"My formula-fed baby sometimes gets a bit constipated. Giving him plenty of plain water in between his feeds really helps to loosen things up."
Lydia, 32, first time mum

"My seven-month-old had a cold recently and lost his appetite – his stuffy nose made feeding difficult, so he didn't want to feed for long. The result was a bit of dehydration and no sign of poo for a few days, apart from a couple of pebbly bits! Giving him milk or water little and often eased his constipation and kept him hydrated."
Ronnie, 31, mother of two

What you can do

It's not uncommon for older babies to get constipation once they're on solids, as their bodies are learning to manage new foods. Try gently working your baby's legs in a cycling motion, which may help move stool matter along her intestine. If she's on solids, cut down on constipating foods, such as rice, bananas and cereal.

Constipation is uncomfortable and unpleasant for your baby, and it's not nice for you to see her in pain. However, with your attention, any treatment from the doctor and time, she'll establish easier, regular bowel movements.

When to see the doctor

If your baby is constipated, check with the doctor or health visitor before trying anything to ease her discomfort. You may be asked to bring her in to be examined.

Welcome to parenthood!
0–6 weeks

Your growing baby
6 weeks to 6 months

Your older baby
6 months to one year

Baby healthcare
0–12 months

Intussusception

This is a serious intestinal condition in which a section of the bowel "telescopes" in on itself. This leads to inflammation and swelling that may eventually block or tear the intestine. If left untreated intussusception can be life-threatening, but when caught early it's almost always fixable.

Intussusception is very rare and is thought to affect between four and seven babies in every 10,000. It tends to develop most commonly between the ages of three and 18 months.

Experts don't know exactly why it happens, but there may be a link to infections. In a few cases, a benign growth inside the bowel wall may be to blame, but the vast majority of cases have no apparent cause.

What you can do

If you have any worries about your baby, don't wait for a whole range of the symptoms to appear before getting help.

When to see the doctor

Call your doctor if your baby appears to have intermittent, worsening pain, or if there's blood and mucus in his stools. Your doctor will tell you whether to bring your baby to the surgery or take him straight to the hospital accident and emergency department.

If you can't reach the doctor straightaway, take your baby to accident and emergency anyway. Intussusception is an emergency that requires prompt skilled medical attention and treatment – it won't go away on its own.

Symptoms

Obviously, your baby won't be able to tell you that something is wrong, but if he develops intussusception, he'll seem fine one minute and will then be writhing in pain the next.

Severe abdominal pain that comes and goes is the main symptom of intussusception. During a wave of pain your baby will probably cry hard and draw up his legs, but between spasms he'll seem fairly comfortable. Each episode tends to last two to three minutes. The waves of pain will become gradually more intense and frequent, and your baby will probably go off his food and may vomit.

Your baby may also have bloody, mucus-streaked stools. He may be sweaty and lethargic, and after a few hours may show signs of dehydration, such as sunken eyes, tearless crying, a dry or sticky mouth, a sunken soft spot on his fontanelle on top of his head and fewer wet nappies. As the condition progresses, your baby's stomach may become hard and distended, and you may be able to feel a sausage-shaped mass in the upper mid or right abdomen.

Diagnosis and treatment

If your doctor suspects intussusception, she'll confirm the diagnosis by arranging for your baby to have an ultrasound scan at the hospital.

If your baby is dehydrated because of the vomiting, he will need a drip of fluids before any treatment starts. He'll also be given a nasogastric tube, which goes into his nose and down into his stomach. This will drain off his stomach contents and remove any air that has built up in his tummy, making him feel more comfortable.

Intussusception is usually treated with an enema. Your baby will have a tube inserted into his bottom and air or oxygen released into the bowel. This expands the bowel, allowing the intussusception to correct itself.

If this doesn't work, or if your baby is too unwell to receive an enema, then he will need surgery to remove the blockage. Your baby's surgeon will explain the operation to you fully and will ask you to sign a consent form giving your permission for the hospital to perform the operation. During the operation, the surgeon will squeeze the bowel to push out the inner segment. In some cases, the surgeon will have to take out a small section of the bowel where tissue has died because of the lack of blood flow.

As the condition sometimes recurs soon after either procedure, your baby will need to stay in the hospital for several days, during which time he'll be monitored closely to check his breathing, heart rate and oxygen levels.

He won't be able to eat for the first 48 hours after the operation to allow the bowel to recover, so he'll be on a drip to provide fluids. He'll be able to go home as soon as he is showing signs of recovery. Although intussusception is a frightening condition, when it's caught early, your baby's recovery is almost 100 per cent certain.

Note: Tummy pain and discomfort are common among babies.

The cause of discomfort isn't usually serious – it's usually a sign of trapped wind or colic. However, see your doctor if you're worried.

Gastro-oesphageal reflux

Reflux is the term used to describe what happens when the stomach contents come back up into the gullet or even into the mouth. The medical name for the food pipe is oesophagus. So the long name for reflux is gastro-oesophageal reflux disease, shortened to GORD.

Causes

The diaphragm is the muscle that separates the chest cavity from the abdominal cavity. As the oesophagus passes through the diaphragm, the diaphragm acts like a valve, preventing stomach contents from going backwards up the oesophagus. Doctors refer to this valve mechanism as a sphincter. Sometimes, the valve action isn't as strong as it could be – when you are pregnant, for example. In fact, one of the reasons women get heartburn in pregnancy is due to the baby pushing up onto the sphincter and forcing acid back up the oesophagus.

This also happens to babies, but in their case it is because the sphincter action of the diaphragm isn't developed. During the first year of a baby's life, the sphincter action gradually gets stronger and their chance of having reflux decreases. Around 50 per cent of babies will get some reflux, but in only a small percentage of these is it a real problem. At the age of 10 months, the number is down to about one in 20 babies.

Symptoms

Your baby may regurgitate milk after a feed or have hiccups. He may occasionally cough a little after regurgitating the milk if some has "gone down the wrong way". Or he may cry a lot after every feed, especially if you lie him down. Some babies cry during a feed, too. Both formula- and breastfed babies may be affected.

Simple measures, such as holding your baby in an upright position for 20 minutes after each feed, can be helpful. It's also worth trying smaller but more frequent feeds, although babies don't always agree to this!

Complications

It's always important to see your doctor if you are worried that your baby may

In addition to winding your baby, holding her upright after a feed can help reduce reflux.

What you can do

In severe cases, it can be worth trying antacids or feed thickeners, available on prescription. Only use these on the advice of your doctor, though, and stop them every once in a while to check whether things have got better.

If you look at websites from other countries, you may see drugs such as cimetidine or ranitidine recommended. In the UK, these are used to heal stomach ulcers in adults, but aren't licensed for use in babies. Your doctor is likely to be reluctant to prescribe them without advice from a specialist.

When to see the doctor

Speak to your health visitor or doctor if your baby's reflux regularly happens more than five times a day; if he cries excessively after feeds; if there is regular vomiting or if the coughing becomes a regular occurrence.

have reflux. Your doctor may refer your baby on to a paediatric specialist if there is any doubt about the diagnosis, or if the condition does not get better with simple treatments. Other reasons why your baby might be referred include blood in your baby's vomit; your baby becoming anaemic; or having persistent coughs or frequent chest infections because of the regurgitation. It can also be a cause for concern if your baby fails to gain weight, begins to refuse food or has trouble swallowing.

Thankfully these symptoms are rare, but do see your doctor if you are worried about any of them.

Most babies will suffer the more minor symptoms described earlier, and without complications. Reassure yourself that things will get better as your baby grows.

Welcome to parenthood! 0–6 weeks

Your growing baby 6 weeks to 6 months

Your older baby 6 months to one year

Baby healthcare 0–12 months

Vomiting

ParentsAsk...

When is vomiting a concern?

Sometimes vomiting can be a sign of more serious illnesses. Call your doctor if it's accompanied by any of the following:

- signs of dehydration, including a dry mouth, tearless crying, sunken fontanelle, and fewer wet nappies than usual (fewer than six wet nappies a day)
- a fever, with a temperature of 38°C (100.4°F) or higher if she is younger than three months, or 39°C (102.2°F) or higher if three months or older
- refusal to breastfeed or drink her formula milk
- vomiting for more than 12 hours, or vomiting with great force
- a non-blanching rash, that is a rash that doesn't fade when the skin is pressed (see p.274)
- sleepiness or severe irritability
- a bulging fontanelle.
- shortness of breath
- a swollen abdomen
- blood or green bile in the vomit
- persistent forceful vomiting in a newborn within half an hour of eating
- diarrhoea

It's common for babies to vomit frequently in the early weeks as their bodies develop and they adjust to feeding. You can tell when your baby is vomiting rather than just posseting (bringing up small quantities of milk), because there will be a lot more coming out, not just a few teaspoons' worth trickling down. It can be frightening for your baby, so she's likely to cry.

Causes

Everything from car sickness to indigestion can cause your baby to be sick – even a prolonged bout of crying or coughing can trigger this reflex. So you may see quite a lot of vomiting in your baby's first few years.

An attack of vomiting will generally subside in six to 24 hours without any particular treatment apart from a change in diet. As long as your baby seems otherwise healthy and continues to gain weight, there's usually no need to worry.

During your baby's first few months, vomiting is probably caused by mild feeding problems, such as her tummy being too full. After the first few months, a sudden onset of vomiting is more likely to be caused by gastroenteritis, a viral infection that is often accompanied by diarrhoea.

Your baby may also be sick when she has a cold, a urinary-tract infection (see p.264) or an ear infection (see p.262).

Complications

A little blood or bile in the vomit is usually not a concern. This may happen when the force of regurgitation causes tiny tears in the blood vessels lining the food pipe (oesophagus). Your baby's vomit may also be tinged with red if she has swallowed blood from a cut in her mouth or has had a nosebleed in the past six hours.

However, call your doctor if your baby continues to have blood in her vomit or if the amount is increasing. The doctor will probably want to see a sample of the vomit so, although it may be an unpleasant task, try to save some. Green bile can indicate that the intestine is blocked, a condition that needs immediate attention.

Persistent or forceful vomiting in a newborn within half an hour of eating may be due to pyloric stenosis, a rare condition that is most likely to begin when your baby is a few weeks old, but could show up at any time before she reaches four months.

With this condition, the vomiting is caused when a muscle that controls the valve leading from the stomach into the intestines becomes so thickened that it won't open enough to let food through. The problem is easy to remedy with minor surgery, but needs immediate medical attention.

What you can do

Vomiting in young children is common and even babies vomit at times. Keep your baby well hydrated. When she vomits, she loses fluids. It's important to replace them so she won't get dehydrated. If she's over three months, give sips of oral rehydration solution a few times an hour, alongside her milk feed, and water if she's formula fed. Don't give fruit juices or carbonated drinks, or anti-nausea medicines unless advised to do so by your doctor.

Ease her back into her routine: If she hasn't vomited for 12 to 24 hours, begin moving back to her usual diet, but keep giving plenty of fluids. Start with easily digested foods such as cereal or yoghurt.

Help her rest. Going to sleep may help settle your baby. The stomach often empties into the intestines during sleep, relieving the need to vomit.

If she attends childcare or nursery, keep her at home for at least 48 hours after her last episode of vomiting.

When to see the doctor

Call your doctor if you're worried or your baby is dehydrated or vomiting persists.

Minor concerns

There's nothing like having young children to familiarise yourself with all manners of rashes, bumps and other nuisances. The good news is that most of these ailments are minor, won't harm your baby (beyond the discomfort or itching) and will go away with simple treatment.

Worms

Threadworms are small, white worms that infest the intestines. They look like six centimetre-long pieces of dental floss, and can be seen wiggling around the anus and in your baby's stools. It can be upsetting to discover that your baby has threadworms, but this common childhood malady isn't a sign of poor hygiene or bad parenting! They pose no health risks and are easily eradicated.

How worms are spread
It's rare for young babies to get threadworms, but it can happen, especially if your baby goes to nursery or if her siblings have threadworms. Your baby probably swallowed threadworm eggs after she got them on her hands, possibly from touching a toy handled by a child with threadworms, and then put her fingers in her mouth. (Eggs can survive for up to two weeks on some surfaces.) The eggs then travelled to her large intestine where they hatched. From there, female worms migrated out of your baby's intestines to lay their eggs on her anus.

As worms move, they cause intense itching, which can disrupt sleep. When she scratches her bottom, the eggs get under her nails, and another cycle begins when she puts her hands in her mouth.

Symptoms and diagnosis
If your baby has worms, the only sign may be disturbed sleep and fussiness due to itching. Occasionally, worms also cause an upset tummy.

Confirm your suspicions by checking her bottom and nappy for worms at night with a torch. You can also check by gently pressing a piece of transparent tape to her anus. Eggs stick to it, and you can take it to the doctor for a diagnosis.

If you don't find worms or eggs, anal itching may be a sign of a problem such as dryness from cleaning the area too vigorously with soap. Red, tender skin around the anus could be due to nappy rash, diarrhoea or a bacterial infection, in which case talk to your doctor.

Prevention
You can keep the pests from infecting or re-infecting your baby by taking a few precautions. Clean her nails with a soft brush and keep them short to prevent eggs getting trapped underneath. It's a good idea to bathe her when she wakes up to help eliminate the eggs, and wash your hands when you change her nappy.

Regularly trimming your baby's fingernails to stop them harbouring eggs can help break the cycle of reinfection.

What you can do
Mild cases may clear without treatment, but a severe infestation can cause more serious infections.

When to see the doctor
If you suspect worms, talk to your doctor. She may prescribe medication to kill them and is likely to suggest the whole family be treated. Symptoms usually go within a week of treatment, but the doctor may want to repeat the treatment two weeks later. She'll advise washing clothing and bedding in hot water to destroy the worms and eggs.

After treatment, you may see lots of worms, some moving, in your baby's stools. This is unsettling, but just means the worms are leaving her body.

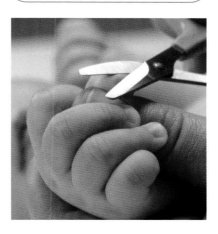

Welcome to parenthood!
0–6 weeks

Your growing baby
6 weeks to 6 months

Your older baby
6 months to one year

Baby healthcare
0–12 months

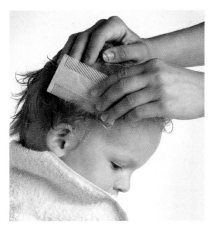

Eradicating lice from your child's head is a time-consuming business. Each member of the family needs to be treated.

What you can do

If your baby has head lice, check the rest of the family and treat if necessary.

Your doctor or nurse can only confirm the diagnosis if a live louse is found in the hair.

When to see the doctor

Talk to your doctor before using a chemical treatment on a baby under 12 months old.

Head lice

These are small, wingless insects that are grey or brown in colour. They are parasites that feed by sucking blood from the human scalp. Newly hatched lice are about 1 millimetre in size (about the size of a pin-head) and a fully grown adult measures around 3mm (just less than the size of a match head). A head louse takes between six and 14 days to become fully grown; then the females mate and lays eggs close to the scalp.

The eggs, also known as "nits" (some people use this name for head lice, too), are a yellow-white colour. They are sometimes confused with dandruff, but are distinguishable because they stick to the hair and are difficult to remove. Eggs take seven to 10 days to hatch and the empty shiny white egg shells are left stuck to the hair shaft. A louse has an average life span of around 21 days, and a female adult can lay up to 56 eggs in just one mating.

Although lice are more common in older preschool and school-aged children, babies can occasionally pick up headlice from older siblings or from nurseries or daycare situations. There are a lot of misconceptions about head lice preferring long, unwashed hair, but they can be found in hair of all types.

Symptoms

Head lice are very well camouflaged in the hair and can be difficult to detect. It is often assumed that itching is the first sign of head lice but, in fact, head lice can live on a head without causing any itching for up to three months. Other tell-tale signs include shiny whitish nits stuck to the hair close to the scalp, often behind the ears and at the back of the neck; shiny white empty egg sacs found further along the hair shaft; live adult head lice visible on the scalp/hair; and a rash on the back of the neck caused by irritation from louse droppings.

Treatment

Head lice have become resistant to some of the chemical pesticides used to destroy them, so there's no guarantee that a one-off shampoo will get rid of them. The Department of Health recommends using either chemical treatments to get rid of live lice (talk to the doctor before using one on your baby) and wet-combing all close family and friends to check for infestation then treat if needed, or using the bug-busting method of systematically removing live lice by wet-combing (see box, left).

Chemical treatment involves two applications seven days apart. You leave the chemical on the hair for anything from 10 minutes to 12 hours depending on the instructions, then rinse and wet-comb to remove dead lice. Although treatments kill any live lice (if they're not resistant to the chemical), they may not destroy all the eggs, so need to be repeated a week later to destroy newly hatched lice.

ParentsAsk...

How can I get rid of the lice without chemical treatments?

You can remove lice from your baby's head by wet-combing. Live lice are removed from wet hair with a special fine-toothed nit comb. By repeating the procedure three more times over 14 days, the lifecycle of the louse is broken and your baby's head becomes louse-free.

Start by washing your baby's hair with ordinary shampoo, then rinse and apply generous amounts of hair conditioner.

Use an ordinary comb or brush to detangle the hair and then use the nit comb, slotting the teeth into a section of hair at the roots and drawing it down to the tips of the hair. Wet, conditioner-coated lice stay still and will be caught in the teeth of the comb. Wipe the teeth both sides with kitchen roll or rinse under a tap to remove lice.

Continue all around the head. When you've finished, rinse the hair, detangle again and then use the nit comb to pick any remaining lice out of the wet hair.

Impetigo

A highly contagious skin infection, impetigo mainly affects children aged between two and six. It's unusual, although not unheard of, in babies. Your baby may have picked up the bacteria that cause it (usually staphylococcus, but sometimes streptococcus) by touching an infected child, or an object that the infected child touched, such as a toy, towel, or pillowcase.

The bacteria invades the skin through cold sores, cuts or grazes, eczema, or other areas where your baby's skin is broken or sensitive, such as just below the nose where he may be constantly wiping away mucus.

Symptoms

Impetigo symptoms vary according to which type of bacteria is causing the infection. Streptococcus bacteria bring on tiny blisters that burst easily and expose wet, reddish skin underneath, while staphylococcus bacteria also cause blisters, but they are larger and more resilient.

As the skin dries, a scabby tan or yellow-brown crust forms over the tender area, making it look as if it's been coated with honey or brown sugar. The crusts gradually heal and don't leave any scarring.

The infection often develops around the nose and mouth, but it can easily spread to other parts of the body. It's not usually painful, but it can become itchy. Your baby may also develop a temperature and swollen lymph glands in his face or neck.

Complications

In most cases, impetigo clears up without any major problems. Occasionally, though, other more serious conditions develop, such as cellulitis (a deeper, more serious skin inflammation); a form of psoriasis that causes sores on the chest, arms, legs and scalp; or blood poisoning (known as septicaemia). In rare cases, scarlet fever can occur as a complication – and, rarer still, a kidney disorder called glomerulonephritis can occur, which is accompanied by high blood pressure and blood in the urine.

Controlling the infection

With impetigo, your baby will have been infectious for four to 10 days before the rash became obvious and, if left untreated, he may be contagious for several weeks. Once antibiotic treatment has started and the rash begins to disappear (usually after 48 hours) or the sores have crusted and healed, he should not be contagious any more.

In the meantime, keep your baby at home and be scrupulous about hygiene. Take care to keep him out of nursery and cancel any arrangements for seeing friends until he has taken antibiotics for at least two days. Don't let anyone share soap, towels, hairbrushes, or other personal items with your baby. Make sure everyone in your household washes their hands regularly with soap and water. Avoid contact with newborn babies until the risk of spreading impetigo has passed.

You can reduce the risk of your baby getting another impetigo infection by ensuring that any cuts and scratches are kept clean and treating episodes of eczema, or other conditions that can lead to broken skin, promptly.

The bacteria that causes impetigo
produces an unsightly red, blistery rash, which can sometimes be itchy.

What you can do

Once you've seen the doctor (see below) keep the infection clean to help it heal and prevent it spreading. Twice a day, gently wash away scabs with soap and warm water. Pat the area dry, using a clean towel each time, and don't let anyone else use it afterwards. Wash your hands before applying cream (if prescribed) to the skin. Trim your baby's nails to prevent him from scratching the infected area, which could spread the infection. Finally, cover the infected skin with a loose gauze dressing or clothes.

When to see the doctor

Always see your doctor if you think your baby has impetigo as it is highly infectious. Impetigo is treated with antibiotics, usually a cream. If the infection is severe or widespread, your doctor may prescribe oral antibiotics. Your baby must take the full course, even if the symptoms clear up quickly.

If the treatment isn't working after a week, your baby develops a temperature and/or the infected area becomes noticeably red and tender, return to your doctor.

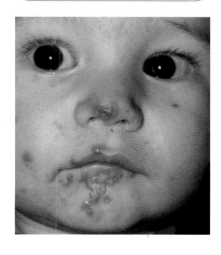

Welcome to parenthood!
0–6 weeks

Your growing baby
6 weeks to 6 months

Your older baby
6 months to one year

Baby healthcare
0–12 months

Cold sores

These are small, red blisters that crop up near the lips or actually on them, and develop into a painful sore. More rarely, they appear on the roof of the mouth. Despite their name, cold sores have nothing to do with colds; in fact, they are caused by the herpes simplex virus – usually the herpes simplex virus type 1. About seven out of 10 adults permanently carry this virus in their nerve endings.

What you can do

Cold sores will go away without treatment, but to ease the pain in the meantime, apply ice to the sore, or give your baby a dose of infant paracetamol suspension. Offer her cool drinks, too. You can use a syringe to give your baby drinks if it will help, squirting the syringe into the side of the mouth, not the back, as it can cause choking.

When to see the doctor

Most babies are protected from cold sores for at least six months by antibodies they received from their mother. However, if your newborn baby does get a cold sore, call your doctor straightaway because, as her immune system is still developing, any kind of herpes virus is dangerous for a very young baby.

Doctors sometimes prescribe an anti-viral medicine when the symptoms are bad. It may not have much effect once the blisters and ulcers are well developed. However, if it is taken early in the infection, it may reduce the duration of the pain and speed recovery a little.

How cold sores spread

If your baby gets a cold sore, it's probably because someone with a cold sore has kissed her, or someone who didn't have a visible sore, but had the virus in their saliva. It is also possible for a newborn baby to get the herpes virus via the birth canal if her mother has genital herpes (caused by herpes simplex virus type 1).

Once your baby catches the virus, it then remains in her body, hiding in nerve cells near the ear. In some people, the herpes virus lies dormant and never causes any particular harm. In others, though, it periodically wakes up and triggers cold sores, which are often encouraged by tiredness, stress, fever, colds or sunburn.

Symptoms

The first time your baby develops a cold sore, she'll start off with swollen gums and a sore mouth. A few days later, you may notice a cluster of small blisters on or near her lips that develop into a shallow, painful sore, possibly accompanied by fever and swollen lymph glands in the neck. In a few days, the sore will crust over and slowly disappear. The whole flare-up lasts for around five to 10 days, during which time your baby may feel miserable and her mouth will be sore. The mouth pain can put your baby off eating or drinking, so you'll need to check that she's not getting dehydrated.

The next time your baby has an outbreak, the first symptoms will be the blisters – not the swelling or mouth pain. It is also possible for your baby to get a cold sore inside her mouth, on her gums, on the insides of her cheeks, on the roof of her mouth or on her tongue.

Prevention

If you have a cold sore, you should avoid kissing your baby until the cold sore goes away. If you have a herpes sore on your breast, as long as you are able to cover it so that your baby does not touch it, you can continue to breastfeed. If you have a herpes sore on your nipple, experts recommend that you should stop breastfeeding from that breast until the sore has healed. Feed as much as you can from the unaffected breast and express milk from the affected breast to keep your milk supply up until the sore on the nipple heals.

There is conflicting advice as to whether the expressed milk should be thrown away or whether it is safe to bottle-feed it to your baby. Contact your midwife, health visitor or breastfeeding specialist for advice.

If your baby has a cold sore, stop her from infecting other parts of her body or giving the virus to someone else by washing her hands regularly and allocating separate flannels and towels to the rest of the family. Try to keep her from picking at her sores.

Try to keep your baby from touching her eyes whenever she has a cold sore, because this can cause ocular herpes, which is a serious eye infection. If your baby develops a painful sore on her eyelid, eye surface or on the end of her nose, call your doctor straightaway. Your baby may need a course of anti-viral drugs to help prevent the infection scarring her cornea.

You don't need to keep your baby away from nursery if she has a cold sore. The best thing you can do is to keep your baby's immune system strong by making sure she has a healthy diet and gets plenty of sleep.

Scabies

Scabies is a skin irritation caused by an infestation of tiny parasitic mites that burrow under the skin. The bumpy rash is an allergic reaction to the eggs and faeces the mites leave behind. The name comes from a Latin word meaning "to scratch", and if your baby has scabies, she's probably doing a lot of that.

Your baby can pick up scabies through skin-to-skin contact with someone who has it. Scabies is very contagious, and anyone can get it, even if they're scrupulously clean. It often shows up in more than one family member or in groups of nursery children.

Symptoms

If your baby gets scabies, she'll develop an extremely itchy rash of scattered red bumps, usually between the fingers,

Fact: Studies suggest that one in 1,000 people develop scabies each month.

The incidence of scabies is more common in preschool children than in babies, although it's not unheard of in babies.

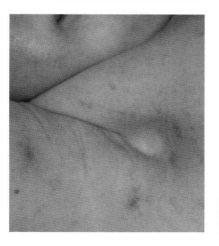

The itchy bumps caused by a scabies infestation typically appear in certain areas of the body, including the armpits.

around the wrists, and on the outside of the elbows, armpits, lower abdomen and genitals. It may also show up on the kneecaps and the sides of the feet.

You may see wavy, light brown or silvery lines where the mites burrow under the skin. Your baby may develop little pustules (inflamed areas filled with pus) or small, water-filled blisters. The itching is usually most intense after a bath or at night, and may keep her awake. Nasty-looking scabs may form over the areas your baby has scratched, and a bacterial infection, such as impetigo (see p.285) could develop.

If this is your baby's first bout of scabies, two to six weeks may pass between when the mites latch onto her and when she begins to itch. If she's had scabies before, her reaction time will be much shorter, possibly a few hours.

Prevention and treatment

All other members of the household, as well as carers, will need to be treated, even if they show no symptoms of scabies. It's best if everyone is treated together, so that one person doesn't reinfect the others.

There's little evidence that scabies spreads through linen and bed sheets, however, you may want to take the extra precaution of vacuuming the floors and then washing all of the clothing, towels and bedding in water hotter than 50°C (122°F). Seal stuffed animals or toys that can't be washed in a plastic bag for a week. Scabies mites can't survive for more than a few days without a human host.

Permethrin cream, the most common treatment for scabies, is thought to be the safest remedy. Talk with your doctor if you have questions or concerns about its safety for your baby.

The only way to avoid scabies is to avoid contact with anyone who might have it. That can be tricky, especially if your baby is around other children often.

What you can do

Keep your baby's fingernails short to prevent her from tearing her skin if she is scratching. Scratch mittens can stop her scratching herself when asleep.

When to see the doctor

Always see your doctor if your baby has an unidentified rash. The doctor may do a painless test that involves scraping off a small skin sample and looking at it under a microscope. Scabies mites, their eggs and faeces are visible when magnified.

Your doctor will prescribe a cream that you'll need to spread over every inch of her body from the neck down. Even parts of the body that don't look infected must be treated. Follow the directions for leaving the cream on the skin (it may be for eight to 12 hours), and then wash it off. As babies put their hands in their mouth a lot when awake, it's best to put the cream on at bedtime and wash it off in the morning.

Also, because it takes some time for the irritants in the skin to die down, itching can continue for up to three weeks after the mites have gone. In the meantime, your doctor may prescribe an oral antihistamine or a mild steroid cream for relief.

Welcome to parenthood! 0–6 weeks

Your growing baby 6 weeks to 6 months

Your older baby 6 months to one year

Baby healthcare 0–12 months

First aid

No matter how many precautions you take, accidents will happen and there won't always be a qualified health professional on the scene. Prepare yourself for the worst by learning some basic first aid so that you can come to the rescue confidently in an emergency.

Action in an emergency

If an incident puts your baby at risk, follow the checklist below to prevent the situation becoming more serious.

● Check for further danger and make sure that your baby's immediate surroundings are safe.

● Assess the seriousness of the incident. Decide whether to call an ambulance, take your baby to hospital, call NHS Direct, or treat your baby yourself.

● Call an ambulance or ask someone else to before you start to give first aid. Give the ambulance service as much information as possible, including your exact location and postcode, if possible.

● Check if your baby is conscious (see right). If he isn't, take 10 seconds to check if he is breathing (see opposite).

● If he is breathing, but unconscious, put him in the recovery position (see opposite). If he isn't breathing, give cardiopulmonary resuscitation (CPR) (see opposite).

● If he's bleeding heavily, raise the injury above heart level, press on the wound with a clean pad and secure with a bandage. If there is an object in the wound, don't remove it, pad around it.

● While waiting for assistance, reassure your baby. Stay calm; you will be more effective at dealing with the situation.

Assessing a baby

The first thing to do after an accident is to make sure that you or your baby aren't in further danger, for example you may need to disconnect the power in the case of an electric shock, or make sure that speeding traffic is diverted away from the scene in a road accident.

Assess the situation

Is it serious enough to call an ambulance, or could you take your baby to accident and emergency, your doctor or treat him yourself? If an ambulance is needed, dial 999 (or ask someone else to) before you give first aid. Emergency situations can be frightening, but your actions could make a real difference; it could be as simple as reassuring and talking to your baby while waiting for an ambulance so he doesn't drift into unconsciousness, or trying to stem bleeding, so that he doesn't go into shock.

Check your baby's response

Try to stay calm. If you panic you are less likely to remember your first aid skills. You also need to be able to reassure your baby, which you can't do unless you're calm, so take a few deep breaths. Assess your baby: does he appear unconscious? Call his name or tap the soles of his feet (never shake a baby). If there's no response, open his airway (see opposite). Take 10 seconds to check if he is breathing. Is his chest rising and falling? If you place your face near his, can you feel his breath against your cheek? If he isn't breathing normally, cardio-pulmonary resuscitation (CPR) will be necessary (see opposite), and you will need to send for help immediately.

Common scenarios

Babies can easily choke on food or small objects in their mouth. If your baby is still able to breathe, cry or cough, the obstruction will probably clear on its own. If it doesn't, you will need to take immediate action to dislodge it and clear your baby's airways (see p.290).

Insect stings are another potential hazard. Look out for any swelling or a rash anywhere else on his body (including his face or mouth), wheezing, a fast heart rate or difficulty swallowing, as this could indicate anaphylactic shock – a severe allergic reaction that can be fatal. If this happens, call an ambulance immediately.

There are many different scenarios that require first aid. It's unlikely that you will do any harm and you could even save your baby's life.

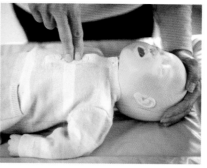

With your baby lying on his back on a flat surface, ensure that his airway remains open by lifting his chin with one fingertip and placing your other hand on his forehead so that his head is tilted back slightly.

Take a breath, then put your mouth around his mouth and nose to create a seal, or close his mouth and make the seal over his nose. Blow into his mouth and nose for one second. Watch the chest rise and fall. Give five breaths.

Put two fingertips on the centre of the chest and press down to a third of the depth of his chest. Release pressure and let the chest rise fully, but don't move your hand. Give 30 compressions at a rate of 100 per minute.

Resuscitation for babies under one year

Call for help

If you need to resuscitate your baby, get someone to dial 999 while you begin cardio-pulmonary resuscitation (CPR) (see right). If you're on your own, give CPR for a minute before dialling 999.

Quickly identify the problem and check your baby's response. If your baby is conscious but choking, follow the steps on page 290 to clear his airway. If your baby has trouble breathing or is unresponsive, take the following steps.

Check for breathing

● Open the airway: lay your baby on a waist-level surface. Push down on his forehead with one hand and lift his chin with a finger of the other to tilt his head back. In some cases, this may be enough to help breathing resume.

● Check for breathing: listen for the sound of breath; look for chest movement; and feel for breath on your cheek. If he's not breathing or his lips are blue, do (CPR) (see right).

Giving CPR

● Ensure that your baby's airway is open and clear.

● Take a normal breath and seal your lips around your baby's mouth and nose.

● Blow gently into the lungs, looking along your baby's chest as you breathe.

● As the chest rises, stop blowing, remove your mouth and then allow the chest to fall.

● Repeat this five times.

● If you haven't done so already, place your baby on a firm surface.

● Find the centre of your baby's chest. Position two of your fingers of one hand on that spot.

● Press down sharply on this point to a third of the depth of the chest.

● Press 30 times, at a rate of 100 compressions per minute.

● After 30 compressions, give two more rescue breaths.

● Continue resuscitation (30 compressions to two breaths) without stopping until help arrives, normal breathing returns, or you are too tired to continue CPR.

Recovery position for babies

The recovery position for a baby is different from that for an older child or for an adult.

Hold your baby in your arms on his side, as though giving him a cuddle. Tilt his head down, lower than his tummy, to prevent him from choking on his tongue, or breathing in vomit. Monitor and record his vital signs, including his pulse, breathing and his response levels while you wait for medical help to arrive.

Welcome to parenthood! 0–6 weeks

Your growing baby 6 weeks to 6 months

Your older baby 6 months to one year

Baby healthcare 0–12 months

Choking

If your baby is suddenly unable to breathe, cry, cough or speak, she may be gagging, or choking, which happens if your baby's airway becomes partially blocked. This makes breathing or coughing difficult, but not impossible. Or the airway can become completely blocked. In babies who have just started solids, eating is a very new experience and they are more likely to choke on food than adults and older children. A baby will become very distressed if she chokes and you will need to act immediately to clear the blockage.

If your baby is choking but still coughing effectively, let her cough – it's the best way to clear an airway.

Knowing how to clear a blocked airway quickly and effectively and, if necessary, resuscitate your baby if she isn't showing any signs of breathing, may save your baby's life.

Give back blows

Hold your baby so that she is lying face down along your forearm with her head lower than her body and her back and head supported.

● Use the heel of your hand to give up to five back blows.

● Turn her over and check her mouth; carefully remove any obvious obstructions. Do not use your finger to sweep inside her mouth because this could push the obstruction further down into your baby's throat.

Give five chest thrusts

If your baby is still unable to breathe, turn her onto her back and give up to five chest thrusts.

● Use two fingertips to push inwards and upwards (towards her head) against her breastbone, one finger's width below her nipple line.

● Try to dislodge the object with each thrust. Don't automatically do all five.

● Check your baby's mouth after each thrust and remove an obvious obstruction.

● If the obstruction does not clear after three cycles of back blows and chest thrusts, dial 999 for an ambulance and continue giving your baby back blows and chest thrusts until help arrives.

If, at any stage during this process, your baby loses consciousness, open her airway and check her breathing, and if there are no signs of breathing, start giving your baby cardiopulmonary resuscitation (CPR) (see p.289), which may help to dislodge the obstruction. Continue until your baby regains consciousness or help arrives.

Even if your baby seems to be fully recovered from the choking episode, if you gave chest thrusts take her to hospital that day for an examination.

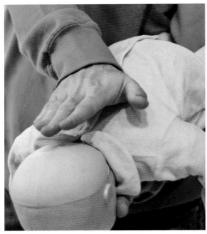

If your baby is in clear distress, unable to cough, cry or breathe properly, lie her face down along your forearm with her head positioned lower than the rest of her body and her body supported. With your free hand, give her up to five sharp blows to the back with the heel of your hand.

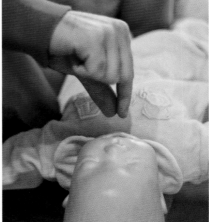

After the back blows, turn your baby over and check inside her mouth. If you can see an obvious obstruction in her mouth, fish it out carefully with your fingertips, but don't be tempted to sweep her mouth with your finger as this could push the obstruction further down her throat.

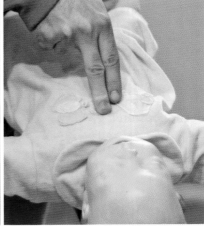

If the blockage still hasn't cleared, keep your baby on her back and place two fingertips one finger's width below her nipple line and give up to five chest thrusts. Push inwards and upwards towards her head. If the obstruction hasn't cleared, repeat all steps three times and then call an ambulance.

Poisoning

If your baby swallows a poisonous substance, try to make her spit out anything in her mouth. Keep a sample in case it's needed for identification. If she has difficulty breathing, throat pain, burns on her lips or mouth, seizures, extreme sleepiness, or is unconscious, call 999 immediately.

What you should do

Don't try to make your baby vomit. Vomiting could further injure her by bringing a burning liquid back up through her throat and mouth. If your baby doesn't have any serious symptoms, it's still wise to take her to accident and emergency. Doctors will want to know your baby's approximate weight, any medical conditions she may have, and information about the substance she has swallowed. Have the container handy, if possible.

External toxins

If your baby gets a poison on her skin, remove any affected clothes and rinse her skin with lukewarm water. If the skin looks burned, continue rinsing for at least 20 minutes and call your doctor. If something toxic splashes her eyes, rinse them with lukewarm water. Try to hold her eyelids open or get your baby to blink. Reassure your baby while you continue flushing the eye for 15 minutes.

If your baby inhales toxic fumes, get her into fresh air as quickly as possible. If your baby isn't breathing, start CPR immediately (see p.289). If possible, ask someone to call 999. If you're alone, give CPR for one minute, then call 999. Resume CPR and continue until help arrives or your baby begins breathing.

If your baby has been exposed to toxic fumes, but doesn't seem to be affected by them, consult her doctor.

Head injury

If a baby falls and hits her head, usually it isn't serious. A cold compress can be comforting and reduce swelling and bruising. If there's a cut, apply pressure over a dressing pad and call your doctor.

Keep an eye on your baby for a while, as with head injuries a serious injury isn't always immediately obvious. If you're unsure, call your doctor or go to hospital.

Complications

Your baby could have concussion, when the brain is "shaken" in the skull. She may lose consciousness for a while, and have vision or balance problems. She'll recover from the concussion, but take her to your doctor or to hospital. Rarely, a head injury causes brain damage, so the doctor may want to monitor her for a few weeks.

If there's serious bleeding, or you see clear fluid or watery blood coming from the nose or ears after a head injury, this could indicate a skull fracture and you need to call an ambulance straightaway.

Sometimes the reaction to a head injury can be delayed, by hours or longer. If your baby develops any of the following, call an ambulance: a headache, irregular breathing, drowsiness, unequal-sized pupils, and not being fully conscious. These indicate a serious condition called compression, which could mean an injury to the brain, bleeding inside the skull, or a skull fracture, and your child will probably need an operation. If she loses consciousness, open her airway, check her breathing and begin CPR if necessary (see p.289).

Shaken baby syndrome

Shaken baby syndrome (SBS) is the name given to a serious brain injury that occurs when an adult violently shakes a baby or young child. Usually, the adult is angry and is trying to get a baby to stop crying, but it can also result from frustration with a toddler or preschooler over toilet training or a tantrum, for example.

If a baby's head is shaken back and forth, her brain hits the skull, causing bruising, swelling, pressure and bleeding in and around the brain. The impact can cause bleeding in the retina: the eye's light-sensitive part that transmits images to the brain. There may also be spinal cord damage and neck and bone fractures. The amount of damage depends on how long and hard the baby is shaken, but in five to 10 seconds a baby can suffer permanent, severe damage or death.

Babies and young children are very vulnerable to this kind of injury as their heads are proportionally larger than their bodies and their neck muscles are weak. Also, the immature skull is thinner and the blood vessels more susceptible to tearing.

Welcome to parenthood!
0–6 weeks

Your growing baby
6 weeks to 6 months

Your older baby
6 months to one year

Baby healthcare
0–12 months

Hypothermia

Hypothermia occurs when the body's temperature drops below 35°C (95°F) (the normal body temperature is 37°C/98.6°F).

Babies are more susceptible to hypothermia because their body's ability to regulate its temperature isn't fully developed. Hypothermia can happen if your baby is not dressed in clothes that keep him warm enough.

Symptoms

The symptoms of hypothermia progress as your baby's temperature drops. In babies, mild symptoms of hypothermia include shivering, fatigue, pink, but cold, skin and feeble crying. Moderate symptoms of hypothermia include violent shivering, difficulty moving, slow, shallow breathing, drowsiness and listlessness and fretfulness.

If your baby is suffering from a severe case of hypothermia, he may stop shivering, become unconscious, have stiff muscles and dilated pupils, his breathing may become shallow or he may stop breathing altogether, and he may have only a weak, irregular pulse or may lose his pulse.

What to do

Call 999 if your baby has severe or moderate hypothermia. He will need urgent medical treatment.

While you're waiting for the ambulance to arrive – or if your baby has mild hypothermia – move him somewhere warmer as soon as possible. Change him promptly out of any wet clothing and wrap him in blankets (or whatever you have to hand). It's most important to wrap up his body and head. Your body heat will also help, so hug him gently. If possible, give him a warm drink or breastfeed him. This will help restore his energy.

Prevention

You can prevent hypothermia by dressing your baby appropriately. Most body heat is lost through the head, so put a hat on him if it's cold. Having a room thermometer in the room where your baby sleeps will help you monitor the temperature. The room should be between 16°C (60.8°F) and 20°C (68°F).

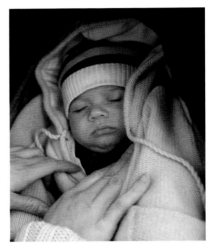

Keep your baby in a warm place, remove any wet clothing and wrap his head and body in blankets or warm clothing.

Heat stroke

Heat stroke occurs when the body's temperature rises while its ability to cool off shuts down. As with hypothermia (see above), babies are especially vulnerable to heat stroke as they are less able to regulate their body temperature. Your baby might get heat stroke if he's outside too long in hot weather, for example, especially if he becomes dehydrated or is dressed too warmly.

Symptoms

If your baby has heat stroke, he may have any of the following symptoms and signs: a temperature of 40°C (104°F) or higher (but no sweating); hot, red, dry skin; a rapid pulse; restlessness; confusion; dizziness; headache (which may make him irritable); vomiting; rapid, shallow breathing; lethargy (he might not respond as strongly as usual if you call his name or tickle him, for example); dehydration; and unconsciousness.

What to do

First, call 999. Then bring your baby's internal temperature down as quickly as possible. Time is of the essence because a baby or child suffering from severe heat stroke can easily slip into unconsciousness. You can lower your baby's temperature by undressing him completely and lying him down in a cool area. While you're waiting for the ambulance to arrive, sponge down his body with a cool, wet cloth, and fan him. Talk to your baby reassuringly to help keep him calm. Don't give your baby any infant paracetamol – this is not recommended because it won't help to lower a temperature that has been caused by heat stroke.

Everyday first aid

Even the most cautious parent cannot be expected to foresee every eventuality. Children are adventurous and their curiosity can sometimes lead them to accidents, even in a baby-proofed home. Prepare yourself for first-aid situations by learning these basics.

Bites and stings

It's common for children to get bitten and stung by insects, and usually it's not something to worry about. In very rare cases, a child may have a severe allergic reaction to a bee or wasp sting. This is known as anaphylactic shock (see p.268).

If you can see the sting still in the skin, remove it by scraping or flicking it out with the sharp edge of your nail; don't grasp it with your fingers or tweezers or you may squeeze more of the venom into your child. Wash the area thoroughly with soap and water.

Once a sting is out, stings and bites can be treated in the same way. You can relieve swelling and itching by applying an ice pack or a cool damp flannel, and/or by giving your baby a children's antihistamine medicine. If your baby is in pain, you can use a painkiller, such as infant paracetamol suspension. Anaesthetic or steroid cream can also be used to soothe pain locally.

Cuts, grazes and burns

If your baby cuts himself, wash your hands and take a look. If he is bleeding, apply direct pressure over a clean dressing and raise the injury until the bleeding stops. (If the bleeding doesn't stop after 10 minutes of direct pressure and elevation, take your baby to hospital.)

After the bleeding stops, check for glass, dirt or other foreign materials in the wound. If you see anything, try to flush it out with cool running water. If that doesn't work, use tweezers to carefully lift off the debris (don't touch anything embedded in the cut). It's not crucial, but applying an antibiotic ointment after washing and drying the area can reduce the risk of infection.

Small cuts and scrapes heal faster when exposed to the air, so unless the cut is likely to get dirty or rub against clothing, you can skip the bandage.

For deeper cuts and scrapes, use an ordinary bandage or dressing, but make sure the skin is clean and dry. Make sure the bandage isn't so tight that it cuts off your baby's circulation.

If your baby has a burn, run cold water over it and take your baby to hospital, or call an ambulance if it's severe.

Bruises

Most bruises are harmless and heal on their own within a week to 10 days. If your baby's bruise is accompanied by swelling, you can apply ice packs for 15-minute periods several times a day during the first 48 hours. A bag of frozen peas may be useful if an ice pack isn't handy, but do wrap it in a cloth first to avoid the cold burning your baby's skin.

Homeopathic or herbal remedies may be helpful too – try arnica cream from your pharmacist. Lastly, don't forget to give yout baby plenty of those healing hugs and kisses!

47% of parents worry about making a first-aid mistake.
Almost half of parents worry that they would do something wrong in an emergency. Find a first-aid course or go online to learn the basics.

Foreign objects

If something gets lodged in your baby's ears or nose, stay calm and reassure him that it's nothing to worry about. The biggest danger is that you will push the object deeper if you try to get it out.

If a foreign object is very close to the surface and clearly visible, clean tweezers are fine to use to remove it. You can use them on splinters and thorns.

Don't poke or press down in the ear or nose, as you may cause damage. Instead, leave the more tricky removals to the health professionals – they have tiny forceps for jobs like this.

If in any doubt, it is best to take your baby to see your doctor. It's important to be aware that some foreign objects can become more problematic the longer you leave them in place. (A bean can swell and become more difficult to remove, for example, and a small watch battery could cause serious damage if left for a long period of time.)

A bump to the head may be soothed by applying a cold compress, which will also help reduce swelling and bruising.

Welcome to parenthood!
0–6 weeks

Your growing baby
6 weeks to 6 months

Your older baby
6 months to one year

Baby healthcare
0–12 months

Special
care
babies

Welcome to parenthood!
0–6 weeks

Your growing baby
6 weeks to 6 months

Your older baby
6 months to one year

Baby healthcare
0–12 months

Your special care baby

There are many reasons why a baby needs special care. Perhaps she was born prematurely and needs extra care in the first important days, or she has a condition that needs early treatment. Fortunately, medicine is constantly improving, and so is the support for parents.

Care after the birth

It's very hard if your baby has to go into the neonatal unit and she will probaby appear very small and fragile. It may feel as though the nurses are doing everything for her and that she doesn't need you, but she does of course. She might be in hospital, but you are still her parent. You're making important decisions for her and you can comfort her just by being there beside her. Talk to her often – she will be reassured by your voice. Give her a bit of clothing, too, that has been next to your skin so that it carries your familiar smell.

The best care

Babies go into the neonatal unit when they're born prematurely, or when they have conditions linked to prematurity (you can read more about these units on pages 28–9). Try to reassure yourself that your baby is in the best possible place, getting all the care she needs to grow stronger in these first important days.

The nurses on the unit should encourage you to care for your baby as much as possible, too. As your baby grows stronger, you will be able to do more and more for her.

Going home

When you finally get to take your baby home, it's exciting, but can feel quite scary. Ideally, you will have time to ease away gradually from the neonatal unit. You may be offered a few days of "rooming in" with your baby before she leaves the hospital, perhaps on the ordinary maternity ward.

If your baby is going home on oxygen or has other medical needs, it's even more daunting. The staff on the neonatal unit should teach you all you need to know about your baby's oxygen before you take her home. If you're unsure on any point, keep asking

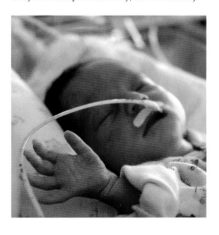

Although daunting, your baby's time on the neonatal ward ensures that she receives the best care to develop and grow stronger.

ParentsAsk...

If my baby was born prematurely, is he more likely to have health problems?

Every baby is different, so there's no single answer to this, but the earlier or smaller a baby is born, the more likely he is to have health problems.

The most extensive study carried out on premature babies was called EPICure. It looked at babies who had no more than 25 weeks in the uterus before birth. Many of these babies were too young or too small to survive. Those who lived were followed up until the age of six. Problems such as slow development, lung conditions or neurological disability were common. However, it's important to remember that this study looked at the earliest, tiniest babies. We don't have such extensive studies for babies born later. In general, the nearer babies get to "full term" (37–42 weeks), the better chance they have for good health. Babies born after 33 weeks generally do well.

questions until you're confident. If your baby does come home when she is still on oxygen or requires extra help such as tube feeding, she'll be followed up by your community home-care team. She'll also be monitored by your doctor and the hospital, and you should have direct access to the hospital's paediatric unit. If you're worried at all, ask for help.

Cerebral palsy

Cerebral palsy (also called CP) is a condition that affects movement and posture. It's caused by brain damage that usually happens before, during or just after birth. The damage may be caused by an infection in pregnancy, such as rubella (German measles), or by a lack of oxygen to a baby's brain during birth. Sometimes no cause can be found.

Cerebral palsy varies from person to person. Some children are hardly affected at all, whereas others may have major disabilities. Some people with cerebral palsy have learning disabilities, speech problems, hearing and physical impairment or epilepsy.

Types of cerebral palsy

There are different types of cerebral palsy. Spastic CP is the commonest form. This causes the body's muscles to become stiff and weak. Athetoid CP affects posture and often causes unwanted movements, while Ataxic CP affects balance. People with Ataxic CP may have shaky hand movements.

Estimates vary on how common cerebral palsy is, but it is thought that around one in every 400 to 500 children has some form of it. Children may be diagnosed in the first year of their life, but a diagnosis can take time as the full extent of the condition may not be apparent until later on.

Treatment

Unfortunately, there is no cure for cerebral palsy. A variety of drugs and treatments can help to alleviate the symptoms and can help to make your child feel better. If your child is diagnosed with cerebral palsy, doctors will guide you carefully through all the different therapies and medications that are available.

The most important therapy for your baby is physiotherapy. Physiotherapy can help teach your child how to control his head movements and sit, roll over, crawl and walk. A physiotherapist will help you, too, showing you how to feed, carry and dress your baby without damaging his muscles. Speech therapy can help if your child has difficulty swallowing or chewing.

It's not always easy coming to terms with a diagnosis of cerebral palsy, but there will be plenty of support and information available to you – and to your child as he grows up.

ParentsAsk...

My daughter has cerebral palsy. I feel so hopeless – how can I help her?

It can be devastating to find out that your baby has cerebral palsy, but you don't have to cope with the diagnosis alone. A team of health professionals should be involved in helping you to look after your baby so that she can reach her full potential. This may include a paediatrician, a health visitor, a physiotherapist and an educational psychologist. Your child will also have an individual care plan drawn up by her key worker (usually a health visitor) who will act as a point of contact between your child and various support services.

Physiotherapists will teach your child exercises that she can do every day as she gets older to strengthen and stretch her muscles. Speech therapy helps with communication difficulties. Your child can also have occupational therapy to improve her posture and maximise her mobility. This helps your child with day-to-day tasks, for example getting dressed, and helps her retain as much independence as possible as she grows.

The charity Scope offers advice and support to families with cerebral palsy (see pp.312–13) and has regional response workers, who work in the local community and can put you in touch with local services.

Early signs of cerebral palsy

The early signs of cerebral palsy vary enormously from baby to baby because there are several different types of the condition. Also, some babies will only be mildly affected, whereas others will have more severe disabilities.

Your baby's development

If your baby has cerebral palsy, he may be slower than other babies to reach his developmental milestones. For example, he may roll over, sit, crawl, smile or talk later than other babies.

Your baby's muscle tone may also be different to that of other babies. His body may seem relaxed, almost floppy, or he may seem quite stiff and rigid. He may also use one side of his body more than the other side.

First steps to a diagnosis

All babies develop at different rates. If you have concerns that your baby may have cerebral palsy, take him to your doctor who can work out what are normal variations in development and what may be a sign of cerebral palsy. Your baby can then be referred to a specialist, if needed, who can examine him and perform any necessary tests.

Children with Down's syndrome experience developmental delays, but many develop to enjoy typical childhood activities, such as riding a bike and learning to read and write.

The future for children with Down's syndrome

Children born with Down's syndrome can thrive well into their fifties and lead fulfilled lives. Many children are successfully integrated into mainstream schools, and residential and job opportunities are being developed all the time.

Your family's support group

If you need help, your midwife, family doctor or health visitor are useful sources of information. Your baby may be under the care of a specialist at the hospital, and a useful starting point can be a social worker based either in the community or at your hospital.

Down's syndrome

Down's syndrome is a genetic condition that affects just over one in every 800 babies born in the UK.

Usually, the 23 chromosomes from a man's sperm come together with the 23 chromosomes from a woman's egg and create a baby with a full complement of 46 chromosomes. With Down's, instead of one number 21 chromosome from the father and one from the mother, a third chromosome creeps in and is duplicated in every body cell. No one knows what causes the extra chromosome, which can come from either parent. There is a link with older mothers.

What we do know is that no one is to blame. Nothing done before or during pregnancy causes Down's syndrome. It occurs in all races, social classes and in all countries throughout the world. It can happen to anyone.

Characteristics

Children with Down's syndrome are slower than "normal" babies to reach milestones, but they will reach them.

Although development is often delayed and is limited, most can walk, talk, ride a bike, read and write, like other children. All children with Down's syndrome have some degree of learning disability.

A baby with Down's syndrome may have looser muscles and joints than other babies. This will improve as he gets older. He may have a lower-than-average birth weight and gain weight at a slower pace than other babies.

Babies with Down's often have eyes that slant upwards and outwards. Their eyelids may have an extra fold of skin that appears to exaggerate the slant, but doesn't affect vision. The back of the head may be flatter than average. Many babies with Down's have a single crease that runs across the palm. However, some babies without Down's have a crease, too.

Complications

Children with Down's syndrome can be prone to chest and sinus infections, but better medical care means these are no longer as serious as they used to be. At

first, some babies with Down's have problems with feeding. They may be slow to coordinate sucking, swallowing and breathing and they may splutter and choke a bit. These problems often settle down in the first few weeks. Some babies with Down's syndrome find it easier to use a bottle, but if you can keep your milk supply going, your baby may eventually take to breastfeeding.

Your baby may need help in learning to control his tongue. Playing games, pulling faces and making noises will help him to exercise face and tongue muscles, and will also help with early sounds and speech.

About one in three Down's children has a heart defect. This may be minor, such as a heart murmur, or more complex, requiring medication and/or surgery. If your baby has a heart defect and you wish to talk to someone whose child has a similar problem, the Down's Syndrome Association (see pp.312–13) can put you in touch with parents who understand what you're going through.

Cleft lip and palate

The word "cleft" means a split or separation. If a baby has a cleft lip, she has a split in the upper lip between her mouth and nose, where separate facial areas didn't join properly. The condition ranges from a slight notch in the lip, to complete separation in one or both sides of the lip, extending up and into the nose.

A cleft palate occurs when the roof of the mouth hasn't joined completely. The back of the palate is the "soft palate" and the front the "hard palate". A cleft palate ranges from a small opening at the back of the soft palate, to a nearly complete separation of the roof of the mouth.

Before treatment (see left), babies with cleft lips may have problems latching on to the breast and creating an airtight seal with their mouths. However, most breastfeed with help from a feeding specialist and by experimenting with positions. A cleft in the palate can make it hard for a baby to suck. You can still express your milk and give it to your baby in a specially adapted bottle.

Causes

Cleft lips and palates tend to run in families. If a woman drinks alcohol and smokes in pregnancy, the risk increases. Some medicines increase the risk. If you take tablets for a condition, talk to your doctor. Older parents are more likely to have a baby with a cleft lip and/or palate.

Congenital heart disease

Congenital heart problems can be minor, as in the case of some heart murmurs, or more serious heart conditions.

Heart murmurs

Around 50 per cent of babies have some kind of heart murmur, but in the vast majority of cases, this isn't serious. A "murmur" describes the extra sounds that blood makes as it passes through the heart's valves and blood vessels, heard through a stethoscope between heartbeats. At birth, murmurs may need a second opinion, but can disappear on their own. A further test for a heart condition is to feel for the presence of a pulse in the groin (the femoral pulse).

Other heart conditions

Most murmurs are normal or "innocent" and cause no symptoms. However, some can be a sign of a heart disorder or congenital heart condition – a condition present at birth, either inherited or caused by a baby's environment.

Examples of heart conditions include openings in the heart's internal wall; a narrowing of the main heart valves or of the main artery; pathway blockages between the heart and lungs; or abnormal connections between the heart's chambers and vessels. Your baby may need further checks or treatment.

Kidney reflux

One of the most common problems associated with baby's and children's kidneys is referred to as reflux or vesico-ureteric reflux (VUR).

Normally, a valve between the bladder and the ureter (the drainage tube from the kidney to the bladder) prevents urine from leaking out of the bladder and into the kidneys. However, for babies with kidney reflux, the valve does not work properly and urine flows out of the bladder back up the ureter to the kidney.

Babies who have kidney reflux will have small amounts of urine remaining in their bladder after they have passed urine. This retention of urine can lead to infections developing.

Outlook

Around one per cent of babies have some form of kidney reflux, but in most cases the condition is a mild one. It's thought that about 30 per cent of children who get urinary tract infections (UTIs) have kidney reflux. Fortunately, many babies and children grow out of kidney reflux.

Diagnosis and treatment

Sometimes, a problem with one or both of your baby's kidneys might become apparent on an ultrasound scan during your pregnancy. If that's the case, doctors might look out for any signs of kidney reflux once your baby is born.

Sometimes, frequent UTIs in babies might be a sign that your baby has kidney reflux. However, most babies and children who develop UTIs don't have kidney reflux.

If your baby has a mild case of reflux, her consultant will monitor her condition and she'll have regular outpatient check-ups at the hospital to check her progress. She may be given a daily low dose of antibiotics to make sure she doesn't get frequent UTIs, which could scar the kidneys. Occasionally, if the problem appears to be severe, an operation can be performed to correct the condition. In many cases, it gets better on its own. The UK National Kidney Federation (see pp.312–13) may be able to offer advice.

Club foot (talipes)

Talipes is a condition that can affect one or both of a baby's feet. Most cases are known as congenital talipes equinovarus (CTE), where the front half of the baby's foot turns inwards and downwards. The condition is commonly referred to as "club foot".

Talipes, or club foot, affects around one in every 1,000 babies and is more common in boys than girls. It's one of the most common abnormalities at birth.

Causes

We do not know exactly what causes talipes, but the condition can run in families – about a quarter of cases are genetically linked. If both parents have the condition, then there is around a 15 per cent chance that they'll pass it on to their baby. There is also a theory that talipes may be caused by some kind of disruption during fetal development.

Although babies don't find the condition painful, it does need to be treated so that they can learn to walk successfully when they are older.

Diagnosis and treatment

Some cases of talipes are discovered during a routine ultrasound scan in pregnancy. This won't tell you how severe the talipes is, though. If it isn't diagnosed during pregnancy, it will be picked up during your baby's routine newborn examination after birth.

Treatment for talipes starts during your baby's first year and the type depends on how severe it is.

Physiotherapy can help, as can gentle manipulation, plaster casts, special splints and boots. In some cases, your consultant may recommend surgery.

The "Ponseti" method, developed by the Spanish born Dr Ponseti, is popular. This uses manipulation and casting methods, together with boots that have a metal bar inside. In 2008, there were 15 registered practitioners in the UK.

Welcome to parenthood! 0–6 weeks

Your growing baby 6 weeks to 6 months

Your older baby 6 months to one year

Baby healthcare 0–12 months

Cystic fibrosis

Cystic fibrosis (CF) is almost always diagnosed in the first three years of life. A baby with CF has a genetic fault that causes his body to make mucus that is so heavy and sticky that it blocks the lungs and pancreas, making breathing and digestion difficult.

CF affects one in 2,500 babies in the UK. About one in 25 people in the UK carry the CF gene. If both parents carry the gene, there is a one in four chance that their baby will be born with CF. The good news is that, in many cases, babies with CF lead normal lives, going to

Regular physiotherapy is an important treatment for cystic fibrosis, helping to clear the heavy mucus from the lungs.

school with everyone else. Also, the prospects for children with CF keep getting better: several decades ago, most children with CF died by the age of two; today, average life expectancy is 31.

Symptoms

In approximately one in 10 babies born with CF, their meconium (the greenish-black substance that is passed through their bowels just after they are born) is so thick that it actually blocks their bowel. Babies born with this problem often need to have an urgent operation to remove the blockage.

Other babies are fine at birth, but they can't seem to put on weight in their first four to six weeks. Repeated chest infections, oily, smelly stools, noticeably salty tasting skin and a persistent cough and wheeze are also symptoms. If you notice any of these in your baby, talk to your doctor.

In the UK, a heel-prick blood test (Guthrie test) is taken from all babies when they're a few days old to screen for various diseases, including CF. Now, all newborn babies are tested for CF, which means that all babies born with CF should receive the best possible treatment early on.

Diagnosis and treatment

Babies with CF have more salt in their sweat than others, so if CF is suspected, your doctor will perform a quick and painless sweat test. If your baby has higher than normal levels of salt, CF may be diagnosed. If the results are borderline, the doctor may get material for genetic testing by gently rubbing the inside of your baby's cheek.

Treatment for CF usually focuses on two areas. The first is clearing sticky mucus from the lungs with physiotherapy, breathing exercises and physical activity. Doctors teach parents these techniques.

The second treatment involves preventing and treating infections, usually with antibiotics. Drugs called bronchodilators treat CF by opening the

airways, relieving tightness and shortness of breath. Steroids are also used to reduce inflammation in the airways, and a drug called DNase breaks down mucus.

Each baby responds to a different combination of therapies, and parents play an important role by watching how their own baby reacts.

Spina bifida

This is a condition that results when something goes wrong with the development of the neural tube during pregnancy. The spinal cord does not fully close, leaving a gap, so the spinal cord and nerves are not properly formed. Spina bifida actually means "split spine".

According to the Association for Spina Bifida and Hydropcephalus (see pp.312–13), spina bifida affects one in every 1,500 babies in the UK. Research shows that women with a very low intake of folic acid are much more likely to give birth to a baby with spina bifida, compared with women who take a daily supplement of 400 micrograms (mcg) of folic acid before conception and during the first three months of pregnancy.

Types of spina bifida

There are three types of spina bifida. The first, known as spina bifida occulta, is the most common type and the mildest form of the condition. With spina bifida occulta, there is a tiny gap between the vertebrae of the spine. Most people who have spina bifida occulta have no symptoms at all, or perhaps just very mild symptoms, and may not even be aware that they have spina bifida. In fact, it is estimated that around five to 10 per cent of the population may have spina bifida occulta without actually realising it.

Myelomeningocele is the most serious form of spina bifida. With this type, a cyst or sac can usually be seen on the back, covered by skin. The cyst contains tissue and also nerves, and the spinal cord is damaged or is unable to develop properly. People who have this serious form of spina bifida usually suffer with some degree of nerve damage or paralysis in some areas, depending on where exactly on the back the cyst is located. They may not be able to walk or control their bladder. Around one in 1,000 babies is born with myelomeningocele.

Most children with this more severe form of spina bifida will also have the associated condition of hydrocephalus, which is when the fluid surrounding the brain cannot drain out into the bloodstream. Certain parts of the brain become damaged before birth, preventing the fluid from draining properly. The increase in pressure compresses the brain even further.

Spina bifida meningocele is a less serious type of spina bifida than myelomeningocele and is also the rarest form of spina bifida. With this type, a cyst contains membranes that can rupture easily.

If your baby has spina bifida, you can get lots of support and information from your doctor or midwife, as well as from the Association for Spina Bifida and Hydropcephalus.

Diagnosis and treatment

Spina bifida may be spotted either during a routine pregnancy ultrasound scan or following an antenatal blood test designed to detect certain abnormalities.

Babies born with a severe form may be given surgery in the first two days after the birth to repair the gap. Some doctors, however, do not use surgery, but leave the area to heal on its own.

Some babies are operated on successfully while they're in the uterus. This type of surgery is still rare, though, as it does hold additional risks to the baby and the mother and so is seen as a riskier procedure.

Babies who have hydrocephalus may need to have a shunt (a hollow tube) fitted to drain the excess fluid from the brain into the abdomen (see box, right).

Living with spina bifida

Your baby may need regular visits to hospital, which can be hard for you both. However, if you strive to have a positive attitude, this can make a real difference to your baby's care and quality of life.

Dealing with hydrocephalus

Most babies with the severe form of spina bifida also have hydrocephalus, which causes a build up of fluid on the brain. The extra fluid is drained away to another part of the body with a device called a shunt, which is flexible like a straw. The shunt is normally put in a few days after your baby is born.

If your baby has a shunt in his head you may worry later about finding him ways in which he can play safely and explore the world. A physiotherapist can show you safe ways of positioning your baby so that he gets as much stimulation as possible.

Bowel and bladder concerns

Nearly all children who have spina bifida have problems controlling their bladder and bowels, and so toilet training needs to be approached differently. Some children have a catheter to help empty their bladder.

Epilepsy

This is a brain disorder that makes a person prone to having seizures. Nerve cells in the brain are constantly sending electrical signals to each other. When the normal process is interrupted – or when the signals suddenly fire at the same time – it can cause a seizure, resulting in a sudden change in consciousness, movement or sensation. Although this is not painful, it can be very upsetting.

If your baby has had one seizure, it doesn't mean that she has epilepsy. If she's had more than one seizure without any known, acute cause, such as hypoglycemia, an electrolyte imbalance (an inbalance in sodium, calcium or magnesium levels), a high fever, or meningitis, then she may be diagnosed as epileptic. Non-acute causes might include a head injury or a structural abnormality of the brain (see below).

Causes

Epilepsy can have a number of causes. Symptomatic epilepsy is caused by brain injury from an accident or illness, for example. In around a third of all cases, the exact cause of the epilepsy is unknown. In these instances, it's called idiopathic epilepsy.

In some babies, epilepsy may be caused by birth defects or by problems that occurred during birth that resulted in the baby being deprived of oxygen, such as the umbilical cord getting twisted.

Researchers think that there may also be a genetic link to a tendency to have some types of epileptic seizures.

Diagnosis

Epilepsy can be difficult to diagnose in babies because there are many other conditions that can cause seizures. In fact, seizures in young children don't usually signal epilepsy; they tend to be caused by high fever (see p.257). If your baby has had a seizure, call her doctor or an ambulance if it was longer than four minutes. Explain to her exactly what happened during the seizure. To find out what might have caused it, she'll do a physical examination. She may refer your baby to a specialist in epilepsy, who may arrange for further tests. One of the most common tests is an EEG test, which records electrical activity in the brain through electrodes placed on the scalp. It's not a conclusive test for epilepsy, but it can be very useful in detecting subtle seizures, and can also provide information about specific types of epileptic seizure.

A MRI scan can provide a more detailed picture of the brain and detect possible causes of epilepsy, such as defects of the structure of the brain.

Treatment

There are treatments that help reduce the chances of your child having epileptic seizures. These anti-epileptic drugs don't cure epilepsy, but do prevent epileptic seizures from happening. The drugs do have various side effects, though, and it may take time to find the right drug or combination of drugs for your baby. Side effects include nausea, drowsiness, abdominal pain and irritability.

The choice of medication will depend on the type of seizure your baby has, your baby's age, the cause of her epilepsy and the potential outcome of that type of epilepsy. For some children with difficult to control epilepsy, a special low-carbohydrate, adequate protein, high-fat diet called a ketogenic diet seems to help.

Diagnosis and treatment

Diagnosing epilepsy can be hard in babies but, following a consultation, your doctor may request these tests:
● an EEG (electroencephalogram), to measure electrical activity in the brain via electrodes placed on the scalp
● an MRI (magnetic resonance imaging) scan

Treatment is with anti-epileptic drugs. A ketogenic diet, one low in carbohydrates, with adequate protein and high in fats, can alter the chemical make-up of the brain, making seizures less likely.

Hearing and sight problems

While the vast majority of babies have excellent hearing and sight, a certain percentage have problems. Checks on both vision and hearing can identify problems early on and, if possible, steps can be taken to improve these functions.

Hearing

Babies are more at risk of impaired hearing if they were born extremely prematurely, were deprived of oxygen or had a severe infection at birth. Babies with a family history of hearing loss are also more likely to have problems.

All newborns are offered a hearing test shortly after birth, either in hospital, at a community clinic or at home. Later, you can ask your doctor or health visitor to check her hearing if you're concerned. Trust your instinct if you're worried. The earlier babies are checked for hearing problems, the better. According to the most recent research, identifying babies who need hearing aids and fitting them with the devices before they're six months old significantly helps their speech and language development.

Make your own assessment of your baby's hearing with some quick tests.
● Under three months: clap your hands behind your baby's head. If she startles, she's fine. Otherwise, repeat a few times.
● Between four and six months: call her name to see if she turns to, or reacts to, your voice. See if she turns her eyes or head to look for an interesting sound.
● Between six and 10 months: see whether your baby responds to her name and to familiar environmental sounds, such as the ringing of the phone or the roar of the vacuum cleaner.
● Between 10 and 15 months: ask her to point to a familiar object in a book. If she can't, she may not be hearing you.

Sight

Babies should be screened for vision problems at birth and at every check-up. Most eye problems and deficiencies can be corrected if they're spotted early enough; the older your child gets, the harder it will be to fix any problems.

You won't be able to detect conditions such as near sightedness, far sightedness and astigmatism (an uneven curvature of the cornea and/or lens) on your own, but keep an eye out for bigger difficulties. If your baby can't focus on, or track, an object (or your face) with both eyes by three or four months, talk to your doctor. Premature babies have a higher risk of developing eye problems such as astigmatism, strabismus (eye misalignment) and myopia (short sightedness), so parents and doctors should pay attention to their sight. Tell your health visitor if your baby has trouble moving one or both of her eyes in all directions; her eyes are crossed most of the time; or one or both of your baby's eyes tend to turn outwards.

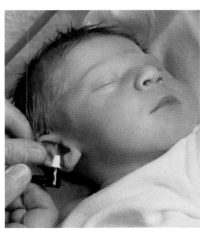

A hearing test carried out soon after birth helps detect infants with hearing problems and allows early treatment.

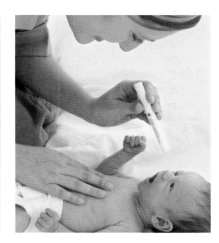

Checking your baby's vision after the birth and at check-ups means that problems can be identified and often corrected.

Welcome to parenthood! 0–6 weeks

Your growing baby 6 weeks to 6 months

Your older baby 6 months to one year

Baby healthcare 0–12 months

Returning to work
your options now

Your new working life

Whether you're returning to work with a heavy heart, or looking forward to new challenges, you need to feel certain that your baby is in the best possible care. The first step to becoming a confident working mum is to find someone trustworthy to care for your child.

Working mum

Some mums find going back to work part-time provides a good balance between work and family life.

"I absolutely love my job, but at the same time I also love being there for my baby. So I decided to try to achieve the best of both worlds by going back to work part-time. I now have three days a week when I'm in adult, professional mode, and it feels great to put on some nice clothes on those days and enjoy some grown up, non-baby related conversaton! However, I always make sure I'm home by 5.30 to feed my baby and do her bedtime routine.

I've got the other four days in the week to be in mummy mode, when I can spend plenty of quality time with my daughter – and catch up on some housework. Working part-time means that someone else isn't spending more time with my daughter than I am – I wouldn't want to be in a situation where she feels closer to her childminder than she does to me! At the moment, this routine is working out really well. The only hard part is having to say goodbye to her three mornings a week."

What you decide

Are you thinking about going back to work, or will you be a stay-at-home mum? Most new parents see money as the main factor in their decision, but there are other things to consider, too.

Some people are lucky enough to have sufficient income so that they don't need to go back to work – they have a choice. For most of us, though, finances are a big consideration. While staying at home means losing a salary, going back to work can be costly, too. A monthly childcare bill leaves little left over for holidays, clothes and other expenses.

Weighing up your options

Disposable income may not be the only factor to consider. Some mums feel pressured to go back to work – maybe their friends have all returned to careers and they feel they should follow suit. Other women are keen to maintain an income separate from their partner's.

It's possible to generalise and say that our society does not always value mothers who stay at home. However, it's probably true to say that the fact that running a family home and caring for children is far harder work than many

Sharing the childcare between you, your partner and perhaps a carer, too, is an increasingly popular choice for many families.

Parents**Talk...**

"When the time came for me to go back to work, I couldn't face being away from my baby for 40 hours a week! I spent every waking minute I could with him at home and knew leaving him would be too much of a wrench. I saw my boss and asked if I would be able to go part-time. Together, we organised my workload so it could function as a job share. I'm so grateful this was possible."
Pippa, 32, first-time mum

"Before I had my daughter, I adored the buzz of the office: the social aspect of going to work, as well as the job itself. Now though, spending time with my daughter is my top priority, so I approached my manager about working from home two days a week. She went for it, and now I feel like I have the best of both worlds."
Fleur, 36, first-time mum

"When my maternity leave was up, I just couldn't face going back to my nine-to-five office job and leaving my baby with someone else. So I set up my own business, a nursery in fact, and now I get to spend all day with my little one!"
Louise, 27, first-time mum

Starting up an office at home can seem an attractive option once you have a baby, but does require discipline and planning.

other jobs, with no financial reward, is often overlooked. This may explain why around half of all mothers return to work by the time their baby is a year old.

Your decision may be influenced by your own experiences. Maybe you feel that your mum gave up too much for you; or perhaps she inspired you by holding down a job while managing the family. Perhaps you loved having her at home and wish to replicate that for your child.

It can also depend on your job. Some jobs offer flexible employment, while others are more difficult to adapt. If your company has a rigid approach to overtime and early morning meetings, it can seem hard to believe that you'll still be part of the team, and not resented by colleagues if you leave at 4pm to pick up your baby. Maybe you're also worried that taking time out now will make it harder for you to advance later on.

It's worth remembering that employers are now legally obliged to offer a more family-friendly approach to working mothers, so the situation may not be as bad as you think.

What works for you

Whether or not you go back to work can also depend on the childcare available. For example, you may feel less anxious if your mother or another close relative can care for your baby.

In other situations, there are different issues. For example, if you're a single mum, you may benefit from the social side of employment by returning to work, and staying at home could feel isolating. On the other hand, maybe you want to reassure your child of your constant presence in her life.

Fact: Flexible working practices are becoming more popular.

Flexible working offers benefits to employers as well as to employees, such as staff retention, improved productivity and a reduction in absenteeism, sickness and stress.

Working from home

Working from home can seem very attractive when you have small children – you can plan your hours around your family and work when it suits. Well, that's the idea anyway! In reality, it needs lots of organisation and discipline.

Making it work

Working from home isn't a soft option, and you'll need support from your partner, family and friends. You'll need to be able to tell them when and how you'd like help.

Even if you held down a stressful job before, if possible, consider something less demanding when you first start working at home. Pressurised jobs with tight deadlines can leave you over-stressed. Also, don't allocate every spare minute to working or checking emails; always build in relaxation time for yourself.

: **Before entrusting the care of your baby** to others, ensure that you are totally
: happy and confident with your choice and take time to help your baby settle.

Your childcare options

It's never too early to start thinking about childcare. However, that doesn't mean you should rush into a decision. Leaving your baby with someone who is, at first, a stranger is a big deal, and you need to be completely happy. You may have to compromise on location or price, but you should never compromise on your certainty that your baby is being cared for by the right person.

What's available

A good starting point when seeking out childcare is to chat to local parents, many of whom will be able to give you first-hand information on the childcare available. Also, get leaflets about local nurseries, and contact the Children's Information Service, the details for which you'll find in your local phone directory. Friends with older children are also great sources of childcare tips.

As you find out about availability and prices, your options will become clearer (see opposite). But don't expect to find childcare immediately. In fact, it's good to see a number of people and places before making a decision so that you get an idea of quality, price and style.

Thorough checks

When you find a childcare option that you like, how do you then make sure it's a safe, trustworthy option? Don't make any assumptions. Ensure that all you've been told has evidence to back it up; if it doesn't, take steps to get facts verified. Check identification: a passport, driver's licence or birth certificate. You can ask a potential childminder for a letter from her doctor confirming that she is mentally and physically fit to care for children. There will be a charge for this, which you should offer to pay. Also, talk

"I took six months' maternity leave, because being a single mum I couldn't really have afforded to take any longer than this. I went back to work for three days a week when my baby was five months old. As he was still so little, I didn't want to bundle him off to a daycare centre with lots of other babies – so he went to my parents for one day of the week, and to a childminder for the other two days, which meant that he had plenty of one-to-one care and attention throughout the week.

This has worked out as the cheapest option for me at the moment, until he'd old enough to go to nursery and then I'll be able to work every day. Money is tight at the moment, but I'm getting by. I wish I could be there for my baby all the time, but luckily I still have four days out of seven I can spend with him."

to her referees. People tend to say things on the telephone that they wouldn't necessarily commit to paper, so you may find that you get a more thorough assessment this way.

In England, all carers who work in a registered childcare setting must be inspected by Ofsted and checked by the Criminal Records Bureau. Contact your local Children's Information Service for confirmation that they are registered.

Overall, the golden rules in finding the right person to care for your baby are to give it plenty of time; don't opt for second best; be thorough in your search; and always trust your instincts.

Childcare options: what to consider

Think carefully about the pros and cons of different childcare options and choose something that suits your family's needs.

Nurseries

These employ qualified and unqualified staff to care for babies and children from about four months to five years of age in a child-centred environment.

Pros They offer a structured environment with clear rules for parents on picking up and drop-off times. They are stable and reliable as they are open regardless of whether a carer is sick or late.

Cons You must conform to opening and closing times and find back-up care if a nursery is closed or your child is ill. Your baby is less likely to get one-to-one care and will be exposed to more germs.

Nannies

A nanny has a qualification in childcare and cares for your child in your home.

Pros At home one-to-one care means your baby can adjust gradually to your absence. A loving nanny is valued and often stays in touch after she has left.

Cons Nannies are expensive. You are her employer and have to pay National Insurance, tax and provide holiday leave. Unless you do a nanny-share, your child is likely to be on his own.

Childminders

They care for your child in their home.

Pros Your baby will be one of a small group, so should have plenty of attention. Childminders have mixed age groups, so your baby will get used to children of different ages. Some care for children from babyhood to secondary school, giving a sense of security. They may be more flexible about pick-up and drop-off times.

Cons The childminder's introductory childcare course is less in-depth than some full-time nursery nursing courses. Also, there may not be back-up childcare if your childminder is ill or on holiday.

Au pairs

These are young people who stay with a family to study English and can help with light housework and childcare.

Pros They are relatively inexpensive. Au pairs can introduce your child to their own culture. You can get help with both the childcare and the housework.

Cons Au pairs rarely have professional experience and seldom take sole charge of babies. They have restricted hours, and you're unlikely to meet her in advance.

Care by a relative

A relative cares for your child in your home or theirs.

Pros Your baby is in a loving, non-institutional environment with one-to-one care from someone you trust. If you pay your relative, your childcare bill is likely to be low.

Cons Some relatives may ignore your views on childcare, which undermines your authority, confuses your baby and can damage relationships. You may feel indebted, which can be awkward. Relatives aren't registered, so you have to trust them to provide a safe, clean and welcoming environment.

Grandparents can sometimes offer the perfect childminding solution, saving money and ensuring a loving environment.

Money-saving tips

Whether you're using a nursery, a childminder or a nanny, with careful planning you can trim your costs.

How to save money

Make sure you get all the tax credits you're entitled to: Child Benefit and, if you're eligible, Working Tax Credit. Your local benefits agency will help.

Some childcare providers charge for late pickups, so always be on time to collect your little one.

Consider splitting the cost of a nanny or au pair with friends who have children. A nanny share gives your baby a playmate, and halves your childcare bill.

Finally, if you have a relative nearby who is happy to help, see whether they would like to care for your child one day a week. This will enable you to save on your childcare bill, and your relative probably won't find it too much of a burden. Your child may well enjoy the variety and look forward to her "granny day".

Returning to work and letting someone else care for your baby is a big step: give yourself and your baby time to adapt.

Systemised mum

Settling your baby into a nursery may take you longer than you first expected.

"The staff at Poppy's nursery have been so helpful about the settling-in process. They suggested that I should first go for an informal visit and stay with Poppy, and then we would go for some short sessions, gradually building up the time apart.

I felt so anxious the first time I left her. Her keyworker told me to say a cheerful goodbye and a promise to be back soon, and I went into another room for 10 minutes. She cried, which was heart-wrenching, but stopped once I left the room.

After that, I left Poppy for longer sessions, starting with half an hour, then an hour, then two, three, and working up to a whole session. The process has taken several weeks, but I feel much happier knowing that she's secure and happy now. The nursery staff don't mind if I call during the day to find out how she's getting on."

Starting childcare

Handing your baby over to the care of someone else – possibly a relative stranger – is a scary step. Can anybody look after your baby as well as you? What if she cries all day? Will she forgive you? Will you forgive yourself?

While this is a difficult time, there are ways that you can minimise the disruptive effects of you returning to work and make the transition as smooth as possible for both you and your baby.

Easing in

First, you need to be confident that the person you choose to look after your child is the right person. Returning to work is bound to be difficult and painful if you're not convinced that your baby is in the best place. It is vital to allow yourself enough time to find the most reliable and professional childcare, and be satisfied that you've made the right choice (see pp.308–09).

It's important for both you and your baby to build a relationship with her carer – this will give you peace of mind and help to make your baby feel more secure. Without being dictatorial, feel free to leave instructions about your baby's favourite toys, how warm she likes her milk, what time she has her naps and any other parts of her daily routine that you would like to be taken into account.

To ease the transition into childcare, arrange to stay with your baby for the first couple of sessions. Most nurseries and childminders will encourage you to do this, as they know that it smoothes the settling-in process for your baby as well as for you. Once your baby has started to grow accustomed to her new surroundings, leave for a short time when she is engrossed in something. Then you can extend the periods that you are apart.

ParentsAsk...

I can't find the right childcare – what should I do?

Finding suitable, good-quality childcare can be difficult, and as the time to return to work draws closer you may find yourself feeling worried. Your first move might be to talk to your employers about the problem: they may be flexible and extend your leave until you have sorted this out.

You may be eligible to take time off under the parental leave regulations. This is unpaid, but it could offer a short-term solution in the absence of an alternative. Fathers are allowed to take this leave, too.

This may be the time to do some detective work. If your searches through agencies or listings of childminders have come to nothing, try another route. Ask if you can talk to some of the mothers at the local nursery – they may know of carers who are just about to have a space, or who are coming back into childcare. Local schools may also know of mums who are qualified childminders.

Do you know of anybody who could help on a temporary basis? Do you have a suitable relative who could help for a month or so until you find a more permanent solution? Perhaps your employer would allow you to return with reduced hours if you can get short-term cover.

Whatever you do, though, don't compromise on your baby's safety: it's more important to take your time and find a carer with whom you and your baby are completely happy.

Coping with the demands of work and home

Life can be extremely tiring for working mums. You can't just come home and flop onto the sofa – there is always something or someone demanding your time and attention.

Getting enough rest

It's a good idea to keep a diary, even if just a mental one, for two or three weeks to identify high and low energy periods of your day, and schedule your main responsibilities accordingly.

When you feel tired at work, try changing tasks, standing up and stretching or going for a walk. Allow yourself breaks. Some jobs (and definitely commuting) are dangerous when you're exhausted. You may feel torn between your family, work and household responsibilities, but if you're sleep-deprived, you'll have an even harder time keeping up with everything.

Try designating one night a week as the one when you hit the sack early, and cut back your morning routine to the bare minimum so you can sleep a bit later. Don't forget to build in relaxation time just for yourself.

Working mum

Returning to work doesn't have to spell an end to breastfeeding.

"I had to go back to work when my daughter was just four months old. It was already going to be a wrench and I really didn't want to have to give up breastfeeding as I wasn't keen on stopping before the recommended six months was up.

My mum offered to look after her while I work, so we came up with a plan that I'd express milk each morning so that she had enough for the day. It was a lot of milk, so a few weeks before I was due to go back, I began expressing more to build up my supply. I also introduced my daughter to bottles. Before then, she'd only fed from the breast, so it took some getting used to.

Expressing so much left me feeling really tired at first. It's like any routine though, you soon adapt. That last breastfeed I get to give my daughter every night makes it all worthwhile. My mum is happy that she doesn't have to mess about with measuring out formula, too."

Expressing and storing your milk means that your baby continues to reap the benefits of breastmilk after you've returned to work.

Your working hours

Your baby, like all of us, will respond best if she is introduced slowly to each of the changes in her life. Make allowances for this when you prepare your return-to-work timetable, so that she is prepared gently for her new arrangements. In this way, she should feel more secure, and therefore happier.

If it is possible, arrange to go back to your job on part-time hours for the first week. This will not only help your child, but will also help you because this is likely to be a tiring time for you. Your colleagues will be keen to have you back. Reassure them that while you're raring to get your feet back under the desk, you want to make a gradual start so that you have a chance to test your new arrangements.

Adapting to the changes

It's a really good idea to send your baby to her nursery or the childminder with objects from home that are familiar and special to her. These so-called "transitional objects" signal security and familiarity to your child. They could include teddy bears, dolls, a blanket or even just a piece of material – anything that your baby knows well and links with home and you. Pack some of these favourite items in her changing bag; your baby will recognise them and feel more secure in her new situation because of them.

As if you needed telling, it won't just be your baby who may be feeling a little lost at first, so take your favourite photo of her to work to put on your desk. Also, don't forget to pack some tissues and replacement make-up – your baby will probably be playing perfectly happily as you leave her for work, but you may shed a few tears yourself. Is there someone at work who has children and has gone through this too and knows how you're feeling? Have a chat with them – it will help.

Don't worry if your baby acts differently with you for a short while after starting with childcare. Although she may behave impeccably while she's being cared for, she may well then take it out on you at the end of the day. Be patient; this phase will pass. Just try to remind yourself that we all take things out on the people we love most.

Useful contacts and organisations

Breastfeeding

Association of Breastfeeding Mothers
www.abm.me.uk
08444 122 949

Breastfeeding Network
www.breastfeedingnetwork.org.uk
0300 100 0210

National Breastfeeding Helpline
www.breastfeeding.nhs.uk
0300 100 0212

La Leche League
www.laleche.org.uk
0845 120 2918

Ask a Midwife
www.midwivesonline.com
01274 427132

National Childbirth Trust
www.nct.org.uk
0300 33 00 771

Baby health

Action for Sick Children
www.actionforsickchildren.org
0800 074 4519

Association for Spina Bifida and Hydrocephalus
www.asbah.org
0845 450 7755

Asthma UK
www.asthma.org.uk
0800 121 62 44

British Deaf Association
www.bda.org.uk

British Heart Foundation
www.bhf.org.uk
0300 330 3311

Bliss
Support for families of premature and special-care babies
www.bliss.org.uk
0500 618140

Cystic Fibrosis Trust
www.cftrust.org.uk
0845 859 1000

Changing Faces
Support for individuals with facial disfigurement
www.changingfaces.org.uk
0845 450 0275

Children's Liver Disease Foundation
www.childliverdisease.org
0121 212 3839

Cleft Lip and Palate Association
www.clapa.com
020 7833 4883

Down's Heart Group
www.dhg.org.uk
0844 288 4800

Down's Syndrome Association
www.downs-syndrome.org.uk
0845 230 0372

National Eczema Society
www.eczema.org
0800 089 1122

British Epilepsy Association
www.epilepsy.org.uk
0808 800 5050

National Kidney Federation
www.kidney.org.uk
0845 601 0209

Little Heart Matters
Support for families of children with heart conditions
www.lhm.org.uk
0121 455 8982

British Lung Foundation
www.lunguk.org
08458 505 020

National Meningitis Trust
www.meningitis-trust.org
0800 028 1828

National Autistic Society
www.nas.org.uk
0845 0704 004

Newlife Foundation for Disabled Children
www.newlifecharity.co.uk
08700 707 020

British Red Cross Society
www.redcross.org.uk
0844 871 1111

Royal National Institute for the Blind
www.rnib.org.uk
0303 123 9999

Scope
Information and advice on cerebral palsy
www.scope.org.uk
0808 800 3333

National Deaf, Blind and Rubella Association
www.sense.org.uk
0845 127 0060

Foundation for the Study of Infant Deaths
www.sids.org.uk
0808 802 6868

Support Organisation for Trisomy 13/18 and related disorders
www.soft.org.uk

Steps
Information and advice on talipes (club foot)
www.steps-charity.org.uk
01925 750 271

Turner Syndrome Support Society
www.tss.org.uk
0845 230 7520

UK Thalassaemia Society
www.ukts.org
020 8882 0011

New mum health
Association for Postnatal Illness
www.apni.org
020 7386 0868

Bladder and Bowel Foundation
www.bladderandbowelfoundation.org
0845 345 0165

Family Planning Association
www.fpa.org.uk
020 7608 5240

General Osteopathic Council
www.osteopathy.org.uk
020 7357 6655

Pelvic Partnership
www.pelvicpartnership.org.uk
01235 820 921

Guild of Pregnancy and Postnatal Exercise Teachers
www.postnatalexercise.co.uk

Relate
www.relate.org.uk
0300 100 1234

Crying
Cry-sis
Support for parents dealing with excessive crying
www.cry-sis.org.uk
08451 228 669

Nappies
National Association of Nappy Services
www.changeanappy.co.uk
0121 693 4949

Go Real
www.goreal.org.uk
0845 850 0606

Women's Environmental Network
www.wen.org.uk
020 7481 9004

Childcare
Childcare Directory
www.childcaredirectory.co.uk
01379 898 535

Childcare Link
www.childcarelink.gov.uk

Daycare Trust
www.daycaretrust.org.uk
0845 872 6251

National Childminding Association
www.ncma.org.uk
0845 880 0044

Working Families
www.workingfamilies.org.uk

Rights and benefits
Advisory, Conciliation and Arbitration Service
www.acas.org.uk
08457 474 747

Citizens advice
www.citizensadvice.org.uk

Directgov Tax Credit help
www.direct.gov.uk
0845 300 3900

HMRC Child Benefit help
www.hmrc.gov.uk
0845 302 1444

Inland Revenue Tax Credit help
www.taxcredits.inlandrevenue.gov.uk
0845 300 3900

Working Families
www.workingfamilies.org.uk
020 7253 7243

General
Adoption UK
www.adoptionuk.org
0844 848 7900

Disabled Parents Network
www.disabledparentsnetwork.org.uk
0300 3300 639

Family Rights Group
www.frg.org.uk
0808 801 0366

Family Action
Charity for disadvantaged families
www.fwa.org.uk
020 7254 6251

Gingerbread
Advice and information for one-parent families
www.gingerbread.org.uk
0800 018 5026

Home Start
Support for families in local communities
www.home-start.org.uk
0800 0686 368

National Childbirth Trust
www.nct.org.uk
0300 330 0771

NHS Direct
www.nhsdirect.nhs.uk
0845 4647

National Society for the Prevention of Cruelty to Children
www.nspcc.org.uk
0808 800 5000

Parentline Plus
www.parentlineplus.org.uk
0808 800 2222

TAMBA (Twins and multiple birth association)
www.tamba.org.uk
Twinline: 0800 138 0509

Tommy's, the baby charity
Research on miscarriage, premature birth and stillbirth
www.tommys.org
020 7398 3400

Twinsclub
www.twinsclub.co.uk

Index

Acknowledgments

BabyCentre Acknowledgments:

BabyCentre would like to thank contributing editor Marie Kreft for her work in adapting content from our web pages to make it work on the printed page. Also Victoria Farrimond for her tireless work in managing this project.

Thank you to the BabyCentre team – Daphne Metland, Sasha Miller, Emma Woolfenden, Chess Thomas, Catherine Mendham, Rhianydd Thomas, Bernie Sheehan, Sam Wright, Jenny Leach, and Lynda Hale – for their expertise and contributions. All of our medical articles are checked and approved by the team of health professionals on our medical advisory board, but we'd like especially to thank consultant paediatrician and neonatologist Dr Dwight Lindo, consultant perinatal psychiatrist Dr Andrew Kent MD FRCPsych, and GP Dr Philippa Kaye for their advice and assistance during this project.

And, finally, we'd like to thank Penny Warren, Claire Cross, Helen Murray, Glenda Fisher, Hannah Moore, Kevin Smith, Isabel de Cordova and Saskia Janssen for their hard work in driving this project and for understanding and championing the BabyCentre ethos.

Publisher's Acknowledgments:

DK would like to thank Jemima Dunne for proofreading; Susan Bosanko for the index; Karen Sullivan for editorial consultancy; Joanna Dingley for editorial assistance; Carly Churchill and Sue Prescott for photographic assistance; Vicky Barnes, Roisin Donaghy, Nadine Wilkie and Alli Williams for hair and make-up; Kate Simunek for designing the icons.

Lastly, we would like to thank all of our models: Sharmina Karim and Joshua Allen; Catherine and Elise Allison; Adrian and Imogen May Bewsey; Liza Bowers and Florence Bowers-Stroud; Deborah and Ella Cadby; Rachel Chan and Niamh Chung; Pam Crane and Ava Freeman; Vibeche and Clara Dart; K.C. Jones and Holly Dixon; Katie, James and Isabella Dockray; Zandra Evans; Hannah Wilson and Rocky Ferguson; Matthew, Christina and Annabella Garbutt; Penny, Jemima and Lara Groves-Berry; Hannah and Dilan Guganeswaran; Carla and Alexa Haslock; Dayton Henderson and Isabelle Henderson-Lee; Clarissa Isles and Lakeisha Isles-Joseph; Annina Salo and Nicolas Jenkins; Juliette and Rafael Livesey-Howe; Lesley Manalo, Steven De Castro and Nathan De Castro; Barbara Mandley; Natalie May and Lukas Sattaur-May; Ruth Mbegabolawe and Naomi Okundaye; Lucy and Alex Morley; Lois, Layla and Phoebe Oliver; Rosanne, Amelia and Charlotte Please; Véronique and Bibi Méautte-Evans; Paula Regan and Henry Moran; Perdy Richardson; Viv and Aaron Ridgeway; Nicola and Freya Riley; Anwen and Lydia Russell; Andrea and Mauricio Samayoa; Charlotte Seymour; Alberta and Thomas Starr; Phillipa Strub and Molly Statham; Zai and Rafael Swan; Sophie and Somerset Young; Justyna, Majid and Nicole-Anna Zohreh.

Picture credits:

The publisher would like to thank the following for their kind permission to reproduce their photographs:
(Key: a-above; b-below/bottom; c-centre; l-left; r-right; t-top)
Alamy Images: Bart's Medical Library/Phototake 268; Bubbles Photolibrary 138; Janine Wiedel Photolibrary 23; Christina Kennedy 94; mauritius images GmbH 198; Dionne McGill 127br; Mira 28; Picture Partners 308; Alena Sudová 247; **Corbis:** Cameron 17; Kevin Dodge 12-13; eyetrigger Pty Ltd 155; Adam Gault/Science Photo Library 84; Rick Gomez 25tr, 58; Judith Haeusler 110; David P. Hall 236l; Beau Lark 89tl; LWA-Sharie Kennedy 85tl; Steve Prezant 254; Norbert Schaefer 210; Stock This Way 52; Judith Wagner 83; **Dorling Kindersley:** First Aid Manual 289b, 289tc, 289tl, 289tr, 290bc, 290bl, 290br; Julie Fisher 167tc, 167tl, 167tr; **Getty Images:** altrendo images 73tl, 125bl; Tony Anderson 57; Anthony-Masterson 74; B2M Productions 292; Ian Batchelor 230bl; Michael Blann 231; Stephen Chiang 232; Jamie Grill 179; Frank Herholdt 22; JGI 242; Johner 226br; Jose Luis Pelaez, Inc 14; Catherine Ledner 129; Fabrice Lerouge 158, 304-305; Ghislain & Marie David de Lossy 85tr, 159; Jens Lucking 226cla; LWA 91; Diane Macdonald 29; Regine Mahaux 307; Barbara Maurer 96; Thomas Northcut 183bl; Eric O'Connell 126; PhotoAlto/Sigrid Olsson 234; picturegarden 89br; Sara Press 31tr; Tosca Radigonda 122; Rich Reid 80; James Ross 225; Rachel Weill 125tr; Ross Whitaker 181tl; **iStockphoto.com:** asiseeit 163tc; jkullander 212; Jason Stitt 90; SweetyMommy 175b; **Mother & Baby Picture Library:** Ian Hooton 25tl, 79tl, 79tr, 82, 92, 98, 128, 183tr, 190br, 224tl, 236r, 249, 250, 255, 274, 293; Ruth Jenkinson 51br, 87br, 303br; Paul Mitchell 224b, 310; **Photolibrary:** BSIP Medical 283; Picture Partners 200b; Alicia Romano 111; Westend61 237; **PunchStock:** Brand X Pictures 20; **Science Photo Library:** 270, 277; AJ Photo 295; Dr M.A. Ansary 265; Ian Boddy 244; CNRI 287; Lowell Georgia 271; Ian Hooton 257; Ruth Jenkinson 266; James King-Holmes 303bc; La La 294, 297; Dr P. Marazzi 263, 267, 273, 285; Dr H.C. Robinson 272; **SuperStock:** age fotostock 175t, 251; Glow Images, inc. 235; Mauritius 168-169

All other images © Dorling Kindersley
For further information see: www.dkimages.com